CYRUS HALL McCORMICK

Cyrus Hall McCormick
A daguerreotype made about 1848

CYRUS HALL McCORMICK

SEED-TIME, 1809-1856

WILLIAM T. HUTCHINSON
Assistant Professor of History, The University of Chicago

With Foreword by
WILLIAM E. DODD
Professor of History, The University of Chicago

ILLUSTRATED WITH PHOTOGRAPHS,
CHARTS, AND MAPS

THE CENTURY CO.
New York & London

First Printing

PREFACE

ONE hundred harvests have passed since the summer of 1831, when Cyrus Hall McCormick invented a reaper in the Valley of Virginia. From that time until his death in 1884 his career closely concerned the westward march of the American farmer, the rise of a major industry in the United States, and the increased production of small grains everywhere.

The enduring influence of his genius, both as an inventor and as a manufacturer, confirms the judgment of his contemporaries. By the eve of the Civil War they had seen him perfect his implement; prevail against the skepticism of the farmer; outdistance his competitors year after year, and gain large wealth from the profits of his ever growing factory. These formative years are the subject of the present volume. A sequel will complete the story of his life.

The manufacture and sale of the reaper entailed much correspondence by Cyrus McCormick and his associates at the factory, as well as by agents and farmers throughout the land. These documents, many thousands in all, together with a large number of books relating to agriculture, are preserved by the members of the McCormick Historical Association in their library in Chicago. For permission to use this material, and for many other courtesies, I am deeply in their debt. Mr. Herbert A. Kellar, the librarian, generously shared with me his unrivaled knowledge of Cyrus McCormick and the reaper. Research was the more pleasant and fruitful because of his expert advice and the enthusiasm of Miss Loraine Weber, the assistant librarian.

It is a privilege to join the large company of students of United States history who are united by a common tie of gratitude to Professor William E. Dodd for counsel and sympathetic assistance.

Through the kindness of the late Mr. Cyrus Bentley, I was enabled to examine the rich McCormick files in his office. Several chapters owe much to the criticism of Professor Andrew C. McLaughlin, Professor Marcus W. Jernegan, Professor William T. Utter, and Professor L. Ethan Ellis, and for assistance with special problems I am under obligation to Professor Avery O. Craven, Professor Carl F. Huth, Professor Watt Stewart, and Dr. Carl R. Woodward. To these men; to Miss Helen Woodrow Bones of The Century Co.; and to my wife, Frances R. Hutchinson, who has aided more than she would have me admit, I am most grateful.

WILLIAM T. HUTCHINSON.

July 28, 1930,
The University of Chicago.

FOREWORD

In the evolution of the United States from the old congeries of independent communities of free farmers into the vast industrial, financial and consolidated power which overshadows all States and supervises the conduct of all men, there were many influences in operation and many men who worked unaware of the ends they were bringing to pass. Among these Cyrus McCormick, son of a Virginia farmer and mechanic, deserves high rank. Stimulated by an inventive father, young Cyrus fashioned in 1831 a machine which cut many acres of wheat in a day and gave promise of revolutionizing ancient methods of grain production as Eli Whitney had revolutionized the business of cotton growing. McCormick's strange machine soon acquired the name of the reaper.

Half aware of the future that beckoned him, he procured a patent, busied himself each winter making new machines, and traveled about Virginia in summer demonstrating in heavy or light wheat the efficiency of his invention. Great planters along the James River and lesser farmers in the valley nearer home gathered in their fields to scrutinize his work and to give orders for the next season. But before Virginia was fairly convinced of the value of the reaper, McCormick went into the upper Ohio Valley, engaged mechanics at Cincinnati to build machines under his specifications. Between 1845 and 1848 he was well known in the near West and the demand for his work was so steady that he set up a plant in Chicago and persuaded his younger brothers, William and Leander, to join him there.

William B. Ogden, railway builder and financial wizard of

the Middle West, loaned many thousands of dollars to aid the
Virginia émigrés in the upbuilding of their new business. In
a little while the McCormick buildings on the banks of the
Chicago River were among the largest and most interesting
in the city, and Cyrus McCormick was one of the most widely
known men of the region. William McCormick was busy from
early morning to sunset keeping the books of the new concern
while Leander supervised the thousand carpenters and machinists who before 1860 turned out five thousand reapers a year.
The elder brother traveled far and near advertising his invention at State fairs or upon the farms of well-known grain
growers. Many clever agents visited the towns and river valleys from Pittsburgh to Des Moines selling machines and
showing inexperienced farmers how to make them cut clean.
They sold for cash, on instalment plans and for notes which
often remained unpaid for years. But every year men seeded
more wheat and every year larger shipments of grain and flour
left the wharves of all the lake and river ports of the Middle
West. It was the active, eager, speculative era which preceded
the Civil War, the first period of revolutionary immigration.
If the West was not growing rich, it was becoming populous,
self-conscious and assertive of Western interests and Western
rights.

McCormick was one of the builders of the new region. And
inevitably, he tended to associate with the greater political leaders, particularly with Ogden and Stephen A. Douglas, then ap-
plying his marvelous genius to both the political and the economic up-building of the States and Territories which lay north
of the Ohio and the Missouri rivers and even westward to the
Rocky Mountains. The two had settled in Chicago about the
same time and both of them envisaged a vast, active Middle
West and Northwest that must soon come into larger control of
the United States. But the beneficiaries of Whitney's gin were
spreading their cotton fields over greater areas of the South

and the Southwest every year; and with their development went the slave system which made of Southerners masterful and domineering planters and politicians who looked with resolute jealousy upon the expanding Northwest. Moreover there was in the mid-fifties a rising and a resolute Republican party which had absorbed the abolitionists of the East, the anti-Southern Democrats of the West and most of the Whig party.

With a business yielding an annual net income of three hundred thousand dollars, with increasing shipments of reapers to England and France, McCormick devoted much of his time and all his astonishing political acumen to the cause of the conservative Democratic party, inclining to the more liberal views of Douglas as against the stubborn reactionism of Buchanan and the lower South. Then as now business and politics were close allies; and one need not be surprised to find McCormick in Baltimore at the moment when the Northern Democrats nominated Douglas as their candidate for the presidency as against John C. Breckinridge, the Southern candidate. The inventor saw in this the almost certain success of Abraham Lincoln and his masterful and radical party ally, William H. Seward, which to him meant business disaster, if not civil war.

To avoid this McCormick endeavored to bring about the resignation of his friend Douglas on condition that Breckinridge likewise withdrew. Then both wings of the severed party of conservatism might unite upon another candidate and postpone the imminent sectional conflict. Jefferson Davis, as uneasy as McCormick, worked toward the same end, but there was no third candidate on whom the Southerners and Westerners could unite. McCormick returned discouraged to Chicago, there to unite the "Herald," a Buchanan paper, with the "Times," a Douglas organ. The new paper was known as the property of McCormick, and its editor, James W. Sheahan, quickly proved himself one of the ablest of publicists and advocates of peace in a world which grew more warlike every day. The invention of 1831 had carried its owner a long way. He was one of the great business men of the time; he had won prizes from agricultural societies all over the country; he had been honored by the Government of Great Britain; and he had begun to sell his reapers to hard-fisted Frenchmen. But Abraham Lincoln, whom he knew and feared, was elected President, and William H. Seward, whom he distrusted, was to be Secretary of State. The future was dark in the spring of 1861.

It is the biography of this dynamic figure which is unfolded in the following chapters and the author, Professor William T. Hutchinson, of the University of Chicago, tells for the first time in authoritative form the story of this eager, restless business man. More than three years Mr. Hutchinson has labored through voluminous data gathered during the last twenty years from every known source by the members of the present McCormick family and their assistants, Mr. Cyrus Bentley, recently deceased, and Mr. Herbert A. Kellar, custodian of the collection. Family correspondence covering many years, the files of many agricultural journals and court records, as noted in the Preface, compose the major part of this material which is a veritable storehouse of American economic history. The author has examined these papers without restraint or suggestion and I think he has made one of the most valuable of biographies, a book which is as accurate and just as it is interesting and charming.

WILLIAM E. DODD.

September, 1930.

CONTENTS

ILLUSTRATIONS

CYRUS HALL McCORMICK

CYRUS HALL McCORMICK

CHAPTER I

THE YOUTH AND HIS ENVIRONMENT

ONE midsummer's afternoon in 1831 a few farmers in the Valley of Virginia watched a strange machine cut ripe wheat on the farm of Robert McCormick. Neither Robert's son Cyrus, its builder, who now walked rapidly beside it raking the cut grain from its platform, nor any one of the witnesses realized the lines of diverse experience which converged in this experiment and its significance for the future. Cyrus Mc-Cormick would have said, as he was to say so many times in later days, that its peculiar construction was the result of sudden inspiration, assisted by the efforts of his father, for many years, to build a practical horse-power reaper.

To Cyrus the invention was the product of his boyhood observation, and his realization, through hard experience, of the drudgery of the yearly harvest-time. His assertion that he had never read about or seen any reaper except his father's prior to 1831 is supported by the manner of life in the isolated Valley of Virginia during his youth. Nevertheless, earlier machines in both England and America resemble his and form a necessary part of its background. Each one is an expression of an age-old effort to solve a problem common to all peoples who harvest grain. The McCormick reaper, therefore, must be approached from the standpoint of its inventor and his environment, and as the climax of a process of endeavor which can be traced as far back as the time of the Cæsars.

The Valley of Virginia was at the close of its period of log-

3

cabin economy in the days of President Jefferson. For twenty-five years Indians had not been a serious menace, although in 1809, when Cyrus McCormick was born, Rockbridge County farmers were much concerned about the increasing number of wolves.[1] The new States of Kentucky, Tennessee, and Ohio, on its western flank, assured its people that the era of the stockade was over. They were proud to be a part of the Old Dominion, since Virginia was the home of Thomas Jefferson who best expressed their own ideals. Although they liked to say "plantation" when they referred to a two-hundred-acre farm presided over by a log cabin or a box-like clapboard house, and respected the man who had a few slaves to broadcast his seed wheat between his stumps and stones, their climate, their limestone soil, and their origin were far more Pennsylvanian than Virginian.

By 1800 they were not new-comers in the land. For almost seventy-five years there had been a steady trickle of Scotch-Irish and Germans southward through the Harper's Ferry portal, away from that model government of William Penn which was too insistent upon quit-rents.[2] The trail was easy to follow. The curving crest of the Blue Ridge on the east and the Allegheny sky-line on the west led them up the swirling Shenandoah River to its source. Here they soon met streams running southward to join the James as it broke through the Blue Ridge at Balcony Falls to plunge across the piedmont toward the ocean. Much of the valley floor was heavily timbered and punctured by outcropping rock. Fifteen hundred feet above sea-level, frost and snow were expected from October to April, and the soil and climate were adapted to grain, orchards, and tobacco. Cattle could graze on meadow and hill-

---

[1] Oren F. Morton, "History of Rockbridge County, Virginia" (Staunton, Va., 1920), p. 39. Hereafter cited as "Morton."
[2] Morton, pp. 12-32, tells of the Borden grant and of the coming of the first settlers.

side, and on the mast of the forest razorback swine grew fat
for the autumn killing. The Shenandoah River, with the
Potomac, furnished contact with the seaboard for those who
lived in the lower valley, while the farmers around Staunton
and Lexington expected Lynchburg and Richmond to market
their surplus.

As early as the French and Indian War their grain had
helped to feed the troops of George II and had brought the
Valley its first vision of prosperity. This aid had been rewarded by a proclamation which made their western horizon
a barrier never to be crossed, while down at Williamsburg a
small coterie of big James River tobacco-planters seemed to
believe that no one except tax-gatherers and lawyers should
pierce beyond the Blue Ridge. The thunder of Stamp Act and
tea-tax controversies echoed but faintly among their mountains, but they were assured by Patrick Henry, Richard Henry
Lee, and Thomas Jefferson that the only way to secure justice
in their own State, from these tobacco lords, was to throw off
the tenuous control of a sovereign three thousand miles away.

Joy of battle against England was a part of the inheritance
of every Scotch-Irishman, and, if needs be, the same tactics
could be used in the highlands of Virginia which their forefathers had successfully employed north of the Tweed. Expert
riflemen, grain, and iron were sent to aid the patriot forces
along the seaboard. The Indian menace in the Valley held
many to the defense of their own firesides during the Revolution, but such an opportune stroke as King's Mountain in 1780
made the debt of the coast to the frontier a real one. Jefferson
managed to have brave sayings about liberty and equality incorporated in the Bill of Rights of the Constitution of a free
Virginia in 1776, but the Valley farmers found that the new
order of things still meant under-representation for their back
country in the state legislature and a continuance of planter
control.

Little disposition was shown by the tidewater to build roads through the few passes of the Blue Ridge so that Valley wheat could compete advantageously with that of the low country in the Richmond market. Alexander Hamilton, upheld by Congress, endeavored to make the farmer pay a part of the cost of the late war by taxing the corn which he transmuted into whisky in order to ease his transportation problem. No wonder that the farmers of the Valley of Virginia voted for Jefferson in 1800 when he called upon the plain man to place those in high office who would translate the axioms of agrarianism into law. The millennium did not come, however, and in 1809, as this story opens, Jefferson's attempt to teach the world a way of peace by means of the embargo was stifling the grain-culture of Virginia as effectively as Hamiltonian excise or planter indifference to good roads.

Among those Scotch-Irish who reached Philadelphia in the crowded immigrant ships of 1735 were Thomas McCormick and his wife, Elizabeth Carruth.[3] Assiduous genealogists in recent days have discovered medieval Irish kings and mitered appointees of St. Patrick at the roots of the McCormick family tree.[4] Thomas was probably content to know that his father had distinguished himself at the siege of Londonderry in 1690.[5] Fighting was bred in his blood and until his death in 1760 he found the frontier dangers of Cumberland County, Pennsylvania, as congenial to his disposition as the two hundred

[3] MS. J. H. Shields, "A Scrap of History" (1880), pp. 5 ff.

[4] MS. Gustave Anjou, "The McCormic Family of Ulster Province, Ireland" (undated), pp. 3-15. According to this account, the founder of the family was Cormac Cas, son of Olliol Ollum, King of Munster in 177 A.D., and of his consort, Sabia, daughter of Con of the Hundred Battles, King of Ireland, 148 A.D. MS. "McCormick Family Genealogical Notes" (no date and no author given), pp. 3-6.

[5] Wm. H. Egle, "Pennsylvania Genealogies, Chiefly Scotch-Irish and German" (Harrisburg, Pa., 1896), p. 384. Hereafter cited as "Egle."

acres of limestone soil upon which he erected his homestead.[6]

Thomas McCormick's fifth son, Robert, born in 1738, practised the arts of peace as a farmer and a weaver in Juniata County. His diligence was rewarded with increased property and an advantageous marriage to Martha Sanderson, whose Scotch-Irish father owned broad acres not far away.[7] When the Revolution came, six years later, Robert left his loom and wooden plow and eventually found himself in the Carolinas, helping to push Cornwallis toward the cul-de-sac at Yorktown.[8] For some cause, usually recorded as Indian forays, Robert left his kinsfolk and moved his family to the Valley of Virginia in 1779. He soon used the sales money from his Pennsylvania farm to purchase four hundred and fifty acres and a large log house near Midway, on the boundary line of Rockbridge and Augusta counties.[9]

The Robert McCormick who was the defendant in several suits for debts during the next decade was probably not the owner of the Valley farm whose horses and cattle annually increased during the same period.[10] Although no documents remain to reveal the manner of his life, the Personal Property Book of Rockbridge County for 1792 records that he had at

[6] R. H. McCormick and J. H. Shields, compilers, "The Life and Works of Robert McCormick, Including His Invention of the Reaper" (Chicago, 1910), p. 1. Hereafter cited as "McCormick and Shields."

[7] MS. W. J. Hanna, "Notes on a Virginia Trip" (1885), p. 73. Hereafter cited as "Hanna." MS. written by Mary Caroline Shields, June 17, 1883. Hereafter cited as "M. C. Shields." Anjou, pp. 44-46.

[8] R. McCormick to L. J. McCormick, Jan. 21, 1879, and June 20, 1881. H. A. Johnston, "Three Scotch-Irish Builders of Chicago," in "Proceedings and Addresses of 9th Congress of the Scotch-Irish Society of America" (Nashville, 1900).

[9] MS. Biography of Cyrus McCormick, no author or date given, but written after 1884.

[10] M.S. extracts from Augusta County Order Books, Nos. 17, 18, 19, 20, Courts of Feb. 19, 1782, Mch. 19, 1785, Aug. 18, 1785, and Mch. 24, 1787, respectively.

last acquired one slave.[11] It was about this time that he, stout Presbyterian elder that he was, refused to abide, in the New Providence Church, the substitution of Dr. Watts's hymns for the Psalms of David. With others, he withdrew his membership, and his neighbor Patrick Hall contributed land and materials for the erection of an Old Providence Meeting House, where the true faith could be kept secure from such dangerous innovations.[12] Robert's rise to a place of influence in his neighborhood was a steady one. By 1800 the tax-books show that he possessed three slaves and eight horses. As Colonel James McDowell, who topped the local roster of good society, owned but thirteen slaves and nineteen horses that same year, it is evident that the McCormicks were among those families upon whom the community looked with respect.

Five of Robert's children were born in Pennsylvania, but a last son was welcomed in the new Virginia home on June 8, 1780.[13] He was named for his father, and beyond this fact little else is known of his life during its first thirty years. That he learned to write with a customary disregard for the niceties of spelling, his later correspondence proves.[14] His mother, who

[11] MS. extracts from Rockbridge County Personal Property Books, 1783-1811. In 1783 he owned 4 horses and 14 cattle.

[12] J. A. Waddell, "Annals of Augusta County, Virginia" (Richmond, 1886), pp. 201, 278. Hereafter cited as "Waddell." An Old Providence Church had been erected in 1748. It was later abandoned, but was temporarily reoccupied by the seceders at the time of this schism, which Waddell dates 1789 or 1790. The new church was built on P. Hall's land in 1793. Leander J. McCormick, compiler, "Ancestral Record and Biography" (Chicago, 1896), p. 337. Hereafter cited as "L. J. McCormick." Morton, pp. 172-174. Hanna, pp. 46, 47.

[13] M. C. Shields.

[14] Egle, p. 404: Robert "received an ordinary education acquired at a private school." Leander J. McCormick, compiler, "Memorial of Robert McCormick, Being a Brief History of His Life, Character and Inventions, Including the Early History of the McCormick Reaper," p. 1. (The original of this work was printed in Chicago in 1885. Since this is not available, reference will be made to the photo-engraved reprint of 1898, by

had long been in delicate health, died in 1807 and was buried in the Old Providence churchyard.[15] On February 11, 1808, Robert married Mary Ann Hall, who brought as her dowry, cattle and horses worth one thousand dollars.[16] Her father, Patrick Hall, had come to Augusta County from the vicinity of Londonderry in 1770, and almost at once married Susan McChestney (McChesney) to whom he had been affianced in Ireland.[17] Patrick fought on the patriot side in the Revolution, and, notwithstanding his advanced age, was once more in the field during the War of 1812.[18] Shortly after his arrival in America he exchanged for a farm in the Valley of Virginia the linen he had brought from Ireland. The Hall and Mc-Cormick homes were only two miles apart and it was inevitable that Robert should know the beautiful Mary Ann, whose wit and ready tongue came to be proverbial about the country-side. Their marriage united two Scotch-Irish families whose ancestors had probably been neighbors one hundred years before in northern Ireland.[19]

Robert brought his bride to live in the log home of his father. Here Cyrus Hall McCormick was born on February 15, 1809.[20] Amid more primitive surroundings across the Alleghenies, Abraham Lincoln was then three days old. Both were ultimately to go to Illinois, and the career of each was greatly to help the fortunes of the other, although they were ever to be in disagreement. A severe illness at the age of five became in

J. R. Parsons, Lewis Miller, and J. F. Steward.) The name of L. J. McCormick does not appear on its title-page. It will be cited hereafter as "Memorial."

[15] MS. Rockbridge County Order Book, No. 9, p. 115. Egle, p. 392.

[16] MS. M. C. Shields, "McCormick Genealogical Notes" (undated), p. 8.

[17] *Ibid.*, pp. 1, 2.

[18] *Ibid.*, pp. 5, 6. Patrick Hall was a commissary in the War of 1812.

[19] *Ibid.*, p. 12. Robert and Mary Ann McCormick were members of Old Providence Church.

[20] For descriptions of the manner of building these log houses, and their usual dimensions, see Morton, pp. 38, 107.

after years the earliest recollection of Cyrus's boyhood. Many of the volunteers from the Valley in the War of 1812 had been stationed for a time in the low country about Norfolk, Virginia. Here William Hall, a brother of Cyrus's mother, was stricken with yellow fever and was brought back to his father's house in the mountains to die. His father and mother paid for their care of him with their lives, and Robert, Jr., and Mary Ann came over to the Hall homestead to assist in the emergency.

The vigorous bleeding prescribed by the family doctor helped not at all, and two slaves also were victims of the epidemic. Finally young Cyrus contracted the dread disease. The doctor, by now too much concerned for the welfare of his own family to remain longer, left for home after advising Robert to use the lancet freely. Rejecting a prescription which seemed to lead only to death, Robert immersed his son frequently in hot steam baths containing bitter herbs and whisky. This heroic treatment, together with long drafts of hot tea, proved successful.[21]

This first crisis in Cyrus's life reveals one side of his boyhood environment. Meager medical knowledge, abundant food but a poorly balanced diet, and almost complete lack of information concerning sanitation and quarantine, did much to counteract the healthful climate of the Valley of Virginia. Cuppings, purges, herbs, roots, barks, and various patent medicines were the usual remedies given for all illnesses.[22] The

[21] MS. of M. C. Shields, dated Oct., 1882. M. C. Shields, "McCormick Genealogical Notes," pp. 7, 8. L. J. McCormick, p. 105. Patrick Hall and his wife died on Nov. 19 and 23, respectively.

[22] For patent-medicine advertisements, see "Lexington Gazette" (Lexington, Va.), July 24, Nov. 13, and Dec. 11, 1835. Morton, p. 108. Herbert A. Kellar, "Rockbridge County, Virginia, in 1835; A Study of Ante-Bellum Society," in Louis J. Paetow, ed. "The Crusades and Other Historical Essays" (N. Y., 1928), pp. 361-364. Hereafter cited as "Kellar." Almost every home had its herb bed, growing sage, dittany, boneset, catnip, horsemint, and horehound. Lobelia was used as an emetic; white walnut bark as a purgative; snakeroot for coughs, and elder blossoms for perspiration.

childhood death-rate was particularly high. In 1826, Cyrus's brother Robert, aged sixteen, and his sister Susan, aged thirteen, died on successive days of the "flux," which was then ravaging the country-side.[23]

In 1832, William S. McCormick wrote to his brother Cyrus, who was then in Kentucky: "Our neighborhood has been attended with a good deal of sickness this spring, the measles particularly have been very prevalent, by which some few have been deprived of life. Brother John was very bad with a relapse of the measles, and some of the others had them, but not so bad."[24] In this same letter William remarked that physicians were so increasing in number in the Valley that "after a while they will have to ride two on a horse." Perhaps Cyrus's insistence upon preventive medicines, in his later life, finds its origin in these experiences of his youth.

Although the health of the body was endangered by too little knowledge of disease and its proper care, the welfare of the soul received daily attention. The forefathers of these Valley farmers had been planted in Ireland by a king who found their sturdy Scotch-Presbyterianism a menace to his sovereignty. Due in part to religious discontent, their descendants had come to America during the eighteenth century, bringing doctrines of Calvin and Knox as potent in the sphere of politics as in the domain of the Church. Contact with the hard life of the frontier, where they were surrounded by natural forces which they could only partially master, served to increase their devotion. Their emphasis upon an educated clergy preserved the dignity of their faith amid an environment conducive to superstition. Nevertheless, the camp-meeting with its

Cherry, poplar, or dogwood bark, steeped in whisky, were for fever and ague. May-apple root, walnut bark, and slippery-elm bark were prescribed for dysentery.

[23] Anjou, p. 46. M. C. Shields. L. J. McCormick, p. 340. Robert the father and John, a son, also were ill with "flux" at this time, but recovered.

[24] W. S. to C. H. McCormick, May 1, 1832.

hysteria was a significant religious and social event in their isolated existence. Each day began and ended with family prayers. The Bible and Shorter Catechism were books which children were required to memorize as well as to obey.[25] A schism within the denomination about 1790, over doctrinal matters, merely signified that thereafter each little community would have two Presbyterian churches instead of one.[26] Until Washington College was able to meet the need, Princeton was the intellectual center of their faith and yearly sent forth a trained clergy to protect the faithful from the inroads of the Baptists and Methodists.

Such preachers as the Morrisons and the Browns, whom Cyrus McCormick knew, tilled their own land with the help of their slaves [27] and often found time to instruct the youth of their flock in Latin, Greek, and good manners. The negroes, if they did not have a carefully supervised meeting-house of their own, sat in the gallery of the white people's church and received communion after their masters were finished. Save for the court days at the county-seats and the occasional corn-huskings, house-raisings, quilting parties, and musters, the Sabbath services afforded almost the only opportunity for the Valley folk to meet together. Because morning and afternoon preaching was the rule, church attendance was an all-day business. The recess for lunch permitted an interchange of

[25] Morton, p. 173: Ann Henderson "got the 'jerks'" at a meeting at Timber Ridge in 1805. Samuel Houston told her not to dance during preaching and helped her from the building. He was charged with disturbing public worship, but pastor and congregation supported his action. M. C. Shields.

[26] Waddell, pp. 201, 278.

[27] Rockbridge County Property Book, 1837, p. 15: The Rev. James Morrison had 5 slaves and 9 horses this year. In 1842 (p. 21), he was listed with 6 slaves and 10 horses. For a picture of the religious life of the county in 1835, see Kellar, pp. 326-333.

Mary Ann McCormick

weekly news budgets and the inception of many a courtship.[28]

As willing sharers of this intensely sincere, if narrow, religious atmosphere, Robert McCormick and his wife Mary Ann brought up their increasing family in the stern regimen of a Scotch-Irish household. Besides Cyrus, and the two who died in 1826, five children were born between 1815 and 1822, William S. in 1815, Mary Caroline in 1817, Leander J. in 1819, John P. in 1820, and Amanda J. in 1822. Of these five, all save John lived for many years, and they will appear frequently in the course of this narrative. John died in 1849, and his twenty-nine years of life remained only an indistinct and pleasant memory when his brothers and sisters attempted long afterward to recall the days of their youth.[29]

Mary Ann McCormick, or "Polly" as she was familiarly known, enjoyed a reputation for efficiency. By the fireside or in the harvest fields she was equally in her element. She was determined to thrust herself and her family ahead in the world, and her children found her ready at all times to listen sympathetically to their dreams. She took pride in her silver, her peacocks, and her stylish carriage, and she liked to drive rapidly along the rough country roads, behind a spirited team. Her attention to dress and her love of display made less prosperous neighbors wag their heads and gossip about her extravagance and pride. Impulsive of tongue, she nevertheless had many friends, and the home at Walnut Grove entertained much company.[30] Under her direction the McCormick household

[28] Pamphlet, "Mt. Carmel Presbyterian Church, Steele's Tavern, Virginia, 1920." Morton, pp. 108, 109, 173 ff. "A Narrative of a Visit to the American Churches by Andrew Reed and James Matheson" (N. Y., 1835). Hanna, pp. 46, 51: Old Providence Church had outside staircases at each end of the building, leading to the galleries where the negroes sat.

[29] McCormick and Shields, p. 10. Anjou, p. 46.

[30] Hanna, p. 73, Miss Polly Carson remembered in 1885: "The mother was rather a large woman. She was a great business woman, very thrifty,

was well managed, and her children in later years centered their recollection of her about her love for them. Her nervous energy and business talent well supplemented the less aggressive character of her husband. She lived until June 17, 1853, and the evening of her life was brightened by the success of her eldest son. In him she chiefly saw her own ambition fulfilled.[31]

Robert McCormick was well loved by his children and respected by his neighbors.[32] The few existing letters of these early years serve to confirm the opinion of his associates. In his honesty and fervent attention to religion he was a typical Scotch-Irish farmer of the Valley of Virginia. His interest in local politics and in the transportation needs of his neighborhood was not unique in his day.[33] Because of his studious,

a grand good housekeeper who looked after everything and was full of energy." She would often work in the fields and help others with their haying if the weather was precarious. M. C. Shields. H. N. Casson, "Cyrus Hall McCormick, His Life and Work" (Chicago, 1909), pp. 23 ff. L. J. McCormick, p. 339. Copy of "Daniel Matthews vs. Robert and Cyrus H. McCormick," Augusta County, Index, Chancery Cases, 1838-39, p. 267. Hereafter cited as Matthews vs. McCormick. R. McCormick to C. H. McCormick, Dec. 5, 1831.

[31] Hanna, p. 41, statement of Mrs. Hamilton Ware. The mother visited Cyrus after the factory was started in Chicago. Upon her return she exclaimed, "Well, I feel just like the Queen of Sheba, for the half had not been told me."

[32] MS. "Sketch of My Life," by C. H. McCormick, Aug. 4, 1876. MSS. of M. C. Shields, Oct., 1882, and June 17, 1883. Hanna, pp. 30, 53. McCormick and Shields, pp. 4, 25, 26, 28.

[33] MS. filed under the name of "Jas. Young, 1816," in McCormick Historical Association Library. On Aug. 10, 1816, Robert McCormick was one of those who met at Fairfield, Va., to elect deputies to a convention to be held at Staunton "to take into consideration such measures in concert to secure an amendment to, or reform of, the Constitution of the State of Virga. so as to obtain an equality in the representation of the State in both branches of the State Legislature." R. McCormick to Wm. Massie, May 7, 1826. Wm. Massie to the President and Directors of the Tye River and Blue Ridge Turnpike Co., July 28, 1831. Robert McCormick was a director in this company.

quiet nature, and above all because of his talent for invention, he attracted at least local attention. His reticence denied him a large circle of close friends, but those whom he enjoyed were such substantial men of the neighborhood as James McDowell and William Massie.[34] He had the business ability to double the size of his father's estate, and to dot it with grist-mills and sawmills, a blacksmith shop and a distillery. Nevertheless he failed to specialize, and his inventive genius was spread over such a number of machines that no one of them was ever perfected.

As a good Calvinist, he found true harmony to exist between success in business and the tenets of his faith. His Scotch thrift and the appeal of temperance societies led him to withhold the customary liquor ration from his workmen, but his letters and account-books show that he made whisky and sold it for twenty-five cents a gallon.[35] Lime from his kilns was marketed as far distant as Richmond, and his grain was sold in the same city after a somewhat dangerous batteau trip down the James River.

Two years after his marriage Robert purchased the 532-acre home farm from his aged father for £760 and by 1812 he also owned four slaves and seven horses.[36] His father continued to live with him until October, 1818, when in "a Low state of health but in perfect mind and memory," he willed his chil-

[34] MS. "Sketch of My Life," by C. H. McCormick, Aug. 4, 1876. W. Le Conte Stevens, "McCormick the Inventor," in the "Rockbridge County News" (Lexington, Va.), Feb. 18, 1909. R. McCormick to J. Newton, Jan. 30, 1836.

[35] Morton, p. 181: A temperance movement began in Rockbridge County about 1829. "Lexington Union" (Lexington, Va.), Jan. 17, 1835. "Lexington Gazette," Aug. 14, 1835. Letters of R. McCormick to Wm. Massie, Jan. 22 and Feb. 12, 1826.

[36] R. McCormick to Wm. Massie, June 17, 1824, and Apr. 26, 1828. R. McCormick to Henry Massie, June 22, 1824. Account of R. McCormick with D. and D. Higgenbotham & Co., from Feb. 11, 1820, to Mch. 4, 1821. Rockbridge County Personal Property Book, 1812.

dren "his brass clock and large kittle," a "large old chest," and "his loom and tacklings." [37] Most of his property was bequeathed to Robert, who, ever rising in the world, decided four years later that it was time to exchange the log house for one better suited to his station in life. Stone was brought from his fields and lime from his kilns. A heavy foundation of sixty-five-foot front and fifty-foot depth, was laid. Upon this a red-brick house arose, with a porch, a service wing in the rear, and many windows with white casements. The front door opened upon a broad hallway, and the eight rooms of its two stories were gradually furnished with products of Robert's own skill and the yield of Lynchburg and Richmond stores. High wainscoting, carved wooden mantels, and broad fireplaces added to the comfort and distinction of the interior.

From his deep shady lawn Robert could look down the slope and over his fields to the Blue Ridge. Clustered about his house were his workshops, his barns, and the quarters for his few slaves, while his mills were along the South River, several miles away. Thence he would often walk in the morning, depending upon a negro to bring him his noon lunch and a spare horse for the uphill trip to Walnut Grove in the evening.[38]

Except for a few luxuries, the McCormick estate was self-sufficing. Flax, hemp, and sheep furnished the fiber and wool for spinning-wheel and loom. Robert's cattle and hogs yielded the yearly meat supply for brine barrel and smoke-house, the tallow for candles, and the oil for soap. The hides were taken to a near-by tannery and made ready for shoes and harness. His grain became flour at his own grist-mill or whisky at his own distillery, while he was prepared to make his fruit into cider if the swing-shelves of his cellar were already too heavily

---

[37] L. J. McCormick, p. 339: Robert, Sr., died Oct. 12, 1818. His will of Oct. 9 is in Rockbridge County Records, Will Book, No. 4, pp. 367, 386.
[38] M. C. Shields. R. McCormick to "Dear Brother," Dec. 7, 1822. Hanna, pp. 68-70. Edith T. Sale, in the "Harvester World" (Chicago), June, 1921.

laden with sweetmeats for the winter. When lumber was needed his sawmill could cut it from timber felled upon his own land. Of stone for building purposes and the lime-kiln, there was no end. His mechanical skill found expression at the forge and anvil of his smithy, and he was proud to see that his son Cyrus had inherited his own talent.

In short, Walnut Grove stood for a measure of success in the Valley which entitled its owner to the respect of his fellows. By 1830, Robert was master of about twelve hundred acres of land, nine slaves, and eighteen horses.[39] He had earned the right to indulge his passion for mechanical experiment without fear for the material comfort of his family, in case his inventions did not find a ready market.[40]

A cross-section of Robert's life is preserved in the following letter to his brother in 1822.[41] It shows him not only as a farmer "on the make" but also as the thinker, not quite satisfied with the theology of his fathers.

I commenced the building of a new house this summer and have it nearly completed. I have had good success in carrying it

[39] Extract from Augusta County Land Book, Texas, 1st District, 1830. In 1814 he purchased 376 acres with Patrick Hall; in 1826, 217 acres in one parcel, 453 acres in a second, and 20 in a third. In 1826 he sold 362 acres. The exact reference for each of these transactions would make too lengthy a foot-note, but they may be found in the Order Books and Deed Books of Rockbridge and Augusta counties for the appropriate year.

[40] It should not be understood that Robert McCormick was wealthy. Like so many other Virginians at this time, he was "land-poor." Mary C. Shields, his daughter, wrote in 1883, "The last of September [1832] my school closed and, although I was anxious to go to school longer, father thought he could not afford the expense." McCormick and Shields, pp. 43, 44. W. S. to C. H. McCormick, May 1, 1832: "Father has paid most of his debts, I believe, and has money coming to him yet." Augusta County Order Book, No. 44, pp. 230, 368: On May 29, 1834, Robert McCormick was sued for a debt of $31.47 and in October for another of $28.06.

[41] R. McCormick to "Dear Brother," Dec. 7, 1822. As a result of a controversy with the minister of Old Providence Church, Robert transferred his membership to New Providence in 1823.

on, and have had four children born since you left this country, the eldest a daughter, the next two boys, and the last a daughter born September last. Times are very different in this country from what we formerly experienced. Money scarce and a low price for all kinds of property. I expect to do but a small business this season, my crop being but light. . . .

I believe it more honourable to forgive than to retaliate as our passage through life may be compared to the morning and evening of the passing day. I think it may be said with propriety that we can not commence too early nor continue too late in acts of morality and religion. There appears to be a great revival in this country and wonderful are its effects,[42] but as in political affairs there is a difference of opinion which forms a number of parties. The Armenian sistom I think is gaining ground in this country, and setting aside our early prejudices, I think deserves considerable appreciation. We have been taught Calvanistic Doctrine from our youth, but it is really a hard doctrine to compare with that reason which the Deity has given us for our guide. Many texts are introduced by our teachers to prove Calvanistic tenits, one of which I will make a few remarks on, which is that of the potter and the Clay he having power out of the same lump to make one vessel to Honor and another to Dishonor. This we must admit as fact, and if his vessel made to Dishonor continues in the station for which it was intended has it violated the intention of the maker? Surely not, because upon his own plan it has exactly answered the purpose for which he made it, and if the being so formed be cast into eternal misery it is probable reason would say he is more to be pitied than faulted.

Much more is known about Cyrus McCormick's parents and his environment, during the first twenty years of his life, than of his personal history. No one of the children except Susan is mentioned by name in any existing document before 1830, and concerning her it is simply recorded that her father bought her a handkerchief and a necklace from a Yankee peddler the same year that she died.[43] Fifty years later old residents of the Valley and members of the family tried to

[42] Kellar, p. 334.
[43] MS. account of R. McCormick with Wm. Massie, 1826.

reconstruct these early days.[44] They naturally remembered the picturesque rather than the usual, and in the main a faithful account of the customary life of any son of a prosperous farmer of the Valley of Virginia between 1815 and 1830 would be as accurate as these reminiscences. Miss Polly Carson, a neighbor, stated many years afterward that Robert McCormick "prepared them [his children] for the worst and allowed them to hope for the best." [45]

There remains the picture of a barefoot boy dressed in homespun, helping his father in mill, field, and smithy for long hours each summer's day [46] and seeking solace and enjoyment from his fiddle in the evening. Cyrus disliked the labor of the fields and preferred to work with the tools of the carpenter shop. Early products of his skill, of undetermined date, were a light cradle made of locust wood that allowed him to harvest the ripe grain with less strain upon his tender muscles,[47] and a revolving terrestrial globe upon which he painted the continents and the seas.[48] A daguerreotype, made about 1848, shows Cyrus at the age of forty with thick, dark brown hair, heavy beard, and large dark eyes.[49] His father and mother were each five feet eight inches tall, but the son had added almost four more inches to his own stature. His powerful physique permitted a tireless application to work which in later years was to be the

[44] Most of these reminiscences may be found in Hanna, in the "Memorial," or in McCormick and Shields. The last two are very similar in content.

[45] Hanna, p. 73.

[46] Ibid., p. 30, article entitled, "Inventor and Christian," in the "Interior" (Chicago), Feb. 18, 1909, p. 205.

[47] McCormick and Shields, p. 44. Hanna, pp. 53, 54, Adam McChesney said in 1885: "Old Charley, the father of Old Joe Anderson now living, I bought from Rob't. McCormick for $700. . . . He brought with him the identical cradle that C.H.McC. had made for himself when a boy. I retained the cradle until five years ago, when it was stolen from me. It was a piece of very fine workmanship."

[48] Ibid., p. 52.

[49] See frontispiece. M. C. Shields. Hanna, pp. 55, 57, 78.

despair of associates who were obliged to follow him through his day.

He attended an old field school built of logs and was taught the three "R's," geography, and religion from such texts as the Bible, the New York Primer, Webster's Speller, Dilworth's Arithmetic, Murray's Grammar, and Adams's Geography.[50] Whether he ever played corner-ball, hop-scotch, or hooky with his thirty or more school-fellows, or helped to smoke out the teacher, can only be surmised.[51] How many seasons he trudged across the fields with his books and his noonday lunch, and scratched with his goose-quill pen dipped in home-made ink as he sat on his slab bench, is not known.[52] His first letters show an acquaintance with punctuation and spelling quite unusual for his day, and it seems probable that he was instructed at home or at the parsonage by men more learned and less inclined to use the switch than the typical old field school-master.

One elderly gentleman in 1885 recalled that Cyrus was taught surveying and mathematics in 1823 by a special tutor.[53] Cyrus placed much stress upon correct spelling and as late as 1845 counseled his brother Leander to adopt his habit of carrying a small dictionary about with him.[54] The library of his father's friend Colonel James McDowell was not far away, but there is no reason to believe that Cyrus borrowed from its shelves such volumes as Stith's "History of Virginia," "The Works of the

[50] Kellar, pp. 342, 343.

[51] Hanna, p. 73. "Cyrus Hall McCormick," in the "Interior," Aug. 17, 1884, p. 3.

[52] Hanna, p. 80: Old Joe Anderson, a former slave of Cyrus, stated in 1885, "I used to go to school with him for company along the road to an old field school where about thirty or more scholars met." Morton, p. 185.

[53] Hanna, p. 30, statement of Wm. White of Lexington.

[54] C. H. to W. S. McCormick, Aug. 9, 1845. Cyrus H. McCormick, Jr., was often told by his father that he never attended school after he was fifteen years of age, but that he carefully studied the newspapers in order to improve his spelling and punctuation.

Rev. Thomas Chalmers," Campbell's "The Lives of the British Admirals," and Bickersteth's "A Treatise on Prayer." [55]

A few extracts from letters and memoirs of the McCormick family will illustrate the educational opportunities in Rockbridge County about 1830. Mary Caroline, Cyrus's sister, wrote long afterward:

In the fall of 1829 and 1830 father employed a teacher by the name of Fox of good reputation. The neighbors subscribed as much as they were able, and father, as was his custom, paid the deficiency in the amount necessary to induce Mr. Fox to take the school. So Mr. Fox continued to teach our school two winters, the sessions lasting nine months each, commencing in October. He was a good teacher but used the whip severely. We studied Harris' English Grammar, Adams' Geography, Mrs. D's Natural Philosophy . . . Titler's History, spelling in the dictionary, and we took drawing lessons.[56]

Robert informed Cyrus in November, 1831: "We expect to start Caroline to school to Mr. Morrison on Monday next and the rest of your brothers, probably Amanda, about Christmas to Mr. Metcalf." [57] The next spring the situation had somewhat changed: "Mary Caroline is at school in Staunton which commenced last Monday. Your brothers and sister Amanda are

[55] MS. inventory of the books in the library of Jas. McDowell, 1835. This lists about fifty volumes, mainly religious, legal, medical, and historical. Hanna, p. 55: Dr. S. B. Morrison, a son of the pastor of New Providence Church, stated in 1885 that the parlor of the McCormick home formerly contained many books. No record of their titles has survived.

[56] M. C. Shields. Samuel Fox was a medical student at this time, and about ten years later was a partner of Robert and Cyrus McCormick in their furnace venture. See Chap. VI, p. 136.

[57] R. McCormick to C. H. McCormick, Nov. 17, 1831. The Rev. James Morrison was their pastor. The Rev. Allen Metcalf was pastor of Fairfield Presbyterian Church. Mary Caroline had attended Metcalf's school for several months in the summer of 1831. In Robert's letter to Cyrus of Dec. 23, 1831, he states that "the coldness of the winter" has kept the children at home thus far.

at school at home, Mr. John Steele and myself having employed a teacher who I think is doing tolerably well." [58] At the same time, William S., one of the pupils, confided to Cyrus: "Caroline . . . is now in Staunton and intends going a session there to Mr. Thatcher accompanied by the two Miss McNutts, the squire's daughters . . . and I am now going to a young man by the name of Wamsley from Stafford County who is teaching here; I am studying Gibson which proves to be very tough with me, as he is not very good at explaining it." [59] There seems to have been no inclination to send any of the sons to Washington College, so close at hand in Lexington. In view of his future career, Cyrus's best education was gained in his father's workshops and in the harvest field.

As a youth he was daily instructed in Scripture and Catechism and received a grounding in Calvinism which decisively molded his thought throughout his long life. His earliest letter, still extant, furnishes evidence of his interest in religion even when far from his home church. Writing to his cousin from Woodford County, Kentucky, in the autumn of 1831, he stated:

I have attended several religious meetings in this neighborhood, and suffice it to say, that there is a good deal of opposition both in, and to, the cause of religion in this country. The Campbellites exalt themselves, by sinking and excluding every sect on earth, if I understand them. [60]

New Providence Church was about eight miles from Walnut Grove and it was Cyrus's custom to go there to Sabbath preaching, on the back of his white-footed sorrel, Peacock. [61] The con-

---

[58] R. McCormick to C. H. McCormick, May 4, 1832.
[59] W. S. to C. H. McCormick, May 1, 1832. Probably the "Gibson," to which he refers, is John Gibson's "A New and Improved System of Practical Bookkeeping" (Phila., 1826).
[60] C. H. McCormick to A. McChesney, Oct. 31, 1831.
[61] Hanna, pp. 51-53.

gregation elected him to be their precentor and he led the church singing for several years.[62] The earnest pleading of his father and the persuasion of exhorter and friends induced him to make a public confession of faith during the great revival season at New Providence in the summer of 1834.[63] In 1837, apparently wishing to have a place of worship nearer to Walnut Grove, he became one of the charter members of Mt. Carmel Presbyterian Meeting House at Steele's Tavern.[64]

Besides his fondness for his fiddle, little is known of his diversions. All sources agree that he was an excellent rider, the best in the locality.[65] His skill in the saddle and his love of horses followed him through life. The strict tenets of his faith barred him from the more boisterous rural entertainments of his day and rod and gun seem to have carried little appeal. Walnut Grove could hardly have been a true Virginian farm without a few hounds, but, so far as is known, the bear, deer, fox, and wild turkey of his neighborhood never lured him to the chase.[66] His brother wrote him jestingly in 1832:

Let me know whether you are going to bring those pointers or not. I should like to see them and Dr. Hitt was glad to hear of them, and said he expected and hoped the kentuckians would make a hunter of you before you returned, as he . . . has now some tolerable good hounds I believe. I and he caught two Foxes, in the winter. Our hounds are not very good for Foxes, as they have never been well trained, but Milow is first rate for tracing squirrells.[67]

[62] *Ibid.*, pp. 36, 55, 81, testimony of W. T. Rush, 1885.
[63] *Ibid.*, pp. 1, 52-54, 73. About fifty were converted. It was "like the Day of Pentecost." Morton, p. 174, writes that New Providence Church had 591 members after the revival.
[64] "The New Providence Presbyterian" (Raphine, Va.), May, 1921, p. 4. Pamphlets, "Mt. Carmel Presbyterian Church, Steele's Tavern, Va., 1920," p. 3; "Mt. Carmel Church, Steele's Tavern, Va." (1906).
[65] Hanna, pp. 42, 52, 53, 57.
[66] Morton, p. 5.
[67] W. S. to C. H. McCormick, May 1, 1832.

Cyrus did know how to use a gun and when he was on his way to Kentucky, in 1831, Nat Turner almost gave him a chance to fire it. His usually sedate pen could not hide his excitement:

We journeyed on through wilderness uninterrupted in body or mind, until Sat. night, when within 20 miles of Charlestown, we found the family of Mr. Stockton so much alarmed by fear of an insurrection among the negroes, that we slept none, determined that if an attack was made, to have a round with our long guns, at least. The darkness of the night, the wind that blew, keeping up a constant clapping of the window blinds, and the rain that occasionally fell; together with the increasing noise of the multitude of overgrown rats, constantly pacing over the garret, would probably have favored such an attack, by preventing a discovery, and the scene must have been truly terrific. However, the dawn of day at last brought peace and quiet to our minds, if not repose to our eyes. We set off to Charlestown. . . . While in Charlestown I learned that that was the night fixed upon by the negroes to take the town and then to sweep the valley up and down the river. 'Twas said their plan was first to explode the church and then fire the town, etc. As is usual on such occasions there was doubtless a great deal of exaggeration on that. The finding of several guns, ammunition, etc. in their possession concealed in the mines first gave rise to the suspicion. What their intention may have been is not for me to say. 'Tis supposed that Nat Turner is among them. All the women and children of the town were said to have been collected into 4 houses and guarded one or two nights.[68]

On his first long journey away from the home farm the youth naturally felt much self-satisfaction at his association with an event of national interest.

Those who remembered him as a boy, later testified that he made few close friendships and that his reserve and quiet earnestness were a subject of remark and criticism among his

[68] C. H. McCormick to A. McChesney, Oct. 31, 1831.

fellows.[69] He lived among men who drank deeply and used much tobacco, but he did not follow their example.[70] It was judged that he was conceited, and his attention to dress was extraordinary enough among the plain Valley folk to occasion adverse comment. Those who went barefoot to church could not appreciate his broadcloth coat and black beaver hat.[71]

No record of an early love-affair enlivens this somewhat somber boyhood. One who knew him as a youth concluded that "because of his sedateness he was never very popular with the girls, indeed he made no effort whatever to become so." [72] And yet his former slave Old Joe recalled many years later that "sometimes he and I used to go out of an evening to see our girls, but we was always home again early at night, for late hours was agin the rules of the house." [73] In one of his earlier letters Cyrus was sufficiently sensitive to devote a paragraph to the ladies:

Mr. Hart has two fine daughters, rite pretty, very smart, and as rich probably as you could wish; but alas! I have other business to attend to and can, as I told you, devote but a small proportion of my time to the enjoyment of their society or any others. But if you, Cousin Adam, will continue to confide in my judgments and will send me written authority to act, I will use my feeble influence to, and have no doubt that I could obtain for you the heart and hand of a charming young lady. I have attended several religious meetings. . . .[74]

[69] Hanna, pp. 52, 55: Dr. S. B. Morrison, the son of the pastor of New Providence Church during Cyrus's youth, said in 1885, "He was always regarded as a peculiarly model and upright young man, free from the follies that youth are given to. . . ."
[70] *Ibid.*, p. 42.
[71] *Ibid.*, p. 55. Statement of C. R. McCormick of Patterson, Mo., to W. G. McCormick, Feb. 25, 1912. Morton, p. 39.
[72] M. C. Shields. McCormick and Shields, p. 4. Hanna, p. 55.
[73] Hanna, p. 80.
[74] C. H. McCormick to A. McChesney, Oct. 31, 1831.

About this same time his brother William chided him for his lack of attention to the girls of Kentucky:

I believe you have not so much as named a lady since you went to Kentucky, and I reckon you have got in love with some of them and want to keep it secret until you get here, so I suppose you intend to bring her home with you when you come, but I think you might at least tell us whether they are pretty or not or how they compare with the ladies of Va.[75]

William would attend his brother's wedding, but he would have to wait for over twenty-five years before doing so.

Until 1830, Cyrus McCormick had few opportunities to view the world beyond the mountains. Undoubtedly he frequently rode his horse the eighteen miles to the little towns of Lexington or Staunton, to trade live stock or to listen sympathetically to Democratic oratory from the court-house steps. Court days at the county-seat assured politicians an audience; taverns, brisk business; and negro boys, a chance to make a few coppers by currying the saddle-horses at the tie-rail.[76] Here Cyrus could watch the mail arrive, and the stage-coaches with travelers who told broad tales as they stretched their legs and cooled or warmed themselves at the tavern bar. The trek of the emigrant in his Conestoga wagon, coffles of slaves destined for the new cotton lands of the Old Southwest, and great droves of hogs going north from Kentucky every autumn, must have been familiar sights on the Lexington pike. The local press furnished scant news from over the mountains but told much of remarkable patent medicines and doubtful remedies for wheat blight, spavin, gapes, and Hessian fly. Although no record remains, Cyrus probably often urged a four-horse team over indifferent roads with a two-ton load of farm produce

[75] W. S. to C. H. McCormick, May 1, 1832.
[76] Kellar, pp. 338, 339.

for Scottsville or Richmond, hoping to get back to Walnut Grove within a fortnight.[77]

Life moved slowly in the Valley of Virginia. The farm and the church were the two chief focal points, and in each adherence to the customary was upheld as a virtue. Preachers of new methods to achieve either salvation or bigger crops could expect little sympathy. The oratory of the candidate for office, the periodic exhortations of the revivalist, the roll of the drum at military muster, and the scrape of the fiddle at a barn dance were legitimate ways to relieve the usual monotony of life.[78] It was not a congenial environment for an innovator. Cyrus McCormick, who had inherited his mother's ambition and energy, and his father's talent for invention, learned after fifteen years of trial that his reaper needed the open prairies of the West to give it vigorous life.

[77] Morton, pp. 48, 106, 163-165. Waddell, pp. 241, 242, 252-254.
[78] Kellar, p. 358.

CHAPTER II

INVENTIVE GENIUS AT WALNUT GROVE

THE measure of comfort and prosperity enjoyed by the McCormicks in their Rockbridge County home was due in part to the mechanical skill of Robert and Cyrus. The improvements they effected, or sought to effect, in the farm and mill machinery of their day reflect the backward state of agriculture, not only in the Valley of Virginia but in the world at large. The climax of this series of inventions, the reaper of Cyrus McCormick, will be separately discussed in a later chapter, but both before and after its first appearance other implements were devised in the carpenter and blacksmith shops of Walnut Grove.

For seventy-five years before 1830, efforts had been made in America, through the medium of books, newspapers, societies, fairs, lectures, and model farms, to point out and urge the adoption of improved methods of cultivation and stock-raising. Although Jared Elliot's "Essays upon Field Husbandry in New England," published in 1760, was the pioneer book in its field by an American author, English works had already appeared in the colonies. Following the Revolution, such leaders as John Taylor, John Skinner, and Edmund Ruffin were soon to give much of their attention to the cause of better farming.[1]

---

[1] Edmund Ruffin's famous "Essay on Calcareous Manures" first appeared in the "American Farmer" (Baltimore), III (1821-22), p. 313 ff. It was separately printed and five editions were sold within twenty years. John Taylor of Caroline combined farming, political philosophy, and politics. See his letter "On the Necessity of Defending the Rights and Interests of Agriculture," *ibid.*, III, p. 131.

In the "American Quarterly Review" for March, 1837, twenty-six books, written after 1760 by English and American authors, were listed and recommended for every farmer's library. In that same issue appear the titles of nineteen current American agricultural periodicals, and the editor feared that he had omitted a few.[2]

The emphasis in these magazines naturally varied with the needs of the locality in which each was sold. Assuming that John Skinner's "American Farmer" is as typical as any, the volumes for the period, 1820-30, indicate that most stress was placed upon the following subjects: The farmer should read books helpful in his profession and should urge the formation of an agricultural society in his vicinity.[3] These societies should hold annual fairs and cattle-shows. The present need is quality and not quantity, and premiums should not be awarded simply for monstrosities of animal and vegetable life.[4] The recurrent craze for merino sheep, mammoth bulls, enormous hogs "fit only for soap," and unusual vegetables is to be deprecated.[5] Grape- and silk-culture should be fostered, and every effort

[2] "American Quarterly Review" (N. Y.), I, p. 13. The "Cultivator" (Albany), of June, 1835, p. 51, lists 1 quarterly, 7 monthlies, 1 semi-monthly, and 8 weeklies devoted to agriculture; 2 to horticulture, and 2 to sericulture; 3 of these were published west of the Alleghenies, 6 in New York, 4 in New England, 3 in the South, and the other 5 in the Middle States, exclusive of New York. See "Transactions of Essex Agricultural Society of Salem, Mass.," Pamphlet No. 4 (1834), pp. 78-84, for other lists of agricultural books and magazines. The "Farmers' Register" (Scottsville, Petersburg, Richmond, and Shellbanks, Va.), May, 1839, p. 283, copies an article from the "Genesee Farmer" of Rochester, N. Y., stating that there are 32 agricultural journals, of which nearly half are in their first year of circulation.

[3] The "American Farmer," I (1819-20), pp. 105-107, recommends Home's "Principles of Vegetation," Darwin's "Phytologia," Hunter's "Georgical Essays," Anderson's "Essays," Lord Dundonald's "Connection of Agriculture with Chymistry," Davy's "Agricultural Chymistry." *Ibid.*, III, p. 171.

[4] *Ibid.*, III, pp. 113, 268. This volume, however, devotes much space to the introduction of the llama and alpaca.

[5] *Ibid.*, III, pp. 126, 130, 170.

must be made to improve the breed of live stock and the quality of fruit.[6] Encouragement is needed for new and useful agricultural inventions, and farmers should so prepare their fields that they can employ the horse-rakes, harrows, rollers, cultivators, and seeders already on the market. Threshing machines, corn-shellers, corn-cob crushers, hay-chaffers, fanning mills, hemp-breaks, and riddles for sizing potatoes, deserve a place on every large and well-ordered farm.[7] The tendency to accumulate more acreage than can be cultivated is most unwise.[8] Skinner also gave much space to new fertilizers, grasses, deep plowing, and crop-rotation.[9] He printed a call to the farmer to awaken from his lethargy and keep step with progress in other walks of life:

Farmers are over cautious in admitting innovations in their practice, and discover too much of a jealous reluctance to examine the documents by which the utility of these may be fully proved. . . . The chemist, the mineralogist, the botanist and the mathematician are fellow laborers with the practical farmer and the manufacturer. Vain and unprofitable theories no longer engross the attention of men of science. It can no longer be said, as formerly, that an active and feverish imagination is as distinguishing a mark of a philosopher as of a poet. Philosophers are, in our days, business men.[10]

Notwithstanding the need for such information in the Valley of Virginia in 1830, it was difficult to secure a large reading

[6] *Ibid.*, VIII and X are particularly emphatic upon these topics.

[7] *Ibid.*, I, pp. 107, 357; V, p. 257.

[8] *Ibid.*, V, p. 346. Wm. M. Barton, Vice-President of the Shenandoah Valley Agricultural Society, called this tendency the "grand and prominent error" in the agricultural system of Virginia.

[9] *Ibid.*, I, *passim,* for frequent discussion of Chile wheat, May wheat, Guinea grass and fiorin grass. The third volume gives much attention in its first fifty pages to deep plowing and manures. Better methods of cultivation were necessary to halt declining land values and Western emigration, which went hand in hand.

[10] *Ibid.*, III, p. 57, address of R. Sullivan before the Massachusetts Agricultural Society, Oct. 17, 1820.

public for agricultural periodicals. In Rockbridge County in 1834, there were but eighteen subscribers to the "Farmers' Register," published in the State and one of the best magazines of its kind.[11] The editors of Lexington and Staunton gave considerable space in their newspapers to rural information, but only too often farmers must have come to grief when they attempted to apply their untested and fantastic recommendations and remedies.[12] Citizens of Philadelphia organized an agricultural society in 1785, but those of Rockbridge County, almost wholly devoted to farming, did not establish one until 1827. The latter had a troubled and broken existence until the Civil War, but undoubtedly did good service through its annual fairs. Unfortunately, those who were most interested in such clubs were the farmers who least needed stimulation. In spite of this fact, the yearly exhibition was a social event, and even the farmer most scornful of book learning, who was lured there by the entertainment alone, could not but see that some of his neighbors were excelling him in the quality and quantity of their stock, fruit, and vegetables.[13]

Almost twenty per cent of the population of Rockbridge County was slave in 1830, and, although most of the negroes were concentrated upon a few estates, their presence added an additional handicap to agricultural improvement in this area.[14]

[11] "Farmers' Register," I (1833), p. 774, Supplement. The McCormicks were not among the number.

[12] "Lexington Union," which became the "Lexington Gazette" in July, 1835. "Staunton Spectator and General Advertiser" (Staunton, Va.).

[13] "Farmers' Register," III, pp. 607, 608, letter of R. R. Barton to the editor, Dec. 28, 1835. To paraphrase: Our agricultural society drags on a feeble existence, but under its present officers we hope to revive its usefulness. The stock exhibition at our last show was not very creditable, but the display of domestic manufactures was highly so. We must interest our women in silk and vineyard culture. If this can be done, and if the legislature will aid with bounties and internal improvements, fewer will leave the State to endure the pestilences and privations of the far West.

[14] Morton, pp. 142-145. Waddell, pp. 244, 245.

Hilly, stumpy, and rocky farms also gave little incentive to the use of many new implements. Most farmers were satisfied to scratch their land three or four inches deep with an iron-sheathed wooden plow, broadcast their seed by hand, harrow it in with a crude implement made at a local smithy, and roll the field with a log pulled by a horse.[15] Grain could be cut fast enough with scythe, sickle, and cradle, if the workmen were furnished sufficient liquid refreshment, and centuries of use prescribed the hickory flail and horses' hoofs for threshing grain.[16]

If an acre yielded thirty bushels of corn, fifteen of wheat, or thirty of oats, the farmers were satisfied.[17] Their barnyards and stables furnished all of the manure which they needed, and they cared little to know about the usefulness of Nova Scotia plaster, lime, and the calcareous deposits of their own county. To plant clover or other green crop and then plow it under for the good of the soil seemed sinful waste. At least they would let their cattle graze over it for a time before they used their plows. The meadows would serve for pasturage if they were flooded once a year, and native grasses were as satisfactory and less trouble to raise than clover and alfalfa.[18] Sheep throve best when they were least cared for; and the purer the breed of any animal, the more ills to which it was susceptible.[19] Com-

[15] "American Farmer," I (1819-20), pp. 107, 357.
[16] Statement of Peter Hite to H. A. Kellar, Sept. 6, 1919. A MS. inventory of the estate of James McDowell, Sr., 1835, lists the following implements: 16 plows, 3 harrows, 2 straw-cutters, 10 cradle-scythes, 6 mowing scythes, 13 hoes, 12 forks, 2 mattocks, 1 grubbing hoe, 2 flax hackles, 12 spinning-wheels, 2 looms, 3 churns, candle molds, sausage-stuffers, stills, surveyor's outfit. He was one of the large landowners of the Valley of Virginia.
[17] "Farmers' Register," Feb., 1835, pp. 548-550.
[18] Ibid., Jan., 1837, pp. 547, 548: Dr. Alfred Leyburn, in an address before the Rockbridge County Agrl. Society on Oct. 13, 1836, recommended "the use of clover as the sheet anchor of the farmer."
[19] Ibid., Jan., 1834, p. 485.

plicated rotation systems savored too much of book farming. Apples might be so sour that the pigs squealed when they ate them, but they would at least make good cider, apple-butter, and apple-jack. Wheat smut, blight, Hessian 'fly, and locusts were visitations of God's wrath, and it was idle, if not wicked, to seek remedies. Eggs should not be expected in winter-time. Ginger for heaves, and the lancet for colic were bound to cure —if they did not kill.

Against such apathy and superstitions a few leaders in Rockbridge and Augusta counties raised their voices, and among these Dr. Robert Barton was one of the most insistent. In an address before the Rockbridge Agricultural Society, in 1834, he urged the need of agricultural education as the only cure for the prevalent prejudice against innovations:

> None of the *learned professions,* as they are called in common parlance, require such a range of knowledge as ours. . . . But so great is the prevailing error on this subject, that all our youth, esteemed the most promising, because the most pert and precocious, are destined to expound the law to us—to dose us with physic— or to teach us our duty to God and man. This will account for the increase of pettifoggers, charlatans, fanatics, and I may add, of mere clod-hoppers. I mean no disrespect to either of the professions. . . . I entreat you then . . . to commence the work of reform . . . spare no pains towards educating your sons as farmers, and after they have acquired a thorough knowledge of the sciences, lop off an hundred acres of your farms to each, and let them shift for themselves. . . . It is our own faults if we are the "hewers of wood and drawers of water" for every other class. If not prepared by *education* we do not deserve to share the loaves and fishes.

He thought that a "taste and fondness for rural life" could be fostered by the establishment of colleges "on the manual labor system, or, pattern or experimental farms." [20]

[20] *Ibid.,* Feb., 1835, pp. 548-550: Barton was president of the society. On Jan. 11, 1836, an agricultural convention was held in Richmond and

Among those farmers of Rockbridge County who sought to respond to the challenge of leaders like Barton were Robert and Cyrus McCormick. The son wrote in 1876:

My father was both mechanical and inventive, and could and did at that time, use the tools of his shops in making any piece of machinery he wanted. He invented, made and patented several more or less valuable agricultural implements, but, with perhaps less inventive speculation than some others, most of his inventions dropped into disuse after the lapse of some years. Among these were a thrashing machine, a hydraulic machine, a hemp-breaking machine, with a peculiar horsepower adapted to it, and others.[21]

He omits mention of a blacksmith's bellows, a grist-mill improvement, and "an improvement in teaching the art of performing on the violin." By "inventive speculation" was meant the business energy necessary to advertise his inventions and to assure them an extended sale. Robert devoted his attention to too many new devices simultaneously and thus failed to promote any one of them with undivided vigor. He patented neither his bellows nor his threshing machine, and these, together with his other inventions, commanded his interest in

ex-Governor Jas. Barbour presided. The legislature was petitioned to establish an agricultural professorship at the University of Virginia, with a salary of $1,500 a year; to create a State Board of Agriculture, and to make an agricultural survey of the State. "Albany Cultivator," Mch., 1836. In view of Barton's speech it is interesting to note that on Nov. 7, 1835, Robert and Mary Ann McCormick deeded Cyrus a slave and a farm. Perhaps they had listened to Barton's address. Rockbridge County Records, Deed Book, Index, "T," p. 108. Barton's appeal to the farmers is perennial in U. S. history. In Jan., 1848, the editor of the "American Agriculturist" (N. Y.), VII, p. 1, struck the same note: "Farmers, when will you arouse yourselves to the dignity and importance of your calling, and educate yourselves to that height of intelligence which will make you the *rulers* instead of the *ruled* of the other professions?" *Post*, p. 237, ftn. 26.

[21] MS. "Sketch of My Life," by C. H. McCormick, Aug. 4, 1876. C. H. McCormick to H. Baldwin, Jr., Mch. 7, 1867.

1830 and 1831.[22] He used his automatic "self stopper for stopping the motion of mills" in his own grist-mill, but apparently sold none. By this device the machinery stopped of itself when all of the grain had run out of the hopper.

His patent upon an "Improvement in a Hydraulic Machine for Working Machinery" was granted on October 1, 1830, and over a year later it still held a prominent place in his thoughts. "I have done but little as yet but think upon plans for the hydraulic machine," he wrote to Cyrus in November, 1831, "and I think the time not wasted as I feel satisfied I have thought of some improvements." [23] Early in the following month a Lynchburg firm encouraged him to build one,[24] but just before Christmas he once more told his son: "I have done nothing toward building the hydraulic machine but have studied much on the principle and I think the time not lost in value. I think I discovered about the best that can be done." [25] And so the next spring came with the device still unperfected, and Robert advised his son not to attempt to construct one in Kentucky.[26] No sources after May 4, 1832, mention the machine, and so far as is known there was none manufactured under the patent.

Robert McCormick was one of the many, on both sides of the Atlantic, who invented a threshing machine. Meikle of East Lothian, Scotland, led the way in 1786, and twenty years later C. Hoxie of Hudson, New York, announced that he was prepared to make and sell his threshers for $100 and to guarantee them to thresh out fifty or sixty bushels of wheat in a

[22] "Copies of the Patents of Robert McCormick, Jr., Certified by the Commissioner of Patents." His grist-mill device was patented on Apr. 20, 1831.
[23] R. McCormick to C. H. McCormick, Nov. 17, 1831.
[24] Idem to idem, Dec. 5, 1831.
[25] Idem to idem, Dec. 23, 1831, and M'ch. 27, 1832.
[26] Idem to idem, May 4, 1832. This letter contains detailed information about the machine.

working day.[27] By 1830 numerous inventors were advertising
their machines, and at least two attempts had already been
made to combine a reaper and a thresher in a single implement.[28] Although Robert McCormick did not patent his
thresher and horse-power, he built and sold at least five by the
close of 1834. In that year he advertised that he would sell
them for $70 each, or for about one half of the usual price of
a thresher, and that his invention differed "entirely from any
hitherto used in this section of the country." A description was
added to support this claim.

Four horses were required to operate his machine, and its
mechanical beaters not only threshed twenty bushels of wheat
(or forty dozen sheaves) an hour but delivered the straw unbroken as well.[29] This was a considerable advance in speed over
the Hoxie machine of twenty-five years before, although there
were others on the market in 1830 which were warranted to
thresh as much in a day as the McCormick. Why Robert did
not continue the manufacture of this implement is not known.
His blacksmith's tub bellows also left few records. He made
them at Walnut Grove between 1830 and 1833 and during

[27] Edward H. Knight, "American Mechanical Dictionary" (3 vols., N. Y.,
1877), III, p. 2556. "Farmer's Magazine" (Edinburgh), Dec., 1810, pp.
511, 512. Robert Brown, "A Treatise on Agriculture and Rural Affairs"
(Edinburgh, 1811), II, p. 33. "The Balance and Columbian Repository"
(Hudson, N. Y.), V (Jan. 28, 1806), p. 28.

[28] "American Farmer," III, pp. 106, 396; V, pp. 91, 92, 126, 258; X, pp.
107, 137, 214, 258. "American Museum and Repository of Arts and Sciences" (Washington, D. C., 1822). "New England Farmer's and Mechanic's
Journal" (Gardiner, Me.), I (May, 1828), p. 120. Knight, III, pp. 1890-91.
These references mention, and in some instances describe, twelve different
threshing machines invented and advertised for sale by citizens of the United
States between 1815 and 1830.

[29] "Lexington Union," Feb. 22 and Aug. 16, 1834. MS. receipt of R. Mc-
Cormick to Thos. Willson, Dec. 15, 1834. McCormick and Shields, pp. 6, 7,
contains a somewhat unsatisfactory description of the thresher and horse-
power. Hanna, p. 52. "Memorial," p. 11.

those years sold at least fifteen for twelve dollars and a half apiece.[30]

At this time almost every farm of moderate size in the Valley of Virginia grew at least a little hemp, although its culture was largely experimental.[31] The fiber was used to make coarse clothing, bagging, and twine, but it was most difficult to harvest and prepare for the loom. Hemp ripened in late August and was then pulled. One man could pull about one quarter of an acre a day or cut twice that amount. The plants were left on the ground for several days, to cure. The stalks were then stripped of their leaves, tied in bundles, and stacked in a corner of the field. Early in the winter the hemp was spread on the field to ret and this operation, known as dew-retting, usually required several months. Some farmers retted their hemp by soaking the stalks in water for a time, but, in either case, the process was accomplished when the lint could be separated easily from the stalk. It was then time to "break" it. In 1842, to the editor of the "Genesee Farmer," Henry Clay described this work:

I task my hands 80 lbs. per day, and allow them a cent per lb. for every pound beyond that. I have known, in some instances, as much as 250 pounds per day broken out. As each handful is broken out, the shoes, that is the little particles of the stalk which adhere to the lint, are carefully beaten off, so as to make it clean, and the hemp is laid away, and at night tied up in a bale or bales, and carried to the Hemp house. . . . All attempts to substitute horse, water or steam power for the hand brake, and there have been many, have hitherto failed.[32]

[30] R. McCormick to Wm. Massie, Mch. 4, 1830. MS. Receipt of Hancock & Brown of Lynchburg to R. McCormick for two tub bellows, Dec. 3, 1831. R. McCormick to C. H. McCormick, Dec. 5, 1831, May 1 and May 4, 1832. W. S. to C. H. McCormick, May 1, 1832. McCormick and Shields, p. 7.

[31] "American Farmer," III, pp. 289, 290, 305, 413; X, pp. 106, 344.

[32] "Genesee Farmer" (Rochester, N. Y.), Apr., 1842, p. 59.

One of those unsuccessful attempts was made by Robert McCormick between 1830 and 1832. At the outset he was sufficiently encouraged by the results of his experiments to write to his friend William Massie:

About two weeks ago I finished my new modeled hemp machine and wheel . . . and have been agreeably disappointed finding it has gone beyond every calculation that I had made, both as respects the machine itself, and the wheel by which we give it motion. I have not had a sufficient opportunity of knowing what quantity of hemp we could break fit for market in any given quantity of time, as our hemp was not at home, and we have had but small quantities to try it on. . . . It however performed with masterly power on hemp on last Saturday. I broke out the remaining part of my crop of flax, which was 62½ dozens of such handfuls as are broke on a common break, in two hours and a quarter.[33]

With this evidence of his success, Cyrus accompanied his father to Washington in late July, 1830, and was a witness to his application for a patent.[34]

Hemp-breaks sold slowly in the Valley, and after a year only three prospective buyers had been found.[35] Kentucky was the great hemp country in that day, with Henry Clay in Congress to secure it tariff protection. In the autumn of 1831, Cyrus McCormick started on horseback over the mountains to build hemp-breaks for his father in that State and to attempt to sell county rights for their manufacture. He was in Lexington, Kentucky, by October 14. "The landscape was now changed from dreary, to the most beautiful that eyes probably ever beheld, in America at least," he wrote his cousin as he first saw the West, in which so much of his later life was to be spent.

[33] R. McCormick to Wm. Massie, Mch. 4, 1830.
[34] "Copies of the Specifications and Patents of Robert McCormick, Certified by the Commissioner of Patents," Patent of Oct. 1, 1830.
[35] R. McCormick to C. H. McCormick, Oct. 26, Nov. 10, Dec. 5, 1831, and Mch. 26, 1832. The first machine, besides the one in use on the home farm, was built for Jas. McDowell, Sr.

I went to the house of Mr. Robt. Breckinridge, but had not, nor have I yet had the pleasure of seeing him, he being in Danville. I then proceeded to Mr. Hart's his uncles, for whom I am now building a machine for breaking hemp. A good deal of anxiety prevails generally with the farmers on the subject, so far as I can learn. They all say that if a cheap machine can be had to answer the purpose well, it will be almost universally adopted, but having been so very frequently deceived by men and disappointed by their own calculations on the subject, they have generally speaking, concluded that no machine will do but the hand break. . . . Some time will doubtless be necessary to remove the prejudices of many. I expect to have one in operation 2 or 3 weeks here. . . .[36]

Cyrus soon discovered that it cost more and took longer to build machines in Kentucky than in the Walnut Grove black-smith shop. As early as mid-November, Robert McCormick wrote him to inquire when he expected to start for home.[37] By the beginning of the next month the father's concern for his son had increased.

The present is a critical period with you in our business. . . . We had thought that if you could so wind up your business as to come home this winter it would be well, but of these things you will have to be the judge. If your circumstances require more money we will expect you to give us notice. . . . Your mother requests you to get a few flannel clothes for the winter. We have been much visited and you have been much inquired after. We wish you to remember that we want you to write frequently.[38]

Illness, the extremely cold weather, and other interruptions of which only hints remain, delayed until February, 1832,[39] the

[36] C. H. McCormick to A. McChesney, from Woodford County, Ky., Oct. 31, 1831.
[37] R. McCormick to C. H. McCormick, Nov. 17, 1831. This letter was directed to Versailles, Ky.
[38] *Idem* to *idem*, Dec. 5, 1831.
[39] *Idem* to *idem*, Feb. 6, 1832: "In my opinion, we have had the coldest winter ever seen here by the present inhabitants."

completion of the machine which Cyrus was building. He then advertised in the "Kentucky Reporter" of Lexington, inviting attendance on March 1 at the farm of David C. Humphrey, where the hemp-break would be shown in operation. He thought that the machine would cost about $125 and he expected it to break about one hundred and twenty pounds of hemp per hour, with the help of five or six men and two horses. County and state rights to manufacture the implement were offered,[40] and a letter of Cyrus McCormick to his father indicates that he was asking $1,000 for the Woodford County monopoly alone. An account of the exhibition can best be given in Cyrus's own words:

Never before have I . . . so much felt my want of the assistance and advice, of one so capable of giving it as yourself. . . . A good many attended and a good many were pleased, notwithstanding our crank broke before we had timed it. A few, however, as is to be expected, spoke unfavorably of it. Mrs. Harts thought it perfect, one of whom has employed a workman to build him one to be driven by water power, and I think can be put in operation within a month. I am to make it break 100 lbs. per hour of water-retted hemp, in which case his father agrees to build another. Mr. Woodfolk . . . says he will build a mill next summer with a view to attach one to it. . . . I could not have expected more encouragement than I received. The next day I had a new crank made and put in, and the next morning I commenced with the intention of breaking all the day, but one of the pins in the lever broke. After putting in an iron one we broke in an hour 141 pounds of long hemp, with roots . . . It operates more powerfully, I think, than any I ever saw. . . . Mr. Humphrey said he will undertake to sell some for me, if I will break 1000 pounds without pushing in a day, which I calculate on doing this week. . . . I think to make it profitable it is probable I should stay here some time yet.[41]

[40] "Kentucky Reporter," Feb. 22, 29 and Mch. 7, 1832.
[41] C. H. to R. McCormick, from Versailles, Ky., Mch. 6, 1832.

These high hopes quickly fell, for reasons which must have been detailed in letters to his father during the next month. By March 27, Robert again urged Cyrus to return:

I think you will soon know whether the tide of opinion is for or against you and I wish you not to be the least discouraged, as your lost time, if you were not to effect sales at all, is but a small matter. . . . I think you are among people who can counsel together and perhaps at your expense.[42]

Three days later Robert informed his son: "Our business at home requires our united attention and I think our interest too."[43] Letters for the next two months are missing, but in early May, Robert was still advising a speedy return and inclosed ten dollars, "having anticipated your situation as being somewhat critical. . . . I think as there is considerable doubt about the hemp breaking machine taking generally in that country you had best as much as possible study safety."[44] The son returned to Walnut Grove sometime that month and explained long afterward that his failure in Kentucky was caused largely by the fact that his father's machine was constructed to break water-retted rather than the dew-retted hemp of the West.[45] In the meantime Robert McCormick had sold at least three hemp-breaks in the Valley, and had two other purchasers in prospect.[46] Details are lacking after Cyrus's return from Kentucky, but since hemp-culture in Virginia did not prove to be profitable, the home market for Robert's invention probably soon disappeared.

[42] R. McCormick to C. H. McCormick, Mch. 27, 1832.
[43] Idem to idem, Mch. 30, 1832. This letter implies that Cyrus had sold several breaks. Messrs. Humphrey and Hart are the only two purchasers mentioned by name in the correspondence.
[44] Idem to idem, May 4, 1832.
[45] MS. "Sketch of My Life," by C. H. McCormick, Aug. 4, 1876.
[46] Robert's sales are incidentally mentioned in the letters to his son, which have been listed in the previous foot-notes of this chapter.

At the same time that the hemp-break engaged the attention of father and son Cyrus invented a plow which was particularly designed for hillside work. Many farmers in Virginia still used the age-old wooden implement whose point and sides were protected by iron strips. Thomas Jefferson and his son-in-law, Thomas M. Randolph, had designed plows for turning horizontal furrows on sloping fields, and they were only two of many who had endeavored to solve the same problem.[47] Horizontal plowing eventually terraced the hillside and thus helped to prevent erosion, but denuded slopes, due to heavy rainfall and improper cultivation, were all too common in the United States. In 1819, Stephen McCormick, of Fauquier County, Virginia, a distant kinsman of Cyrus, patented a cast-iron moldboard plow which was extensively used throughout the State for many years.[48] Twelve years later a patent was granted to Cyrus McCormick for "an improvement in a hill-side plough."[49] It was made of cast- and wrought-iron, and the moldboard was so fashioned that it could be reversed at the will of the operator, while the share remained stationary. Thus all the furrows could be turned uphill on a slope. The idea of a shifting moldboard dates back to at least the sixteenth century in England, and apparently at the time Cyrus received his patent the Germans were using plows constructed similarly.[50]

In 1831, Cyrus McCormick contemplated a partnership for

[47] "American Farmer," I, pp. 107, 357.

[48] J. C. Shields, "Developement [sic] in Rockbridge," in the "Buena Vista [Va.] Advocate," Jan. 17, 1890. "American Farmer," V, p. 371. S. McCormick to John Randolph of Roanoke, Nov. 26, 1829; to Wm. Weaver, July 1 and Sept. 29, 1828, May 27 and Oct. 8, 1829; to Clerk of Superior Court of Law and Chancery, Lexington, Aug. 6, 1846. "Farmers' Register," Sept. 30, 1842, p. 411. "American Farmer," VIII, p. 145: He presented one to Lafayette in 1825.

[49] "Copies of the Specifications and Patents of Cyrus McCormick, Certified by the Commissioner of Patents." Patent issued June 13, 1831.

[50] "Southern Agriculturist" (Charleston, S. C.), May, 1835, pp. 272-274.

the manufacture of these plows with a Dr. Cobbs.[51] This was not effected, possibly because Cyrus decided to go to Kentucky that autumn and sell hemp-breaks for his father. In September, 1831, the month before he left, he sold his first plow, for $7.00, to his friend William Massie.[52]

A year now passed before he was ready to advertise his implement for sale at Lexington and Staunton stores. In the "Lexington Union" for January, 1833, Robert McCormick and Son announced that they were "engaged in the manufacture of their late Patent Hill Side Plough . . . and respectfully inform the public that they will at all times have on hand an assortment of said Ploughs. . . . These ploughs will be found upon examination and trial, to be more durable than the common plough, equal in point of fact to two ploughs, being double and without any increased weight." [53] Eight months later Cyrus stated in the same paper that he had satisfactorily tested the implement and intended "to get it into operation as extensively as practicable by selling patent-rights or otherwise." Four testimonials were added, one by Colonel James McDowell, who had bought two in the spring of 1832 and was so pleased that he believed they were "the best ploughs for a hilly country ever invented." [54]

While sales of his plow were increasing, Cyrus raised its price to $9.00, remodeled it, and made it self-sharpening.[55] This meant that the operator could turn over the shares of the implement at the end of each furrow and wear their points equally on top and bottom. A patent was secured for this, and

[51] C. H. McCormick to Wm. Massie, May 12, 1831. R. McCormick to C. H. McCormick, Dec. 5, 1831.
[52] MS. receipt from C. H. McCormick to Wm. Massie, Sept. 29, 1831.
[53] "Lexington Union," Jan. 12, 1833.
[54] Ibid., Aug. 17, 1833.
[55] MS. receipts of C. H. and R. McCormick to Wm. Massie, Mch. 31 and May 19, 1835.

other improvements, on November 19, 1833.[56] During the previous month, the inventor had intended to exhibit it at the fair of the Rockbridge County Agricultural Society, but for some unknown reason he was confused as to the date of the meeting and arrived at the show-grounds after most of the crowd had left.[57] Nevertheless three farmers who had seen it there, certified in the "Lexington Union": "We believe that it is destined to take an important stand among the agricultural improvements of our country, as we have never seen a hillside plough which combines more decided advantages." [58] Dr. Robert Barton, to whom reference has already been made, mentioned the plow, in a letter to his friend Edmund Ruffin, editor of the "Farmers' Register" of Richmond.[59] In this way news of the implement crossed the Blue Ridge for the first time and by 1835, both the "Mechanics' Magazine" of New York and the "Southern Agriculturist" of Charleston had given it space in their pages.[60]

The Rockbridge County Agricultural Society named Cyrus McCormick one of the judges of the agricultural implements exhibited at its autumn fair in 1835, but no premium was offered for the best plow. In all likelihood he did not find his appointment onerous, and if he concurred with the report of

[56] "Copies of Specifications and Patents of Cyrus McCormick, Certified by the Commissioner of Patents."

[57] "Lexington Union," Oct. 26, 1833. He exhibited it at Fancy Hill, at the fair-ground, and at Lexington the next day. At this fair Robert McCormick was a member of the Committee on Mechanical Improvements. *Ibid.,* Sept. 18, 1833.

[58] *Ibid.,* Feb. 22, Apr. 5, and Aug. 16, 1834.

[59] "Farmers' Register," Jan., 1834, p. 487.

[60] "Mechanics' Magazine and Register of Inventions and Improvements" (N. Y.), Feb., 1834, pp. 70-72. Cuts of the plow are shown. "Southern Agriculturist," May, 1835, pp. 272-274. "Journal of the Franklin Institute" (Phila.), VIII (1831), p. 338; XIII (1834), p. 318. "American Railroad Journal and Advocate of Internal Improvements" (N. Y.), Mch. 22, 1834, p. 167.

the society after the meeting was over, he thoroughly enjoyed the exhibition:

It was truly a noble sight to see the bone and sinew of the country assembled together under such a cheering aspect. . . . Much of the beauty, fashion, and good housewifery of the country and town have not only manifested their good wishes for our success, by honouring us with their presence, but have made such an exhibition of their skill, ingenuity and quality of household manufacture exhibited by them, as reflects lasting honour both on themselves and the country of which they may be truly said to be its highest ornament.[61]

For four years after 1835 the McCormicks were so occupied with a smelting furnace that the plows were temporarily laid aside. Not until December, 1839, when the iron venture seemed doomed to failure, did Cyrus McCormick once again advertise that he intended to resume their manufacture.[62] The next year he exhibited them on court days at Staunton and began again to collect certificates of their worth from farmers who had used them. The lease of the furnace in January, 1841, slowed up their manufacture, although he was then selling them as far away as Lynchburg.[63]

The increasing reaper sales after 1841 quickly thrust all other projects into the background. In 1842 his plows were still displayed at a Staunton store, and the next year a field trial with two rivals in Loudoun County resulted in a doubtful defeat for the McCormick.[64] Long trips to the West, the press of reaper-making at Walnut Grove, and the illness and death

[61] "Lexington Gazette," Nov. 20, 1835.
[62] "Richmond [Va.] Enquirer," Dec. 12, 14, 17, 1839, and Jan. 28, 1840.
[63] "Staunton Spectator," Feb. 20 and 27, Sept. 17 and 24, and Oct. 1, 1840. The price was $10 for a plow with wrought-iron shares, and $8.50 for one with cast-iron shares. C. H. McCormick to Wm. Massie, Mch. 25, Aug. 16 and 29, 1840; Feb. 10, Apr. 3, and Dec. 30, 1841.
[64] "Staunton Spectator," Mch. 3, 1842. "Southern Planter" (Richmond, Va.), July, 1843, pp. 163, 164.

of Robert McCormick in 1846, combined to end the plow
business. In early 1847, when Cyrus was planning to establish
his reaper factory in Chicago, he, for the moment, talked of
resuming plow-making in the old blacksmith shop on the farm.
He so announced in the "Richmond Enquirer," flinging a challenge to the world that his implement was the "only perfect
self-sharpener in use." [65] The patent was about to expire, however, and his failure to secure its renewal meant that every
blacksmith in the land could make his plows without interference from the inventor.[66] Thereafter McCormick's self-sharp-
ening horizontal plow passed into history, although its inventor
recalled it with pride when he told his friends of his youth.[67]

These inventions did not have a wide sale, even in the Valley
of Virginia, and they were not of great importance in the agricultural history of the time. The plow alone enjoyed a local
reputation for more than a decade, but Cyrus McCormick had
neither enough capital nor a sufficiently unique implement to
compete successfully with the big plow-makers of his neighborhood. The ironmasters of the Valley often manufactured plows
in connection with their furnaces,[68] and their success played its
part in leading Cyrus to his unfortunate venture in the iron
business in 1836.

[65] "Richmond Enquirer," Mch. 19, 1847, McCormick wrote: "Other pressing engagements have hitherto prevented much attention from being bestowed upon its general introduction."
[66] Salem G. Pattison, compiler, "McCormick Extension Case of 1848"
(Chicago, 1900), Sec. III, C. H. McCormick to E. Burke, Commr. of
Patents, Feb. 12, 1848. Hereafter cited as "Pattison." "Congressional Globe,"
30th Cong., 1st Sess. (Mch. 10, 1848), p. 450; 30th Cong., 2d Sess. (Dec.
27, 1848), p. 92.
[67] "Sketch of My Life," by C. H. McCormick, Aug. 4, 1876. C. H.
McCormick to H. Baldwin, Jr., Mch. 7, 1867. Memo. of a conversation
between C. H. McCormick, W. J. Hanna, and C. H. McCormick, Jr., Mch.
14, 1882. Henry Howe, "Adventures and Achievements of Americans"
(Cincinnati and N. Y., 1859), pp. 153-157.
[68] J. C. Shields, "Developement [sic] in Rockbridge," in the "Buena
Vista Advocate," Jan. 17, 1890.

It is important to note the close association of father and son in the manufacture and sale of the hemp-break and the plow. In the eyes of the world, Walnut Grove was the factory site of "Robert McCormick and Son," and although it seems certain that no legal partnership existed, the son was an associate rather than an employee of his father. Because Cyrus made his father's hemp-breaks in Kentucky, and Robert's blacksmith shop was used for the manufacture of Cyrus's plows, those in the Valley who did not share the confidence of the Mc-Cormicks had difficulty in separating the identities of father and son as inventors.

Each patented the products of his own skill, however, and the correspondence of the two men during the years 1831-32 makes it clear that coöperation in manufacture rather than in invention was the rule. Cyrus suggested improvements in his father's hemp-break and hydraulic machine, but never regarded these implements as his own property.[69] In like manner Robert associated with his son for a brief period in the manufacture of "their . . . plough," [70] but his letters leave no doubt that Cyrus was the inventor. A realization of this close business relationship is necessary as one approaches the story of the invention of the reaper. This implement was first constructed by Cyrus while he and his father were engaged in the hemp-break and plow business, and there is every reason to suppose that they adopted in relation to its patent and sale the same practice which they were following in making and marketing the implements mentioned in this chapter.

Despite the fact that these minor inventions did not bring wealth and renown to Robert and Cyrus, they do illustrate the new spirit in American agriculture. As Robert had in 1822 questioned the justice of Calvin's doctrine of predestination, so

[69] R. McCormick to C. H. McCormick, Dec. 23, 1831, Feb. 6 and May 4, 1832.
[70] "Lexington Union," Jan. 12, 1833.

he was also ready to substitute more efficient farming implements for those sanctioned by long usage. To secede from his
church was a personal matter which could be accomplished
without the consent of his neighbors, but it was an infinitely
more difficult task to persuade his fellow-farmers to give up the
flail for his thresher or to prepare their hemp with his break.
Lacking the aggressiveness to lead a revolt, he nevertheless, by
his refusal to accept humbly the teaching of the fathers both in
the domain of the Church and on the farm, was an insurgent
against the conservatism of his locality toward its two major
interests. The son accepted the father's Presbyterianism, but his
inherited inventive talent and business ability enabled him to
play a noteworthy part in the agricultural revolution of the
generation preceding the Civil War.

CHAPTER III

THE MECHANICAL BACKGROUND OF THE McCORMICK REAPER

DURING the youth of Cyrus McCormick steam- and water-driven machinery was gradually replacing the manual skill of the artisan in the field of manufacturing. For almost one hundred years textile-makers had been the chief beneficiaries of inventive genius, while conservatism and age-old inertia still ruled the country-side. The industrial revolution, well under way in America by 1830, impelled farmers to produce a surplus of raw materials and food for the supply of the factories and factory employees, so rapidly increasing in number.

Coincident with the growing capacity of the cities to purchase agricultural products, soil-exhaustion was lessening the yield per acre along the Eastern seaboard.[1] Each year much new soil in the West was broken by the plow, but if a means of transportation to market were lacking it was a sheer waste of land and labor to harvest more than could be used in the farmer's home. The lure of the West and of the city kept farm wages high and workmen few. With a doubtful labor supply, the landowner, in so far as uncertain weather conditions would permit, accommodated the size of his crop to the number of his helpers. The invention of horse-driven farm implements was therefore urgently needed to permit agricultural production to keep step with the quickening pace of city life, but

[1] Avery O. Craven, "Soil Exhaustion as a Factor in the Agricultural History of Virginia and Maryland, 1606-1860" (undated, Urbana, Ill.). Hereafter cited as "Craven."

substitutes for manual labor would avail little unless the farmer were taught to prepare his fields for their use and his hired men were persuaded that machinery was not their enemy.

Although land, labor, transportation, markets, education, and inventions suggest six of the chief needs of the American farmer in 1830, no one of these could be filled without affecting each of the others; nor would the satisfaction of any one of them yield its fullest benefits until all of the rest had also been successfully met. More concretely, the reaper deserves much emphasis in a study of the agricultural renaissance in America after 1830, but its wide use and great importance depended in no small measure upon other tendencies and inventions which it also stimulated. Among these were the extension of railroad lines, the westward movement, the increasing immigration from Europe, the growth of manufacturing and of a city population, the employment of better methods of cultivation, and the increased production of cereals. Causes and effects so merge that they cannot be clearly differentiated.

The American farmer in 1830, however, was far better prepared to welcome a new day in his occupation than were the peasants of Europe. He was a freeholder, and was not held by a customary tenure to a minute patch of land which had been tilled for generations by his forefathers. America, of necessity, signified movement. The American farmer had been forced to earn his land from Nature in a way unknown to the European husbandman of his own day. He was accustomed to change, for in his new country change was necessary to life. The unusual was to be expected and energy was constantly required to keep his arable land from reverting to the wilderness from which he had wrested it. The English squire could rely upon great bands of Irish laborers crossing the Channel to help in each harvest season, but the American farmer found last year's immigrant settled beside him, with his own grain to cut. His environment compelled him to be acquisitive, and he was prone to add more acres to his freehold than he could well keep under cultivation. Since lines of communication were needed to bind together the enormous expanse of America, if the nation were long to endure, transportation was inevitably a first concern of government. In short, the character of the farmer, the abundance of land, the scarcity of labor, the coming of railroad and steamboat, and the growth of cities, in some measure explain why the most significant agricultural inventions in modern times were made in the United States.

Of all the inventions during the first half of the nineteenth century which revolutionized agriculture, the reaper was probably the most important. Grain was a staple crop throughout the temperate zones the world over, and the appearance of a machine which permitted the farmer to reap as much as he could sow brought changes in cereal-culture as far-reaching in their importance as those which attended the cotton-gin of Eli Whitney in the South. Without the stimulus of the latter upon the production of cotton, the improvements in spinning and weaving machinery, made by Hargreaves, Crompton, Arkwright, and others, would have been largely futile. The gin was an essential link in the chain of machinery which had to be forged before men and women would make cotton as well as woolen clothing their usual attire. As Whitney's invention was important in its effect upon one of the basic necessities of human life, so the first successful reaper was of great significance in its influence upon the food supply of the world. This machine was necessary if the increasing millions of city dwellers were to have low-priced bread. City and country life must be complementary for industrial society to exist, and the few inventors who have conspicuously aided in maintaining this equilibrium deserve much emphasis.

In view of the long and urgent need for a horse-power reaper, it is surprising that the sickle held an unchallenged sway over the harvest fields of the world for so many centuries.

The farmer continued to use his hand implements until a machine appeared which cut the grain effectively; handled it so
gently that the ripe kernels were not shaken from the ear; and
left the severed stalks so well arranged that the binder could
make an orderly sheaf without difficulty. This standard of
performance was first attained by a reaper in 1831, and Cyrus
McCormick, its inventor, labored fifteen years longer before he
convinced many grain-growers that he had found a way.

The McCormick reaper is a combination of seven essential
parts.[2] In spite of the one hundred years of use and experiment
since its invention, no alteration which materially changed any
one of these parts has been found advisable. Forerunners of
Cyrus McCormick had used one or more of the seven prior to
1831, but he was the first to unite them all into an effective
whole. A familiarity with these few basic principles is essential
to an understanding of the work of McCormick's predecessors
and the history of his reaper.

The motive power must draw rather than push the reaper
forward through the grain.[3] When the machine is propelled
from behind, there is great difficulty in guiding it in a straight
line across the field and particularly in turning it at the end of
each course. Furthermore, because the animals cannot walk in
front of the knife without damage to the crop, they are placed
at the stubble side of the reaper. This side draft, as it is called,
permits the use of a horizontal knife, vibrating close to the
ground at right angles to the direction in which the reaper
advances. To aid in separating a swath from the standing crop,
and to turn it toward the blade, a divider of wood and iron,
roughly triangular in shape, extends from the grain end of the

[2] R. B. Swift, "Who Invented the Reaper," in the "Implement Age," Apr.
15, 1897. Letter of C. H. McCormick to the editor of the "North British
Agriculturist" (Edinburgh), for Oct. 14, 1863.
[3] This discussion does not include the header, an implement still used
to-day, which clips the heads from the stalks and leaves the latter standing
in the field. The header is normally propelled from the rear.

cutter-bar. On this bar, above or above and below the knife, is a row of projecting guards or fingers, perhaps four or five inches apart. Their points enter the grain just ahead of the vibrating blade and hold the straws in a vertical position while these are being severed. They serve the same purpose as the hand or knee of a carpenter, which steadies a board while he saws it.

The cutter, fingers, and divider work close to the ground, but a device is also necessary to bend the heads of the grain gently toward the knife and to push the severed stalks back upon the platform of the reaper. This double task is performed by the reel. Its arms or wings of thin slats, each parallel to and about as long as the cutter, revolve in a clockwise direction above the knife, as the machine moves forward. When a gavel has accumulated on the horizontal surface of boards back of the blade, known as the platform, it is raked to the ground by a man who walks beside the machine. Without the platform, the reaper would deliver the cut grain in swath and the labor of binding the strewn stalks would be greatly increased. Finally, a large ground wheel carries most of the weight of the implement. As the horses pull ahead and this wheel turns, the power thus generated is transmitted by cogs and bands to the reel and the cutter.

Thus, side draft, vibrating horizontal knife, divider, fingers, reel, platform, and main wheel are the seven essential parts of the reaper. Each of these is related to and dependent upon most of the others, and all interlock to solve the difficult problem of harvesting grain. The reel throws the grain on the platform with the heads toward the rear of the machine. Therefore the reel and the platform—not separately, but together—handle the cut grain effectively. The dividing process is accomplished by the divider and by the forward motion of the reaper, the reel which swings the swath against the knife, and by the fingers which make the necessary minute separations within the swath itself. All parts save the platform are essential to the cutting, and neither this nor the orderly division and handling of the grain could be effected without the main wheel to furnish the power for the reel and the cutter. Therefore a machine with six but not seven of these elements, or even with all of them included but not harmoniously working in conjunction, might well be a total failure. Perfection in proportion and in construction is essential even when all of the necessary principles are present.

An effective combination of elements already well known may be patented. That is to say, no one of the parts necessary to the success of a machine needs to be original with the inventor, but all must have been for the first time so united as to produce the long-sought-for result. "He who fails of making a successful machine, although he approaches within a single step of success, is not regarded as the inventor, nor entitled to the protection of the law; while he who supplies the necessary link in the chain of invention, and makes the machine a successful one, is regarded as the true inventor whose right is to be protected." [4] This right of protection presumes that the inventor has secured a patent from the Government and has manufactured (or provided for the manufacture of) his machine so that the public may have the opportunity to enjoy its use. An implement, such as a reaper, which has no commercial value, has no value at all. "A single machine made and practically hidden away shall not be allowed to defeat a patent when

[4] "In the Patent Office of the United States. In the Matter of the Application of Cyrus H. McCormick for the Extension of His Patent for an Improvement in Reaping Machines, dated Jan. 31, 1845," pp. 199-202, deposition of Edmund Burke, ex-Commr. of Patents, July 9, 1856. This volume will be cited hereafter as "McCormick Extension Case, Patent of 1845." *Grant vs. Raymond,* 6 Peters 318; *Seymour vs. Osborne,* 11 Wallace 518; *Imhaeser vs. Buerk,* 101 U. S. 647; *Parks vs. Booth,* 102 U. S. 96; *Loom Co. vs. Higgins,* 105 U. S. 580; *Clough vs. Barker,* 106 U. S. 166. "Decisions of the Commissioner of Patents for 1869" (Washington, 1870), p. 6.

a subsequent inventor has shown due diligence." [5] The patentee of a new device may consider as the date of its origin the time when he first successfully employed it, rather than the day on which he received his patent.[6] These mechanical and legal principles will find frequent application in the course of this narrative.

At least as early as the first century of the Christian era men were endeavoring to reap grain by horse-power. About 70 A.D., Pliny the Elder noted that "in the vast domains of the provinces of Gaul a large hollow frame, armed with teeth and supported on two wheels, is driven through the standing corn, the beasts being yoked behind it; the result being, that the ears are torn off and fall within the frame." [7] The attendant of this historic header probably assisted in guiding the severed ears into the cart.[8] Palladius, a writer of the fourth century, elaborated upon Pliny's description and implied that the machine was still in use in Gaul.[9] How long these implements continued to be em-

[5] Knight, "American Mechanical Dictionary," III, p. 1891. Robert L. Ardrey, "The Harvesting Machine Industry," in the "Scientific American" (N. Y.), LIV, Supplement, pp. 22544-22547. Letter of C. H. McCormick in the "No. British Agriculturist," Oct. 14, 1863, p. 50.

[6] For a slight qualification of this generalization see *post,* p. 438, ftn. 25.

[7] J. Bostock and H. T. Riley, translators, "Natural History of Pliny" (6 vols., London, 1853-57), IV, p. 103.

[8] Bennet Woodcroft, compiler, "Specifications of English Patents for Reaping Machines" (London, 1853), pp. 2 ff. Hereafter cited as "Woodcroft." Robert L. Ardrey, "American Agricultural Implements" (Chicago, 1894), p. 41. This writer states that at Ungarisch-Altenburg near Vienna is a model of a primitive reaper copied from a stone carving in the vicinity. It has a revolving cylindrical drum, carrying a projecting circular knife at its base, and a notched rim above to aid in delivering the grain in swath. Ardrey surmises that this implement was used by the Carthaginians who colonized there about 150 B.C.

[9] Since R. T. Ae. Palladius (cir. 350 A.D.), "De Re Rustica" (T. Owen, trans., London, 1803), Book VII, Tit. II, is little more than a poetical rendition of Columella, a writer of the first century A.D., it is probable that he made no effort to learn whether the Gallic header was still in use. Cuts of the Gallic header are in Peter T. Dondlinger, "The Book of Wheat" (N. Y.,

ployed is unknown. About twelve hundred years intervened before another reference was made to a mechanical grain-cutter. Conrad Heresbach (1496-1576), a prolific writer of the court of Cleves, in his "Four Books of Husbandry" mentioned the Gallic machine, but was certain that it would be useless in his hilly homeland.[10]

The beginning of the modern history of reaping machinery came almost simultaneously in England and America. Arthur Young published in his "Annals of Agriculture" for 1784 a description of the primitive header of the Gauls, while in the preceding year the Society for the Encouragement of Arts, Manufactures, and Commerce in Great Britain began its practice of offering a gold medal for an effective reaping and mowing machine.[11] As a result of this offer and of Young's account of the ancient machine, William Pitt of Pendeford in 1786 constructed an implement in which a circular motion was given to the Gallic stripping device. Gearing from the wheels of a cart revolved a horizontal cylindrical cutter that was expected to head the ripe grain as the machine was pushed through the field. The heads, when severed, fell upon a platform and thence into a box from which a man with a fork transferred them to a cart for carriage to the barn.[12] The machine was never pat-

1908), pp. 80-84, and Jean A. Barral, "Dictionaire d'Agriculture" (4 vols., Paris, 1885 ff.) III, under "Moissonneuse (mécanique)."

[10] Barnaby Googe, translator, "Conrad Heresbach's Foure Bookes of Husbandry" (London, 1577, 1601, 1614), pp. 39, 40.

[11] Arthur Young, "Annals of Agriculture and Other Useful Arts" (London, 1784-1808), IV, p. 205. "Journal of the Society of Arts" (London, 1783 ff.), I, pp. 63, 107. A prize was offered annually for about thirty-five years, but was never awarded. *Ibid.*, XXXI (1883, n.s.), pp. 324-327, it is stated that the first offer was made by the society in 1780. "Scots' Magazine" (Edinburgh), 1762, p. 404.

[12] Young, VIII (1787), p. 161: Cut and description of the machine. Knight, *op. cit.*, III, p. 1890. "The Complete Farmer, or a General Dictionary of Husbandry" (4th ed., London, 1793); the page headed "Rag," gives two cuts of it, and there is a description on page "Rea." "American Agriculturist," 1854, No. 3, p. 35.

ented and seems to have given little if any actual service, but it was the first attempt to operate a grain-cutter by power transmitted from the wheels.

About seven years later a very similar implement was constructed in the United States to gather clover heads, but horses pulled rather than pushed it through the grass.[13] Adam Walker in his "System of Familiar Philosophy in Twelve Lectures" (seventh edition, London, 1795) pictured a reaper consisting of a circular cutter of seven scythes revolving over a plate with sharpened steel points. There was also illustrated a sweep-rake on a vertical axis to deliver the cut grain in gavels from the platform of the machine. Although no other reference to this machine has been found, it seems to have been the first to employ a circular cutter, fingers, and self-rake.[14]

In 1799, Joseph Boyce of Marylebone, England, was granted the first patent ever issued for a reaper. Boyce used six curved knives fitted radially on a vertical spindle. These cutters were geared from the wheels and were protected by guards that also aided in holding the grain to the knife. The severed stalks were delivered in swath as the machine was pulled through the field.[15] The next year, another Englishman, Robert Meares of

[13] "Transactions of the Society Instituted in the State of New York for the Promotion of Agriculture, Arts and Manufactures," I (Albany, 1792), pp. 77, 78. A cut and description of the machine will be found in Ezra L'Hommedieu, "On the Raising of Red Clover Seed," in "Gleanings from the Most Celebrated Books on Husbandry, Gardening, and Rural Affairs" (Phila., 1803), p. 80. Two clover-seed collectors are described, one of which is a header.

[14] Woodcroft, p. 6. John P. Alexander, "American Harvesting Machines," in the "American Inventor" (Washington), Aug. 1, 1901, p. 3. "Agricultural Chronicle, Machinery, and Horticultural Gazette" (London), May, 1902, pp. 29 ff. Lincoln-Young, "Agricultural Survey by the Board of Agriculture" (London, 1799), pp. 69, 70.

[15] "Abridgement of Patent Specifications Relating to Agriculture, Div. 1, Field Implements, 1618-1866," p. 30. "Gardeners' Chronicle and Agricultural Gazette" (London), Sept. 4, 1852, p. 569. Hereafter cited as "Gardeners' Chronicle." "Prairie Farmer," XII (1852), pp. 86-88.

Frome, patented the first cutter based upon the action of a pair
of shears. In fact, the machine was little more than a large pair
of long-handled garden shears mounted on wheels, although
there was a gathering bow on the back of each blade.[16] Three
years later (1803) the first reaper patent in the United States
was granted to Richard French and John J. Hawkins of New
Jersey for an implement with scythes revolving on a pivot.[17]
After twenty years of experiment, therefore, the side draft,
fingers, platform, and utilization of power from the wheels,
four of the seven essential parts of a modern reaper, had been
more or less clearly foreseen.

The accompanying chart illustrates the mechanical development of the reaper in England and America from 1799 to 1831,
the date of Cyrus McCormick's invention. Most of the significant early grain-cutters were constructed by Englishmen. Both
the push and the pull principles were employed before 1830,
with a decided preference for the former. Theoretically it
seemed to be more justifiable to apply the power in the rear,
since with the horses in front a swath had to be cut by hand before the reaper could start in the field. With the shafts in front,
and the cutter at one side and behind the horse, the weight of
the machine was so distributed that it could not be drawn
forward with ease. There was an unequal drag upon the two
flanks of the animal which tended to pull him from a straight
course parallel to the grain. And yet if the motive power were
to be in the front, the cutter must obviously extend to one side.
This side-draft evil, as it was known, was to be an object of
concern to McCormick and his rivals for many years. Placing
a heavy main driving wheel directly behind the horse went

[16] "Copies of Specifications of English Patents," XXXI, No. 2404. Woodcroft, p. 7. For a cut of the machine see the "American Agriculturist,"
Sept. 27, 1854, p. 35.
[17] Harper's Encyclopædia of United States History (N. Y., 1905), VI,
pp. 68-70. "Orchard and Farm" (San Francisco), Feb., 1910, p. 7.

Date	Inventor	Draft	Traction	Knife	Fingers	Divider	Reel	Delivery	Remarks
1786	Wm. Pitt, Pendeford, England.	Push.	Two-wheel cart, with gearing to the cutter.	Horizontal, cylindrical stripper which could be raised or lowered.	None.	None.	None.	Combined platform and cart.	A header.
1799	A. Walker, England	Push.	Wheelbarrow-form carriage.	Circular cutter of 7 scythes, which could be raised or lowered by altering size of wheel.	The scythes revolved over plate having sharp steel points.	None.	None.	Sweep-rake on vertical axis to deliver grain in gavels.	Probably never used.
1799	Jos. Boyce, Marylebone, England.	Pull.	Two-wheel cart, with gearing to the cutters.	Six curved knives, fitted radially on vertical spindles.	Knives protected by guards which aided in holding grain to be cut.	None.	None.	In swath.	First patented reaper.
1800	Robt. Meares, Frome, England.	Push	Two-wheel frame, pushed by hand.	Pair of long shears worked by hand.	None.	None.	None.	Gathering bow on back of each blade.	First shear-action cutter.
1805	T. J. Plucknett, Surrey, England.	Push or Pull.	Two-wheel cart, with spindle geared from axle.	Circular, serrated-edge, plate knife, suspended under frame of machine on vertical spindle.	"Leaders or horns" with sharp upper edges, projecting from carriage to guide grain to cutter.	"Horns" seem to have served as divider.	None.	In swath.	First attempt to provide a divider.
1806	Gladstone, Castle Douglas, Scotland.	Pull.	Two-wheel cart, with cutter geared from axle. Cutter could be thrown out of gear.	Circular disk cutter of 6 pieces on revolving, vertical axis. A fixed emery wheel made the knife self-sharpening. Disk adjustable in height.	Wooden fingers just above cutting disk.	None(?).	None.	Attendant raked grain off in gavels from cutting platform. By 1815, a rotary rake on a vertical axis, to strip the teeth. Probably first ever used, unless Walker reaper was actually operated in 1799.	
1807	Salmon, Woburn, Bedfordshire, England.	Push.	Two-wheel cart, with cutter geared by a crank and pitman to axle.	Two sets of horizontal, shear-like knives, the upper set vibrating over the lower, stationary one. Adjustable in height.	Projecting fingers to gather grain and hold it while being cut.	None(?).	None.	A rake, suspended and reciprocating sideways to discharge grain from platform in gavels.	
1811	Jas. Smith, Deanston, Perthshire, Scotland.	Push.	Two-wheel cart, with cutter geared to axle.	Revolving circular cutter of 6 steel segments. Could be revolved in either direction; was adjustable in height, and could be lifted to clear obstacles in field.	None.	None.	None.	Cutter was fixed on base of drum which revolved and threw off cut grain in swath. Drum was shaped like frustum of a cone, with base uppermost.	First reaper to use conical drum principle of delivery.
1811	Donald Cummings, Northumberland, England.	Push.	Triangular-shaped cart with cutter geared from wheels.	Revolving circular cutters on vertical spindles.	Projecting bars guided grain to cutter.	None.	Gatherers or "holdfasts," consisting of radial arms on a revolving spindle.	Endless apron on fluted rollers to deliver grain at side in swath.	First use of device to serve as a reel, but unlike the modern one.
1814	Jas. Dobbs, Birmingham, England.	Push.	Wheelbarrow-form carriage with 2 small wheels in front. Cutter revolved as operator turned windlass.	Revolving cutter with sickle teeth. Shears were mentioned as alternative.	Revolving rollers just above knife to hold grain while being cut.	Triangular shaped projecting arms to guide grain to rollers.	None.	Tilt platform by which grain could be delivered in gavels.	Apparently first machine to use triangular dividers and tilt platform.
1815	M. Scott, Ormiston, England.	Pull.	Two-wheel frame, with cutter geared to axle. Cutter could be thrown out of gear.	A circular cutter ring, to which were screwed 16 blades with serrated edges.	Revolving drum had 24 hook-shaped "collectors" or rakes.	None(?).	None.	A revolving drum by which cut grain was thrown off in swath.	
1820	Jos. Mann, Cumberland, England.	Push or Pull.	Seems to have been first to put main wheel directly behind horse.	Revolving polygonal cutter with 12 equal sides.	Revolving rakes acted similarly to fingers.	None.	Revolving rakes in part fulfilled function of modern reel.	Six vertical revolving rakes to deliver grain in swath, with aid of a comb which stripped cut grain from rakes. Rakes revolved on a drum.	
1822	Henry Ogle, Rennington, and T. and J. Brown, Northumberland, England.	Pull.	Two-wheel cart. A horizontal working beam was vibrated by cogs from each wheel.	Straight edge, vibrating, horizontal blade on a cutter bar.	Teeth three inches long projected from cutter bar.	None.	A cylindrical horizontal revolving rake, consisting of 8 vanes.	A tilt platform, placed at side and behind main driving wheel.	First use of a reel which resembled the modern one.
1822	Jeremiah Bailey, Chester Cy., Penn.	Pull.	Two-wheel cart with cutter geared to axle.	Circular cutter of 6 self-sharpening scythes, suspended under frame of cart on shaft.	None.	None.	None.	In swath.	Resembled a mower. Peter Gaillard of Pennsylvania had a similar one in 1812.
1825	Jas. Ten Eyck, Somerset Cy., N. J.	Push.	Two-wheel cart with cutter geared to wheels.	A horizontal cylinder with spiral knives cutting against straight edges.	Below revolving cylinder were several fingers, each about 9 inches long.	None.	None.	In swath.	The cutting cylinder resembled McCormick's reel in shape but not in function.
1827	Patrick Bell, Mid Lioch, Scotland.	Push.	Square frame on 2 large wheels of equal size, with cutters geared to axle.	Two sets of horizontal, steel-edged, shear-action blades. Upper set vibrated over lower. Together they formed mechanical scissors.	Stationary iron fingers projecting between the blades.	None(?).	A small reel with 6 vanes. Could be adjusted to height of grain.	An endless apron made of a canvas sheet on rollers. Carried cut grain to stubble side of machine and discharged it in swath.	Never patented.
1831	Wm. Manning, Plainfield, N. J.	Push.	Two-wheel cart, with cutter geared from axle.	Spear-shaped cutters, attached to a vibrating bar. Cutters were sharpened on each edge.	Just below cutter were fingers 6 or 8 inches long, fixed on a bar.	Triangular divider.	None.	In swath.	First reaper patented in U. S. which had a divider.

These seventeen reapers were probably the most important of the thirty-three English, twenty-two American, two French, and one German machines which appeared in the period from 1786 to 1831. For more or less complete lists of these early reapers, see: Bennet Woodcroft, compiler, "Specifications of English Patents for Reaping Machines" (London, 1853); Wm. Elliott, "Patentees' Manual" (Washington, 1830); M. F. Miller, "The Evolution of Reaping Machines," United States Department of Agriculture, Office of Experiment Stations, Bulletin, No. 103; and the Journals of the Franklin Institute of Philadelphia.

far toward a solution of the difficulty. Mann, in 1820, was probably the first to experiment in this direction.

Prior to the McCormick machine, four cutting devices had been tried, a revolving horizontal knife-rack such as is used to-day in lawn-mowers; a cutting disk or a series of scythes turned by a revolving vertical pivot; mechanical scissors; and finally the principle which was ultimately to supersede all others, a horizontal knife vibrating at right angles to the line of draft. Such a knife might be one long blade or it might consist of individual knife-plates or teeth bolted on a cutter-bar. Minute variations in the length and the shape of the teeth and the angle between them and the projecting fingers, seemingly unimportant, sometimes made all the difference between success and failure.

Many harvests were to pass before the exact proportions for most effective cutting were finally determined. Cutters whose distance from the ground could be varied according to the length of the stubble desired, had been provided as early as the Pitt machine in 1786. Except in the Manning machine of 1831, which was too late to affect the experiments of McCormick in the same year, this vibrating knife had always been smooth-edged. Several, however, had used rotating plates or scythes with indented or serrated edges. Serrations aided in holding the grain to the knife and also lengthened the cutting edge. Fingers or their equivalent had been utilized by many of the early inventors, but no one had yet thought of making a double one with a slot through which the knife could vibrate. This would serve to protect the knife from obstructions in the field and at the same time hold the blade in line and increase its cutting efficiency.

Three chief methods of handling the severed grain had been discovered. A horizontal plane of wood back of the cutter had been frequently employed, and at least two men had experimented with a tilt-platform by which the grain could be dropped off at the side in gavels ready for binding.[18] Although the tilt-platforms were forerunners of the later droppers, neither of them worked well, and a man usually walked beside the machine to rake the grain from the platform in sheaf-size gavels. Several machines had a revolving drum above the cutter.[19] When the stalks fell against this rotating cylinder, they were spun around to one side and thrown off in swath. This rough treatment shelled the grain and also laid the stalks at angles to the line of draft varying with the speed of the machine. Because of this, drum delivery required the binders to make their own gavels, and often laid the grain in such fashion that orderly sheaves could not be made.

Endless webs or aprons of canvas on rollers had been invented to carry the grain from the knife and lay it in swath at the stubble side of the machine.[20] Automatic rakes also had been tried.[21] These were designed to sweep the grain from the platform when enough had accumulated to make a sheaf. The heyday of the self-rake, however, was not to come until after 1855. Side delivery was an essential, no matter how achieved, if the reaper were not to halt at the end of each course through the field and wait for the binders to catch up with the cutting. Otherwise the horses would tread upon the cut grain when they returned on their next round. If neither platform, drum, nor endless apron was employed, the grain would, of course, merely fall in swath at the back of the cutter and be trampled upon when the next course was run. Rear delivery would serve for mowing hay, but grain required more careful handling.

The very earliest machine of Pitt had geared the cutter

[18] Dobbs and Ogle. For cuts illustrating different cutting devices see Knight, II, p. 1489.
[19] Those of Smith, Kerr, Scott, etc.
[20] By Cummings and Bell.
[21] By Walker, Salmon, Gladstone, and Mann.

to the wheels. The whole subject of the most effective cranks, cogs, and pitman rods to vibrate or rotate the cutter and turn the reel is too technical to have place here. It can be appreciated, however, that the blade must rotate (or vibrate) many times faster than the ground wheel turns which furnishes the power. Therefore gearing is necessary, to transmit the power generated by the wheels and to effect this acceleration. The gearing must be kept free from dust and grain stalks so that it will not clog; and, too, it should be covered for the protection of the operator of the machine. Gladstone had discovered a method of throwing the cutter out of gear so that the reaper might move along the road without rotating the knife. Most of the predecessors of McCormick merely used a two-wheel cart as a frame, with no thought of one large driving wheel and a small caster to carry the blade at the side. The question of the proper distribution of weight, to make the draft of the machine as light as possible, also is involved in the structure of the frame. Even the width of the tread of the wheels is an important matter, because the rim will sink in the soft ground if it is too narrow, and will add unnecessarily to the weight if too broad.

The need for a device to bend the grain toward the knife had been foreseen by Cummings as early as 1811, but Ogle about ten years later was the first to use a horizontal reel which resembled the modern one. This fan is rotated by a belt from the wheel, and is turned with a speed proportioned to the forward motion of the machine and the velocity of the knife. It is about the same length as the cutter-bar, and its distance above this corresponds to the height of the grain. It must rotate gently if its wings are not to beat out much ripe grain.[22] A divider to extend ahead of the cutter on the grain side of the machine was the element most infrequently

[22] The Ten Eyck machine of 1825 had a revolving rack which resembled a reel, but its primary function was to cut.

used before 1831. The 1831 Manning patent was the first in America to describe one, although early English machines had appliances which were intended to answer much the same purpose.

Any one of these early machines might have cut well for a short time if the grain were upright and the field level, but such favorable conditions were infrequently, if ever, met at harvest-time. Tangled and lodged grain is to be expected, and land is rarely smooth. To construct a machine which would cut under all save the most extreme conditions, and also deliver the stalks in good order for binding, would alone serve to lift mechanical reaping from the realm of interesting but futile experiment to that of utility to the farmer. The need of skilful and exact coördination of the many parts essential to such success, helps to explain why the first practical reaper was so long delayed in its appearance. The problems of mowing and threshing were simple when compared with those which were faced in grain-harvesting. In the first, no thought had to be given to the handling of the cut grass, and in the second the grain could be fed to the machine in a manner best suited to its particular construction. Furthermore, experiments might be made with a thresher at all seasons of the year, but each harvest-time was very short and the inventor who found that his reaper did not work in practice was forced to await another summer before he could try again.

An intelligent farmer was obviously the man most likely to understand all phases of the problem of grain-cutting. If he was mechanically adroit he realized that the point of his sickle acted as a divider, his hand served as the reel and fingers, and the draw motion of his blade severed the stalks with the least effort. Cyrus McCormick had worked in the harvest every summer since he was old enough to swing a scythe, and his talent for mechanics permitted him to translate his ideas into tangible form. The conditions common to grain-fields on both sides of the Atlantic led men in England and America to quite similar conclusions concerning those general elements which necessarily comprised a successful reaper. It is not incredible, or even very surprising, that McCormick should combine in his machine certain parts which had been tried by others without his knowledge.

But these early experiments had too often been made by men who were unfamiliar with the farm. Meares was a dyer, Gladstone a millwright, Smith a cotton-spinner, and Ogle a school-teacher. James Dobbs of Birmingham was the most interesting of all. He was an actor and used his ingenious reaper to promote realism on the stage. In the "Birmingham Gazette" of October 10, 1814, appeared this curious advertisement.[23]

J. Dobbs most respectfully informs his Friends and the Public, that having invented a Machine to expedite the Reaping of Corn, etc., but having been unable to obtain the Patent till too late to give it a general inspection in the field with safety, he is induced to take advantage of his Theatrical Profession and make it known to his Friends, who have been anxious to see it, through that medium. . . . To conclude [the performance] will be presented the celebrated farce of Fortune's Frolic. The part of Robin Roughhead will be taken by Mr. Dobbs, in which he will work the Machine in character, in an Artificial Field of Wheat, planted as near as possible in the manner it grows.

Of all the early machines, that of Henry Ogle most closely resembled the first reaper of Cyrus McCormick. This implement had a reel, reciprocating smooth-edged knife, fingers, side draft, and platform. Apparently the only significant differences of construction between it and the McCormick were in the arrangement of the gearing, the shape of the frame, and the absence of a divider. Although a description of the machine was published in English magazines several years

[23] Quoted in Woodcroft, pp. 16, 17.

before 1831, Cyrus McCormick denied that he had ever heard of it.[24] But the Ogle reaper did not operate successfully throughout a single harvest. Forgotten after 1823, it was recalled at the time of the London World's Fair of 1851, when some one who had seen it thirty years before remembered that the McCormick reaper bore a striking resemblance to it. McCormick was at once charged with copying from it.[25] Why the Ogle machine did not succeed is open to question. The usual blame is placed upon its costliness, its defective construction, and hostile English labor.

A more prolonged attack upon the McCormick reaper was made by those who contended that Patrick Bell of Mid Lioch, near Dundee, Scotland, was the inventor of the first practical grain-cutter. Bell had made a model of his implement in 1827, and two reapers were tried with some success in the harvest of the following year.[26] Until 1831 he received flattering notice in the press of his own country, and twelve or fifteen machines which operated "with more or less success" were built by a Dundee firm.[27] Most of these reapers had been sold to purchasers within Bell's home county. After 1832 the outside world lost sight of the implement and its manufacture

[24] "Mechanics' Magazine, Museum, Register, Journal, and Gazette" (London, 1823 ff.), Nov. 12, 1825, p. 50. Thomas and Joseph Brown, founders of Alnwick, were so closely associated with Ogle, that the machine is sometimes attributed to them as well as to the schoolmaster.

[25] Ibid., Feb. 14, 1852, p. 123, letter of Benj. Cheverton. This is the earliest mention of the resemblance of the two reapers that has been found. "Gardeners' Chronicle," Sept. 4, 1852, p. 569. "London Times," Sept. 1, 1852, letter of Chas. May. John Wilson, "Lectures on the Results of the Great Exhibition of 1851" (2d ser., London, 1853), pp. 14-27. "Journal of the Society of Arts" (London), XXVIII, pp. 499 ff., and XXXI, pp. 324-327.

[26] "Quarterly Journal of Agriculture" (Edinburgh), I (1828-29), pp. 136, 217-219, 331. "Gardener's Magazine and Register of Rural and Domestic Improvement" (London, 1827 ff.), V, p. 557.

[27] John C. Loudon, "An Encyclopædia of Agriculture" (London, 1831), pp. 422-427. "Gardener's Magazine," etc., VI, p. 295; VII, p. 103, for long letters of P. Bell.

was virtually suspended.[28] Only one seems to have been operated in each harvest from 1837 to 1851, and that was used on the farm of the inventor's brother, George Bell,[29] in Scotland. In 1852, the year following the successful introduction of the McCormick reaper to England, William Crosskill, a manufacturer of that country, exhumed Bell's implement from its grave. It was at once proclaimed to be the model from which McCormick had copied and the first successful reaper ever invented.[30]

These chauvinists maintained that one or more Bell machines had been sold in America in the early 1830's, and that McCormick undoubtedly had adopted its principles as his own.[31] The skeptics who asked why the Bell reaper had not been a success in its own land between 1828 and 1852 were reminded of the lack of readiness of the English farmer for its reception, of the many ridges and furrows in the fields of Britain, and of the influx of cheap labor from Ireland every harvest season which made its use at that time either impossible or unnecessary. Of course, said they, when the potato famine caused a large Irish migration and death-rate, the Englishman had to find a substitute, and the long-forgotten Bell reaper came at once into its own.[32]

[28] James Jackson, "A Treatise on Agriculture and Dairy Husbandry" (Edinburgh, 1840), pp. 113, 114. "Mechanics' Magazine," etc. (London), LVII, pp. 233, 234.
[29] "Transactions of the Highland and Agricultural Society of Scotland" (Edinburgh), 3d ser., V, p. 183.
[30] "Notes and Queries" (London), Nov. 27, 1852, p. 506. "Economist" (London), Aug. 14, 1852, pp. 899, 900. "Quarterly Review" (London), CIII, pp. 419, 420. "Journal of Soc. of Arts," VI, pp. 698-700.
[31] "Gardeners' Chronicle," Jan. 24, 1852, p. 59; Sept. 4, 1852, p. 569. "Edinburgh Review," XCVI, pp. 155, 156. "Farmer's Magazine" (London), Sept., 1853, pp. 241-246. "Prairie Farmer," Jan., 1853, p. 14. "Canadian Journal" (Toronto), I (Sept., 1852), p. 39.
[32] "Gardeners' Chronicle," Sept. 25, 1852, pp. 618, 619; Jan. 24, 1852, p. 59; Aug. 14, 1852, p. 523; Dec. 25, 1852, p. 826; Sept. 17, 1853, pp. 601, 602. "Farmer's Magazine" (London), Jan., 1852, pp. 1, 14.

Time and again between 1830 and 1850 the English press deplored the scarcity of labor and the lack of a successful mechanical way to reap grain.[33] Many English articles during these years refer to the sickle, scythe, Hainault scythe, and hook as the sole effective harvesting tools for grain. Some few of them regret that the Bell machine had failed because it was too complicated and of defective construction.[34] The abundance of these accounts and the constant dissatisfaction because a better way had not been discovered, disprove the assertions of those champions of Bell that England was not ready for a reaper before 1850, and that the fault lay with the times and not with the machine. The joy with which the McCormick reaper was hailed at the Great Exhibition of 1851 is evidence of the satisfaction felt at the final solution of the problem of harvesting grain.[35]

[33] Alexander Jamieson, "A Dictionary of Mechanical Science, Arts, Manufactures, and Miscellaneous Knowledge" (London, 1827), II, p. 876. James Cleghorn, "System of Agriculture," in Encyclopædia Britannica (7th ed., Edinburgh, 1831), p. 269. John Sinclair, "The Code of Agriculture" (London, 1832), pp. 117, 118, 350. John R. McCulloch, "A Descriptive and Statistical Account of the British Empire" (London, 1847), pp. 468, 472, 476, 486-488, 573-580, 584, 586, 588. Charles F. Partington, "The British Cyclopædia of Arts and Sciences," etc. (2 vols., London, 1833-35), II, pp. 582, 583. R. Baldwin, "British Husbandry" (London, 1837), II, pp. 188-193. Cuthbert W. Johnson, "The Farmer's Encyclopædia and Dictionary of Rural Affairs" (London, 1842), p. 1033. David Low, "Elements of Practical Agriculture" (4th ed., London, 1843), p. 312. John Sproule, "Elements of Practical Agriculture" (3d ed., London, 1844), p. 270. M. Doyle and W. Rham, eds., "A Cyclopædia of Practical Husbandry and Rural Affairs in General" (London, 1844), p. 494.

[34] L. Herbert, "Engineers' and Mechanics' Encyclopædia" (London, 1836), II, p. 179. J. M. Wilson, "The Rural Cyclopædia," etc. (4 vols., Edinburgh, 1852), IV, pp. 27-29. "Farmer's Magazine" (London), 1838, pp. 115, 116. "Illustrated London News," Aug. 16, 1851, statement of J. S. Mechi. "Economist," Aug. 16, 1851, p. 899. "Farmers' Register," Aug., 1834, pp. 132-134, quoting from the "Quarterly Journal of Agriculture." "Journal of Soc. of Arts," VI, pp. 698-700, statement of Alfred Crosskill.

[35] *Post*, Chap. XVI.

If this were not enough, the fact that the Bell reaper, which was sold to a Mr. John B. Yates of Chittenango, New York, did not reach its destination until 1835, makes its arrival in the United States five years too late to affect the McCormick reaper of 1831.[36] If others came to America before or after that date, no record of their importation has been found. Furthermore, even when the Bell machine was promoted, after 1851, it gained no distinguished success other than before Scotch juries, until its manufacturers adopted the McCormick knife.[37] It is true that a description of the machine appeared before 1831 in English agricultural magazines which had a few American subscribers.[38] McCormick asserted on a number of occasions that he had never heard of the Bell reaper or read of it until twelve years after the first successful trial of his own.[39] It is impossible to prove that his statement is false, and the two machines are so unlike in construction that the contrasts between them are more striking than the similarities. Bell's was pushed, used a reciprocating scissor-action knife, and had a tiny reel two and a half feet in diameter and no

[36] "Gardener's Magazine," etc., XII, p. 704. "Scientific American," Oct. 30, 1852, p. 54. "Supreme Court of the United States, No. 34; Cyrus H. McCormick, Appellant, vs. Waite Talcott, Ralph Emmerson [sic] Jesse Blinn, and Sylvester Talcott, survivors of John H. Manny, Appeal from the Circuit Court of the United States for the Northern District of Illinois," pp. 741-751. Hereafter cited as *McCormick vs. Manny*, II.

[37] "Mechanics' Magazine," etc. (London), Dec., 1853, article by Lord Kinnaird. Letter of C. H. McCormick in the "No. British Agriculturist," Oct. 14, 1863. "Transactions Highland and Agrl. Soc.," 3d ser, XII, pp. 123-147, paper by J. Wilson. "Journal of Soc. of Arts," VI, pp. 698-700.

[38] See p. 67, ftns. 26, 27. "New England Farmer" (Boston), VIII, p. 189, copying from the "Fife Herald." "New York Farmer" (N. Y.), Apr., 1831, pp. 103, 104.

[39] Letter of C. H. McCormick in the "Scientific American," Nov. 13, 1852, p. 70. "Award on Reaping Machines at the Great Hamburg International Exhibition of 1863, Invention of the Reaper; Discussion of Merits between the Editor of the North British Agriculturist and others, and Cyrus H. McCormick," undated pamphlet printed in London,

platform.[40] McCormick's was a side-draft machine, with a reciprocating draw-cut blade, a reel six or eight feet in diameter, and a platform. The Bell machine was never patented and had virtually no sale outside its own county until a McCormick reaper was working in almost every State of the Union and in England.[41] But still, to-day, Bell is remembered in Great Britain as the inventor of the first successful grain-cutter.[42] In the parish church at Carmylie, Scotland, his old home, are memorial windows in his honor.[43]

In spite of the many attempts before 1830 to construct a successful reaper, the agricultural press in both England and America continued to deplore the slowness of the hand methods still necessarily employed in the harvest field.[44] Jonathan

[40] *Ibid.* Letter of C. H. McCormick in the "Scientific American," Nov. 13, 1852, p. 70. C. H. to L. J. McCormick, June 17, 1878, postscript.

[41] See p. 65, ftns. 28, 29.

[42] "Gardeners' Chronicle," Aug. 25, 1866, p. 817; Oct. 13, 1866, p. 978; Jan. 5, 1867, p. 11; Jan. 19, 1867, p. 58; Jan. 26, 1867, pp. 89, 90; July 13, 1867, p. 741; Oct. 5, 1867, pp. 1031, 1032; Nov. 30, 1867, p. 1229; Feb. 1, 1868, p. 109. The Highland and Agricultural Society of Scotland presented Bell with a silver salver inscribed "Inventor of first efficient reaping machine," and £1,000. Bell died Apr. 22, 1869. "Glasgow Herald," Sept. 8, 1926. James M. McBain, "Eminent Arbroathians, 1178-1894" (Arbroath, Scotland), pp. 363-378.

[43] There are a few temperate statements on this subject in English magazines. "Journal of Soc. of Arts," XXVI, pp. 369, 370. "Mark Lane Express" (London), Oct. 26, 1863.

[44] "New York Farmer," VII, p. 113, and "Farmers' Register," Aug., 1834, pp. 132-134, both copying an article by the Rev. Jas. Farquharson, "Cutting Grain Crops with the Common Scythe, as Practised in Aberdeenshire," in the "Quarterly Journal of Agriculture." Farquharson wrote, "It is certainly a remarkable circumstance in the history of mechanical science in this country, that the art of cutting down the cultivated crops should be so inadequately supplied with instruments." Thomas Sullivan, "On Reaping and Harvesting Grain Crops," in "Farmer's Magazine" (London), XII, pp. 101-105. Merritt F. Miller, "The Evolution of Reaping Machines," in "U. S. Dept. of Agriculture, Office of Experiment Stations, Bulletin No. 103" (Washington, 1902). Hereafter cited as "Miller." He notes 2 French, 1 German, 33 English, and 22 American machines before 1831.

Roberts, president of the Pennsylvania Agricultural Society said in 1823:

> In practical husbandry the expense of labor is a cardinal consideration. Since the year 1818, farmers have very sensibly felt that labour has been much dearer than produce. We can not speedily look for their equalization; a mitigation of this effect may be sought in some degree by improved implements. . . . Nothing is more wanted than the application of animal labour in the cutting of grain. It is the business on the farm which requires the most expedition, and it is always the most expensive labour. Such an invention can be no easy task, or the ingenuity of our fellow citizens would, ere this, have effected it. But we have no right to despair where there is not a physical impossibility. A liberal premium might well be employed to obtain such an object. . . . The scythe is improving from year to year—not so with the sickle—thirty years ago it was better than it is now.[45]

When harvest-time came every grain farmer in the world was faced with the same problem. There was imperative need of extra helpers to cut the ripened crop before the grain dropped from the heads and was lost. Heat hastened this process, and usually a farmer could not rely upon having more than a week or ten days in which to cut his grain without serious loss from shelling. Consequently every member of the family, sometimes an entire village, was called to the harvest field to assist in the reaping. This seasonal pressure for labor was largely due to the lack of effective harvesting implements. In other fields of agricultural work—such as plowing, seeding, soil-cultivation, grain-threshing, and hay-raking—horse-power had already been successfully applied, but a farmer had little use for grain-drills and threshing machines unless the intermediate step of reaping could be mechanically achieved.

Reaping hooks and sickles were the harvesting tools most frequently used in 1830.[46] The hook was a broad, heavy curved

[45] "American Farmer," V, pp. 307, 356, 361.
[46] "Penny Magazine" (London), IX, pp. 337 ff.

knife with a smooth edge, set in a wooden handle. The sickle, while varying in detail, was similar to the modern implement but had a saw-tooth blade. These implements had been employed for reaping for thousands of years, although for a long time prior to 1830 the scythe and the cradle-scythe had been winning more and more favor with the farmers of America. The hook and the sickle are manipulated with one hand, but the scythe has two grips on its long, bent wooden stock. The curved blade of the scythe is smooth-edged, and on its upper side, as it is held by the operator, may be affixed a cradle, consisting of three or more narrow, parallel strips of wood, shorter than the knife but curving similarly and fastened together with small crosspieces. The cradle is useful for laying the grain straight in the swath, with all the ears in one direction.

Viewed from a shady vantage-point, the business of reaping by hand has seemed since the days of Ruth and Boaz to be an appropriate subject for song and story.[47] In reality there were few tasks of the farmer less idyllic or more back-breaking and exhausting. The sickleman bent to his work, holding a few stalks of grain together in his left hand while he cut them close to the ground with a quick draw of his implement. When he had thus reaped a handful, he laid the straw on the stubble and repeated the process, from sunrise to sunset. Following him came one or two binders (bandsters), who tied the grain into sheaves, using straw for their cord. Others assembled from ten to fifteen sheaves into a shock, straw butts on the ground, heads together, and all capped with an additional sheaf to prevent moisture from penetrating to the grain. A woman or a boy usually brought up the rear with

[47] Holy Bible, Ruth, II. "Quarterly Journal of Agriculture," I, pp. 136-155: There are strong prejudices against the use of agricultural machinery. Many think it will destroy the gaiety and charm of rural life in harvest-time. "Lexington Gazette," June 15, 1843.

a large rake to clear the stubble of any loose straws and to carry the gleanings to the binders. If the grain was very ripe and tangled, much was wasted from the ear by shattering. After the harvest, hogs were often turned into the stubble to fatten on the leavings.

Working all day, one reaper with the necessary number of binders and shockers (stookers) might harvest two acres. In most grain the scythe was more effective than the sickle. A good scytheman in heavy upright grain could cut a seven and a half or eight foot swath of from ten to fifteen inches in depth at each stroke, and keep two or three assistants busy with the binding and shocking. But at best not much over three acres a day could be harvested in this manner. The owner of the grain, whether one of the laborers or one affluent enough to view the scene from horseback, would counsel speed, low cutting, and careful handling and gleaning. Often a wagon followed the workmen, carrying one barrel of water and one of some less innocent liquid—"ra-al Monongehely" or a mixture of molasses, ginger, and water.[48] Seventy-five cents or one dollar was the usual daily wage for an able-bodied man in harvest-time, but he would sometimes take a bushel of grain in payment of his hire.

Looking ahead to the age of the reaper, the manual methods of harvesting were most expensive by comparison. In 1830 a force of six laborers might harvest two acres of wheat a day. Thus the wage cost of the harvest per acre would be about

---

[48] "Southern Planter," July, 1848, p. 211: "The next best thing to the 'ra-al Monongaly' to string up the nerves of those who wield the scythe, is a drink composed of five gallons of iced water well mixed with half a gallon of molasses, one quart of vinegar, and two ounces of ginger." "American Farmer," July, 1853, p. 3; 5 gals. water, ½ gallon molasses, and ¼ lb. ginger, mixed and served hourly, "invigorating, refreshing, and safe, no matter how cold the water may be. The cooler the water, the more grateful will it be to the palate,—the more refreshing to the system, the surer of giving tone and strength to the harvester."

$3.00. If the acre yielded twenty bushels of grain and the market price of wheat was $1.50 per bushel, the farmer would receive a gross income from his crop of $30 an acre. It is impossible accurately to compute the cost of raising twenty bushels of wheat. Probably one third of the gross return can safely be considered the average net profit per acre. The cost of the seed (five to eight pecks an acre); the cultivation; the fertilizer, if any; the depreciation on the farm implements employed; the interest on the money invested; the cash value of the owner's time; and the expense of reaping, threshing, winnowing, bagging, and hauling to market would total two thirds of the sale price of the wheat.

In any event, the margin of safety was not great, and if labor was too high, transportation too long, or the market price too low, it did not pay the farmer to grow a surplus. If he did plant in excess of his own needs under such circumstances, it was often less costly (or perhaps slightly more profitable) to turn his stock into the grain and transform the cereal into pork and beef.[49] A Western farmer would occasionally offer workmen one half of his crop if they would aid him in his harvest. It was fortunate for the farmer in that day that he was usually self-sufficing and could eke out a bare livelihood even if he shut himself away from the outside world. But it was not so happy for the city dweller who depended upon the country for his food and the material for his clothing.

The first McCormick reaper of 1831 could harvest ten acres of grain a day with a force of eight men and one or two horses. One dollar an acre would be a liberal estimate of the cost of the harvest, without taking into account the increased

---

[49] "Ohio Cultivator," Oct. 15, 1853, p. 315: A bushel of corn will make 15 pounds of pork and 6 barrels of corn will make $11.25 worth of pork at $.02½ a pound. This is more profitable than selling corn at $.25 a bushel.

speed and the sale value of the bushel of grain which would normally have been lost by shattering if a cradle had been used. Five scythemen and about ten helpers would be required to harvest a like amount in a day. The saving in man-power by the use of the reaper was thus about one hundred per cent.[50] With good care the reaper would harvest one hundred acres per year for ten years. Consequently, with the machine selling at $100, the yearly depreciation cost was not very great. The area which could be sown in grain after the advent of the reaper was potentially multiplied many fold, granting always that the ground was fairly level and smooth.

The inventors who have been mentioned in this chapter were unquestionably striving to reach a glorious goal. It is indeed strange that it should be first attained by one who lived in a region abounding in stones and hills, distant from markets, and isolated from the main current of world affairs.

[50] "Albany Cultivator," Jan., 1851, pp. 40, 41. In a letter in this issue Cyrus McCormick estimates the saving from the use of his reaper as follows: It cut on an average of 16 acres of grain a day. The cost of hand-harvesting this amount, using 8 cradlers and 8 binders at $1.25 each, was $20. To do the same work with a reaper:

```
2 men, or 1 man and 1 boy, @ $1.25 and $1.00..............$ 2.25
5 binders @ $1.25.........................................  6.25
4 horses (change at noon).................................  1.50
                                                          _____
                        Total...........................$10.00
```

Therefore the total labor-saving daily amounted to $10, and to this should be added the value of 16 bushels of wheat saved at $.40 per bushel. Manual harvesting cost $1.25 per acre, and the same work could be done more efficiently by the reaper for just half that amount. Probably 6 or 7 binders, rather than 5, were normally required to accompany the reaper.

CHAPTER IV

THE INVENTION OF THE McCORMICK REAPER

SUMMER in the Valley of Virginia found the farmer busy with his scythe and sickle from the time the barley ripened in mid-June until the last oats were cut, six or eight weeks later. On large estates such as Walnut Grove, where a variety of small grain was grown, the harvest brought the hardest work of the year. Every moment counted when the hot sun was bursting the grain casings and when sudden storms meant costly delays with an extra labor force standing idle. Robert McCormick grew at least fifty acres of wheat in 1832, and it is probable that this was about the amount which he harvested the preceding year. Summer after summer he had worked beside his slaves and hired men, vying with his neighbors for the help of the few expert cradlers who could reap three acres of upstanding grain a day. There was no release from the worry and toil of harvest-time so long as hand implements were the sole dependence.

As a youth, Cyrus McCormick found relief for his tired arms during the harvest season by fashioning a light cradle. His father struck more directly at the problem by striving to construct a horse-power reaper which would lighten the labor of harvesting and at the same time reap with much more speed than the sickle or the scythe. His efforts to make a reaper entitle him to a place on the long roster headed by Pitt in England in 1786. But he worked in the seclusion of his blacksmith shop, unencouraged either by the success of his experiments or by the patronage of an agricultural society, and his reaper inventions were unmentioned in the press of the time and were never patented. The machines listed in the chart of the preceding chapter enjoyed at least a momentary publicity, and in many cases originated some principle which after modification was to find a place in the first practical reaper. Unlike these, the reapers of Robert McCormick emphasized methods of operation which for the most part have been wholly superseded. No record of his machines can be found in any existing document which dates earlier than 1848.

And yet, because Cyrus McCormick in 1831 was unacquainted with the work of such men as Ogle and Bell, the experiments of his father form a more important part of the background of his successful reaper than do earlier machines which incorporated elements of permanency in their construction. In any explanation of the sudden appearance of the first practical reaper, in 1831, the reapers of Robert McCormick take their place beside Cyrus's inherited inventive talent and his intimate acquaintance with the problems of grain-harvesting. The father taught his son the use of tools and through his reaper experiments turned Cyrus's thoughts in the same direction. He unintentionally demonstrated that certain mechanical principles should be avoided as profitless.[1]

The history of Robert McCormick's experiments with a horse-power reaper is most baffling. No certain account based upon contemporary sources can be written, either of the number of machines which he built or of the exact appearance of any one of them. Doubtful testimony alone suggests that they were ever used beyond the limits of his own farm. If the statements of old men, more than fifty years after the event, can be trusted, he abandoned one machine in disgust on the farm of Colonel James McDowell, Sr., of Fairfield, and another with like feeling at Captain John Humphrey's near Greenville,

[1] W. L. Stevens, "McCormick the Inventor," in the "Rockbridge County News," Feb. 18, 1909.

Virginia.[2] Most of the evidence for the existence of Robert McCormick's reapers dates forty years or more after the time of their alleged construction, and the few earlier references to them were made by Cyrus McCormick.

On January 1, 1848, Cyrus wrote to the Commissioner of Patents at Washington: [3]

In the summer of 1831, my father . . . constructed a Machine for cutting grain upon a principle entirely different from mine, and on which he had made experiments years before; and by his experiment in the 1831 harvest he became satisfied that it would not answer a valuable purpose notwithstanding it cut well in straight wheat. Very soon after my father had abandoned his Machine, I first conceived the idea of cutting upon the principle of mine . . .

This is the earliest mention of Robert McCormick's reaper, and no details of its construction are given in the letter. Three years later Cyrus McCormick wrote to Philip Pusey, the Chairman of the Committee on Agricultural Implements of the London exposition:

My father was a farmer in the county of Rockbridge, state of Virginia, United States. He made an experiment in cutting grain, in the year 1816, by a number of cylinders standing perpendicularly. Another experiment of the same kind was made by my father in the harvest of 1831, which satisfied my father to abandon it.[4]

The son had no reason to refer to his father's experiments either to the Commissioner of Patents or to Pusey, and there-

[2] Hanna, p. 52: statement of A. McChesney in 1885. Jas. Houser (eighty-five years of age) to H. A. Kellar, Mch. 24, 1919. J. D. Davidson to C. H. McCormick, Mch. 26, 1871.
[3] Pattison, II, a, C. H. McCormick's attested letter to E. Burke, Commr. of Patents, Jan. 1, 1848.
[4] "Report by the Juries of the Great Exhibition of the Works of Industry of All Nations, 1851" (London, 1852), pp. 495, 496, report of the Committee on Agricultural Implements. "Journal of the Royal Agricultural Society of England, 1851" (London), XII, pt. II, No. 28, p. 614.

fore, because his statements are the earliest, as well as "unconscious" testimony, more reliance can be placed upon them than upon other "conscious" attempts at a later date to remember details about the machines. Since the first of these letters was written for the purpose of supporting his applications for patent extension, and the second was sent to a committee which he hoped would award him a prize for his machine, an unselfish wish to acknowledge his debt to his father's experiments is the only obvious motive for mentioning a matter which would to a slight degree detract from the glory of his own achievement.

Even these statements postdate by seventeen and twenty-one years, respectively, the time when Robert is said to have made a final effort to construct a practical reaper. If Cyrus was correct, there was but one reaper—first built in 1816 and finally abandoned in 1831.[5] Save for his reference in 1863 [6] to the fact that the reaper of 1816 laid the grain in swath, no description of its mechanism has been found prior to several brief biographical sketches written by or for him, during the years 1870 to 1876.[7]

According to these accounts, Robert McCormick's reaper was pushed through the grain by one or more horses, and along its front edge were several vertical cylinders which had projecting teeth on their peripheries. As these cylinders were revolved by

[5] There is a slight difference between C. H. McCormick's statement to Burke on Jan. 1, 1848, in regard to Robert McCormick's machine of 1831, and the account he sent to E. H. Knight on Aug. 4, 1876. In the former he seems to mean that his father built a new machine in 1831, and in the latter that Robert merely resurrected the one of 1816 for a final trial and abandonment.

[6] Letter of C. H. McCormick in the "No. British Agriculturist," Oct. 14, 1863. C. H. McCormick to H. Baldwin, Jr., Mch. 7, 1867.

[7] MSS. Nos. 1, 2, and 7 in McCormick Hist. Assn. Library, dated respectively, Dec., 1870, Aug.-Dec., 1870, and Jan., 1871. There is also a description in a statement dictated by C. H. McCormick to his wife and his niece, Mrs. Amanda Tillman, probably in 1874. Hereafter cited as "C. H. McCormick's statement, 1874." Jas. Parton, etc., "Men of Progress" (Cincinnati, 1871), p. 3.

the power carried by leather bands from the ground wheels, their teeth caught the grain and lifted it across stationary hook-shaped, sickle-edged knives. Thus the stalks were severed, and the cut grain was delivered in swath at the side of the machine by the aid of an endless leather apron studded with nails. This device was impracticable in tangled and lodged grain, because the revolving hooks could not make the numerous divisions of the straw necessary to carry it effectively across the stationary cutters. If all the wheat stood erect, the machine would cut well, but to be of practical value it must cut successfully under the usual harvest conditions.

Although Cyrus McCormick was but seven years of age when the machine of 1816 was built, he might have learned of its construction by personal observation after reaching manhood, for it was stored in an outbuilding at Walnut Grove at least as late as 1848. In 1885 an old Rockbridge County resident described parts of it which he had been shown by William S. McCormick thirty-seven years before and his account agreed with the one of Cyrus written nine years earlier.[8]

Robert McCormick either retried his old 1816 reaper in 1831 or in that year built a new one of the same or of a different principle.[9] The experiment failed, and although the exact date of the trial is unknown, it was probably in May, since the wheat was still green. The only existing source for this month is a letter written by Cyrus on May 12 to his friend William Massie, promising to build him a hillside plow. In mid-June the son was in Washington securing a patent on this implement,[10] and

[8] Hanna, p. 31. "Farm Implement and County Hardware Trade" (Chicago), Apr. 30, 1884, p. 2. J. P. Alexander, "American Harvesting Machines," in the "American Inventor," VII, No. 5, p. 3. "Memorial," p. 14. McCormick and Shields, pp. 11-13. H. N. Casson, "Cyrus Hall McCormick," etc., p. 28.

[9] MS. Memo. of C. H. McCormick, Apr. 10, 1882. C. H. McCormick, "Sketch of My Life," Aug. 4, 1876.

[10] See p. 113, ftn. 52.

during the following month he tested, in an oat-field of his neighbor John Steele, a reaper of his own invention and construction.

In view of the future, the period from May to July, 1831 is one of the most significant in the life of Cyrus McCormick. Unfortunately, no important contemporary record survives to throw light upon the course of events during those weeks.[11] For this reason, the story of the building and the first trials of the McCormick reaper must be almost wholly reconstructed from testimony given many years after 1831. Since these recollections of members of the McCormick family and of neighbors are often contradictory upon small points, they inspire more confidence in their general trustworthiness than would be the case if they were in complete agreement. In many instances they were given under oath and the deponents were cross-examined by business rivals of Cyrus McCormick. So conclusive was this evidence, that Obed Hussey abandoned his treasured claim to priority of invention and admitted to the United States Patent Extension Board in 1848 that his most feared competitor had first operated his reaper in the harvest of 1831.[12] Nor does the testimony of 1848 comprise all the proof of the date of the first experiment. As early as May, 1834, Cyrus McCormick

[11] As a possible explanation of the silence with which the McCormick reaper was greeted in 1831 and 1832, Mr. Herbert A. Kellar has called my attention to the considerable sectionalism within Rockbridge County and the prejudice of the townsmen of Lexington against the farmers of the Augusta County border. Furthermore, Lexington had no newspaper in 1831 and all the files of the Staunton paper for the summer of that year are missing. The gap in the journal of the Rockbridge County Agricultural Society shows that it was temporarily disbanded in 1831. Thus the two or three places where mention of the first trials of the McCormick reaper would naturally have been made, were not available.

[12] Pattison, II, r. O. Hussey to Patent Extension Board, undated, but between Mch. 18 and 27, 1848. The Hussey reaper will be discussed in Chap. VII. See also p. 120, ftn. 73, and p. 164, ftn. 46.

wrote that his machine was "operated on wheat and oats in July, 1831." [13]

With this preliminary word of caution concerning the sources from which the history of the summer of 1831 at Walnut Grove must be written, the story may be resumed from the time when Robert McCormick discovered that his reaper would not cut tangled wheat. Cyrus was closely associated with his father in business at this time and probably assisted in the unsuccessful experiment.[14] Six weeks before Cyrus went to Washington to secure his plow patent in June, 1831, William Manning of Plainfield, New Jersey, patented a reaper with a divider, fingers, and a vibrating knife.[15] There is no reason to believe that McCormick saw a model of this machine when he was in the Patent Office. Manning's knife was quite different in form from Cyrus McCormick's, and reference to the chart of the preceding chapter will indicate the few points of resemblance between the two reapers. It is as reasonable to infer that Cyrus gained the idea of a horizontal reciprocating knife from the crank and vibratory motion of his father's hemp-break.[16]

At first thought, the month—or six weeks at most—in which Cyrus claims to have evolved his reaper seems too short a period for one to have accomplished so much.[17] The first ma-

---

[13] *Post*, p. 92. "Albany Cultivator," June, 1845, pp. 181, 182. Ardrey, pp. 22544 ff.

[14] C. H. McCormick, "Sketch of My Life," Aug. 4, 1876, "At this point then twenty-two years of age, having been present and having closely watched the operation of my father's machine, I applied myself to the study of the principles and difficulties so far demonstrated."

[15] See the chart following p. 58.

[16] Robert was working on his hemp-break in 1831, but the connection between the two machines rests wholly upon surmise. See R. McCormick to C. H. McCormick, Nov. 10 and Dec. 23, 1831.

[17] MS. "Cyrus Hall McCormick, Invention of the Reaper, Dec., 1870." This account was probably dictated by Cyrus. "Finding, as his father also had found, that the difficulty of separating the grain to be cut between each two of the 'cylinders,' when in a fallen or tangled state, was unsurmountable, and that, therefore, to succeed, the grain must be cut with-

The Reaper Invented by Cyrus McCormick in 1831

A restoration

chine, however, was a small experimental one and was mainly designed to test his theory of cutting. It is possible that he made use of a few parts of his father's machine, although he stated later that he built it all with his own hands.[18] This is not necessarily contradictory, but William S. McCormick testified in 1855 that Robert did some of the rough carpentering work upon it under Cyrus's direction.[19] It was the product of the carpenter shop as much as of the smithy, for most of its parts, save the knife, were of wood. This trial machine had a straight, smooth-edged knife,[20] vibrated by a crank and gearing from

out such separation, except at the line of division between the swath to be cut and the grain to be left standing,—at which point the ascertained difficulty of separation had to be overcome,—the question first to be solved was how that was possible. In his reflections and reasoning on this point it occurred to him that to effect the cutting of the grain by a cutting instrument, only a certain amount of motion was necessary, that this was indeed demonstrated by the action on the grain of the cradle. . . . The next thought was that while the motion forward as drawn by horses was not sufficient, a lateral motion must at the same time be communicated to the cutting instrument. . . ."

[18] Pattison, II, a, letter of C. H. McCormick, Jan. 1, 1848, to the Commr. of Patents. C. H. McCormick, "Sketch of My Life," Aug. 4, 1876. MS. Memo. of C. H. McCormick, Apr. 10, 1882: "My father's machine was tried on a green crop and after his failure I then designed, originated and constructed the entire machine by the time the crops were ripe and ready for cutting." Hanna, pp. 78, 80, 81: Harvey Harrison stated to Hanna that McCormick's first knife was only 2½ feet long. "This was before he ever made a full-sized machine." Joe Anderson, Cyrus's slave, said, "He made several little machines (models) before he got one that pleased him."

[19] *McCormick vs. Manny*, II, p. 229, testimony of W. S. McCormick, Aug. 30, 1855: "To the best of my recollection, the complainant [C. H.] himself with his own hands made all the particular parts of it, such as the patterns for the gearing, and that my father, who could himself do rough carpentering, assisted the complainant in its construction." Pattison, II, o: N. M. Hitt deposed on Mch. 17, 1848, that in the summer of 1831 he saw Robert and C. H. McCormick engaged in building a reaper which he saw working on their farm in late July, 1831. Contrast this with ftn. 26, on p. 83.

[20] C. H. McCormick to P. Pusey, "Journal of Royal Agrl. Soc., 1851," XII, pt. II, No. 28, p. 614. Pattison, II, o, deposition of W. S. McCormick,

the main wheel [21]; side draft with the main wheel directly behind the horse,[22] a crude divider,[23] wire or wooden fingers,[24]
and a platform of thin plank supported by a small wheel or a
slide.[25] Cyrus tried it once or twice in a little patch of overripe

Mch. 18, 1848. C. H. McCormick's letters in the "No. British Agriculturist,"
Sept. 30 and Oct. 14, 1863. C. H. McCormick to H. C. Parsons, Sept. 27,
1881.

[21] *Ibid.* There were single bearings in 1831 and double in 1832. Pattison,
II, e, deposition of W. S., L. J., and Mary Ann McCormick, Feb. 17,
1848. The main driving wheel was of wood and was two feet in diameter.
The cog-wheels operated from its axle and gave motion to a crank in
line with the blade. It was attached to the blade by a wooden driver.

[22] Letter of C. H. McCormick in the "No. British Agriculturist," Oct.
14, 1863. Pattison, II, a, letter of C. H. McCormick to Commr. of Patents,
Jan. 1, 1848. Two horses were first used in 1833. "American Gardener's
Magazine" (N. Y.), May, 1834, App. p. 73, advt. of C. H. McCormick.

[23] *McCormick vs. Manny*, II, p. 199: W. S. McCormick testified that the
first divider did not work well. Pattison, II, o, deposition of W. S. Mc-
Cormick, Mch. 18, 1848. C. H. McCormick, "Sketch of My Life," Aug. 4,
1876.

[24] Pattison, II, e, deposition of W. S., L. J., and Mary Ann McCormick,
Feb. 17, 1848. The fingers were two or three inches apart. *Ibid.*, II, o,
deposition of L. J. McCormick, Mch. 17, 1848: Each finger was double,
that is, curved over the edge of the knife, which vibrated in the groove
thus formed. *Ibid.*, II, a: McCormick wrote to the Commr. of Patents
on Jan. 1, 1848, that he thought the fingers of the 1831 machine were of
iron, but, if not, they were of that material in 1832.

[25] C. H. McCormick to H. C. Parsons, Sept. 27, 1881: After the "first
rude trial convinced me that a gathering frame for bringing up the grain
to the cutting apparatus was necessary . . . I immediately had the additions made to the machine, viz., the gathering reel, with a divider for
separating the grain to be cut, from that to be passed by the machine,
fixing at the same time a slide instead of a wheel under the grain side
of the machine; and adding a serrated cutting blade instead of one with
a smooth edge, with improved fingers or guards (over the blade for supporting the grain at the edge while being cut off) at short intervals from
each other. Instead of having the gear wheels of this machine behind the
main driving wheel, they were placed forward of it but outside of the
'driver,' as still used in the machine." Pattison, II, o: W. S. McCormick
stated on Mch. 18, 1848, that he thought a slide was used first but that
a wheel was employed either in the first or second year. *Ibid.*, II, d,
C. H. McCormick to Commr. of Patents, Feb. 2, 1848: The weight of
the machine was mainly (perhaps nine tenths) carried on the main driving

wheat his father had left standing for the purpose.[26] Convinced that he had discovered a practical cutting principle, he went to the tilt-hammer shop of John McCown, and had this locally famous blacksmith make him a new blade with a sickled or serrated edge.[27] Devoting more thought to the equally important consideration of the delivery of the severed grain in a form fit for binding, he remodeled the divider and added a reel.[28] Thus improved, the machine cut about six acres of oats on the neighboring farm of John Steele in late July, 1831. So far as is known, not more than three or four persons, besides members of the McCormick family, witnessed this first public trial.[29]

wheel, while under the grain end of the platform was a slide or an oblique wheel.

[26] *Ibid.*, II, g, deposition of N. M. Hitt, Jan. 1, 1848. Hitt stated that he boarded at John Steele's in the summer of 1831 and was told that C. H. McCormick had built a machine. The Steeles and he went to see it operate at Walnut Grove, in wheat. *Ibid.*, II, o: John Steele stated on Mch. 17, 1848, that he first saw it in his own field cutting oats, but that he was not sure whether it was in 1831 or 1832. This somewhat contradicts Hitt's testimony, but in the joint deposition with his wife on Jan. 1, 1848, he agreed with Hitt. *McCormick vs. Manny*, II, p. 228: W. S. McCormick testified that he believed only the immediate family saw its first trial, but that Dr. Hitt, John Steele, and one Paxton witnessed it in operation during the harvest of 1831.

[27] Pattison, II, f, and o, deposition of John McCown, Dec. 31, 1847. McCown stated that he made a blade in 1831 under Cyrus's direction. It was about four feet long, with a straight, serrated, or sickle edge. J. C. Shields, "Developement [sic] in Rockbridge," in the "Buena Vista Advocate," Jan. 17, 1890. C. H. McCormick's letter in the "No. British Agriculturist," Oct. 14, 1863.

[28] Pattison, II, g, deposition to N. M. Hitt, Jan. 1, 1848. See p. 82, ftn. 25.

[29] Pattison, II, a, C. H. McCormick to Commr. of Patents, Jan. 1, 1848. Hanna, p. 74: Miss Polly Carson stated in 1885 that she saw the machine going to Steele's farm to cut oats in 1831. "Old Joe" Anderson and Anthony, slaves of Cyrus and Robert McCormick, held the horses to keep them from running away because of the rattle and the flapping canvas of the machine. The neighbors who saw it operate told her that it was "a right smart curious sort of thing," but "nobody ever believed it would come to much." Memo. of C. H. McCormick, Apr. 10, 1882. Pattison, II, g, tes-

Cyrus always admitted that the first reaper did not cut the grain perfectly. The significance of 1831 in the history of agriculture lies in the fact that for the first time a machine was tried which included all of the basic parts of the modern reaper.[30] The seven essential mechanical principles, or elements, had never before been combined in one implement. To coördinate those parts so that the machine would render its best service under almost any harvest conditions, required fifteen more years of thought and experiment. Each one of the principal parts was considerably refashioned prior to 1846, but no change in construction of primary importance was found to be necessary. McCormick was the harshest critic of his own reaper during these years, and so skeptical was he of the worth of his implement that he waited until 1834 to patent it, and it was 1840 before he felt justified in seeking a wide market.[31] This contrasts sharply with his alacrity in patenting his hillside plow in 1831. In spite of this caution, he maintained such faith in the ultimate perfection of the machine that his father, who had tried vainly to build a practical reaper, found that advice to the son to turn his attention to other affairs was largely unheeded.[32]

timony of J. Steele, Jr., and Eliza S. Steele, his wife. In the "Mechanics' Magazine," etc., of New York, for May, 1834, Cyrus McCormick wrote that the machine operated in wheat and oats in July, 1831, and that its work was "witnessed by many persons." See p. 92.

[30] "Farmers' Advance" (Chicago), Jan. and May, 1883. "Farm Implement and County Hardware Trade," Apr. 30, 1884, pp. 1-3. R. B. Swift, "Who Invented the Reaper," in the "Implement Age," Apr. 15, 1897, pp. 20, 21. "L'Agriculture Moderne" (Paris), July 1, 1900. For citations of statements of C. H. McCormick and other members of his family that the machine did not work perfectly in 1831, see post, p. 85, ftn. 33.

[31] C. H. McCormick in the "No. British Agriculturist," Oct. 7 and 14, 1863.

[32] Ibid., Oct. 7, 1863: "During this interval [July, 1831-June, 1834] I was often advised by my father and family to abandon it [the reaper] and pursue my regular business, as likely to be more profitable, he having given me a farm." In truth, the deed for the farm was not recorded until 1835, although of course the gift may have been made before its legal

One great defect in the first machine lay in the operation of the divider. As it moved ahead of the knife to effect the separation between the swath to be cut and the rest of the standing grain, it tended either to root up some of the tangled straws in its path or else to flatten them uncut upon the ground. The reel was not steady in its operation and it would not properly coördinate with the divider as the reaper bumped along over rough ground. The band which connected the reel with the main wheel often slipped out of place and stopped its motion altogether. The reel-support in front of the cutter caught some of the straws and kept them away from the knife. The rim of the main wheel was so narrow that it sank in the soft ground of the field. Grain or weeds lodged between the fingers and the knife and clogged the cutter so that it would not vibrate. The man who walked beside the machine raking off the gavels from the platform had a very difficult task if the grain was heavy. These were some of the imperfections which had to be obviated before the reaper would recommend itself to thrifty and conservative farmers.[33]

The harvest of 1831 was almost over at the time of the trial in John Steele's oat-field. Nothing more could be done with the machine until the following June, and Cyrus, after selling a few plows, left for Kentucky to construct hemp-breaks for his father. Late that winter he wrote to Robert McCormick, asking for advice on the subject of reaper-making in Kentucky. His father replied on March 27, 1832: "I think the building of a grain machine in that country might be attended with

transfer. Memo. of a conversation between C. H. McCormick, W. J. Hanna, and C. H. McCormick, Jr., Mch. 14, 1882.

[33] "Supreme Court of the United States, No. 108; William H. Seymour and Dayton S. Morgan, Plaintiffs in Error v. Cyrus H. McCormick," pp. 185-187, testimony of W. S. McCormick, Oct. 18, 1851. Hereafter cited as *Seymour & Morgan vs. McCormick*. *McCormick vs. Manny*, II, p. 199, testimony of W. S. McCormick. C. H. McCormick to H. C. Parsons, Sept. 27, 1881.

difficulty, as it will require a good deal of new modeling which when done at home is free from the watchful and jealous eye of strangers." [34]

This is the earliest known document in existence which refers to the McCormick reaper. It furnishes almost incontestable proof that the machine was built in 1831. Probably it is the "paper" to which Cyrus refers in his letter of March 12, 1848, to his brother William, when preparing to demonstrate the priority of his reaper over Hussey's: If there should be any questions asked "you can say that you had written evidence in your possession of the year, dated 1831—as can also Mother and Leander . . . and from the paper of father when I went to Kentucky referring to the reaper, can also add that it was in operation in 1831." [35]

Cyrus returned from Kentucky to Walnut Grove in May, 1832, and added improvements to his machine before the harvest. The fingers were now made of iron: the platform was arranged so that it could be adjusted to the height of the knife, and the gearing was slightly changed.[36] Mary Caroline, Cyrus's sister, came home from school in Staunton in early July and saw the reaper cut grain on the home farm. About fifty acres of Walnut Grove wheat were harvested with the machine that season and one or two public trials were held.[37] Many years later, the inventor recalled that a score or more of witnesses in 1832 watched him cut the wheat of Colonel S. McDowell

[34] The letter of Cyrus to Robert McCormick which occasioned this reply has not been found.

[35] *Post,* Chap. XII.

[36] C. H. McCormick's letter in "No. British Agriculturist," Oct. 14, 1863.

[37] C. H. McCormick's statement, 1874. C. H. McCormick, "Sketch of My Life," Aug. 4, 1876. McCormick and Shields, p. 3. C. H. to W. S. McCormick, Mch. 12, 1848: "Caroline can say that she was at school in 1832, that I returned then from Kentucky, and she saw the reaper work in a field near Cochran's."

Reid, near Lexington.[38] His reaper was exhibited in the court-house square of that town during the summer, and tradition has it that its inventor saw his first vision of its possible significance when a teacher of the Ann Smith Academy told him in the presence of many onlookers that he believed that the machine was worth $100,000. Cyrus later recalled that he thought at the time how well the professor merited the title of a "scholar and gentleman," but that he would be willing to sell all rights in his reaper for half that amount. Nevertheless before the harvest was over he was dreaming of one million dollars as the fruit of his invention.[39]

If any trust can be placed in the remembrance of a process of thought forty years after its occurrence, it is possible that the trial on the farm of William Taylor, near Lexington, was the cause of his rising optimism.[40] The exhibition in Taylor's wheat was unanticipated, since it began, as previously announced, on the adjoining estate of John Ruff. In the presence of seventy-five or more spectators, including some of the most prominent men of the neighborhood, the reaper moved over the rough field, stopping frequently for slight repairs, shelling considerable grain with its revolving reel, and crushing down some of the straws with its protruding divider. Ruff, a farmer with a hasty temper and great pride in his grain, told young Cyrus that he wished his wheat reaped rather than threshed and ordered the machine from his land.

Evidently Ruff's anger was momentary, for about a year later his signature appears under a testimonial to the great

[38] The Reid exhibition of 1832 rests wholly upon a statement in a letter of C. H. McCormick to H. C. Parsons, Sept. 27, 1881, and the inventor's memo. of Apr. 10, 1882. Possibly he confused it with another in 1834, when Reid publicly testified to the value of his reaper. *Post*, p. 96, ftn. 60.

[39] *Ibid.*, C. H. McCormick, "Sketch of My Life," Aug. 4, 1876. C. H. McCormick's statement, 1874.

[40] Taylor was a member of Congress twenty years later, and was a brother-in-law of Jas. McDowell, later Governor of Virginia.

value of the McCormick hillside plow.[41] However that may be, Cyrus McCormick must have felt keenly the humiliation of ridicule before so many of the best farmers of the vicinity. Taylor saved the situation by inviting the youth to bring the machine into his wheat and to reap there as long as he desired. As his field was much smoother than Ruff's, the reaper performed quite satisfactorily for several hours.[42] So ended the harvest of 1832, with the name of Cyrus McCormick and his reaper known at least eighteen miles from Walnut Grove—at Lexington, the county-seat of Rockbridge.

The growing reputation of the reaper becomes apparent for the first time in the harvest of 1833. The previous winter had been chiefly devoted, by Robert and Cyrus, to the manufacture of plows, but when the wheat ripened in June an improved grain-cutter was ready to take the field. Cyrus had added to the original divider a long straight brace extending backward and upward from its point to the top of the reel-post. Covering the lower part of the frame thus formed was a strip of canvas two or three feet wide which stretched back along the left side of the machine to the rear edge of the platform. This improvement steadied the reel and supplemented the divider-point in its function of turning the swath toward the knife.[43] There were possibly two reapers now—a larger new one and the original

[41] "Lexington Union," Nov. 2, 1833. The writer is not certain that the Reid trial preceded the Ruff-Taylor one. McCormick stated in his memo. of Apr. 10, 1882, that it was "probably after Ruff's." The court-house exhibition may have followed both. C. H. McCormick to H. C. Parsons, Sept. 27, 1881.

[42] Hanna, pp. 57-61: Description of the Ruff and Taylor farms, now within the city limits, and statements of witnesses. J. C. Shields, "Old Iron Masters of South River Valley," in the "Buena Vista Advocate," June 26, 1891. Shields also was a witness. H. N. Casson, "The Romance of the Reaper," in "Everybody's Magazine" (N. Y.), Dec., 1907, pp. 758 ff. A dramatic account. The trial seems to have continued from 10 a. m. to 4 p. m.

[43] "Lexington Union," Sept. 14, 21, 28, 1833.

implement. The former had been built with a longer knife and platform and with a larger reel, but it seems to have been unwieldy and Cyrus laid it aside temporarily with the thought of improving its draft the following year by pushing it forward into the grain.[44] The harvest at Walnut Grove was reaped, the machine was used by Cyrus to cut the wheat of several local farmers, and at least one public exhibition was viewed by a numerous assemblage near Lexington.[45]

James McDowell, Sr., was so pleased with the reaper that he either purchased one or ordered one to be built for him.[46] In view of the inventor's later statement that he sold none until 1839, the exact meaning of McDowell's testimonial is open to question. The implement demonstrated that it would cut ten or twelve acres a day—over three times the amount harvested by an expert cradler. Of the Lexington trial, a local paper reported, "A large crowd of citizens were present at the trial of it, and

[44] McCormick's letter in the "No. British Agriculturist," Oct. 7, 1863.

[45] McCormick and Shields, p. 43, statement of Mary C. Shields, Jan. 17, 1883: "In the harvest of 1833, I saw this reaper cut wheat again in the field near to Mr. John Weir's." "Lexington Union," Sept. 14, 1833: John Weir stated that he had seen the reaper operate for two seasons and that it had cut for him in 1833, and Archibald Walker wrote that he had used the machine on his farm and that it would harvest an acre in an hour on level land or on steep smooth land. Jas. McDowell stated on the same day that he had used the machine for an hour in the harvest, "and calculated . . . it would cut in a day about twelve acres." In this same paper, a week later, Wm. Moore certified that C. H. McCormick's reaper cut 11 acres of wheat for him on July 6, that it was a good machine and worthy of the attention of the public. Hanna, p. 81, Joe Anderson stated in 1885: "But I remember going to Billy Moore's to cut one Saturday. . . . We cut eight acres of wheat and I raked off walking on the ground. Machine worked well, but had been working right smart before that."

[46] "Lexington Union," Sept. 14, 1833, Jas. McDowell stated, "I was so satisfied that I bought one." C. H. McCormick wrote to the Commr. of Patents on Jan. 1, 1848, "From the experiment of 1831 until [for] the harvest of 1840, I did not sell a single reaper except one which I afterwards took back. . . ." Possibly the machine which A. McChesney recalled that Robert McCormick left at McDowell's was in reality the reaper of Cyrus. See *supra*, p. 75.

although the machine (it being the first) was not as perfectly made as the plan is susceptible of, yet we believe it gave general satisfaction." [47]

This article in the "Lexington Union" of September 14, 1833, deserves more than passing mention. It is the first printed notice of the reaper, and fortunately includes a detailed description of its construction. This is too technical to quote here, but it proves beyond a doubt that the machine embraced all of the essential parts of the modern reaper. There were the side draft with the horse in shafts; the main wheel, two feet three inches in diameter, directly behind the horse; the gearing from this to the knife and reel; the vibrating sickle-edged knife, four and a half feet long; the platform five or six feet long; the cloth partition and the divider; the horizontal reel as long as the knife, six or seven feet in diameter with eight ribs, and the wire fingers "projecting before it [the knife] within two or three inches of each other." The knife could be raised or lowered to leave the length of stubble desired. The reel was said to draw all grain back to the knife "whether straight or tangled, upright or leaning, unless below an angle of 35 degrees." [48]

The cited article, accompanied by the testimonials of three farmers, was soon copied in Edmund Ruffin's "Farmers' Register" [49]; the "New York Farmer," [50] and the "Mechanics' Magazine" [51] of New York City. For the first time the fame of the McCormick reaper had crossed the mountains, and the inventor was soon asked by the New York editors to furnish additional information concerning its con-

[47] "Lexington Union," Sept. 14, 1833. The article is entitled "Important Invention."
[48] *Ibid.*, and an article by C. H. McCormick in the issue of Sept. 28, 1833.
[49] "Farmers' Register," Oct., 1833, p. 301.
[50] "New York Farmer," Nov., 1833, p. 347.
[51] "Mechanics' Magazine," etc. (N. Y.), Nov., 1833, p. 260.

struction and operation.[52] This reputation was not based upon sales but upon practical field tests in which Cyrus either rode the horse attached to the machine or raked beside it as it moved ahead in the grain. By the close of the year he probably felt that it was time to apply for a patent.

The testimonials which he published in 1833 indicate that he was preparing to make his reaper for sale. More than ten years were to pass before he judged that it had attained perfection, but at least a local market was possible in 1834 if he was on hand to make repairs and instruct farmers in its use. He was not ready to warrant that it would cut a minimum number of acres a day, but since it had attracted favorable notice from papers outside of the Valley, it was high time to protect himself by patent from unscrupulous imitators. The final urge in this direction undoubtedly came when he saw in the "Mechanics' Magazine" of April, 1834, a cut and description of a reaper patented late in 1833 by Obed Hussey. With characteristic boldness McCormick immediately sent his rival the following challenge and warning, in the form of a letter to the editor:

> *Rockbridge, Va., May 20, 1834*
>
> Dear Sir:
> Having seen in the April number of your "Mechanics' Magazine" a cut and description of a reaping machine, said to have been invented by Mr. Obed Hussey, of Ohio, last summer, I would ask the favor of you to inform Mr. Hussey, and the public, through your columns, that that principle, viz., cutting grain by means of a toothed instrument, receiving a rotatory motion from a crank, with the iron teeth projecting before the edge of the cutter for the purpose of preventing the grain from partaking of

---

[52] *Ibid.*: The editor invited Cyrus to send further particulars about the machine, its price, and a drawing. So, also, the editor of the "New York Farmer." Cyrus evidently was unprepared to forward a cut of his reaper, so he sent one of his plows, which appeared in the "Mechanics' Magazine," Feb., 1834, p. 71.

its motion, is a part of the principle of my machine, and was invented by me, and operated on wheat and oats in July, 1831. This can be attested to the entire satisfaction of the public and Mr. Hussey, as it was witnessed by many persons; consequently, I would warn all persons against the use of the aforesaid principle, as I regard and treat the use of it, in any way, as an infringement of my right.

Since the first experiment was made of the performance of my machine, I have, for the mutual interests of the public and myself, been laboring to bring it to as much perfection as the principle admitted of, before offering it to the public. I now expect to be able, in a very short time to give such an account of its simplicity utility and durability, as will give general, if not universal satisfaction.[53]

This was the first shot in the war of the reapers in America, which, when resumed in 1843, was to continue in the case of Hussey until his death in 1860. For the moment, however, the issue was not joined, since the silent Hussey had not yet invaded Virginia with his machine. By the next year McCormick's energies were temporarily diverted to another direction.

This incident probably influenced him to present his patent application more speedily than he had originally intended. If he anticipated that the commissioner would hesitate to grant a patent to an inventor whose machine included certain parts which resembled the implement of a previous patentee, he was pleasantly disappointed. At this time no effort was made by the overworked staff of the Patent Office to investigate the originality of the device for which a patent was sought. In fact, neither the Secretary of State nor the Attorney General prior to 1836 had the power to reject a patent application.[54] This

[53] "Mechanics' Magazine," May 31, 1834, p. 306.
[54] Senate, 45th Cong., 2d Sess., "Misc. Docs.," 50, pp. 19, 209-214, 266, arguments before the Committees on Patents of the Senate and House of Representatives. "Farmers' Register," Aug., 1836, pp. 197, 198. As the law was construed in practice, the Secretary of State had no power to refuse a patent for want of novelty or usefulness. The only inquiry which he made,

was a fruitful source of future lawsuits, but in the case of
Hussey and McCormick it was to be evident later that the Virginian rightfully claimed priority of invention and that there
was enough difference of construction and operation between
the two machines to warrant a patent on each. In so far, Mc-
Cormick acted hastily in writing the letter of May, 1834, but
many years were to pass before the matter was removed from
the realm of controversy.[55]

Cyrus McCormick, after paying thirty dollars to the treasury
of the United States and petitioning for a patent, was issued
a fourteen-year monopoly on June 21, 1834, extending him
"the full and exclusive right and liberty of making, constructing, using, and vending to others to be used, the said improvement." This patent was signed by President Andrew Jackson
and Louis McLane, Secretary of State, and was certified by
the Attorney-General, B. F. Butler, to be conformable to law.

The best evidence that McCormick moved ahead for his
patent faster than he wished to go, lies in the fact that the
specification places more stress upon a push-machine than upon
one with the horses in front. The latter is mentioned as an
alternative only, and this is most strange, for the reapers of
1831, 1832, and 1833 had been pulled rather than pushed,
and the machine which was operated in the harvest of 1834
was similarly drawn. The only plausible explanation, and one
which is later supported by McCormick's own recollection, is
that he decided that a heavy machine with an enlarged platform
and a longer knife would have too much side draft if pulled.

concerned the applicant's compliance with the prescribed procedure. Consequently, a considerable number of patents was worthless and void—conflicting with earlier ones, or embracing public rights, not patentable. Some
rogues copied models at the Patent Office, got a patent, and peddled patent
rights.

[55] John F. Steward, "The Reaper and Binder," in the "New York
Tribune," Dec. 22, 1897. Steward, "Hussey, the Real Inventor," in "Deer-
ing's Farm Journal" (Chicago), Feb., 1898.

He therefore concluded that the only possible method of operation was to attach a tongue to the rear of the reaper. With no opportunity to test this in the harvest, he nevertheless secured to himself in the patent whatever advantages might accrue from this historic method of propulsion. As soon as the grain was ready to be cut he quickly found that he had been in error and restored the shafts to their original position in front of the main wheel.[56]

The McCormick reaper has already been described with some fullness, and only those improvements in the machine that are detailed for the first time in the patent specification need mention here. In 1834 the inventor devised a better method of raising and lowering the reel, and the earliest reference is made to fingers which bend over the edge of the knife and back for some distance below its under side. This formed an opening under the blade from which the vibrating knife could discharge particles of straw that otherwise would wedge between the fingers and the knife and clog the cutter.[57] In order to

[56] McCormick's letter in the "No. British Agriculturist," Oct. 14, 1863: "The application of the power at the rear . . . only having been experimented with in a machine *constructed* immediately preceding my application for the patent, but which was not continued afterward. The *side draught* had first been used with a single horse in shafts, when it was *thought a wider machine might* be propelled to advantage from the rear: hence the experiment."

[57] Testimony in later years indicates that McCormick had used these bent fingers in earlier machines—e.g., Pattison, II, o, deposition of W. S. McCormick, Mch. 18, 1848. C. H. McCormick's letter in the "No. British Agriculturist," Oct. 14, 1863. In view of the later dispute with Hussey over the origin of the open-back finger, it is important to note that McCormick's patent provided for a hook-shaped finger with the opening beneath and the knife-edge vibrating in the groove. Three months before McCormick's patent, Hussey had described his reaper fingers in the "Mechanics' Magazine" (N. Y.), Apr., 1834, p. 194. "The teeth are formed of two parts, one part above and one below, and joined at the points, forming a range of mortices, through which runs a saw with the teeth sharp on both sides." So Hussey apparently did not use an open-back guard as early as 1834.

coördinate more effectively the operation of the reel and divider, he made the cross-arms at the grain end of the reel-spindle, to which the ribs of the reel were fastened, shorter than those on the opposite end. This produced a spiral effect and withheld the operation of the reel from the tangled grain straws until the divider had an opportunity to straighten and separate them properly. A raised board, eight to twelve inches wide, was attached to the back of the platform to prevent the cut grain from shaking off until a gavel had accumulated which could be removed in an orderly fashion by the raker.[58] Mention of these improvements seems necessary because they illustrate the continuous refining process which ultimately produced a machine that could be fully warranted by the inventor.

The reaper of Cyrus McCormick gained additional publicity from its use in the harvest of 1834.[59] In the "Lexington Union" of August 9 of that year, it was noted with pleasure that the machine "promises to introduce much additional expedition and economy into one of the most expensive and critical operations of agriculture." During the same month, a less optimistic contributor to the "Farmers' Register" predicted that "the locomotion necessary to a reaping-machine when in the performance of its work, will always present an obstruction to the perfection of its construction." Another public exhibition of the reaper was held in a rough and hilly field of oats near Lexington. A dozen of the most prominent residents

[58] "Certified Copies of the Patent Specification and Patent of June 19 and 21, 1834."
[59] "American Gardener's Magazine," 1834, App., p. 73. Here is shown a cut of his machine as well as a description, but the latter is based in part upon sections from the patent specification which are not used in the reaper employed in the field. "American Railroad Journal and Advocate of Internal Improvements," June 14, 1834, p. 360. McCormick and Shields, p. 6. It is here stated that in 1834 or 1835, three machines were constructed, one of which was sold to John Umphries. About a year later, there were seven built, several of which were sold. No substantiation of this has been found in any other place.

of the vicinity, including several who had or were to achieve a national reputation, certified to its "usefulness and value." James McDowell, Jr., later Governor of Virginia, and William C. Preston, a United States Senator from South Carolina, wrote for publication that

the cutting was rapid and extremely clean, scarcely a stalk of grain being left, and little, if any, being lost by shattering from the working of the machine. Some small quantity of grain was uncut where sudden turns of direction at sharp angles had to be made, but it was altogether unconsiderable. Upon trial made for that purpose they ascertained that this machine, drawn by two horses with a boy to drive and a man to collect the grain into sheaves for binding, cut, when moved at its ordinary speed, about the third of an acre in ten minutes, and cut it, as they think, much cleaner than it could have been done by hand. The forming of the sheaf, however, which has to be bound by other hands was more difficult and less perfect than might be desired. . . .

They witnessed its operation for an hour or two with much satisfaction and cannot but regard it as an invention of a most singular and ingenious kind, and one which is entitled to public favor. . . . As a first thought, the machine is admirable, reflecting great credit on the mechanicle [sic] capacity of its youthful inventor, and when improved in detail as experience shall suggest, will, as they confidently expect, be an acquisition of value and importance to the general husbandry.[60]

---

[60] "Lexington Union," Aug. 9, 16, 23, 30, 1834. Other spectators who signed a testimonial to the value of the reaper were Saml. McD. Reid, Clerk of the Circuit Court and Assemblyman; Hugh Barclay, later Presiding Justice of Rockbridge County; J. W. Jordan, ironmaster; John Alexander, Sheriff of Rockbridge; William Taylor, later a Congressman, and the Rev. J. W. Douglas of Lexington. On Samuel McDowell Reid, see Ulrich B. Phillips, "Life and Labor in the Old South" (Boston, 1929), p. 314. Hereafter cited as "Phillips." In the "Rockbridge County News," Mch. 14, 1907, A. Alexander tells of C. H. McCormick and a negro using the reaper in his father's wheat for some days. He was not sure of the date but thought it was "66 or 68 years ago," which would have placed it about 1839. Since the Alexander farm was near Lexington, the episode may be the same one to which the father certified in 1834.

This report might have been much more complimentary, and most likely its judicious praise represents quite accurately the status of the reaper in 1834. Its inventor realized that some changes in construction were needed, and although the machine continued to cut each season upon the McCormick farms, in all probability it was not publicly exhibited again until 1839.[61] It was more than a coincidence that the manufacture of Robert McCormick's various inventions ceased forever at about the time when the son's reaper and plow entered four years of eclipse.[62]

There are several explanations of this period of pause, besides Cyrus's determination not to advertise his machine until he had more nearly perfected it.[63] A succession of crop failures and the Hessian fly in Virginia, beginning in 1835, brought a situation unfavorable to the sale of agricultural implements.[64] The natural conservatism of the average farmer was reinforced by hard times and a consequent lack of money with which to purchase expensive machines. The rocky, stumpy, and hilly farms of the Valley of Virginia, usually small in acreage, could not under the most favorable conditions furnish a broad market for the reaper. In 1835, Robert deeded to Cyrus a farm of over four hundred acres and the work necessary to bring this under profitable cultivation at a time when old established farmers were finding it difficult to make a livelihood, afforded

[61] *Seymour & Morgan vs. McCormick*, pp. 102, 186, testimony of W. S. McCormick, Oct. 18, 1851. *McCormick vs. Manny*, II, pp. 192, 214, 215, 227-229, testimony of W. S. McCormick. Statement of P. J. Hite in June, 1910, in re. Cyrus McCormick in 1836. *Post*, p. 180, ftn. 8.

[62] Statement of C. H. McCormick, 1874.

[63] "American Farmer," Aug. 17, 1842, p. 101. C. H. McCormick to Commr. of Patents, Jan. 1, 1848, in Pattison, II, a. "Staunton Spectator," July 18, 1839, statement of C. H. McCormick. U. S. Patent Office Records, "Mc-Cormick Extension Case, 1848," C. H. McCormick to Commr. of Patents, Feb. 18, 1848.

[64] "Albany Cultivator," July, 1838, p. 73; Jan., 1837, p. 170. "Farmers' Register," IV (1837), p. 549. "Lexington Gazette," July 17, 31, 1835.

little opportunity for the manufacture of plows and reapers at Walnut Grove. Beginning the following year, the McCormicks engaged in an iron-furnace business which demanded their entire attention and rapidly absorbed whatever surplus capital they possessed.[65]

Before the story of the iron venture can be told, the invention of the McCormick reaper must be reviewed from a different standpoint. Because of the nature of the evidence, it is believed by the writer that Cyrus McCormick was without doubt the inventor of the machine which bears his name. Nevertheless, a counter-claim, advanced in behalf of Cyrus's father, has drawn some support during recent years and demands consideration at this point in the narrative. If Robert McCormick were the inventor of the reaper, Cyrus McCormick would still deserve remembrance as one of the most successful manufacturers in America's first era of "big business," but his chief title to fame would be transferred to the name of his father.

[65] See Chap. VI.

CHAPTER V

THE McCORMICK REAPER CONTROVERSY

SEVENTEEN years after the harvest of 1831, Cyrus Mc-
Cormick moved to Chicago, and there, with the assistance
of his two younger brothers, William S. and Leander J., organized one of the great industrial establishments of the time.[1]
Already the acknowledged head of the family, charged
with initiative and incomparable energy, he led every movement and decided every vital issue connected with the business. He traveled far and near, introducing the reaper,
superintending its operation in the harvest field, and making

[1] The subject of this chapter has received more attention than any
other topic in the career of Cyrus McCormick. Little, however, has been
printed in answer to the evidence published by those who espouse Robert
McCormick as the inventor of the McCormick reaper. The following
manuscripts, and particularly the first named, have been invaluable to the
present writer: Cyrus Bentley, "The Invention of the McCormick Reaper";
R. H. Parkinson, "Invention of the Reaper"; John H. Latané, "Early History of the McCormick Reaper." The first two, legal in viewpoint, were
written by prominent lawyers. The third is by a well-known historian, and
emphasizes the sources up to 1860. Letters written by Herbert A. Kellar,
librarian of the McCormick Historical Association, to Cyrus Bentley in
1924 and 1925, also were most helpful. The evidence unfavorable to Cyrus
McCormick's claim will be found chiefly in two published volumes already
referred to: L. J. McCormick, "The Memorial of Robert McCormick," and
R. H. McCormick and J. H. Shields, "Robert McCormick, Inventor"
(Chicago, 1910). These mainly consist of affidavits and statements dating
between 1878 and 1910. A manuscript collection of similar statements, but
mostly supporting Cyrus McCormick, is W. J. Hanna, "Notes on a Virginia Trip," 1885. For the Robert McCormick position, see also, "Official
Retrospective Exhibit of the Development of Harvesting Machinery" (Paris,
1900), and Paul Gilbert and Charles L. Bryson, "Chicago and Its Makers"
(Chicago, 1929), p. 632.

contracts with the growing force of agents. He attended state fairs for the wider advertisement of the machine, and received the highest awards of the world expositions at London in 1851 and at Paris in 1855, after defeating his greatest rivals, in spectacular contests.[2] As a party to long controversies in Congress and the United States courts, his figure became as well known at Washington as that of the most eminent of public men.[3] Nor was he always gentle and engaging in the business war which raged about him. He asserted his mastery over rivals and subordinates, and his brothers were never in doubt concerning his leadership.

Leander McCormick, less ambitious but adept in the art of mechanical contrivance, supervised the building of the reapers in the expanding manufacturing plant. He contributed to the enormous growth of the undertaking and observed with an increasing and pardonable pride the stream of new and improved reapers which moved each year in larger numbers from the factory to the farmer. He had married Henrietta Hamilton in 1845, an attractive and ambitious woman who was anxious for her husband to merit a dominating position in the new urban environment.[4] Together they made a comfortable home in Chicago after 1849, and Cyrus McCormick lived with them for some time, although he was frequently away from the city on matters of business.[5] During the nine years following 1850 both Leander and William S. McCormick profited from their shrewd investments in Chicago real estate, and were numbered among the most successful men of their city by the time of the Civil War.[6] Nevertheless, despite their invaluable assistance in the factory, Cyrus McCormick was the responsible head of

[2] *Post,* Chap. XVI.
[3] *Post,* Chap. XVII and XVIII.
[4] "Memorial," p. 16, statement of Henrietta McCormick, Aug. 1, 1885.
[5] *Post,* Chap. XI.
[6] *Ibid.*

the business, advertisements ran in his name, and he paid the salaries of his brothers and the wages of all concerned. To him alone were voted the high honors and coveted awards by the agricultural juries of fairs and exhibitions throughout the United States and abroad.

The work of William S. McCormick during these formative years at Chicago covered the supervision and guidance of the department of sales, collections, and the purchase of supplies. He and his wife, Mary Ann Grigsby, played their part in the social life of the old North Side and soon had a home large enough to entertain five hundred guests in honor of Cyrus McCormick's marriage to the beautiful Nancy Fowler in 1858.[7] Late in the following year the three brothers formed a partnership for the manufacture of the reaper, and, according to the contract, each was to bear a definite responsibility and receive a definite share of the profits. William had not been long in Chicago before he wished to return to his idyllic Valley of Virginia, and the increasing and exhausting indoor tasks at the factory undermined his health.[8] The younger brothers began to wonder whether the honors and duties of the partnership were fairly divided, and both became a little critical of Cyrus, whose work absorbed his mind and kept him everlastingly on the road.

The heat and passion of the Civil War added to the problems of Cyrus McCormick and accentuated the growing differences between the partners. It was a trying time for good Virginians in the seething and warlike city of Chicago, with Joseph Medill of the "Tribune" and Norman B. Judd, boss of the Republican party of the West, in control. The inventor worked earnestly but vainly for peace, now as the owner of the influential "Chicago Times" and again as the Democratic candidate for a

[7] *Post*, Chap. XIX, pp. 459, 460.
[8] *McCormick vs. Manny*, II, pp. 202, 208, 236, 237, testimony of W. S. McCormick.

seat in the national House of Representatives.[9] His courageous
stand in behalf of principles long held, brought him only
broken friendships and unrestrained public criticism. He re-
sided in New York City for several years after the war.

Cyrus McCormick spent many months abroad during the
conflict, leaving William and Leander to make the reapers and
manage the complicated business. The war demand and the
failing crops of England greatly increased the yearly harvest
of American wheat and the brothers were more successful than
ever. Without always heeding the advice that Cyrus frequently
sent to him from Europe, William S. McCormick profitably invested the partnership funds in gold and in real estate. Long
in ill health, he collapsed under the strain and anxieties of the
time and died on September 27, 1865.[10] The administration
of his estate caused sharp differences of opinion between the
two surviving brothers.[11]

Cyrus McCormick believed in a business policy of world expansion which found small favor with his youngest brother.
Conservative and cautious by nature, Leander dreaded the
possible financial outcome of an overseas penetration so costly
to initiate and so doubtful of success. He wished Cyrus to pay
the retail price for those machines designed for foreign exhibition or sale, and felt that the awards received at the fairs

[9] Franklin W. Scott, "Newspapers and Periodicals of Illinois, 1814-79"
(Springfield, 1910), pp. 65, 66. Arthur C. Cole, "The Era of the Civil
War," 1848-70 (Vol. III, "Centennial History of Illinois," Springfield,
1919), pp. 303, 304. "Chicago Tribune," June 3 and 4, 1863, and Nov. 7,
1864.
[10] McCormick and Shields, "Robert McCormick, Inventor," p. 10. L. J.
McCormick, pp. 306, 307. Statement of Mrs. Nancy F. McCormick, widow
of Cyrus, on Apr. 24, 1913, to Cyrus Bentley and Mrs. Anita Blaine.
Statements of 'Mrs. Mary A. Chapman and Robt. M. Adams to W. G.
McCormick (son of W. S.), Apr. 7, 1913 (?).
[11] Statement of Robt. M. Adams to W. G. McCormick, Apr. 8, 1913.

should be given to the company and not to his brother alone.[12] He was content to lead the field of reaper-makers in America, and happy, now that the great war was over, to go frequently to Virginia and visit his numerous kinsfolk and the friends of his youth.[13] But Cyrus McCormick looked toward those in high place in his own country and in Europe for his friendships, and although he still loved the Old Dominion, he preferred to spend his vacations at the mineral springs of New York and Vermont.[14]

Although Cyrus and Leander McCormick were so unlike both in character and viewpoint that a difference of opinion upon almost every subject of large moment was inevitable, there was no manifest antipathy before 1866. In that year Leander opposed his brother's wish that he should assign certain mower patents to the firm, and he was also irritated on rereading one of his letters to Cyrus in 1845. In this he had offered suggestions for improvements to the Virginia Reaper, and he now was convinced that Cyrus had patented these ideas as his own in 1847 and had thereby gained large and unmerited profits.[15] He nursed this grievance in silence for some years, although it probably helps to account for the feeling which

[12] Memo. of a conversation on Mch. 14, 1882, between C. H. McCormick, W. J. Hanna, and C. H. McCormick, Jr., relative to European machine costs in 1878-79. Cyrus McCormick took great pride in the honors which came to him because of his invention of the reaper.

[13] Leander McCormick visited the Valley for periods of from two to ten weeks during each year between 1865 and 1871, and in 1875 and 1878.

[14] Cyrus McCormick seems to have visited the Valley but once between 1865 and 1878, and that was in 1875 when he spent five or six weeks there and in West Virginia. "Lexington Gazette and Citizen," Oct. 8, 1875. H. A. Kellar has listed 199 calls for money from residents or former residents of Virginia between 1865 and 1878. These totaled about $250,000, and in response Cyrus McCormick granted 39, totaling $63,000; refused 25, and ignored 135. See also, Cyrus McCormick's address to the Virginia Society of Chicago, in the "Daily Interocean" (Chicago), Feb. 24, 1880, and his letter in the "Chicago Times," July 5, 1866.

[15] See Chap. IX.

prompted him to confide to a friend in October, 1866: "I have not written him [Cyrus] a line since last winter or spring. I don't know *when I shall again.*" [16]

The difficulty was still unsettled in the following February, when Cyrus McCormick wrote, "I of course hope he [Leander] may be able to take a more proper view of my cause, and thus make the situation admit of a restoration of good feeling." [17] From this time until the climax came, about a decade later, there were frequent disputes over details of machine-construction, the yearly contracts, the admission of partners, the selection of a site for the new plant, the purchase of patent rights, and the share of each in the profits arising from their use. The brothers occasionally renewed their friendship, as in 1870 and early 1871, when Leander was much gratified by the kindness shown to his son, Robert Hall McCormick, by Cyrus and his wife.

After the Chicago fire of 1871 had destroyed the McCormick factory, the partners disagreed as to the scope with which it should be rebuilt. At the time of the disaster, Leander owed Cyrus McCormick $100,000. The younger brother had insured Cyrus's properties in Chicago for that sum and had given him the policies to hold as security for the repayment of the loan. After the fire, Cyrus collected the insurance and consequently lessened his losses by that amount. This exasperated Leander, and as late as 1899 he wrote to the widow of his brother, "Would I not appear to have been entitled to some consideration when through my loan from him of this large sum, he recovered so large an amount?" [18]

[16] L. J. McCormick to W. T. Smithson, Oct. 12, 1866. C. A. Spring, Sr., to C. H. McCormick, Sept. 28, 1866.

[17] C. H. McCormick to C. A. Spring, Jr., Feb. 27, 1867. In a letter to C. H. McCormick on Feb. 13, 1867, Leander accused his brother of robbing him of his partnership rights. Good feeling had not been restored when he again wrote to Cyrus on Apr. 23, 1868.

[18] L. J. McCormick to Mrs. Nancy F. McCormick, Nov. 3, 1899.

ventor and that he was persuaded by his wife to give the machine to his eldest son for the benefit of the whole family.[29]

However trustworthy these recollections may be, there is no
doubt that by 1878 the reaper controversy was well defined.
On June 17 of that year Cyrus McCormick sent the following
challenge to his brother Leander:

As I understood you to say to me on Friday last that you did
consider the *experiment* made by my father in 1831 to cut grain
by Horse power, and the machine then made by him for that purpose (although that experiment was an entire failure, and was thus
wholly abandoned as such), as containing the original principles
found in my invention made during the harvest of 1831 and
patented in 1834 (June 21) or so much the same as to affect my
claim to the "invention of the Reaping machine,"—and that you
had so expressed yourself,—I now repeat what I then asked you
to state to me,—viz.—"What part or parts of my father's Machine, referred to by you, resembled any such corresponding part
of my invention?"

Should you fail to respond to this, as you so declined to answer
me when asked verbally, or to make some satisfactory explanation
to me in the premises, I have to say that I shall feel compelled, in
defense of my just rights, to publish a full description of my
father's Machine, that I may not be subject to any slander from
misrepresentations of such sacred rights, whether so meant and
designed or not.[30]

For seven years following the receipt of this letter the
younger brother accumulated evidence to prove the truth of his
charges—now in Virginia, among the neighbors who had been

[29] Letter of Mrs. Jennie C. Adams to Mrs. Anita Blaine, Jan. 31, 1912.
Report of an interview between W. G. McCormick and Mrs. Amanda S.
Tillman, Jan. 9, 1912. On Apr. 24, 1913, Cyrus Bentley and Mrs. Anita
Blaine were told by Mrs. Nancy McCormick that she had never heard
about the reaper controversy until after her husband's death in 1884.

[30] Apparently Leander did not answer this letter, and no "full description"
of Robert's reaper, published by Cyrus after the date of this letter, has
been found.

his friends since his boyhood,[31] now from his wife whose memory of conversations at the old homestead forty years before was remarkably definite and comprehensive,[32] and again from his sister Mary Caroline Shields, who, notwithstanding the passage of a half-century, recalled many mechanical details about her father's reaper, although she confessed that machinery held small attraction for her in those dim distant days.[33] Nor were incidents lacking, between 1878 and 1885, to spur on Leander in his diligent search. The French Academy of Sciences admitted Cyrus McCormick to its select membership [34]; a Virginia poet sang his praises [35]; the New Orleans Cotton Exposition did him much honor; his eldest son, albeit a youth, demonstrated his fitness to direct the factory, and when Leander presented the University of Virginia with a very large telescope a leading scientific magazine accredited the gift to his brother.[36]

By now Leander McCormick no longer proudly supervised reaper-construction at the factory; the directors of the corporation dared to censure him in spite of his long years of faithful service, and his son Robert Hall was denied a responsible position in the firm. At the same time, Cyrus McCormick, often confined to his room with illness, continued to receive the plaudits of the world. After his father's death in May, 1884, Cyrus McCormick, Jr., then president of the company, published a eulogistic volume in his memory.[37] Believing that an answer was called for, Leander prepared to publish much

[31] By Aug., 1878, Leander McCormick was in the Valley of Virginia and secured at least two of the seven statements which he published in 1885.
[32] "Memorial," p. 16.
[33] McCormick and Shields, pp. 43, 44. *Post,* p. 115, ftn. 60.
[34] "Chicago Tribune," Jan. 1, 1880.
[35] Henry C. Parsons, "The Reaper and Other Poems" (N. Y., 1884).
[36] "Scientific American," L (new ser.), May 24, 1884, p. 321. There is no evidence to show that Leander knew of this error. The gift is correctly attributed to him, *ibid.,* LXXXII (1900), p. 154. "New York Weekly Tribune," XXXI (1872), No. 1, p. 614.
[37] A copy of this volume was sent to Leander McCormick in June, 1885.

of the material which he had collected during the preceding seven years. W. J. Hanna, a trusted friend of Cyrus Mc-Cormick, was in the Valley of Virginia in search of evidence to disprove the whispered charges, and possibly the news of this mission also played its part in impelling Leander McCormick to take action.[38]

"The Memorial of Robert McCormick," compiled by Leander, appeared in the late summer or early autumn of 1885. The first sixteen pages of this little volume contain not only the statements of Leander McCormick and his wife but also the written recollections of five aged relatives or residents of the Valley of Virginia who had known the family at Walnut Grove.[39] These men were Leander's friends who knew what he desired to accomplish, and at least one of them was willing to have a failing memory assisted by Leander's suggestions.[40] A few of the writers had cause to dislike Cyrus

[38] W. J. Hanna was in the Valley from May to Sept., 1885. Leander arrived there in July, and so learned of Hanna's visit at least by that month.

[39] William S. McCormick was 76; Robert McCormick, 76; Thos. S. Paxton, 77; Horatio Thompson, 80, and Zachariah McChesney, 82. "Memorial," pp. 7, 10-13.

[40] Ibid., pp. 7-9. McCormick and Shields, pp. 14, 25-27. Leander McCormick wrote to Cousin William S. McCormick of Patterson, Mo., seven times between Oct., 1878, and June, 1881. William replied with two letters on Nov. 7, 1878, and with one each on Jan. 21 and 28, Dec. (?), 1879, and June 20, 1881, and with a statement on June 5, 1880. The two letters of Nov. 7, 1878, furnish a most interesting problem of historical evidence. The longer one recalls many more details about the invention of the reaper than the shorter one, and the differences between the two are most surprising, as is also the contrast between the shorter letter of Nov. 7, 1878, and the statement of June 5, 1880. One of two conclusions seems to be warranted—either that the longer letter of Nov. 7, 1878, was written several months later than its date or was not written by William. Leander, however, printed only the longer letter of Nov. 7, 1878, in the "Memorial," but both appear in McCormick and Shields. In Leander's letter of Feb. 6, 1879, he told William that he had repeatedly instructed him about the cutting device of Robert's reaper. The editors of McCormick and Shields noted that Leander and William described the machines of 1831 and 1832 in

McCormick [41]; four of them died before their reminiscences were published,[42] and no opportunity for cross-examination was afforded at the time that the statements were made. Several of the men clearly did not understand the meaning of "inventor" and "invention," and merely asserted that the credit for the McCormick reaper was rightfully Robert's, because he had made a machine before Cyrus began to experiment.[43] W. J. Hanna found two men in the Valley in 1885 who contradicted the statements which they had given but a short time before either to Leander or to his agent.[44] The manuscript

almost identical terms. This similarity of expression naturally arouses suspicion as to the origin of William's knowledge. See also below, ftn. 44.

[41] Leander and Henrietta McCormick should be placed in this category. In 1866 Cyrus McCormick ignored a request for aid from the Rev. Horatio Thompson. Although his statement does not appear in the "Memorial," J. M. McCue wrote in the "Southern Planter" of Aug., 1881, that Robert was entitled to the entire credit for the reaper. Cyrus had ignored or refused pleas for help from McCue and members of his family in 1867 (letters of Apr. 11 and 24), in 1868 (letter of May 16), in 1876 (letter of Jan. 1), and in 1880 (letter of Sept. 28). The descendants of John McCown also were hostile to Cyrus. On Nov. 21, 1878, McCown's grandniece wrote to Leander that John McCown had invented the serrated sickle of 1831. McCown's relatives had vainly besought Cyrus for aid. See *post*, p. 114, ftn. 61.

[42] H. Thompson, Z. McChesney, and Cousins Robert and William McCormick died between 1878 and 1885.

[43] "Memorial," pp. 11-13, the statements of T. S. Paxton, H. Thompson, and Z. McChesney. Success was apparently not a factor in their definition. So also, J. M. McCue in the "Southern Planter," Aug., 1881, where he writes that Robert is entitled to the entire credit, since he was "the originator of the idea."

[44] Joe Anderson, Cyrus's slave, affixed his mark to a statement in good English, in 1881, saying that Robert McCormick was the inventor. Leander McCormick did not publish this in the "Memorial," probably because he knew that it was absurd to believe that "Old Joe," who had loved Cyrus since the latter's babyhood, would knowingly injure the man who had given him a cabin and cared for him in his old age. However, the statement was printed in 1910, in McCormick and Shields, p. 35. In 1885, Joe described to W. J. Hanna how Cyrus McCormick invented the reaper. (Hanna, pp. 81-83) "Ole Massa Robert gave up working on the reaper

"Notes on a Virginia Trip," which William J. Hanna compiled in defense of Cyrus McCormick, is entitled to as much credence as the material in the "Memorial," but both are virtually worthless as historical evidence in view of the circumstances prompting their preparation, and the veil of a half-century which those who were interviewed found so difficult to draw aside.

The "Memorial of Robert McCormick" also includes several extracts from letters written or testimony taken in 1848, when Cyrus was seeking a renewal of his original patent of 1834. Attention is called by Leander McCormick to the fact that he, together with his mother and his brother William S., jointly deposed that Cyrus had a reaper "constructed" in 1831, but that they were careful to avoid saying that he "invented" the machine.[45] However, the most significant testimony in the extension case is not given in the "Memorial," as both Mary Ann, the mother, and William S. McCormick stated separately under oath at that time that Cyrus invented the reaper which was patented in 1834.[46]

Over thirty of the sixty-one pages of the "Memorial of Robert McCormick" are devoted to material designed to prove that most of the elements of the 1831 reaper had been anticipated by other inventors.[47] If its compiler had been concerned

when Massa Cyrus said thought it could be done. It is like de good Lord who sent his son to save sinners. 'He [Robert] began de work, but his son did de work and finished it." So, also, Hanna questioned T. S. Paxton (*ibid.*, p. 76, and "Memorial," p. 11), and although Paxton clung to his story that Robert was the inventor, he admited that if Cyrus had not taken up the work where his father failed, there would not have been a McCormick reaper in existence. In like manner, Zachariah McChesney, who in *ibid.*, p. 13, states that Robert McCormick invented the reaper, signed a testimonial to the value of Cyrus H. McCormick's reaper, in the "Richmond [Va.] Semi-Weekly Whig," of Oct. 27, 1843.

[45] "Memorial," pp. 17-20.

[46] Pattison, II, o. U. S. Patent Office Records, "McCormick Extension Case of 1848," Photostats, papers No. 17 and No. 18.

[47] "Memorial," pp. 21-51, 58-60.

primarily with a vindication of Robert McCormick he would hardly have laid so much emphasis upon the lack of originality of his alleged invention. Patrick Bell and Obed Hussey are the heroes of this half of the book. A reprint from the "Chicago Tribune," and another from the "Farmers' Advance," both highly praising Cyrus McCormick, are then included,[48] but these merely serve as a foil to make more impressive the climax and close of the volume—an article violently attacking Cyrus McCormick as an inventor, which first appeared five years before in the "Factory and Farm," a trade journal never favored with advertisements of the Virginia reaper.[49] Robert McCormick's name is mentioned in only one of these three reprints. In brief, an examination of the "Memorial of Robert McCormick" leads to the conclusion that Leander's real purpose was to discredit his elder brother, who had died the year before its publication. He was willing that the reader should accord the highest honor for the invention of the first successful horse-power reaper either to Bell or to Hussey if the evidence presented by him in behalf of his father were not deemed conclusive.

Nevertheless Leander McCormick hoped the "Memorial" made clear that his father had experimented with a reaper as early as the year of Cyrus's birth (1809), and that by 1816, or at least by 1831, he had evolved a machine now

[48] *Ibid.*, pp. 52-57. "A Brief History of the Origin of the McCormick Reaper, Including a Few Incidents from the Life of Robert McCormick," in the "Farmers' Advance" (McCormick Harvesting Machine Co., publication), Mch., 1882. "The Trade Boom," in the "Chicago Tribune," Jan. 1, 1880, tells of the honors Cyrus McCormick received in Europe in 1878.

[49] "Memorial," pp. 58-60. "Was McCormick the Inventor of Harvesting Machinery?" in "Factory and Farm" (Chicago), Jan. 15, 1880. One sentence from this article will suffice to illustrate its nature: "He [C. H. McCormick] not only did not invent the said machine [the reaper], nor mechanically assist in the combination of the inventions of others which produced it, but he never produced or invented any essential elementary part of any reaping or harvesting machine from first to last."

wrongly accredited to the eldest son.[50] Cyrus McCormick had coaxed his mother, so the story went, and she, never able to resist her favorite child, persuaded her husband to give him the invention after Cyrus had promised to share its profits with his brothers and sisters, if profits there should be.[51] But Cyrus was said to have disregarded his pledge, and in his pursuit of world fame to have gloried for fifty years in honors which were not his due. Even the hillside plow was a product of Robert McCormick's skill,[52] since, in truth, Cyrus had no genius, save his cleverness in masking a lack of it.[53] The mechanical talent of his father had been inherited by Leander alone, according to the "Memorial," and it was Leander who had devised the valuable appliances covered by his brother's patent of 1847, and other important improvements which greatly increased the worth of the original machine of Robert McCormick.[54]

Leander McCormick lived for fifteen years after the publication of the "Memorial of Robert McCormick," and neither the appearance of his brother's name on Machinery Hall at the Chicago World's Fair in 1893, as one of the thirty great inven-

[50] "Memorial," pp. 1, 2, 7, 10, 14, 15. McCormick and Shields, pp. 11, 25. L. J. McCormick, p. 301. Egle, pp. 404, 405. J. M. McCue to Mrs. Nancy McCormick, May 22, 1885.

[51] "Memorial," pp. 10, 11, 16. McCormick and Shields, pp. 29, 30, 43, 44. For a brief discussion of this "gift story," see *post*, pp. 116-118.

[52] "Memorial," pp. 3-5. McCormick and Shields, pp. 38-41. This charge is refuted by the correspondence quoted in the discussion of the plow in Chap. II; e.g., C. H. McCormick wrote to Wm. Massie on May 12, 1831, "Although I feel indebted to you for your friendship and early patronage, yet I confess I did at one time regret a little that I had consented to let you have a plough without having obtained a patent for it." See also "Mechanics' Magazine" (N. Y.), III (Jan.-June, 1834), pp. 70, 71.

[53] "Memorial," pp. 58-60. A few of the many letters of Cyrus McCormick which prove his mechanical ability are those of Aug. 6-9, and Sept. 6, 1845; Oct. 13 and Nov. 15, 1846, and Dec. 11, 1862.

[54] "Memorial," pp. 5, 16. W. S. McCormick always disclaimed inventive genius. See *McCormick vs. Manny*, II, p. 205.

tors of history,[55] nor the general acceptance of his title to fame
by those who wrote history texts for the youth of America, nor
the elaborate preparations at the factory for the Paris Exposition of 1900, was calculated to allay his discontent.[56] He
secured, and carefully filed away for future use, at least eight
more statements similar to those he had published in 1885.
Nine years after his death in 1900, his son Robert Hall Mc-
Cormick and his nephew James Hall Shields viewed with keen
displeasure the admission of Cyrus McCormick's portrait to
the Farmers' Hall of Fame at the University of Illinois, and
the marked recognition accorded by the press to the one hun-
dredth anniversary of his birth.[57] In the following year they
published a book entitled "Robert McCormick, Inventor,"
which reprinted the statements of the "Memorial," occasionally
altered and "improved," [58] as well as three others which Lean-

[55] C. H. McCormick, Jr., to the chief of the Drafting Department, World's
Fair Columbian Exposition (undated). Jewell N. Halligan, "Illustrated
World's Fair" (Chicago), Sept., 1893, p. 643. L. J. McCormick to R. B.
Swift, Sept. 7, 1893.

[56] L. J. McCormick to H. F. Mann, June 20, 1898, photostat. "Chicago
Record-Herald," Nov. 21, 1898. "Chicago Times-Herald," Nov. 27, 1899.
L. J. McCormick to Mrs. Nancy McCormick, Nov. 3, 1899, referring to
an article in the "Implement Age" of June 1, 1898, as "insulting."

[57] "Chicago Tribune," Feb. 21, 1900. L. J. McCormick died on Feb.
20, 1900. For illustrations of the widespread attention given to the hun-
dredth anniversary of Cyrus McCormick's birth, see the "Implement Trade
Journal" (Kansas City), Nov. 11, 1909; "Orchard and Farm," Dec., 1909;
"Bulman's Farm Crops Magazine" (Winnipeg, Man.), Dec., 1909; the
"Farm Home" (Springfield, Ill.), Dec., 1909, and the "Religious Telescope" (Dayton, O.), LXXV (1909), No. 50.

[58] Punctuation, paragraphing, and spelling are frequently changed in
these reprints, but probably this was unintentional. In the "Memorial,"
pp. 8, 9, will be found Cousin William S. McCormick's letter of Nov. 7,
1878, which closes, "This is about as well as I can recollect so far back."
This sentence is omitted in the 1910 reprint, p. 26. Perhaps it was a
printer's error, but if so, it was most opportune, since as William grew
older the detail included in his letters becomes phenomenal. In his statement of June 5, 1880 (dated Jan. 5 in McCormick and Shields, p. 27), he
remembers not only mechanical parts but dimensions, after a lapse of

der McCormick had not seen fit to include in his volume of
1885,[59] and the eight of more recent date, mentioned above.
Of these last, all except one are based on hearsay, and in
several instances the writers attempt to prove so much that
they destroy the confidence of the reader which they had hoped
to inspire.[60] In general, the same criticisms are as applicable to
this book as to the one of 1885.[61]

---

fifty years. In the 1885 edition of his letter of Nov. 28, 1878, he writes,
"The sickle, or cutter, was straight and cut with a crank motion," and
he closes by saying, "I believe I have given you about all the information I can respecting the first wheat-cutter made by your father, and if I
can do anything more for you in that line it will be most cheerfully done."
In the reprint of 1910 the first sentence is altered to read, "The sickle or
cutter was vibrating and cut with a crank motion," and the last sentence
of the letter is shortened by omitting all after the word "father." Compare
also the statement of H. Thompson in the 1885 volume, p. 12, and in
the reprint of 1910, pp. 30, 31. For full title of "Robert McCormick,
Inventor," see *supra*, p. 7, ftn. 6.

[59] These are the affidavit of Joe Anderson, Mch. 16, 1881; the short letter
of Cousin William McCormick of Nov. 7, 1878, and the statement of Mary
Caroline Shields, of Jan. 17, 1883. McCormick and Shields, pp. 2-5, 25,
26, 35, 43. The probable causes for the omission of the first two from
the "Memorial" have already been given. *Supra*, p. 109, ftn. 40, and p. 110,
ftn. 44. Why Mrs. Shields' statement was not included in the earlier volume
is not known.

[60] McCormick and Shields, pp. 3, 32, 33, 43. Henry Schultz, aged 71,
recalled the exact words his father told him that Robert McCormick's
father told Robert some time before his death in 1818! Mary Caroline
Shields was fifteen years of age in 1832. In her statement of 1883, over
fifty years later, she wrote that she saw her father's reaper operate in
1832, and that it had a "reel . . . vibrating sickle . . . and . . . platform."
It is difficult to credit her with this remarkable memory for distinct
mechanical parts, particularly when she states, five sentences later, "At
that time and at my age I did not think much about the value of machinery." John H. B. Schultz alone asserted that he was told directly by
Robert McCormick in 1845 that the reaper was "a family concern." Of
course, this was true in the sense that Robert was manufacturing the
reaper in that year.

[61] Several of those whose statements appear in this volume (pp. 33, 36-41)
had cause to dislike C. H. McCormick. T. H. McGuffin had owed him
money. J. D. Davidson to C. H. McCormick, Jan. 8, 1881. Cyrus sued

The historical problem involved in this controversy is a relatively simple one. As the preceding chapter has shown, there was a reaper constructed and tested in 1831 which became known as the "McCormick." Two years after its first appearance, and one year prior to the date of the patent, it was first noticed in the press, and was called the invention of Cyrus McCormick, by the editor and also by those farmers of Rockbridge and Augusta counties who testified to its value.[62] In a rural community where each family shared its problems and its news with its neighbors, the inventor of a mechanical curiosity such as a reaper, which needed the open fields for its operation, could not long remain unknown. Since the implement was called "Mr. Cyrus H. McCormick's Reaping Machine" as early as 1833, the story that Robert gave it to his son at the time of the patent in 1834 can hardly be true.[63] If other evidence on this point were lacking, it would at least seem doubtful that a father

Wm. Withrow when he was engaged in the iron business in 1843. "Augusta Circuit Court, Common Law Causes, 1848, Robert McCormick and Company vs. William Withrow." A. Horace Henry had been an unsatisfactory reaper agent about 1860, and J. H. Shields and R. H. McCormick were opposed to Cyrus McCormick for business reasons.

[62] "Lexington Union," Sept. 14, 1833: "We have omitted until now to furnish our agricultural friends with an account of a machine for cutting grain, invented by one of our ingenious and respectable countrymen, Mr. Cyrus H. McCormick." In the same issue John Weir, a neighbor of McCormick, stated, "I have seen Mr. Cyrus H. McCormick's Grain Cutting Machine in operation for two seasons." In the same paper for Aug. 9, 1834, the editor wrote of a "grain cutting machine of Cyrus McCormick." Jas. McDowell, Jr., and Wm. Preston referred to the reaper as "reflecting great credit on the mechanicle [sic] capacity of its youthful inventor," and seven others signed a testimonial that they had seen in operation a "reaping machine invented by Mr. Cyrus H. McCormick."

[63] Ibid., Sept. 21, 1833, testimonial of Wm. Moore. For this story see "Memorial," pp. 10, 11, and McCormick and Shields, pp. 3, 4. On Sept. 10, 1878, Leander McCormick, then in Virginia, secured a statement from T. S. Paxton of Fairfield, which includes the earliest known reference to the "gift story." Possibly it had its origin here, but family reminiscences place it much earlier.

hard pressed for money and with six children to support would
transfer the product of years of effort to his eldest son, particularly when he deeded a large farm to him at about the same
time.

Robert McCormick manufactured the reaper in his shops
for several harvests preceding his death in 1846. His will not
only fails to mention the machine as his invention, but directs
the executor to pay Cyrus fifteen dollars for each reaper which
he (Robert) had made and sold at Walnut Grove in 1846.[64]
That this is a patent fee admits of little doubt, and Cyrus
McCormick so designated it in a letter to the Commissioner of
Patents two years later.[65] If this fee had been merely a commission for selling reapers, Cyrus would not have received it on
those machines which were marketed without his help.

Robert McCormick's estate was still unsettled in 1856. In
that year William S. McCormick, the executor, referring to his
father's will, wrote to Cyrus as follows:

Caroline and Amanda were to have *profits* on ten machines, I
believe it was, and I have told them would give them *something*
when settled anyhow, etc. They say they have each expected $100

[64] Robert's will, made on June 19 and 22, 1846, bequeathed Cyrus two
slaves, and mentioned $149.72 as due him upon a settlement made on
Feb. 3, 1846, "as also in the further sum of fifteen dollars on each machine
made and sold this season, the sale of which may or will have been actually
real."

[65] Cyrus McCormick wrote under oath to the Commr. of Patents on
Jan. 1, 1848, "By agreement with my father (and afterwards provided
for in his will) $15 was made due me as a patent fee on each sale made
of the 75 Reapers built for the harvest of 1846." Pattison, II, a. *McCormick
vs. Manny*, II, pp. 275-278, 283. Here is printed an account between
Robert and Cyrus, showing the father paying the son $20 per machine in
1844 and 1845. The death notice of Robert McCormick in the "Lexington
Valley Star," edited by John Letcher, and Sam'l Gillock, both Robert's
friends, does not mention his invention of the reaper. The "Valley Star"
for July, 1846, is missing, but the "Staunton Spectator," of July 23, 1846,
copies the notice.

and I propose to give each two hundred without regard to figures. I have settled up with them every way to their [?] satisfaction I believe . . .[66]

In view of the fact that Mary Caroline Shields was to state so emphatically at a later date that her father had given Cyrus McCormick the reaper with the understanding that he would share the profits with his brothers and sisters, it is significant to note that in 1856 she considered two hundred dollars twice as much as her due. In a confidential letter dealing with the settlement of his father's estate, William would doubtless have mentioned the family interest in the reaper if such interest had existed.

For six years before the death of his mother, Mary Ann Mc-Cormick, in 1853, Cyrus had been making large profits from his Chicago factory, where his two brothers were assisting him, not as partners, but as salaried employees.[67] There is no reference in his mother's will to the pledge which he is said to have made at the time of the alleged gift of the reaper to him by his father. If such a promise were ever given, his mother must have felt by 1853 that he was faithless, because he had not shared his reaper profits with his brothers and sisters. Quite on the contrary, she bequeathed him her "Bed and Bed Furniture," and named him one of her executors.[68]

Five years before her death she testified under oath that Cyrus invented the McCormick reaper.[69] This statement was given in the patent-extension case of 1848, and at the same time several of those who had witnessed the first trials of the

[66] W. S. to C. H. McCormick, May 16, 1856, L.P.C.B., No. 1, p. 523. For Mary Caroline Shields' statement, see McCormick and Shields, pp. 3, 4.
[67] "Cyrenus Wheeler, Jr., vs. C. H. and L. J. McCormick, in Equity, U. S. Circuit Court, Northern District of Illinois, 1870," pp. 634, 636, 850, testimony of L. J. McCormick.
[68] Rockbridge County Will Book, No. 13, pp. 25, 26; No. 14, p. 12; No. 19, p. 412.
[69] *Supra,* p. 111, ftn. 46.

machine in 1831, including William S. McCormick, corroborated her testimony.[70] Even Leander McCormick, who led in the attack upon his elder brother after 1878, gave testimony, in this and later cases, which can only be interpreted to mean that Cyrus was the inventor. On March 17, 1848, he stated under oath that he "had no right in the machine in any way myself and if I should Build any I will expect to pay for the Privilege of Building." [71] About ten years later, in the suit of *Obed Hussey vs. Cyrus McCormick,* Leander and his two brothers testified jointly that Cyrus invented the reaper which was patented on June 21, 1834.[72] When the chief plaintiff disproves his own charges by his own testimony the student of history is obliged to regard the motives for the attack, and not the validity of the accusation, as the principal focus of his research.

Obed Hussey, the most persistent rival of Cyrus McCormick in these early days, visited the Valley of Virginia in 1848 in search of evidence to show that Cyrus was entitled neither to priority of invention over him nor to an extension of his 1834 patent. Any rumor that the McCormick patent had been fraudulently obtained would have been music to his ears, as it would have furnished him a weapon with which he could strike down his most feared competitor, not only to defeat but

[70] *Ibid.* When William S. McCormick was asked if he had any interest in the reaper patent of 1834, he deposed on Mch. 17, 1848, "I have none as my Father's will on record in the County of Rockbridge would more clearly shew." See also his statements in *McCormick vs. Manny,* II, pp. 205, 227-229; *Seymour & Morgan vs. McCormick,* pp. 104, 186.

[71] *Supra,* p. 111.

[72] "Record in O. Hussey vs. C. H. McCormick, U. S. Circuit Court, Northern District of Illinois, 1857-59" (undated, Washington), pp. 10, 14, 15, 17, the Answer of C. H., L. J., and W. S. McCormick to Hussey's Bill of Complaint. W. S. and L. J. McCormick also stated that since 1850 they had "no interest whatever of any kind in the business of making and vending reaper machines, either in Chicago or elsewhere." This case will be cited hereafter as *Hussey vs. McCormick.*

to disgrace.[73] This was equally true of the many other rivals whom McCormick met in the harvest fields and in the courts.[74] Charges of pirating inventions were often to be brought against him, but never did his opponents employ the most effective accusation of all—that he was a masquerader and a criminal guilty of fraud, because his original reaper was the work of his father. Probably no inventor and his machine have been so subjected to "pitiless publicity" as have Cyrus McCormick and his reaper.

Cyrus McCormick, time and again from 1833 to the date of his death in 1884, asserted his claim to the invention of the reaper, and spoke of the unsuccessful efforts of his father— with a boldness which would be incredible if he had known that he was depriving of their just rights relatives who had it in their power to crush him at will.[75] For forty years he was universally recognized as the inventor of the McCormick reaper, and neither did he nor any member of his family nor any one else, publicly or in intimate family letters, so far as has been discovered, even so much as hint that the reputation

[73] See O. Hussey's letter to B. M. Rhodes in the "American Farmer," X (June, 1855), p. 383. Here he contends that he made the first successful reaper, and that Cyrus McCormick until he had copied from Hussey was not successful. But in spite of this charge, Hussey calls Cyrus the inventor of the McCormick reaper. In 1848, Hussey not only sought testimony in the Valley favorable to his cause but also cross-examined McCormick's witnesses. Pattison, II, i, Hussey to the Commr. of Patents, Feb. 21, 1848.

[74] In 1850, Cyrus McCormick sued Seymour & Morgan for infringements of his 1845 and 1847 patents. The defendants reviewed the whole question of McCormick's right to be recognized as the inventor of the reaper. The country was searched for evidence unfavorable to Cyrus. Certainly if there had been a rumor of Robert's claim, it would have been aired in court. Cyrus McCormick won the case, and Hussey was one of the witnesses for the defendants. See 3 Blatchford 216.

[75] For examples, see letters of C. H. McCormick in "Mechanics' Magazine" (N. Y.), May 20, 1834; "Richmond Enquirer," Nov. 19, 1844, and Feb. 26 and Dec. 19, 1845. Pattison, II, a. "Journal of Royal Agrl. Soc. for 1851," pt. 2, No. 28, p. 612. "Scientific American," Nov. 13, 1852, p. 70. "No. British Agriculturist," Sept. and Oct., 1863.

was undeserved.[76] His whole character and his long career, as the later pages of this narrative will show, are a refutation of the charge. Commissioners of Patents, committees of Congress, learned societies, presidents, and kings hailed him as the inventor.[77]

Offsetting this proof—which, save for the absence of explicit statements in 1831 by Robert and Cyrus McCormick, is as convincing as the most critical student could wish—are about twenty reminiscences, written after 1877 by or at the request of relatives hostile to Cyrus McCormick, wherein it is again and again asserted that it was a persistent family tradition and always well known in the Valley of Virginia that Robert McCormick was the inventor and that he had given the

[76] Samples of the numerous family letters, which "unconsciously" disprove the charge are, C. H. to L. J. McCormick, Jan. 8, 1847, and to W. S. McCormick, Oct. 13, 1846. In the latter Cyrus wrote of his brother John, who had not been so generously remembered in his father's will as the other children, "I can not but hope that it will have a good effect as such, in which case I for one shall feel disposed to *assist* him if prospects be realized." Cyrus would hardly have so written if he had pledged to share the reaper profits with his brothers and sisters. Note also C. H. to W. S. McCormick, Mch. 12, 1848; to L. J. McCormick, Nov. 5 and Dec. 12, 1867; J. H. Shields to C. H. McCormick, July 23, 1872. The son of Mary Caroline here refers to Cyrus's "kindness and thoughtfulness for me as well as for Mother and Amanda in the past, and at all times feeling highly grateful to you for all that you have done for us." He then asks that his mother may be permitted to invest some money in the reaper business. Compare this with his statement in McCormick and Shields, pp. 36 ff.

[77] Senate, 32d Cong., 1st Sess., "Reports of Committees," No. 160, Mch. 30, 1852, pp. 1, 2: "That testimony was thereupon taken [in 1848] . . . and by the proof submitted on the part of the said M'Cormick [Cyrus] it appears conclusively that he invented the machine, and first practically and publicly tested its operation, in the harvest of 1831." "McCormick Extension Case, Patent of 1845," Opinion of Jos. Holt, Commr. of Patents, Jan. 28, 1859. "McCormick Extension Case, Patent of 1847" (Washington, 1861), Opinion of D. P. Holloway, Commr. of Patents, Oct. 20, 1861. See also *post,* Chap. XVI.

reaper to his eldest son.[78] Surely, if this were true there must have been a conspiracy of silence for forty years within a large family and throughout an entire neighborhood, unexampled for the completeness of its observance even by those who were being injured by their reticence.

One of the strangest aspects of the controversy lies in the fact that the champions of Robert McCormick did not seem to realize that the man whom they were attempting to honor would be dishonored if they proved their case. If Robert permitted Cyrus to patent a reaper which was not his own, and to take oath falsely that he was the inventor, he was a procurer of perjury, who according to the law in force in 1834 was liable to a maximum of five years in prison at hard labor and two thousand dollars fine.[79] Both Robert and Cyrus had previously taken out patents; both understood the law, and both

[78] See the statements of H. Thompson, Z. McChesney, J. H. Shields, H., R. H., and K. M. McCormick, in the "Memorial," pp. 12, 13, 16, and in McCormick and Shields, pp. 40-43. Note a statement of similar purport in a letter of Wm. Withrow to L. J. McCormick, Sept. 3, 1879, in Hanna, p. 96. L. J. McCormick's letters to Cousin William McCormick in 1878 and 1879 show that there was no such family tradition, but that Leander was writing as one seeking information about a matter in which he would like to believe. For statements of Valley of Virginia residents who deny that there was any such tradition, see W. T. Rush to W. J. Hanna, May 23, 1885, and those of P. J. Hite, W. H. Cash, E. D. Robertson, W. L. Poague, and Mrs. Holbert, dated June 9 and 10, 1910.

[79] Certified photostat of the patent of 1834: "*Whereas,* Cyrus H. McCormick . . . hath made oath that he does verily believe that he is the true inventor or discoverer of said improvements . . ." See *Stearns vs. Barrett,* 1 Mason R. 153, F.C. 13337, C.C.D. Mass. 1816; *U. S. vs. Ambrose,* 108 U. S. 336; *U. S. vs. Bartow,* 10 Fed. Repts. 873; *U. S. vs. Bailey,* 9 Peters 238; 2 "Opinions Atty. Genl.," 700; *U. S. vs. J. Sonaschall,* 4 Bissell 425; *U. S. vs. Clark,* 1 Gall. 497. Patent Act of Feb. 21, 1793, Sec. 10; Act of Apr. 30, 1790, Sec. 18. "U. S. Statutes at Large," I, Act of Mch. 3, 1825, sec. 13." *Ibid.,* IV, p. 118. The law required proof beyond all reasonable doubt to overcome the presumption that the patentee was the actual inventor of what he patented. The presumption in favor of the patentee increased as time passed, while rights under a patent were being asserted and recognized. *Cantrell et al. vs. Wallick,* 117 U. S. 689.

were known as honest men. If the father invented the reaper it is strange that he was willing to perform a criminal act for the sake of his son, when the same end might have been reached by a simple legal assignment of his right in the patent after it had been issued to him.[80] Notwithstanding this fact, in the same statement in which his daughter Mary Caroline Shields characterizes him as "kind," "generous," "upright," "reliable," "of high moral worth," and his word "as good as his bond"— all of which was true—she also unwittingly gives evidence that he should have been in prison for procuring perjury and consenting to fraud.[81] In like manner, both she and Leander, judging from their statements, did not bear in mind that the reader would naturally conclude that their beloved mother swore to the truth of a falsehood in the McCormick patent-extension case of 1848.

A careful study of the published statements of Leander McCormick between 1885 and his death, about fifteen years later, warrants the belief that he wished those from whom he sought information, to state more than his own cautious nature permitted him to assert over his own signature. Even in his account in the "Memorial" he does not explicitly write that his father invented the same reaper which was patented in 1834; nor does he mention the "gift story." [82] On June 2, 1898, he wrote to Henry F. Mann, "Rest assured that my Brother C. H. was not its [the reaper's] inventor, but again don't use my name. . . ." [83] The same year, in a speech re-

[80] An assignment of patent was permitted under Sec. 4, Act of Feb. 21, 1793, if such an assignment was recorded in the office of the Secretary of State. Since the McCormicks knew that the Hussey patent had been issued in 1833, and incorporated some mechanical features similar to those of Cyrus's reaper, they would be particularly careful to observe the law in every respect.

[81] McCormick and Shields, p. 4.

[82] "Memorial," pp. 1 ff.

[83] Photostats of letters of L. J. McCormick to H. F. Mann, June 2, and 20, 1898.

ported in the "Chicago Record-Herald" of November 21, he
eulogized his father, but went no further in definite statement
than to say, "He built the first reaping-machine that ever was
constructed." [84] The third chapter has made clear that this
assertion is untrue, but it is significant that he was so reticent
about the reaper patented in 1834, and his father's share in its
invention. In the Mann statement he put it negatively; in the
speech he made a generalization which was merely eloquence;
but in each case he wished it to be understood without definitely
committing himself that Robert McCormick invented the reaper
which was almost universally accredited to Cyrus.

In 1899, Leander's letter to Mrs. Nancy F. McCormick, the
widow of Cyrus, is equally instructive:

The point which I have made which he [Cyrus, Jr.] has seen
proper to attack, is just as I have stated—that my Father was the
original inventor of the first successful Reaping Machine. I have
made that statement and I shall continue to make it, and I want
no better proof of the position I take than is found over Cyrus'
signature, when he says "My Father's machine cut well," but even
this only represents my situation in part, as I can show written
and sworn testimonials to the same effect.[85]

Here Leander apparently misquotes the statement which Cyrus
McCormick made in his letter to the Commissioner of Patents
on January 1, 1848: "By his experiment in the 1831 harvest he
[Robert] became satisfied that it [his reaper] would not answer
a valuable purpose notwithstanding it cut well in straight
wheat." In his letter Leander once more does not state explicitly that the 1831 reaper of Robert McCormick was es-

[84] Leander McCormick was celebrating the fiftieth anniversary of his
arrival in Chicago with a banquet at the Virginia Hotel. He also said:
"I built the foundation for the present reaper works. . . . It is but fair
to say that my father . . . was the genius of the family." See also the
"Chicago Times-Herald" of Nov. 27, 1899, and the "Chicago Tribune"
of Feb. 21, 1900.
[85] "Memorial," p. 17.

sentially the one which was patented by his eldest son, Cyrus, in 1834. He was too experienced in the reaper business to believe that a machine was of practical value if it could work only in a field of upstanding grain. If this was all that he wished to prove, then he and Cyrus were virtually in agreement and the whole controversy was based upon a misapprehension. The preceding chapter has emphasized the complete lack of similarity between the Robert and Cyrus McCormick reapers of 1831, and that the son's machine of that harvest, without basic change in its construction, was patented by him in 1834.

For forty years after the first appearance of the McCormick reaper, Cyrus was recognized as its inventor by all, including those who were being materially injured in purse and in reputation if his title were not a just one. Because of this fact, contrary evidence of the most decisive character, dating from 1831, will alone be deserving of serious consideration. The reminiscences in the "Memorial of Robert McCormick" and "Robert McCormick, Inventor," even if the interested motives which inspired their preparation are forgotten, are valueless when compared with the overwhelming volume of proof in Cyrus McCormick's favor. When continuous, contemporary records contradict a tradition which did not exist for almost two generations after the time of the alleged event, no reliance can be placed upon the tradition. Much diligence has been exercised to collect documents and books relating to the subject of the invention of the reaper and to the career of Cyrus McCormick. This wealth of material on agricultural history, assembled over a period of twenty-five years, makes certain beyond a doubt that Cyrus McCormick invented the reaper which bears his name.

CHAPTER VI

A VENTURE IN IRON, 1836-46

THE family controversy of the preceding chapter was far in the future in 1835, when Cyrus McCormick temporarily put aside his reaper and gave his attention to the farm of almost five hundred acres on the South River recently deeded to him by his parents.[1] Farm life with its drudgery and subjection to ceaseless routine was distasteful to him, but no other course was open so long as money was lacking and his neighbors confined their interest in his unperfected machine to congratulations in the local press.

For a man twenty-six years of age, who was a master of an estate large enough to provide a safe, if not a large, income, the custom of the country-side prescribed a wife. No courtship, however, enlivens the record of McCormick's life at this time. The recollections of his enemies agree that he considered himself better than his fellows, and doubtless his friends were chosen with much care. His aloofness, combined with his attention to dress, may easily have been interpreted, by those who did not share his confidence, as conceit. His resolve to live upon a lonely farm, attended by only a few slaves and hired men, suggests a love of solitude and a willingness to be forgotten, quite at variance with his nature. Since he suddenly emerged from obscurity within a year, his thoughts during this period of isolation were probably turned in a direction quite consonant with his usual ambition.

Cyrus McCormick was always attracted by the speculative.

[1] Rockbridge County Records, Index, Deed Book, "T," p. 108, 198. This gift totaled 473 acres. During 1836, Cyrus purchased two other tracts, amounting to 113¼ acres.

Mental courage without action was failure. Action followed thought with such speed as his material resources permitted, and the restless boldness which drove him on through life brought him his most satisfying victories as well as his most bitter defeats. To plod up the natural sequence of steps toward his goal was irksome to him. Until he attained enough wealth to employ competent helpers, he occasionally suffered from his refusal to devote sufficient attention to necessary although burdensome details. He must leap for the prize, and, having gained it, cherish it not so much for itself as for the use he could make of it to secure something even more desirable which showed above his new horizon.

Combined with his determination to test the worth of his dreams, were a joy in battle and a will to continue to fight even after the cost of the conflict exceeded the material rewards which victory would bring. Such tenacity in the pursuit of his aims won notable successes after he had amassed enough wealth to wear out his rivals by his persistence. In these early days, however, when he attempted to soar, without previous experience, from the tedious commonplace of a Valley farm to the heights on which the local ironmasters dwelt, he missed his objective and momentarily carried his family down with him in the crash.

The mountains which bound the Valley of Virginia and make it beautiful are ribbed with iron. For over fifty years this metal had been a source of wealth and a road to supreme local reputation for the few who had wrestled with it successfully. Smelting west of the Blue Ridge probably began as early as 1760,[2] and iron from Rockbridge County mines was shot from patriot cannon at Yorktown.[3] The Weavers, Mayberrys, Jor-

[2] Morton, p. 170.
[3] "Staunton Spectator and General Advertiser," Jan. 23, 1889. J. C. Shields, "Developement [sic] in Rockbridge," in the "Buena Vista Advocate," Jan. 17, 1890.

dans, and Bryans were ironmasters in the 1830's who had found wealth and local social prestige in their slave-manned ore-banks, furnaces, and forges.[4] Bar-, pig-, wrought-iron, and castings were sold in the neighborhood and were freighted down to Richmond at considerable expense by way of Scottsville and the canal.[5] If an ore-bank could be found with wood and water-power close at hand, six or eight thousand dollars would be sufficient to erect the plant and secure the mine and the timber. A similar amount annually would meet the cost of operation, and, so long as the 1836 price of about fifty dollars per ton held at Richmond, three or four thousand dollars a year could be cleared from the venture.

Such a return made the hand-to-mouth economy of a Rockbridge farm seem negligible. Looking back upon this period from a perspective of almost forty years, Cyrus McCormick stated: "In 1836, full of enterprise and not satisfied to rest on my oars nor on my inventions, an opportunity was presented to me to engage in the iron business. . . . The dignity and position of an iron-master was somewhat enviable." [6] Hopes of manufacturing his plow and reaper may also have strengthened his determination to enter this industry.[7]

It is not clear that Cyrus McCormick made his resolve before the opportunity came, but if such was the case the proposal of Daniel Matthews in 1836 must have seemed quite providen-

---

[4] "Lexington Gazette," Oct. 9, 1835, and Mch. 1, 1883. "Lexington Union," May 1, 1835. "Farmers' Register," Sept. 10, 1842.

[5] *Matthews vs. McCormick,* testimony of Thos. Mayberry, Sept. 18, 1839, and of John Montague, Oct. 26, 1839. From this point to page 135 the story is based upon the testimony taken in this case, unless otherwise noted.

[6] C. H. McCormick's statement, 1874. On Sept. 14, 1839, T. Croson testified in the case of *Matthews vs. McCormick* that C. H. McCormick told him he had entered the iron business because "farming was too slow a way of getting before the common order of people."

[7] "Southern Planter," XLII (1881), pp. 469-471. "Scientific American," LIV (1902), Supplement, pp. 22544 ff. J. C. Shields, "Old Iron Masters of the South River Valley," in the "Buena Vista Advocate," June 26, 1891.

tial. Matthews was an ironworker of experience in the Valley who had lost all except faith in himself and a belief that boldness would restore his fallen fortunes. Although pursued by his creditors, he persuaded two Augusta County farmers to allow him a few months to find the money necessary to purchase a valuable ore-bank on the South River and a near-by tract of timber, essential for fuel.[8] He vainly sought for some one who would advance the requisite funds and at the same time guarantee him one third of the profits from the business. The land was known to be rich in ore, and few mines in the neighborhood had water-power so conveniently located. Those who were attracted by these advantages were repelled by the prospect of a business association with Matthews. Nevertheless, because of his experience in the iron industry, he would, if properly curbed, be invaluable to novices, and after he had somewhat eased his terms, Robert and Cyrus McCormick closed a bargain with him. This was on September 12, 1836, when fortunate owners of metal were receiving fifty or fifty-five dollars per ton for it in Richmond.[9]

Robert McCormick had been one of the first to learn of the promotion scheme, as he, knowing how to write, had been called upon in May of that year to draw up the articles of agreement between Matthews and the owner of the ore land. Cyrus McCormick was at once on the alert, investigated the iron shelf, and persuaded its owner to give him a first refusal in case Matthews failed to raise the money needed for its purchase.[10] Robert, at first hesitant to engage in the business, talked during the summer with Edward Bryan, an iron-

[8] Agreement between Matthews and J. Cress for the latter's ore-bank of 103 acres, and with Henry McCormick for his 520 acres of timber. These contracts were dated May 12 and 17, respectively.
[9] The normal price was from $34 to $38 per ton.
[10] J. T. Cress testified in the case of *Matthews vs. McCormick* that Robert McCormick told him he would not have entered the business if it had not been for Cyrus.

master,[11] and by mid-September was induced by his eager son to join in the venture.

How Cyrus McCormick acquired enough money by 1836 to enter the iron business is not clear. He said long afterward that his father contributed only enough to be of encouragement to him and that he had just completed a successful year of farming.[12] But surely his profits for a year did not total $6,000, which was the approximate sum required to launch the new enterprise. Very likely his investment represented all the slow accumulation of his youth. However this may be, Robert and Cyrus McCormick, partners, paid $585 for the 103-acre tract containing the ore,[13] and $1,750 for over 550 acres on South River, suitable for a furnace site and partially timbered.[14] Daniel Matthews agreed to work faithfully for four years under the McCormicks' direction, as manager of the furnace, and was to receive approximately one fourth of the net profits as compensation. At the end of four years he would be granted a quarter-interest in all the movable property of the firm and receive in money one fourth of the initial cost of the erection of the plant. A furnace would be constructed immediately and a careful account of all business would be kept.[15] Whether or not Matthews by this arrangement became a partner rather than an employee was later to be a moot question. The contract was loosely drawn by Cyrus McCormick, without the aid of a lawyer, and in the subsequent controversy each side took refuge

[11] Robert McCormick was told by Edward Bryan in June, 1836, that he did not consider Matthews to be a reliable manager for an iron furnace.

[12] C. H. McCormick's letter in the "Chicago Times," July 5, 1866, and his statement in 1874.

[13] Deed of Sept. 12, 1836, from J. Cress and wife to R. and C. H. McCormick.

[14] Articles of Agreement between Henry McCormick and Robert and C. H. McCormick, Sept. 12, and 13, 1836.

[15] Articles of Agreement between Matthews and Robert and C. H. McCormick.

in its ambiguity.[16] Whatever may have been the original intention, the style of the firm was at first "Robert & C. H. Mc-
Cormick."

Perhaps Robert McCormick entered the business with great
reluctance and felt that he had been driven to a hard bargain
for the land,[17] but there is no doubt that for a time during
the next year he shared the enthusiasm of his son and visualized
large profits.[18] At one moment he sought to increase the capital
by drawing Henry McCormick and William Massie into the
venture, and at another he talked of buying out his rivals the
Bryans. At the same time the latter endeavored in vain to acquire Cotopaxi, as the McCormick furnace was now called.[19]

During these months of buoyant hope, work upon the furnace
started and Cyrus McCormick was out about the Valley, searching for laborers. He carried a letter from James McDowell,
Jr., designating him "a friend of mine," "a meritorious young
man"; and "he and his security I have no doubt are entirely
good for any obligation into which they may enter." [20] The
winter of 1836-37 was unusually cold, and the furnace site,
almost four miles from Walnut Grove, impresses the visitor
even to-day with its oppressive loneliness.[21] Under such circumstances it was no easy task to cut, haul, and saw logs for
lumber and charcoal; to build a road over a mile long from the

[16] Robert and C. H. McCormick's Answer (June 10, 1839) to Matthews's
Bill of Complaint: "We were induced to give him ¼ of the profits for
we were ignorant of the business and thought if the venture failed, we
would lose less than if we paid him wages."
[17] M. Shaw testified in *Matthews vs. McCormick* that the McCormicks
paid about $1,000 too much for H. McCormick's land and five times too
much for the other tract.
[18] R. McCormick to "Dear Sir" (probably Wm. Massie), Feb. 12, 1837.
[19] Testimony of M. Bryan and W. Lusk in *Matthews vs. McCormick* that
Cyrus McCormick told them he would not sell for less than a $6,000 profit
and "was indifferent about that."
[20] Jas. McDowell to T. W. Gilmer, Dec. 20, 1836.
[21] Hanna, p. 49.

ore-bank to the furnace site; to cart stones and erect a stack and the necessary buildings about the furnace, to construct a raceway, and install a water-wheel and bellows.

Matthews soon proved to be an unsuccessful manager, and Cyrus McCormick, with the aid of an assistant, largely took his place, sparing neither himself nor his men. Five weeks of illness in the early spring and a depleted labor force were the price which he paid for this extraordinary exertion. It was not until late April that he was again able to resume his work. By that time, however, Robert McCormick could write: "We are gitting along with our furnace as well as could be expected. Our maschinery, Bellows, and [?] are made and we expect to blow in about six weeks. Our stack is also built. Hearth and inwalls yet to put in." [22] North Mountain and a neighboring quarry supplied the rock needed to finish the work, and by June 10 the furnace was ready for its first blast. The price of metal sharply tumbled in Richmond during the next month.[23]

The workmen were not contented under Cyrus McCormick's management, after he superseded the indulgent Matthews in January, 1837. He refused to issue the customary liquor ration; the best cuts and much of the fat were said to be missing from the beef sent down from Walnut Grove for their supply; and he forbade the sale of goods from the company store to a laborer when their value exceeded the wages which were due.[24] He was charged with close bargaining and with using negroes to reduce the wage-level. Although he worked side by side with his men in the erection of the stack and the hauling of rock, some said that he was gruff and maintained an offensive

[22] R. McCormick to "Dear Sir," Apr. 21, 1837.
[23] W. Weaver and J. Jordan testified in *Matthews vs. McCormick* that the drop in price to about $40 per ton, the usual quotation from July, 1837, to Jan., 1838, was due to the preparation of the banks to resume specie payments.
[24] R. McCormick to "Dear Sir," Apr. 21, 1837.

air of superiority. For every accusation of this nature a contrary statement can be found. Despite the discontent, the work was done quickly, but the dislike of Robert and Cyrus for meticulous bookkeeping prepared the way for a nice financial tangle, still unsolved. Cyrus was handicapped by inexperience, and his effort to buy out or to discharge Matthews created much dissatisfaction among the employees. Matthews finally left in the autumn of 1837, carrying with him a promise of fifty tons of metal, but threatening to sue on the grounds that he was a partner and could not be discharged. The present significance of the wearisome court action which dragged along from 1838 to 1843 consists wholly in the abundant testimony taken, without which the story of the early years of the furnace venture could only be surmised. The McCormicks eventually won the suit.

The five years after the completion of the furnace were so filled with trouble that the few months when Matthews and the weather had been an annoyance must have seemed halcyon by comparison. Matthews was discharged with comparative ease, but no action by the firm could keep up the price of iron at Richmond or call enough capital into being to tide it over the prolonged hard times. It was a fatal but unavoidable misfortune that just at the time when the McCormicks were ready to begin production, a financial panic of unexampled severity drove money into hiding and made the entire Van Buren administration a business nightmare. From a broad historical point of view, the story of Cotopaxi merely affords an illustration of the efforts of one very small unit of the nation's industry to ride out the storm. The full blast of the hard times was not felt in the Valley before 1840, but as early as the autumn of 1837 the McCormicks had lost much of their initial optimism and were searching for monetary aid. When the price of metal began to fall in the summer of 1837, it seemed to be good business sense to hold back shipments until the market became more favorable. But there was no recovery, and those who refused to move their iron when the dealers were offering forty dollars a ton eventually had to unload it at twenty-five dollars.[25]

As the price of metal tended downward, the McCormicks reduced wages, and the disgruntled laborers were more than ever convinced that they were working for hard masters.[26] As Richmond and Lynchburg brokers were unable to give specie for shipments of iron, money could not be secured in sufficient amounts to pay the laborers. Owing to this fact, and because of the distance from the furnace to a village, the partners were obliged to engage in storekeeping; receiving goods of all sorts from their consignees and paying their workmen in kind.[27] A competent founder for the furnace was hard to find and, probably in desperation, Cyrus McCormick, although inexperienced, attempted to perform, himself, this very particular work. After the wood supply failed in the immediate neighborhood of the furnace, a long haul of six or seven miles was necessary, over uncertain roads. On several occasions the furnace chilled or the fires were banked, due either to the cold weather, or to the inability of wood-choppers or charcoal-makers to keep up with the fuel demand, or because the water in the South River fell so low that the stream in the

[25] Hanna, pp. 31, 80, statements of W. T. Rush and Joe Anderson in 1885. Anderson said: "I waggoned pig iron to Scottsville on James River, six days round trip, six horse team, bringing back plaster. Two tons was a big load." Dealers in Richmond were confident of a recovery in price and wanted to make standing contracts for iron for $40 a ton.

[26] J. Montague testified in *Matthews vs. McCormick* that from July, 1837, to Sept., 1838, there were 28 or 30 negroes and 8 or 10 white men customarily employed.

[27] Receipt of J. Fulton to T. N. Blair, Oct. 31, 1837, shows that the McCormicks were buying molasses, sugar, rice, chocolate, powder, shot, sheeting, pen-knives, buckets, calico, cambric, books, shoes, coffee, etc. On May 9, 1839, the firm offered $10 a ton for hauling to Scottsville, and were ready to pay half in cash and the balance in merchandise.

raceway was not sufficient to operate the bellows. The blast was sometimes suspended for weeks at a time, and if it was necessary to "heave-off" when ore was in the furnace, a great loss of time, material, and labor was the price.[28]

The ore was easy to mine, but it was of uncertain grade and mixed with much sand. In the spring of 1838 the McCormicks decided to make castings, as well as bar- and pig-iron, and bought flasks and patterns for that purpose. The molders now contended that the iron was too variable in quality for such use.[29] About the same time a hot-blast was installed, with a hope of improving the metal and speeding up production, but although this device accomplished its design it proved expensive to install and operate.[30] To add to their troubles, the canal which paralleled the James River from Scottsville to Richmond was not always open, and when it was not they could no longer ship to their main market by the cheapest route. Such, in summary, is the story of smelting at Cotopaxi from the summer of 1837 to the close of 1840. In spite of these difficulties, about twelve hundred and fifty tons of metal were produced, besides a number of plows and the ironwork of a few reapers.[31]

The financial life of the firm, which was partially recorded in books "singularly and carelessly kept," [32] reveals the methods by which the enterprise sought to outlive the hard times, the

[28] Between June and Oct., 1837, 18 or 19 tons of metal a week were made; 7 or 8 tons more a week could have been made if the charcoal supply had been adequate.

[29] By converting pig metal into hollow ware and plow molds, Valley ironmasters saved some of the cost of transportation. A flask is a frame to hold the sand, etc., forming a mold.

[30] The hot-blast was of recent English origin and had not been used before in the Valley of Virginia.

[31] "R. and C. H. McCormick vs. John S. Black, Court of Law and Chancery of Augusta County, Va., 1843." Black stated in this case that almost 2,000 tons was the correct total. See McCormick's advertisements in the "Richmond Enquirer," Dec. 12, 14, 17, 1839, and Jan. 28, 1840.

[32] *McCormicks vs. Black*, McCormicks' Bill of Complaint, Nov. 20, 1844.

desperate circumstances to which the family was finally reduced, and the development, under stress, of the character of Cyrus McCormick. If five examiners in 1843 and 1844 were unable to disentangle the accounts in order to ascertain the exact liability of each of the partners and effect a satisfactory settlement,[33] it is obviously impossible to-day, with even fewer records to study, to succeed where they failed. Private and partnership transactions were inextricably mingled; the exact investment of Cyrus and Robert is unknown; no value was assigned to much of the foodstuffs furnished by the McCormicks for the laborers' use, and sums paid from Cyrus's plow and reaper receipts to cancel furnace debts can never be ascertained.

Except for one loan of $800, repaid within six weeks, father and son financed the business for about a year without outside aid.[34] Nevertheless, by the autumn of 1837, partners whom they had sought a year before, to expand the scope of their enterprise, were needed to bolster their credit so that they might extend the amount of their loans. By good fortune, in September when Rumor said that Cotopaxi was making its owners a profit of $40 to $50 a day,[35] John S. Black, a thrifty young bachelor with at least a local reputation for wealth, joined the firm and was guaranteed one quarter of the profits,[36] At the same time Dr. Samuel S. Fox, a former teacher of several of the McCormick children, invested about $4,000 in

[33] Post, p. 141. McCormick vs. Manny, II, pp. 275 ff., R. McCormick's account.

[34] Copy of statement of account from the Day Book of Wm. Massie, by whom this loan was made.

[35] Matthews vs. McCormick, Matthews's Bill of Complaint, and the testimony of W. J. Steele, J. D. McGuffin, and J. Brooks, in 1839 and 1840.

[36] Hanna, p. 96. Wm. Withrow stated that Black had a $10,000 farm and 20 slaves in 1837. See also John Newton's testimony on p. 20 of a pamphlet (no place of publication given) entitled "Black's Executors vs. Black's Heirs, Court of Appeals of Va., Lewisburg, Va. (1848)."

exchange for another quarter's interest in the venture.[37] Fox lived in Botetourt County and never shared actively in the work of the furnace. Late in 1837, when the McCormicks anticipated increased profits due to the installation of a hot-blast, a financial concession was made to Fox and he was induced to give up half of his share to Robert. Fox died in 1839, and in November of that year Black bought his remaining one-eighth interest from the executor of his estate. Therefore, by the close of the decade Black was a three-eighth's shareholder and the remaining five eighths was divided between Robert and Cyrus McCormick.[38] The name of the firm then became McCormicks & Black rather than McCormicks, Black & Co.

Black's participation was most opportune. In addition to his own investment, his reputation for wealth aided the company's credit, and by the close of 1838 he had borrowed at least $3,100 for the use of the partners.[39] Helped by these loans, two more timber tracts were purchased,[40] and the furnace was reported to be "doing very well and making 26 or 28 tons a week." [41] During the first ten months of 1839, four hundred tons of metal were produced, besides castings, plows, and a reaper. The letters of the time, however, show that conditions were becoming more and more serious. Since Black had recently lost $5,000 in another venture, he found his financial

[37] Hanna, p. 52, statement of A. McChesney. *McCormicks vs. Black,* Black's Answer to McCormick's Bill of Complaint of Nov. 20, 1844.

[38] Pamphlet, "Conveyance between J. S. Black and J. S. Newton, in trust for Jane B. Black, and others, Oct. 30, 1841" (no date or place of publication given), pp. 38-44.

[39] C. H. McCormick to Wm. Massie, Feb. 3, 1844. "R. and C. H. McCormick vs. J. Harper, Augusta County Circuit Court, Common Law Causes, Reversed, 1843."

[40] "A. Fitzpatrick [assignee of A. Shultz] vs. R. and C. H. McCormick, Rockbridge County Order Book, Superior Court, 1841-45," p. 39. One tract of timber was purchased in March, 1838, and the second in the following winter.

[41] *Matthews vs. McCormicks,* testimony of J. McClure, Sept. 18, 1839.

credit shaken and was loath (or unable) to sink more money in Cotopaxi.[42] Ill feeling soon arose between the partners, and Black was later accused by the McCormicks of reimbursing himself without their authorization, from the company's money in his charge.[43] Under such circumstances, and before the crisis of the late autumn of 1840 broke the partnership in twain, Robert and Cyrus turned for help to their close friend William Massie, a member of the state legislature and the owner of a large estate and many slaves.

Massie admirably summarized the situation during the next four years when he wrote, "I was told in 1839 that some Bank accommodation for a while would enable them to get their resources into market when they could do without borrowing, but instead of getting easy they were deeper in, and upon the whole, I have no confidence whatever in the iron business." [44] In March, 1839, Cyrus McCormick secured a loan of $2,500 for four months from the Lynchburg bank.[45] This was extended for a like period when it fell due in July, and in September the company, anticipating its maturity, wrote a draft on T. R. Blair of Richmond, endorsed by William Massie.

Blair was a broker to whom the firm shipped some of its iron, and with this draft the dangerous practice was started of calling for money from a consignee at some future date, trusting that enough metal could be forwarded to him in the interim to equal its value. It was presumed that the broker

[42] "McCormicks vs. N. C. Kinney, Augusta County, Index, Chancery Cases," Court of June 13, 1840, p. 267. "Robert and C. H. McCormick vs. John S. Black, et als., Superior Court of Augusta County, Va., 1845," Answer of Black to McCormicks' Bill of Complaint, Apr. 21, 1845. This case will be cited hereafter as *McCormicks vs. Black, et als.*

[43] C. H. McCormick to Wm. Massie, Feb. 3, 1844.

[44] Part of a letter of Wm. Massie, of unknown date, filed with his letter to Robert McCormick of May 30, 1841. On the Massie family see Phillips, pp. 238 ff., 310 ff.

[45] C. H. McCormick to Wm. Massie, Feb. 3, 1844.

would have the money to meet the draft on its maturity, and usually, although not always in these desperate days, his consent had been obtained before it was drawn. In this instance Blair was unable to make the payment, and Massie was informed by the Lynchburg bank that he was liable for the debt.[46] The company tried in vain in the winter of 1839-40 to forward enough iron to Massie's commission merchant to meet the debt, but by this time it was in such straits that promissory notes were given for small obligations, instead of cash.[47] The winter set in, snow blocked the roads, and new in-walls had to be put in the furnace. July came before the debt was paid, but during the next month the McCormicks borrowed $2,900 from the Lynchburg bank, with Massie again standing security for its payment.[48]

Despite the financial assistance of William Massie, the venture could not survive the hard times, and in January, 1841, the furnace was leased. Notice was given in the press that "the partnership . . . has been dissolved, for this year, with a view to the settlement and winding up of the business . . . for which purpose the whole of the funds, property, etc. . . . have

[46] Notice of W. B. Everett, notary public, to Wm. Massie that this draft was protested for non-payment, on Nov. 27, 1839. R. and C. H. McCormick to Wm. Massie, Dec. 5, 1839.

[47] In Dec., 1839, a promissory note was given to one John Bare for hauling wood. In Apr., 1840, the firm was unable to meet debts of $50 and $62.50. "R. and C. H. McCormick vs. John Bare, Augusta Circuit Court, Index, Common Law Causes, Reversed, 1849." "D. Maury [Assignee of R. Overholt] vs. McCormicks & Black, Augusta Circuit Court, Index, Common Law Causes, Direct 1841." "Thos. McCorkle [Assignee of J. Hartigan] vs. McCormicks & Black, Augusta Circuit Court, Index, Common Law Causes, 1841."

[48] C. H. McCormick to Wm. Massie, Mch. 25, 1840. Promissory note of McCormicks & Black, dated Lynchburg, May 18, 1840. R. McCormick to Wm. Massie, July 9 and Sept. 19, 1840. C. H. McCormick to Wm. Massie, Aug. 16 and Aug. 29, 1840. R. and C. H. McCormick to A. McChesney, in trust for Z. J. McChesney, Nov. 17, 1842, Rockbridge County Records, Index, Deed Book X, p. 27.

been placed in the hands of the undersigned [Robert and Cyrus McCormick], who have . . . undertaken to attend to it." [49]

According to Black, he was the only one in the business who had actually suffered loss. Robert was as well off financially, and Cyrus had been raised to independent circumstances by a venture which apparently yielded no profits.[50] The story of the next five years proves the absurdity of this charge, although it is true that the annual tax-lists do not reveal any significant decrease in the number of slaves and the amount of land owned by either of the McCormicks.[51] They answered that Black left them with all the debts to pay,[52] and to make certain that his funds should not be drawn upon he gave his property in trust to a lawyer, who could use it only to satisfy certain specified creditors, most of whom were owed money because of transactions distinct from the furnace business.[53] Furthermore, as Black alleged that he was most heavily indebted to his mother, the McCormicks openly charged that such an obligation was calculated to void all of Black's responsibility.[54]

[49] "Staunton Spectator," Mch. 18, 25 and Apr. 22, 1841.
[50] *McCormicks vs. Black.* Black's Answer to McCormicks' Bill of Complaint of Nov. 20, 1844. Black believed he could prove "from indisputable data that the losses of the firm have been the gain of some of its members." He charged the McCormicks with listing *all* their debts as company liabilities.
[51] Rockbridge County Record Books, 1836-44. In 1836, Robert McCormick had 9 slaves and 13 horses and mules. In 1841 he had 11 slaves and 31 horses and mules. In 1835 he was taxed on 1,208 acres of land; in 1840, on 735 acres, and thereafter until his death in 1846, there is no change shown in his real-estate holdings. See also Augusta County Land Book, Taxes, 1st District, 1836-44; Rockbridge County Land Book, Taxes, 1836-44.
[52] *McCormicks vs. Black,* Bill of Complaint of R. and C. H. McCormick.
[53] Pamphlet, "Conveyance between J. S. Black and J. S. Newton in trust for Jane B. Black and others, Oct. 23, 1841." By a separate indenture of Oct. 29, 1841, Black authorized Newton to sell his property after July 4, 1842, if he could not satisfy his creditors before that date.
[54] *McCormicks vs. Black et als.,* Bill of Complaint of R. and C. H. McCormick, Mch. 6, 1845.

Black also transferred his interest in the furnace to the same trustee, John Newton, for the benefit of one Sampson Pelter, to whom it was alleged the company owed $1,475. If Pelter's debt could not be paid within the year, Newton was authorized by Black to sell the furnace property for his benefit on December 25, 1841.[55] The McCormicks forestalled this arrangement by conveying the entire plant, four days before that date, to Matthew Bryan and Lorenzo Shaw for "230 tons of average gray pig metal." [56] Robert and Cyrus McCormick haled Black before the courts to force him to contribute his share toward the settlement of the firm's indebtedness. The only immediate result of these attempts was to place him in a debtor's prison, where it was necessary to feed him at the company's expense.[57]

For five years after 1841, the history of Cotopaxi is mainly concerned with the struggle of the McCormicks to pay the furnace debts and their efforts to compel Black to assume some of the liabilities. Without doubt, Black believed that his course was justifiable. He protested that the bookkeeping of the firm had been faulty (and of this there is no question), and that if the truth were ever known it would be found that he had paid in for the company's use far more than his due share. All that he desired, said he, was a fair settlement of money matters between the McCormicks and himself, and to effect this his erstwhile partners should be ordered to "open the books." He did not hesitate "to admit that the reflection that thereby [his trust deeds] the complainants [Robert and Cyrus]

[55] Indenture of Oct. 28, 1841, between J. S. Newton and J. S. Black.
[56] Agreement of Dec. 21, 1841, between R. and C. H. McCormick and M. Bryan and L. Shaw. This sale included, besides the furnace, other buildings and all equipment, about 1,700 acres of land, reserving to the McCormicks only "an anvil in the Smith's shop and some small cast-iron pipe lying below the casting house." The 230 tons of pig metal at the furnace were worth about $5,750, or about the initial cost of the erection of the plant and of the necessary land in 1837.
[57] Account-Book of W. S. McCormick, for his father, under months of Mch. and Apr. 1843. *McCormick vs. Manny*, II, pp. 275-278.

would be subjected to the whole burden of the outstanding partnership debts, occasioned him very few qualms of conscience." If by placing his property beyond their grasp he could force them to disgorge, he would not consider it "a very distressing incident." [58]

Very probably Black's reputation for wealth, in 1837, had been unwarranted, for his mother controlled most of the property which he was supposed to own and set her face sternly against any use of it to pay Cotopaxi debts.[59] With much legal subtlety his lawyers spun out the negotiations before an arbitration board and the courts to wearisome length,[60] and the impatient Cyrus McCormick, too busy with his reaper business to be called upon constantly for testimony, finally wrote to his brother William, on April 2, 1845, from Cincinnati:

I would therefore consider it better to take anything Black would give to be forever done with the infernal crew than to be compelled now to attend to it. I think you will so see it. Then see Newton first, and say that I would have to return a little sooner than had been intended to attend to it, and that something less than had been spoken of *might be* taken *as a compromise to be done with it,* and ascertain whether, or what Black will do, at once. . . . I *think* he would give $2,000, and that it is a favorable time to try him—his lawyers had intimated $1,000. You can consult lawyers.[61]

[58] *McCormicks vs. Black,* Answer of Black to the McCormicks' Bill of Complaint, dated Nov. 20, 1844. *McCormicks vs. Black et als.,* Answer of Black to the McCormicks' Bill of Complaint of Apr. 21, 1845.

[59] Pamphlet. "Conveyance between J. S. Black and J. S. Newton in trust for Jane B. Black and others, Oct. 30, 1841." The will of Jane Black of Apr. 10, 1841, is given on pp. 38-44. By this she deeded her property to her son, but with the proviso that none of it should be used to settle "the unjust debts" which the McCormicks claimed to be due from him. She released him from a debt of about $4,000 owed her since Oct. 23, 1841. This date coincides with Black's deed of trust to Newton.

[60] The whole story may be found in the references given in ftn. 58.

[61] C. H. to W. S. McCormick, Apr. 2, May 12, and 15, 1845, and to J. D. Davidson, Feb. 17, 1845.

In spite of Cyrus McCormick's wish for a settlement, another year passed before he accepted $500 from Black and declared the matter closed.[62] By this time Black's mother was dead and he appears again during the few remaining years of his life as a man of considerable property in land and slaves.[63] His mother, perhaps with pardonable foresight, had saved his inheritance for better days, but the coincidence of his renewed prosperity and his release by the McCormicks from Cotopaxi debts made the latter even more convinced that he had hidden his wealth during the preceding five years, with the purpose of escaping his just obligations.

During these years of controversy with Black, the McCormick family exerted every effort to pay the furnace debts. William Massie continued to place his credit at their disposal so that they might borrow from the Lynchburg bank, and the $2,900 for which he stood sponsor as the year 1841 opened had grown to $4,600 by early summer.[64] Drafts for over half of this amount on Richmond metal merchants, who were expected to purchase iron, had not been honored, and when the loans came due, the bank fell back upon Massie for reimbursement.[65] Robert McCormick assured his friend, "My honour is

[62] "Agreement of R. and C. H. McCormick with J. S. Black, June 2, 1846," Augusta County Circuit Court, Common Law Order Book, No. 3, p. 288, court of June 6, 1846. In an arbitration agreement of Mch. 7, 1843, Black agreed to pay at once company debts amounting to $1,200. There is no record that he did so, but if he did, this sum should be added to the $500 stipulated in the final settlement.

[63] Jane B. Black died about Sept., 1845, and her son before Aug. 30, 1847. See the agreement between S. S. Abney, curator of the estate, and T. Johnston and S. Black, Aug. 30, 1847.

[64] C. H. McCormick to Wm. Massie, May 12, 1841. Cyrus was on his way to Richmond to see his brokers, and had "not been able to make arrangements for the payment of the whole of our Lynchbg. debt at this time."

[65] Day Book of Wm. Massie; Account with McCormicks & Black, 1841. C. H. McCormick to Wm. Massie, June 11, and July 5, 1841; C. H. McCormick to J. and T. R. Blair, June 12, 1841.

pledged as well as my property that you shall never lose a Dollar on account of our liabilities," [66] and Cyrus, with more emotion than he was accustomed to reveal, wrote to Massie:

I am frank to say that I scarcely know how we would have got along through these difficult times but for your assistance—times that have brought low many of the most noble, the adventurous spirits of the land,—and yet, surely nothing has been intentionally misrepresented, nothing promised (on my part) that was not intended in good faith to be performed; and, the reports of calumniators to the contrary notwithstanding, I would lose every dollar that I own, in preference to making dishonest conveyance to avoid payment of just debts.[67]

Nevertheless William Massie himself was weathering the storm with difficulty, and after writing Cyrus McCormick that a protested draft was "exceedingly degrading," and much more with equal frankness,[68] he added in a note to Robert:

I am now as willing as ever to aid you in any way I can consistent with self preservation but feel unwilling to go in farther until old scores are wiped out. . . . If I had money to spare I would rather lend it to you than my credit. I owe debts to various persons of more than $20,000, and, should this money be wanting, my credit at the Bank is my only resource for obtaining it. . . . In conclusion, I must advise and beg you to jog your Junr. Partners up about this $4,600 or $4,700 debt. It is more difficult to manage than young and inexperienced heads might suppose.[69]

[66] R. McCormick to Wm. Massie, May 31, 1841; Wm. Massie to R. McCormick, May 30, 1841.

[67] C. H. McCormick to Wm. Massie, Apr. 3, 1841. From this letter it is evident that rumor was about that Black contemplated the step which he did not take until the following October.

[68] Wm. Massie to C. H. McCormick, June 3, 1841: "I must say it is exceedingly to be deprecated that you should have drawn at all, without at least a positive understanding that your Dft. [on Peyton, Dean, & Edwards, brokers] was to be honored. Such jars invariably have the effect not only of weakening one's credit at Bank, but of cheapening the credit of the endorser."

[69] Wm. Massie to R. McCormick, June 3, 1841.

The monotonous sequence of loans, protested drafts, and explanatory letters of the McCormicks to William Massie, to the bank, and to their brokers, which fill the months between the summer of 1841 and the close of 1842, need not be followed here. Frozen assets were the chief cause of the trouble. The quantity of iron on hand was sufficient to pay most or all of the debts, particularly after the furnace property was sold for two hundred and thirty tons of metal at the close of 1841. But the market was so dull that iron could not be turned into cash rapidly enough to meet the liabilities as they fell due.[70] Nevertheless by the close of 1843 the sale of reapers and iron permitted the cancellation of the entire indebtedness to William Massie.[71]

Because the letters of William Massie bulk large among the sources, his assistance to the McCormicks during these troublous times may be overemphasized. He seems to have been a preferred creditor, but others were not so indulgent, and sought the help of the law to force the company to pay its debts. Lawsuits were numerous, even as late as 1844, but only once is it clear that property of the McCormicks was sold at the courthouse in order to satisfy a judgment against them.[72] Many of

[70] C. H. McCormick to Wm. Massie, Feb. 10, Apr. 3, May 31, and July 5, 1841; to J. and T. R. Blair, June 12, 1841.
[71] Day Book of Wm. Massie. Entries under his account with McCormicks & Black, 1842, 1843, and 1844. Receipt of R. and C. H. McCormick to Wm. Massie, Oct. 23, 1845. This mentions a deed of trust to Nelson C. Clarkson, executed by the McCormicks on Nov. 10, 1841, to secure Massie for the funds he had advanced.
[72] "S. R. Moore [for Wyatt & White] vs. C. H. and R. McCormick et als., Augusta County Circuit Court, Index, Common Law Causes, Direct, 1842." *Ibid.*, Common Law Order Book, No. 2, p. 225. In this case 800 bushels of wheat were seized in order to meet a judgment of $692.22, but there is no record of their sale. There is also a hint of distraint of property to pay debts totaling $3,075.11, held by John Newton. See "J. Newton vs. McCormicks & Black, Augusta County Circuit Court, Index, Common Law Causes, Reversed, 1841." The various lawsuits are too numerous to list here. There were at least 9 in 1841, involving $3,700.11; 3 in 1842,

the creditors assigned their debts to Lawyer John Newton for collection, and by January, 1842, the total in his charge was about $3,000.[73] He hesitated to imprison for debt those who were making an honest attempt to market their metal and meet their obligations. Nevertheless Robert and Cyrus McCormick were usually out on bail, and the trips of Sheriff McCue to Walnut Grove became embarrassing because of their frequency.[74] William S. and Leander J. McCormick, the brothers of Cyrus, frequently added their names as security to notes guaranteeing the payment of furnace liabilities. Although they were not partners in the venture, it was natural for them to join in the effort to restore the family fortunes.[75]

The depth of misfortune was reached in November, 1842, when in exchange for an endorsement of drafts and notes totaling over $2,000, Robert and Cyrus McCormick transferred to a relative, Adam McChesney, in trust for Zachariah McChesney, the five-hundred-acre homestead of Walnut Grove "with all its appurtenances." If the McCormicks were able to meet all their obligations to Zachariah, the farm would be returned, but if they failed to do so he could sell the property for his own reimbursement, after giving thirty days' notice.[76] It was January 22, 1846, before this deed of trust was destroyed and Robert McCormick once again received a clear title to the old farm.[77] Although the exact date of the transaction cannot

bringing judgments totaling $2,654.11; 2 in 1843, $387.26; and 1 in 1844, $67.66. The total is thus $6,809.14. Many debts were settled out of court, but their amounts are unknown.

[73] *John Newton vs. McCormicks & Black.* On Jan. 17, 1842, Thos. McCorkle, who had won judgments in four cases against the firm for $1,308.93, assigned his claim to John Newton.

[74] C. H. McCormick to John Newton, Aug. 31, 1842.

[75] Wm. Massie to R. McCormick, June 3, 1841. "S. Pelter vs. R., C. H., W. S., and L. J. McCormick, Augusta Circuit Court, Index, Common Law Causes, Reversed, 1843." *John Newton vs. McCormicks and Black.*

[76] Rockbridge County Records, Index, Deed Book, X, p. 27.

[77] *Ibid.,* Deed Book, Z, p. 27.

now be ascertained, probably at this juncture in 1842, Cyrus McCormick returned to his parents the farm on the South River which they had given him seven years before.[78]

These incidents make the year 1842 seem the darkest in the life of Cyrus McCormick, but in reality the worst of the crisis was over and the outlook steadily brightened during the ensuing months. Reaper sales increased in the 1843 harvest, and by the opening of the next year Cyrus McCormick assured William Massie that he had "been doing well . . . and after a while will get afloat again, I trust." [79] The seasons of 1844 and 1845 were even more profitable, and when Robert McCormick died—in July, 1846, less than a month after the final settlement with Black—he had the satisfaction of knowing that his property was unencumbered with debt; that his friend William Massie had been fully repaid, and that his eldest son was on the road to fortune and also qualified to assume the leadership of the family.[80]

The collapse of Cotopaxi has been variously attributed to the panic of 1837, the inexperience of the partners, the rascality of Black, faulty bookkeeping, the depletion of the ore-bank,

[78] This was apparently a temporary transfer which would hold good only as long as Walnut Grove was used as security for the McChesney debt. In proof of this, four days after the cancellation of this deed of trust, Cyrus McCormick sold all of his land in Virginia, including this South River farm, to Leander. *Post,* p. 240. Mr. Herbert A. Kellar calls attention to the fact that Leander acquired this farm shortly after his marriage, and that probably it was a wedding gift from his father. In support of this theory it should be remembered that Robert gave Cyrus a farm in 1835 and left Walnut Grove to William, in his will. He would hardly have been less generous to Leander. If this is true, Cyrus, without legal transfer, yielded the South River farm, once and for all time, to his father in 1842, and his deed to Leander in 1846 was merely a fiction to satisfy the law. But see *post,* p. 233, ftn. 11.

[79] C. H. McCormick to Wm. Massie, Jan. 2, 1844.

[80] W. S. McCormick was selling the balance of the furnace iron as late as 1849. W. S. McCormick to Wm. Massie, Feb. 10, 1849.

lack of capital, and inadequate transportation facilities.[81] Older
iron-furnaces during those years, contending with the same
hard times and difficult marketing conditions, weathered the
storm and made profits while doing so.[82] The existing accounts
of McCormicks & Black permit a reasonable doubt whether
the actual money loss of the firm was very large, but certainly
the financial return was not commensurate with the capital,
time, and effort expended. Tradition tells that Cyrus McCormick came out of the venture with his honor, one slave, a horse
and saddle, and $300.[83]

But the yield in experience to Cyrus McCormick largely offset more material profits. These stormy five years were most
important in developing his character and business acumen.
With his father, he paid the debts of the company in spite of
discouraging odds, and thus felt the satisfaction of a victory far
more gratifying than would have resulted from his triumph as
an ironmaster. He had become a man of iron in business in a
broader sense than he had hoped, and had discovered within
himself a will to fight, unsuspected at the outset of the venture.
If he sought in 1835 to seclude himself on a farm where he
could live apart from neighbors who scoffed at his dreams, and
were unsympathetic with his pride, by 1846 he had won the

[81] Hanna, pp. 32, 91, 94, statements of W. T. Rush, A. H. H. Stuart,
and Wm. Withrow. C. H. McCormick's statement, 1874. Helen A. Smith,
"One Hundred Famous Americans" (N. Y., 1902), pp. 28-31. Sherman
Williams, "Some Successful Americans" (Boston, 1904), pp. 79-87.
[82] *Matthews vs. McCormick,* testimony of John Steele, Jr., Aug. 8, 1839.
[83] Statement of W. T. Rush, May 6-8, 1893. In his statement to his wife
and niece in 1874, C. H. McCormick said that he was "left as nearly as
could be estimated, even with the world." In his letter in the "Chicago
Times" of July 5, 1866, he wrote: "While I don't mind being said to
have been 'not worth a red cent' at one time, I was not 'poor white trash.'
If they [the editors] can *profit* by referring to *that* [my poverty] they
may; but not by associating my name with 'poor white trash.'" *McCormick
vs. Manny,* II, p. 235, W. S. McCormick testified that when his brother
made his trip to the West in 1844 or 1845, he "had not a single red cent."
For another view see Chap. X, p. 233, ftn. 11.

respect, if not the love, of his fellows, and realized that the proper way to convince the world of his worth did not lie in retirement from it.

Cotopaxi had been his school of business. His experience had brought him a knowledge of iron, marketing, management of workmen, business ethics and law, and court procedure. The manufacture and sale of his reapers supplied him with a field to put this information into practice, and Cyrus McCormick was later to look back upon the iron years as a most valuable period of preparation.[84] He began as a farmer with a penchant for machinery, but on leaving he was ready to manage with extraordinary skill the larger enterprise of reaper-building. Even before the Cotopaxi chapter of McCormick's life was closed, he was known, not as the ironmaster but as the inventor and manufacturer of the Virginia Reaper. This new title was earned during the same years in which he tried so hard to deserve the other.

[84] C. H. McCormick's statement in 1874: "And all this [my furnace experiences] I have ever since felt to be one of the best lessons of my business experience. If I had succeeded in the iron enterprise I would perhaps never have had sufficient determination and perseverance in the pursuit of my reaper enterprise to have brought it to the present stage of success."

CHAPTER VII

THE RISE OF OBED HUSSEY, 1832-42

DURING the mid-thirties many Americans shared the belief in a permanent prosperity which lured Cyrus McCormick and his father into the lean years following the panic of 1837. In June, 1835, a Massachusetts farmer, undaunted by the signs of ruin all about him, was confident that "these dark ages with respect to agriculture are rapidly flitting by us, and the sun that has been so long hid in clouds and darkness, is now breaking forth in its meridian splendor, dispelling the fogs and mists in which our land has been so long enveloped." [1]

Shortly thereafter, Judge Jesse Buel, editor of the "Albany Cultivator," assured the New York State Agricultural Convention, that "the production of our agricultural labor may be doubled in ten years and trebled in twenty." [2] The future was to justify the prediction, but, even as the subscribers of his magazine were reading his address, the first warm weather of spring released the plague, and by midsummer this same publication complained of the "almost unprecedented" devastation of the Hessian fly in the middle States and Virginia. [3] By De-

[1] "Albany Cultivator," Aug., 1835, pp. 91, 92, letter of J.A.B. from Plainfield, Mass., June, 1835.
[2] *Ibid.*, Mch., 1836, p. 22, address of Judge J. Buel, Feb. 8, 1836.
[3] *Ibid.*, July, 1836, p. 73. In the issue for Jan., 1837, p. 170, the editor blamed crop failures mainly on unpropitious weather, insects, and the scarcity of labor. "The labors of agriculture have been diminished by the multiplicity of public works going on, which have employed a great number of laborers; by the great extent of emigration which transformed many thousands of producers into mere consumers,—and by the unprecedented spirit of speculation." The grain farmers suffer; stock farmers prosper.

cember, 1836, wheat was worth two dollars a bushel,[4] and a year later flour sold for twelve dollars a barrel.[5] This doubling of price did not mean that farmers were growing rich. On the contrary, it signified crop failures, and "the disgraceful necessity of importing wheat while we [the Americans] are in the possession of a soil, which God, in his infinite mercy, seems to have created expressly for the purpose." [6]

"Acts of God" and President Van Buren, particularly the latter, were blamed for this season of despair with its financial panic, bread riots, unemployment, Seminole War, and Hessian fly. Although he was the innocent victim of circumstance, the people arose in 1840 and turned out the "Little Magician" whom they charged with practising the black art to their detriment. Amid the crash in the West of paper towns, railroads, and road and canal speculations, the persistent creak of the Conestoga wagon could be heard. The East's loss of men was the West's gain, and the open prairie best suited the reaper. As evidence that the people were always right, Presidents Harrison and Tyler were the heralds of a slowly returning prosperity, a new boom-time during which the reaper was to come into its own.

During this period of chastening, the wisest farmers sought the causes of their trouble. The "Farmers' Register" of May, 1839, rejoiced to learn that the number of agricultural magazines had almost doubled in a year and that there were more than a hundred thousand farmers' families reading about the ways and means to raise bigger and better crops and stock.[7]

[4] *Ibid.*, Dec., 1836. "Farmers' Cabinet" (Phila.), Dec., 1836.

[5] "Albany Cultivator," Dec., 1837. "Farmers' Cabinet," Dec., 1837.

[6] "Journal of the American Institute" (N. Y.), Sept., 1837, pp. 646, 647, letter of "Agricola."

[7] "Farmers' Register," May, 1839, p. 282, copying from the "Genesee Farmer," of Rochester, N. Y. About one tenth of the farmer families of the United States were reading agricultural magazines, according to this estimate. *Supra,* p. 29, ftn. 2.

The decennial census of 1840 was the first to collect statistics of interest and value to the producer. By 1841 a renewed optimism was evident in the agricultural press, and in August of that year, the "Albany Cultivator" was certain that "speculation has had its day"; that a fair, steady, and "compensating price" had returned; that the hard times had educated the nation to a proper estimate of the value of the farmer; and that yearly advances were being made in efficient tillage and stock-raising.[8] This new confidence became more evident during the next two years.[9]

A hasty reading of the "American Agriculturist" of New York for 1843 shows that the change of emphasis from that of the "American Farmer" for 1820 to 1830, already described,[10] was one of degree rather than of kind. There was the same attention given to new implements; to Durham, Devon, and Hereford cattle; to Cotswold, Southdown, and Merino sheep, and Berkshire hogs. Less space was devoted to domestic manufactures, but more to the problem of soil-saving. Coal, ashes, ground glass, plaster of Paris, dock mud, lime, gypsum, clover, marl, and city manures were all discussed. The one hundred and thirty-five daily papers of the country were urged to print more agricultural information; agricultural societies, institutes, and schools were advocated, and the model farm and traveling lecturer encouraged. Articles about the agriculture of Cuba, the products of Oregon and "Wiskonsan" illustrate the

---

[8] "Albany Cultivator," Aug., 1841, p. 123. "Farmers' Cabinet," Aug., 1841.

[9] "American Agriculturist," May, 1843, p. 42. After writing of cotton reaching a "new low" recently, but of its certain rise due to the failure of culture in India, the editor continued, "The rise of cotton will affect other products more or less; so that with the present superabundance of capital, both in this country and abroad, we are satisfied that we are now entering upon a new career of prosperity." Internal improvements—railways and canal digging—will change more producers into consumers. *Ibid.*, Jan., 1844, p. 1: "We think it disgraceful any longer now to speak of hard times."

[10] *Supra*, Chap. II.

drift of empire, while the emphasis upon stock-raising reflects both a leading occupation of the State in which this magazine was printed and the beginnings of the meat-packing industry in the West.[11]

The reaper was unmentioned in this volume, although by 1843 the implement had aroused considerable interest in several of the chief grain areas of the United States. Seven years before, when the farmers shared the current enthusiasm of Jackson's second term, the editor of the "Farmers' Cabinet" of Philadelphia was confident that the age of mechanical harvesting was about to open:

We have long been firm in the faith that the time would come when most of the operations carried on in the growth of corn and grain, would be done by machinery. . . . We have no doubt that ploughing will be done successfully by steam, and that mowing and reaping will be done by the same Herculean power. For a long time our farmers were opposed to the threshing machines,—this opposition arose from imperfect machinery, but still this very opposition retarded the perfection of the very machines it opposed. So in reaping and mowing, some imperfect attempts have been made which were not perfectly successful; and hence the whole scheme has been condemned.[12]

Thus, while the McCormicks endeavored with might and main to earn a fortune in the iron business, the growing interest of the country in the possibility of a successful reaping machine led Obed Hussey and others almost to the very goal of Cyrus McCormick's ambition. As early as 1825, William

[11] "American Agriculturist," 1843, *passim.* In the Nov., 1843, issue, p. 289, it is noted that the packing industry had virtually arisen in one year in the West, due to the lowering of the English import duties upon provisions. At Chicago 500 to 700 barrels of beef were packed daily in the busy season, and the packers were willing to pay more than $1.50 to $2.00 per cwt. for beef if farmers would improve their stock.

[12] "Farmers' Cabinet," Dec. 15, 1836, p. 174. "Albany Cultivator," Aug., 1836, p. 89.

and Thomas Schnebly of Hagerstown, Maryland, built a reaper with a reel, a double-edged scissor-action knife, guard fingers, a divider, and a revolving apron to discharge the cut grain in gavels. They made three or four machines for experimental purposes before they gave up in 1837, but they failed to win either the patronage of the farmer or the notice of the press.[13] The William Manning machine, patented in 1831, was unique for its spear-shaped cutters attached to a vibrating bar, but, like the Schneblys', its chief importance was academic rather than economic.[14]

In the same year that Cyrus McCormick received his patent, Enoch Ambler of Montgomery County, New York, also secured one for a grain- and grass-cutter with a divider, and a scythe over six feet long with peculiar concave blades, vibrating over open-slotted fingers. It was primarily a mower and about one hundred acres of grass were cut with it in 1835. A firm of Spencertown, New York, bought the patent right for the region east of the Hudson River, and early in 1836 advertised it for sale at sixty and seventy dollars. Apparently only three purchasers were found, but the American Institute, at its annual fair in Niblo's Garden, New York City, awarded it a discretionary premium in 1837. Probably no machines were sold after this year, but in 1854 and 1855 five old ones were purchased by reaper manufacturers who wished to use them as evidence in lawsuits. In fact, Ambler's chief claim to remembrance rests upon the possibility that he anticipated Hus-

[13] "McCormick Extension Case, Patent of 1845." Section of book headed "Ralph Emerson, Jr.'s Abstract of Testimony," p. 71, testimony of Wm. Schnebly of Hackensack, N. J. *McCormick vs. Manny,* II, pp. 788-801, testimony of Wm. Schnebly. A few machines were used successfully by others who made them with his permission. "Journal of Franklin Institute," XV (1835), p. 406.

[14] The Manning patent of 1831 was the first issued in the United States for a machine with a divider. See chart in Chap. III.

sey by more than a decade in the use of guard fingers with open slots to prevent clogging.[15]

Not far away, in Oneida County, New York, Abram Randall constructed a reaper in 1833 and two years later, after exhibiting a model at the Utica Mechanics' Fair, he secured a patent. A rake, devised to discharge the grain automatically from the platform, failed to work successfully, and a raker's seat was substituted. There were scissor-like knives, a reel, a divider, and covered gearing. About twenty years later the inventor testified that he had seen a cut of Bell's machine before he finished his own, that his cutters choked, and that about 1840 he abandoned the only reaper which he made.[16] Once again the future interest in this machine was occasioned not by its lack of success but by the efforts of its inventor to construct a practical automatic rake and raker's seat.

Far more publicity at this time was gained by Captain Alexander M. Wilson of Rhinebeck, New York, and his grain- and grass-cutter. Like so many earlier English machines, this reaper was pushed through the grain by two horses, and its cutter consisted of several knives on the periphery of a revolv-

[15] "Journal of Franklin Institute," XVI (1836), p. 30. "Mechanics' Magazine" (N. Y.), Apr., 1836, p. 253. "Albany Cultivator," Aug., 1835, p. 84; Apr., 1836, p. 31; May, 1837, p. 51. "Record in Hussey vs. Bradley et als., U. S. Circuit Court, Northern District of New York (1861-63)," pp. 231 ff., 393. "Record in Hussey vs. Whiteley et als., U. S. Circuit Court, Southern District of Ohio (1860-61)," *passim.* "Record in Aultman vs. Holley et als., U. S. Circuit Court, Southern District of New York (1860)," pp. 1227-1229. These cases will hereafter be cited, respectively, as *Hussey vs. Bradley, Hussey vs. Whiteley,* and *Aultman vs. Holley. McCormick vs. Manny,* II, pp. 715, 719, 728-730. The Ambler machine was said to cut 15 or 20 acres of grass or grain a day. By 1837 its price had risen to $130.

[16] *McCormick vs. Manny,* II, pp. 363-365, 753, 755, 760, 764 ff. testimony of Abram Randall. *Aultman vs. Holley,* pp. 487-506, testimony of Ogden M. Randall, the son of Abram, who was but nine years old in 1835. "McCormick Extension Case, Patent of 1845," adverse testimony, pp. 18-29. "McCormick Extension Case, Patent of 1847," pp. 169-181. "Genesee Farmer," Jan. 24, 1835, p. 26.

ing horizontal wheel. In fact, Wilson's reaper-mower closely resembled the 1811 machine of James Smith of Deanston, Scotland. In 1836, Wilson advertised to sell his implement for $225 and to lease manufacturing rights. He momentarily pleased the farmers of his locality and received a gold medal and a certificate of first premium from the American Institute in 1836 and 1837. A writer in the "Journal of the American Institute" was happy to announce that "the present season [1837] has brought forth the climax of the farmers' hopes, in the great success of *Wilson's Mowing Machine*. . . . With this machine, accompanied by the horse rake, the hay and grain fields lose their terrors; for the small portion of manual work left to perform, is rather a pleasure than a toil." [17]

An exhibition during the same year at Flushing, Long Island, before a gathering said to number two thousand persons, was a disappointment due to frightened horses and a rough meadow. A second trial was more successful, and the jury certified that it performed "to our entire satisfaction," and "ought to be of great value on our western prairies." Wilson

[17] "Journal of the American Institute," Nov., 1836, pp. 85, 92; July, 1837, p. 557; Sept., 1837, pp. 646, 647; Oct., 1837, pp. 25, 32. "American Harvester Patents, 1825-51," patents of Dec. 30, 1835, and May 15, 1837. "Journal of Franklin Institute," XVIII (new ser.), 1836, p. 46; XXX (new ser.), 1838, p. 111; XV (3d ser.), 1848, p. 25. In the "Albany Cultivator," for Mch., 1836, a cut is given and the testimonial of thirteen prominent New York farmers. *Ibid.*, Oct., 1836, p. 128; Aug., 1837, p. 99; Sept., 1837, p. 115; Jan., 1838, p. 177. "Prairie Farmer," Jan., 1846, p. 24; Sept., 1846, pp. 284, 285; July, 1846, p. 202. "Maine Farmer" (Winthrop, Me.), Sept. 5, 1837, p. 238. Francis S. Wiggins, "American Farmers' Instructor" (Phila., 1844), p. 447. It seems to have been manufactured at Southport, Wis., in 1846. Although it is impossible to establish the connection between the machine of Smith of Deanston and that of Wilson, a Smith machine was probably brought to New York in 1835. It was not called Smith's, in the press, but the description tallies. See "Farmers' Register," Aug., 1835, p. 224. "New England Farmer," July 15, 1835, p. 5. "Genesee Farmer," July 25, 1835, p. 238. "Mechanics' Magazine," Nov., 1835, pp. 265-267; Dec., 1836, p. 289.

said that he received thirty-five orders as a result of the award of the American Institute, and he seems to have sold a few machines in the next decade, chiefly along the Hudson River.

Hazard Knowles, chief machinist of the Patent Office, made a reaper in 1837 and exhibited it in Judiciary Square in Washington. It was unique for its hinged finger-bar which permitted the horizontal knife to be raised when not in use. Knowles sold one half of his interest in this machine to a Shenandoah Valley farmer, who abandoned it in 1841 when laborers in his neighborhood threatened its destruction.[18] A patent granted to Jonathan Read of New York City in 1842, for a reaper whose vibrating steel blade had alternating reverse-angle serrations, was to cause McCormick and other big manufacturers some trouble in the courts about fifteen years later.[19]

Finally, there were a few men prior to 1844 who sought to build machines that would not only reap the grain but also thresh, winnow, and even bag it in the field.[20] As early as 1828, Samuel Lane of Hallowell, Maine, invented a reaper-thresher which is remembered only because it was the first one of its kind patented in the United States.[21] Two more successful ones were the Moore-Hascall machine of 1835 and the Churchill harvester of six years later. Hiram Moore of Climax Prairie,

[18] *Aultman vs. Holley, passim.* "U. S. Patent Office. In the Matter of the Application for the Extension of the Reissues of the Patents of J. E. Brown and S. S. Bartlett for Grain and Grass Harvesters, of Jan. 2, 1855, Testimony" (Washington, 1868), pp. 85 ff., 101-105. "U. S. Patent Office. Sylla and Adams, Extensions, Harvesters, II, Opponents' Proofs" (Washington, 1867), pp. 1-55. "Senate Journal," 3d Sess., 25th Cong., 1838-39, p. 116. *Ibid.,* 1st Sess., 26th Cong., 1839-40, pp. 104, 117, 320. *Ibid.,* 2d Sess., 26th Cong., 1840-41, p. 71.

[19] "Journal of Franklin Institute," XII (3d ser., 1846), p. 117. *Seymour & Morgan vs. McCormick,* pp. 132-137. "Western Farmer and Gardener" (Cincinnati), Oct., 1839, p. 57. "Albany Cultivator," Sept. 12, 1835, p. 294; Aug., 1835, p. 84; Dec., 1841, p. 191. "Scientific American," LXX (1894), p. 3. C. H. to W. S. McCormick, Sept. 29, 1856.

[20] There were twenty harvester patents issued between 1836 and 1843.

[21] "Journal of Franklin Institute," II (new ser., 1828), p. 251.

Michigan, joined John Hascall, a lawyer, to secure a patent in 1836. The Moore machine was a header, requiring from fourteen to sixteen oxen or horses and almost as many men to operate it, and selling for prices ranging from $500 to $700. It was too expensive for the usual farmer, but several were in use in Michigan for twenty years following 1835. One was carried to California in 1854, and from it an unbroken descent can be traced to the present-day header in the far West. Its main interest for this story lies in the probability that Moore and Hascall, like Ambler, used open-slot guard fingers for eight years prior to their adoption by Hussey.

As early as the autumn of 1841, Alfred Churchill of Avon, Illinois,[22] was confident that his machine would be as important to the West as the cotton-gin was to the South. Solon Robinson, the traveling Indiana advocate of better agriculture, prophesied, late in the same year, that this new implement bade fair to supersede all reapers. But the big header-thresher could not work through a ripe wheat-field without scattering much grain, and farmers, even if they could afford to buy the machine, hesitated to harvest their crop while it was still green.[23]

Probably not over thirty or thirty-five of these machines already named were sold in the period prior to 1844. They aroused curiosity and hope, and the inventors were often pioneers in the use of some mechanical device which was later to find extensive use. At the time, their effect upon agriculture

[22] "N. Y. Farmer and Mechanic," Oct. 10, 1844, p. 215; June 28, 1849, p. 309. *Hussey vs. Bradley,* pp. 109-113, 319-322. "Hussey Extension Case, Patent of 1847" (Washington, 1861), pp. 161-173. *McCormick vs. Manny,* II, pp. 771-787. *Seymour & Morgan vs. McCormick,* pp. 161 ff., *Hussey vs. Whiteley, passim.*

[23] "Journal of Franklin Institute," III (3d ser., 1842), p. 340. "Union Agriculturist and Western Prairie Farmer" (Chicago), May, 1841, pp. 31, 41; Aug., 1841, pp. 61, 64; Apr., 1842, pp. 36, 37; Sept., 1842, p. 73; Nov., 1842, p. 93. "Illinois State Register" (Springfield), July 2, 1841. "Albany Cultivator," Dec., 1841, pp. 196, 197. "Southern Planter," Sept., 1846, p. 115.

Obed Hussey

was too small to be recognized and their appearance merely symbolizes the growing effort to bring science to the service of the farmer. There was one inventor, however, whose reaper merits more detailed consideration, because it was McCormick's chief rival during the years before 1850. Prior to 1843, it held first place among all the reapers then in use.

Little can be written of Obed Hussey during the first forty years of his life, beyond the facts that he was born in Maine, of Quaker stock, in 1792, and moved to Nantucket at an early age.[24] Life in that village led him to the sea, and, according to his own story, he rowed more than once after whales in the Pacific Ocean.[25] Why he left the sea, and under what circumstances his attention was turned to the problem of reaping, are unknown. The black patch over his sightless left eye is equally a mystery, but it at least helped to make him a man marked among his fellows. He has been characterized as "sensitive, modest, and unassuming," but his letters make clear that these are attributes which a Quaker sometimes lacks. The McCormick-Hussey battle of the reapers will show that neither rival asked for quarter, and that each fought the other with every weapon at his command.

In 1833, Hussey was living on the farm of Judge A. Foster, near Cincinnati, Ohio. Here he constructed a reaper which performed so well in preliminary trials[26] that he took it to the Hamilton County Agricultural Society Fair at Carthage on July 2. Although several parts broke during this exhibition,

[24] Follett L. Greeno, "Obed Hussey, Who, of All Inventors, Made Bread Cheap" (Rochester, N. Y., 1912), p. 5. Hereafter cited as "Greeno." Obed Hussey's relationship to Christopher Hussey, of Nantucket whaling fame in the early eighteenth century, has not been traced.

[25] Greeno, pp. 16-18, letter of Hussey to E. Stabler, Mch. 12, 1854.

[26] E. Stabler, "A Brief Narrative," etc., in J. R. Parsons, L. Miller, and J. F. Steward, "Overlooked Pages of Reaper History" (Chicago, 1897), pp. 3-47. Hussey testimonials of 1833 will be found here. Only one machine was built in 1833 and that was not sold.

the test was enough of a success to win the written approbation of the society.[27] Hussey was penniless, but a Mr. Jarvis
Reynolds of Cincinnati advanced money for the manufacture
of his machine in that city. In December, 1833, Hussey secured
a patent [28] and news of his reaper had already traveled through
the great grain region of the Genesee [29] and as far as doubting
Boston. "So many novelties have been brought forward of
late," the editor of the "New England Farmer" quoted, "and
so few have answered the expectations at first held out of their
utility, that we are supposed to be somewhat cautious and incredulous." [30]

As described in the patent of December 31, 1833, the Hussey reaper consisted of a framework carried upon two wheels
of equal size. Astride the second of the two horses, in line,
that pulled the machine, was a boy who kept the animals on a
straight course through the field.[31] A platform extended to one
side, with its front edge lined with a "series of iron spikes" or
guards. These fingers were seven or eight inches long and
were made of two pieces joined at the tips. Through the
grooves thus formed vibrated a horizontal cutter, consisting of

[27] "New York Farmer," Apr., 1834, p. 111. "Niles' Weekly Register"
(Baltimore), July 27, 1833, p. 355. The Carthage trial is mentioned, but
Hezekiah Niles is skeptical.

[28] Greeno, op. cit., pp. 10, 13-15, 43. Patent Office Records, "Hussey
Extension Case, Patent of 1847," pp. 111, 116, testimony of A. Garrett
Williamson and of Algernon Foster, son of the judge. Hussey vs. Bradley,
pp. 145, 413, testimony of Williamson and Foster. Seymour & Morgan vs.
McCormick, pp. 141, 146, testimony of O. Hussey.

[29] "Genesee Farmer," July 27, 1833, p. 240, copying from the "Cincinnati
Advertiser."

[30] "New England Farmer," July 24, 1833, p. 15, quoted from the "United
States Gazette."

[31] Hussey, in a letter in the "Southern Planter" of Mch., 1843, pp. 68,
69, states that his machine originally used "two horses abreast." The earliest
cut does not support this statement. "Journal of Franklin Institute," XIV
(new ser., 1834), p. 37. The editor notes that the Hussey reaper, save
for its double beveled teeth, resembles Manning's.

a series of triangular steel plates with double-beveled edges, bolted to a straight, flat, iron rod. These cutter-plates were three inches wide at the base and four and a half inches long.[32] The guards formed double bearers above and below for this cutter-bar, and Hussey contended that it made little difference whether the knives were sharp or dull.[33] There was no reel, and the severed grain was pushed to the ground in gavels, from the rear platform, by a man who rode on the machine, wielding a specially made rake with a paddle-like motion.[34] This rakeman was also expected to extend his implement ahead of the knife into the grain and gently bend the straw toward the cutter. In short, he was a human reel, with as onerous a task as the walking raker who accompanied the McCormick reaper.[35] Because of the absence of a reel, it was most difficult to cut grain which was blowing or bent away from the machine.

The Hussey knife, consisting of triangular steel plates, and combined with the closed fingers, was the outstanding novelty. This type of guard finger, improved in 1847 by a slot through its under side to permit the discharge of chaff, was, after some further modifications, to become the standard one for use in harvesting machinery.[36] And yet McCormick, not to mention

[32] Miller, pp. 24-26. "Albany Cultivator," May, 1841, p. 81, letter of Hussey dated Apr. 9, 1841.

[33] "New Genesee Farmer," Nov. 30, 1839, p. 409, letter of Hussey, Nov. 15, 1839. "Farmers' Register," Mch., 1835, pp. 593, 594. A Hussey admirer states that the knives must be sharpened for about fifteen minutes a day.

[34] *Ibid.,* Nov., 1836, p. 413; July 31, 1841, p. 434, letter of W. B. Harrison, Upper Brandon, Va., July 12, 1841. Another gang of slaves and new horses are needed in the afternoon unless a two-hour dinner rest is allowed.

[35] "New York Farmer," Apr., 1834, p. 111. *Seymour & Morgan vs. McCormick,* p. 146. Hussey testified that he tried a reel but found it unnecessary.

[36] Ardrey, "The Harvesting Machine Industry," in the "Scientific American," Supplement, Dec. 20, 1902, pp. 22544 ff. Pattison, II, r, letter of O. Hussey to the Board of Examiners, U. S. Patent Office, no date, but between Mch. 18, and 27, 1848: "My machine entirely depends for its

Ambler, and Moore and Hascall, had used for several years
after 1833, if not before, a hook-shaped finger which, with its
under part cut away, was in general identical both in principle
and purpose with the famous Hussey open-back guards of
1847.[37]

Hussey's original reaper lacked still another element of the
modern machine. It ran on two wheels of equal size while
several smaller ones supported its rigid platform. Because of
this construction it was heavy of draft and difficult to turn.[38]
Several years later the inventor adopted the McCormick principle of one main wheel and a small caster under the grain end
of the platform.[39] As pictured in the "Mechanics' Magazine"
of April, 1834, it had no divider, but this is probably an error,
since the patent provided for a triangular wedge which must
have closely resembled the divider used in the first McCormick
reaper.[40] Nor did Hussey employ side delivery—a principle
regarded as essential to-day. The cut grain, which was pushed
to the ground directly behind the machine, had to be removed
by the binders before the reaper made its next round.

Due either to insufficient gearing or to faulty cutters, the
Hussey machine did its best work when the horses were driven
at a trot.[41] Probably the absence of a reel also contributed to

efficiency as a Reaper on a row of lancet-point blades arranged on a rod,
side by side, in combination with, and vibrating through or into, double
fingers. The lancet blades are not original, but the combination is my
own invention."

[37] *Supra,* p. 94. J. P. Alexander, "American Harvesting Machines," in
the "American Inventor," VII, No. 15, p. 34.

[38] Due to the rigidity of its platform, it could not follow the unevenness
of the field, and generally left a "washboard" stubble. R. B. Swift, "Who
Invented the Reaper?" in the "Implement Age," Apr. 15, 1897, pp. 20, 21.

[39] Greeno, pp. 13-15.

[40] *Ibid.,* pp. 9, 13-15. "Mechanics' Magazine," Apr., 1834, pp. 193, 194.
"American Railway Journal and Advocate of Internal Improvements," Apr.
19, 1834, p. 228.

[41] Stabler, *op. cit.,* p. 19, prints a certificate of C. D. Wallace, of Cincinnati, Nov. 20, 1833, and of nine other Ohio men during the same season.

this necessity, since the implement had to strike the grain with sufficient impact to throw it on the platform with its heads toward the rear. This speed, together with the weight and heavy draft of the machine, quickly tired both horses and the rakeman, who had to remove the cut grain as rapidly as it fell upon the platform. Even with the horses at a trot, the cutter was prone to clog, particularly in wet grain. This defect was not remedied until the open-back finger was adopted, the double bevel-edged knives abandoned, and the angle which the cutters made with the fingers considerably widened.[42] Doubtless its construction was simpler and more durable than that of the early McCormick reaper, but simplicity meant insufficiency, and durability meant unwieldiness and excess weight.

Without reel or side delivery and with two wheels equal in size, the machine of Obed Hussey more nearly resembled a mower than a reaper. Save for the originality of his cutter and its usefulness in grain, he deserves remembrance chiefly as a pioneer of successful mechanical mowing. As has been emphasized before, reaping involves two major problems of equal importance—cutting the grain and carefully handling it. Hussey gave his attention to the first and neglected the second, and the modern mower suggests his early machine stripped of its platform and raker's seat.[43] About ten years after his first experiment, he discovered that if he made a detachable platform for his reaper it would cut grass well, and thereafter

They state that the team must move at least five miles an hour for the reaper to do its best work. *Ibid.*, p. 100. An early cut of the machine shows the horses at a trot. "Farmers' Register," Mch., 1835, p. 593. "New York Farmer," Apr., 1834, p. 111. "Farmers' Cabinet," Dec. 15, 1836, p. 174; Feb. 15, 1838, pp. 198, 199. Greeno, *op. cit.*, p. 58.

[42] Miller, p. 25. U. S. Patent Office: "Specification Forming Part of Letter Patent No. 5227, dated Aug. 7, 1847, to Obed Hussey." In this specification Hussey admitted that his blade, as described in his patent of 1833, "choked."

[43] "Farmers' Register," Mch., 1835, pp. 593, 594, letter of Wm. C. Dwight.

until 1854 he gave up the attempt to make a separate mower.[44] As the years passed, the knives and framework of his machine were altered to resemble the McCormick, while the Virginian derived some profit from a study of Hussey's cutter and guards.[45]

Hussey always contended that he invented the first practical and successful reaper.[46] In the sense that his implement was patented six months before McCormick's and had been worked in at least eight States before his rival's had left the Valley of Virginia, he was correct. But McCormick, as Hussey ac-

[44] *Hussey vs. McCormick,* pp. 84, 85. In Hussey's patent of 1833 a smaller platform for use in mowing is mentioned, but the inventor later tried to construct a separate machine for this purpose. "American Farmer," Apr., 1854, p. 330.

[45] The McCormick knife was beveled on only one side. By adopting this principle and by shortening and broadening the knife-plates, so that a more obtuse angle was formed with the shoulder of the guard finger, the manufacturers of the Hussey reaper tended to substitute the McCormick "draw-cut" for Hussey's original "chop-cut." The long and pointed Hussey knives made a 10- to 20-degree angle with the fingers; McCormick's, broad and stubby, formed a 60- or 70-degree angle. A shear-cut knife operates like scissors; a draw-cut, like a saw. The mower sections to-day are beveled on the upper surfaces only. Swift, pp. 22-27. Greeno, pp. 121-126. Miller, pp. 25-27.

[46] "American Agriculturist," Feb. 21, 1855, p. 371. "Scientific American," Dec. 23, 1854, p. 120. "American Farmer," June, 1855, p. 383. Hussey writes: "I can prove my reaper to have been entirely successful as early as 1833, while my friend McCormick was so unsuccessful between 1831 and 1834, that his father and family advised him to abandon his Reaper. . . . He sold no machines until 1840 and his machines were of no practical value till 1845, while my Reapers had been perfectly successful for twelve years." Hussey submitted old testimonials in proof of this assertion. Of course McCormick had similar evidence, dated as early as 1833. Hussey also asserted that all other reapers, without exception, were "indebted to my invention for the essential features which make them of any practical value as Reaping and Mowing Machines." He added that McCormick had exchanged his original straight blade for a toothed one, vibrating between double guards, and that this was identical in principle with his (Hussey's) original invention. Certified copy, "Court of Claims Record, No. 1654, Hussey vs. U. S.," Hussey's sworn statement of Apr. 18, 1848: "I alone have been successful with a reaper in the United States and now believe myself without a rival in any country." Miller, pp. 27, 28.

knowledged, used his reaper two years before the Carthage trial. He incorporated all seven of the essentials of a modern reaper in his earliest machine, while Hussey used but four of them. Detach the binding apparatus from a modern reaper, and there remains an improved edition of the McCormick machine of 1831. Remove Hussey's platform and raker's seat, and the present-day mower may easily be visualized.

Early in 1834, when Hussey was in New York City, he appointed a manufacturer and agents, and pleased the editor of the "New York Farmer," who saw his reaper "work perfectly in cutting a little artificial field of grain." [47] He was soon in the Genesee Valley, where he left a machine on exhibition at a store in Moscow, and arranged for several fields to be cleared of stones so that it might be used in the harvest. When summer came, at least one order was placed with a local mechanic who had been granted manufacturing rights, after the reaper had cut wheat so effectively on the Genesee flats that one farmer was of the opinion that it "cheated the hogs." [48] Meanwhile Hussey, who had returned to Cincinnati, planned to introduce his invention to the farmers of Illinois, but although a reaper which was shipped to that State in the spring was used in Sangamon County wheat, Hussey was not on hand to superintend its operation. [49]

[47] "New York Farmer," Apr., 1834, p. 111.

[48] *Ibid.*, July, 1834, p. 220. Hussey wrote to the editor that he had left his reaper at Moscow in care of Dr. Wm. C. Dwight, Mr. Horsford, and Mr. Holms, and that they would advertise it and give it a trial. *Ibid.*, Dec. 6, 1834, p. 388, letter of Dwight of Nov. 14, 1834. It was usual to permit hogs to glean after the harvest. "Genesee Farmer," May 17, 1834, p. 154; June, 1835, p. 112; July, 1835, pp. 211, 212. "Maine Farmer," July 11, 1834, p. 206; Dec. 26, 1834, p. 385. "Farmers' Register," Mch., 1835, pp. 593, 594.

[49] Greeno, p. 127. Here will be found a letter of John E. Canfield of Spring Creek, Sangamon County, Ill., dated Oct. 4, 1854, in which the writer asserts that he used a Hussey in 1834 and that it performed well, save that it choked in wet wheat. See also *Seymour & Morgan vs. McCormick*, pp. 141, 142, 147, for Hussey's testimony that he believed three

Even less is known of his course in 1835, despite his assertion nineteen years later that he built twelve or fourteen reapers
for that harvest.[50] This is probably an exaggeration, although
at least one or two were made at Cincinnati, and possibly one
in New York City. A sales agent for New York State was
appointed, with authority to lease county, town, and individual
rights of manufacture "on liberal terms." There were two
exhibitions in the Genesee Valley [51] and the machine may also
have been used during the summer in Illinois, Ohio, Indiana,
and Missouri. Two were sent from Cincinnati to Maryland, but
they arrived too late for the harvest.[52]

Prospects brightened for Hussey in 1836, when his future
rival, Cyrus McCormick, temporarily turned his attention to
an iron-furnace. Tench Tilghman, of distinguished Maryland
family, read in the "Genesee Farmer" of the successful exhibitions of the Hussey reaper in New York and induced the
Agricultural Society of Talbot County to invite the inventor
to come East. Hussey thereupon gave up his residence in Cincinnati and, bringing "one mowing and one reaping machine"
with him, lived for several months as Tilghman's guest.[53] He
so pleased his host by cutting one hundred and eighty acres of
grain on Tilghman's estate that an exhibition was arranged
for July at Oxford, Maryland, before the local agricultural so-

or four of his reapers were used in 1834, and that one of them was sent
to Mexico.
    [50] *Ibid.*, p. 148, testimony of O. Hussey.
    [51] "Genesee Farmer," July 25, 1835, pp. 234, 238; Aug. 15, 1835, pp.
258, 260.
    [52] "Farmers' Cabinet," Feb. 15, 1838, pp. 198, 199. Greeno, *op. cit.*, pp.
56, 131. *Hussey vs. Bradley*, p. 413. *Seymour & Morgan vs. McCormick,*
pp. 141-147.
    [53] "Cyrenus Wheeler, Jr., vs. C. H. and L. J. McCormick, in equity.
Baldwin Private, C. C. of U. S., N. D. of Ill., 1870," pp. 157 ff., testimony
of Tench Tilghman, of Easton, Md., then president of the Maryland and
Delaware R.R. Co. *Aultman vs. Holley*, pp. 477-481, testimony of Tench
Tilghman. "Farmers' Register," Nov., 1836, pp. 413, 414.

ciety. Here his machine reaped fourteen acres between ten o'clock in the morning and half-past seven in the evening and this feat was widely admired in the press.[54] "Its performance may justly be denominated perfect as it cuts every spear of grain, collects it in bunches of the proper size for sheaves, and lays it straight and even for the binders." [55] Hussey was awarded a "pair of silver cups," and other exhibitions that summer on the eastern shore of Maryland added to his reputation. He also staged a trial in oats within the Baltimore city limits, but the owner of the field halted the cutting because the reaper left too long a stubble and the onlookers trampled down his grain.[56]

Hussey needed success. If his recollection of 1836 is correct, "I could not go to meeting for many weeks for want of a *decent coat,* while for economy I made my own coffee and ate, slept in my shop, until I had sold machines enough to be able to do better. . . . My machines then cost me nearly all I got for them when counting moderate wages for my own labour." [57] In all probability his "shop" was the barn of Horatio Watkins of Hagerstown, with whom he now associated in the manufacture of reapers for 1837.[58] The Maryland "factory"

[54] "Genesee Farmer," Oct. 15, 1836, p. 336. "New England Farmer," Jan. 4, 1837, p. 204. "Maine Farmer," Dec. 19, 1836, pp. 353, 354. "Farmer and Gardener," Aug. 9, 1836, and Oct. 4, 1836.

[55] "Farmers' Register," Nov., 1836, p. 413. Hussey gave a public exhibition at Easton, Md., on July 12, under the direction of the same agricultural society, and another a few days later at Trappe. Testimonials noted that oyster-shells stopped the machine if the knife was too low, but that it could be operated by any intelligent and careful negro.

[56] "New England Farmer," Aug. 24, 1836, p. 52. "Farmers' Cabinet," Dec. 15, 1836, pp. 174, 175. The trial was on the field of a Dr. Hitch, but there were few spectators. Hussey went twice around the six-acre plot before its owner stopped the trial. *Hussey vs. McCormick,* pp. 23, 24. Patent Office Records, "Hussey Extension Case, Patent of 1847," pp. 81-83.

[57] Greeno, pp. 16-18, letter of Hussey to E. Stabler, Mch. 12, 1854.

[58] "Maine Farmer," Oct. 24, 1837, p. 293. "Farmers' Cabinet," Jan. 1, 1838, pp. 166, 167. *Seymour & Morgan vs. McCormick,* pp. 141-149.

supplied the six or less machines sold in that State, while for the same harvest a Mr. White of Cincinnati made a few which were marketed in Indiana and Missouri, as well as in Ohio.[59] In this year Hussey also used his machine for mowing, and adopted a main driving wheel in place of the two of equal size.[60] In 1838 he constructed a few reapers at Easton or Dorchester, Maryland, instead of Hagerstown. His machine received the praise of the venerable Philadelphia Society for the Promotion of Agriculture, and, on the advice of Tench Tilghman, he moved to Baltimore in August.[61] From 1838 until his death, over twenty years later, Baltimore was the home of the Hussey reaper.

Ten or twelve machines were made for the 1839 harvest,[62] and for the first time Delaware farmers were introduced to the reaper. On July 4, at Cantwell's Bridge, after the Society of St. George's and Appoquinimink Hundreds for the Promotion of Agriculture had listened to the Declaration of Independence,

[59] Certified copy, "Court of Claims Record No. 1654, O. Hussey vs. U. S." *Hussey vs. Bradley*, p. 413. Patent Office Records, "Hussey Extension Case, Patent of 1847," p. 111. Greeno, p. 39. Henry W. Ellsworth, "Valley of the Upper Wabash, Indiana" (1838), pp. 62-73, 103, 104. Jonathan Perriam, ed., "Encyclopedia of Agriculture" (1881), p. 785. Here it is stated that the Hussey reaper was first used in Pennsylvania in 1838.

[60] "Farmer and Gardener," Oct. 24, 1837, pp. 206, 207. "Farmers' Cabinet," Feb. 15, 1838, pp. 198, 199; Jan. 1, 1838, pp. 166, 167. In *Seymour & Morgan vs. McCormick*, p. 149, Hussey testified that four machines built before 1840 were mowers, one of which was used in 1835, and the other three in 1836, but he was very uncertain of his dates.

[61] *Ibid.*, pp. 141-149, 161. Greeno, p. 139. In 1838, Col. Edward Lloyd, of "Wye," Talbot County, one of the largest wheat-growers in Maryland, bought one. "Farmer and Gardener," Sept. 25, 1838, p. 170. Hussey opened an agency in Philadelphia. "Farmers' Cabinet," Apr. 15, 1839, p. 282; July 15, 1839, p. 380; Aug. 15, 1839, pp. 38, 39. "New Genesee Farmer," Nov. 23, 1839, p. 386. *Aultman vs. Holley*, pp. 477-481.

[62] *Ibid.*, p. 485. Certified copy, "Court of Claims Record No. 1654, Obed Hussey vs. U. S.," Hussey's affidavit of Feb. 2, 1848. Here Hussey affirms that he made sixteen machines in 1839.

"while the greatest order and attention prevailed" and after an "excellent dinner" had been served, Hussey gave such a convincing trial in wheat that the society immediately purchased his machine.[63] Press notices became more frequent and laudatory and the inventor was so encouraged by a degree of popularity never before attained by a maker of reapers that he wrote in the autumn:

The first account of a Reaping Machine . . . is given by Pliny. . . . English scientific works also teem with accounts of unsuccessful efforts. . . . More attempts of a like nature have been made in this country within the last fifty years, than all others put together since wheat was reaped at all. Among those. . . I consider myself alone successful. . . . Every previous attempt has totally failed . . . and . . . gone into oblivion. . . . My next year's machine will be much superior to any which I have before made, and to which I apprehend but little improvement can be subsequently added.[64]

There was good reason for his optimism, but Hussey likely had not read about the success of the McCormick reaper in the Valley of Virginia in July of that same season.[65] Established in Baltimore and looking forward to the harvest of 1840 with confidence, he sought to improve his machine by altering its gearing. This proved to be a serious mistake, because, accord-

[63] "New England Farmer," Sept. 4, 1839, p. 73. "Albany Cultivator," Aug., 1839, p. 116. "Farmers' Cabinet," Aug. 15, 1839, p. 25; Nov. 15, 1839, p. 119; Dec. 15, 1839, p. 164. "Farmers' Register," Aug. 31, 1839, p. 455; Sept. 30, 1839, p. 534. Patent Office Records, "Hussey Extension Case, Patent of 1847," pp. 185, 186, affidavit of B. Hoyle, of Jefferson County, O., who purchased a Hussey reaper in 1839, and also bought for $100 the right to manufacture the machines for sale in his county.

[64] "New Genesee Farmer," Nov. 30, 1839, p. 409. "American Farmer," July 17, 1839, p. 62; July 24, 1839, p. 69; Nov. 20, 1839, pp. 204, 208; Dec. 11, 1839, p. 227. "Richmond Enquirer," July 23, 1839.

[65] *Post*, pp. 180 ff.

ing to his own statement, he made thirty-six for this harvest
and "the credit of the machine suffered a retrograde." [66] His
market, doubtless also affected by the hard times, decreased
during the next three years, and in 1843 he sold but two.[67]
Nevertheless, in 1840, he introduced his reaper to Virginia
planters, and his brother, T. R. Hussey, started production as
a sub-manufacturer at Auburn, New York.[68]

The number of his sales dropped almost fifty per cent in the
next harvest, and although testimonials were more numerous
the commendation was usually half-hearted.[69] As certificates
of approval were easy to procure and often extravagant in
their praise, a qualified recommendation was scarcely better
than a condemnation. Farmers admitted that his reaper was
"perfect in dry wheat," but they did not concur as to "the
economy of its use." In 1841 he sent two machines to William
B. Harrison, the distinguished owner of Brandon's Neck,
Prince George County, Virginia. Harrison had agreed to give
them a fair trial in his own wheat and the inventor arrived in
late June to supervise. After three days' test the planter was
only sufficiently enthusiastic to write, "I think on the whole
that the securing of our crop has been somewhat expedited by
the use of these machines." At least it was "not a humbug,"
but much depended upon the condition of the ground and

[66] Certified copy, "Court of Claims Record, No. 1654, Obed Hussey vs.
U. S.," Hussey's affidavit of Feb. 2, 1848, and his testimony of Apr. 18,
1848.

[67] Patent Office Records, "Hussey Extension Case, Patent of 1847," pp.
185, 186. "American Farmer," Jan. 1, 1840, p. 249; Jan. 29, 1840, p. 284;
Feb. 5, 1840, p. 296.

[68] *Obed Hussey vs. U. S., supra,* testimony of O. Hussey on Apr. 18,
1848. Jas. R. Brookings of Virginia made one or two machines for Hussey
at this time and paid him a patent fee of $24. "Albany Cultivator," May,
1841, p. 81. "Farmers' Register," May 31, 1840, p. 294; Oct. 31, 1840,
p. 634; May 31, 1841, p. 302.

[69] "American Farmer," Feb. 10, 1841, p. 304; Mch. 10, 1841, p. 332;
Apr. 7, 1841, p. 366; May 26, 1841, p. 8.

grain, the skill of the operator, and the docility of the horses or mules.[70]

Some farmers complained that Hussey's machine left too long a stubble and others that the cutter clogged in damp grain and would not reap when the stalks were bent away from the knife. It did its best work in heavy wheat, in the hottest part of the day when the stalks were dry. The cradler, on the other hand, cut fastest in light wheat, in the cool of the morning or early evening. Therefore the reaper might serve to supplement hand harvesting, but would never entirely supersede it.[71] This was the judgment of Virginian planters in July, 1841, as Hussey hastened north to visit the harvest in the Genesee valley. Here he found the farmers more generous with their approval.[72]

[70] "Farmers' Register," May 31, 1841, p. 302. Hussey wrote to the editor on Apr. 14, 1841, "The opposition and *designed* awkwardness of a class of cradlers, whose interest it is that the machine should fail, and the apprehension thus created that the machine may not prove useful, will be very likely to tire the patience of the farmer." *Ibid.*, July 31, 1841, p. 434, letter of W. B. Harrison, in which he states that the reaper is not more economical than a band of cradlers, reaping two acres a day per man. *Ibid.*, June 30, 1842, pp. 274-276. Edmund Ruffin here states that Hussey's will be used by Harrison at Upper Brandon unless superseded by a better. *Ibid.*, July 31, 1841, p. 435; Aug. 31, 1842, p. 388. R. B. Bolling tried Hussey's machine on his Sandy Point estate in Virginia. He reported that it needed more mechanical perfection and would not cut wet wheat, but that he would purchase two for the next harvest. See Phillips, p. 235. "American Farmer," June 9, 1841, p. 9; Aug. 11, 1841, p. 92; Oct. 27, 1841, p. 184; Dec. 29, 1841, p. 249.

[71] "Farmers' Register," Oct. 31, 1840, p. 634; Jan. 31, 1841, p. 32. A planter of Halifax, N. C. (probably one of the Burgwyn family, *post,* pp. 370 ff.), inquired about reaping machines, saying he intended to sow much wheat. The editor replied that he could not recommend Hussey's, since opinions differed concerning its worth. *Ibid.,* Mch. 31, 1841, p. 129: "We still need a good machine."

[72] "New Genesee Farmer," July, 1841, p. 97; Oct., 1841, p. 155. "Albany Cultivator," Dec., 1841, pp. 196, 197, letter of Solon Robinson, Sept. 9, 1841. "Farmer's Magazine" (London), July, 1841, p. 60. For the first time the news of Hussey's reaper reached England. Nevertheless it aroused no interest there and was forgotten.

Except for a ten-dollar premium which his brother received when he exhibited the reaper at the Cattle Show and Fair of the New York Agricultural Society at the famous Bull's Head Tavern on the Albany-Troy postroad, the season of 1842 brought little save discouragement to Hussey.[73] He placed two machines of different size on the market, offering the larger for $170 and the smaller for $100, but Cyrus McCormick was selling for $105 at Richmond.[74] The loss of favor which Hussey had sustained since 1840 was too severe to be overcome, now that a real competitor was in the field for the first time, and he found only ten purchasers during the harvest season.[75] As the new year opened he wrote a letter to the editor of the "Richmond Southern Planter" which caught the eye of his rival:

My first machines were very imperfect, but the work was always well done, the chief difficulties being the liability to get out of order, the failure to cut wet grain, and the severe labor on the shaft horse. The first has been obviated, so far as strength and good workmanship will do it, the second measurably so, and the third is entirely removed; but carelessness and bad management in the field cannot be guarded against. . . .

I see in your last Planter an account of another reaper in your State, which is attracting some attention; it shall be my endeavor to meet the machine in the field in the next harvest. I think it but justice to give this public notice that the parties concerned may not be taken unawares, but have the opportunity to prepare themselves for such a contest, that no advantage may be taken. Those

[73] "Albany Cultivator," Nov., 1842, p. 174, letter of Solon Robinson. "Southern Planter," Feb., 1842, p. 45.
[74] *Obed Hussey vs. U. S.*, deposition of Hussey on Apr. 18, 1848, that his manufacturing cost was about $80 per machine.
[75] "American Farmer," Feb. 23, 1842, p. 319; June 15, 1842, p. 29; Aug. 17, 1842, p. 101; Aug. 24, 1842, p. 106.

gentlemen who have become prudently cautious, by being often deceived by humbugs, will then have an opportunity to judge for themselves.[76]

Cyrus McCormick rarely refused to accept a challenge of this nature, and the year 1843 marked the opening of the "first war of the reapers" in America.

[76] "Southern Planter," Mch., 1843, pp. 68, 69. "Farmers' Register," Nov. 30, 1842, letter of Corbin Braxton of Chericoke, Va. The planters were even then comparing the merits of the McCormick and Hussey reapers.

CHAPTER VIII

THE FIRST WAR OF THE REAPERS, 1839-47

THE early careers of Cyrus McCormick and Obed Hussey present few similarities and many contrasts. Hussey was forty years of age when he brought forward his first machine, while McCormick had just reached manhood in 1831. The former spent his early life in an occupation far removed from the harvest field, while the latter, born to the soil and reared in a home accustomed to invention, unconsciously schooled himself for his life work by long observation of the reaping problem. Hussey invented his reaper in the West and came to the East to locate his factory. This proved unfortunate, because the grain center of the United States was gradually moving into the smooth prairie belt where the reaper could render its best service. McCormick, with more foresight, followed the wheat as soon as his machine found favor in Virginia and the Cotopaxi fiasco was over. As later pages will show, Hussey had the misfortune or the poor judgment to be absent from places of crisis when he should have been present, or, if on hand, to be unprepared to meet the emergency.

His biographer concludes that Obed Hussey was no business man, and his entire career warrants this generalization.[1] After fifteen years of labor with his reaper, he wrote to the Commissioner of Patents in 1848 that he doubted whether his estate would net five hundred dollars if all his debts were paid.[2] The iron business reduced McCormick to similar straits by 1844,

---

[1] Greeno, p. 42.
[2] Certified copy, "Court of Claims Record No. 1654, *Obed Hussey vs. U. S.*," Hussey's affidavit of Feb. 2, 1848.

but four years later he was firmly established in Chicago and future prospects seemed very bright. McCormick possessed that rare combination of business and inventive talent which Hussey lacked. McCormick enjoyed conflict, but as a battle-ground he preferred the harvest field or the courts to the press. Hussey would push a contest of words to the limit in the news-papers, but usually shunned resort to the law, save as a witness, and did not often show to advantage beside his rival in a field trial. When the occasion required, McCormick could use his pen so effectively that both Hussey and the champions of Bell gained small satisfaction from such a contest.

Hussey has been pictured as a martyr who because of his modesty and lack of business ability did not gain proper recog-nition from his contemporaries, although his machine was equal in quality to the McCormick as a reaper. A feeling of sym-pathy for the loser in a hard conflict is natural, but the modesty of Hussey is a myth, and McCormick could not have won if the farmer had not been on his side. McCormick's aggressive-ness and shrewd advertising policy would have been futile if his implement had not demonstrated its superiority in the har-vest field. The farmer, usually hard pressed for funds, did not select his machine on sentimental grounds, and the steadily mounting popularity of the McCormick reaper cannot be as-cribed, in largest measure, either to its inventor's business genius or to Hussey's want of it.

When McCormick reëntered the lists with his reaper in 1839, Hussey had been in the field for six consecutive years and had worked his reaper in a half-dozen or more States. He enjoyed the patronage of Tench Tilghman and had made a little money, at least, during the period of the panic. On the other hand, McCormick was saddled for six years, after the revival of his reaper, with the cares and debts of a disastrous business ven-ture. It was his good fortune to reintroduce his reaper at a time when the country was emerging from the depression of a period of financial crisis, and he was skilful enough to ride to success on the mounting crest of a new wave of prosperity and optimism. Hussey, by ill chance, made unwise alterations in his machine just at the moment when his rival resumed manufacture, and at the very time when his sales might otherwise have widened with the returning years of plenty.

Cyrus McCormick withheld his reaper from the market until he could place it with confidence in the hands of the farmer. Hussey promoted sales from the year of the first trial of the machine, and the purchaser suffered with the inventor during the period of experiment. This difference in policy may be too much emphasized, because many other factors, such as lack of enthusiasm, bad crops, Cotopaxi, and panic, also influenced McCormick to lay aside his machine temporarily. Furthermore, the two reapers that he sold in 1840 did not work well, and he was to write in 1848 that his machine was of little practical value before 1845. Hussey, in like manner, admitted that he had finally given the world a good reaping machine just as his original patent expired in 1847.[3] These statements will be misinterpreted unless they are placed in their context. Both men were judging from the viewpoint of the time when they wrote, and by 1848 the standard for gaging reaper efficiency was far higher than eight years before, when Hussey and McCormick, as well as many farmers, were pleased with the operation of both machines. Certainly the 1840 implement of neither inventor could have been sold in 1848, for the grain-grower became more exacting as the reaper moved toward perfection.

Furthermore, Hussey and McCormick were seeking extension of their patents when they thus minimized the worth of their early machines. Such statements were natural under the circumstances, for the Patent Board was more willing to grant

[3] *Post,* pp. 286 ff.

an extension if profits under the original monopoly were negligible, and if it was evident that the patentee had sought with diligence to improve his invention. Both Hussey and McCormick were to claim that they had made no money under their respective patents of 1833 and 1834. This also is true if a proper compensation for their labor and time is awarded them, and if their increased sales after 1845 are attributed to important improvements not included in their first patents. In the case of McCormick, much of the early income from reaper sales was utilized to discharge iron-furnace debts, and the successful cancellation of these obligations makes his rapid rise to fortune after 1846 the more surprising.

Prior to 1850 both Hussey and McCormick found it impossible, for financial reasons, to keep the manufacture of their machines entirely under their own supervision. Money was necessary, transportation facilities very inadequate, and if the reaper was to enjoy a wide market it must be on hand in the principal grain regions of the country when harvest-time came. Therefore, effort was made to sell town, county, or regional rights of manufacture. The machines made by those paying for the privilege were known as the "McCormick" or the "Hussey," and if they were poorly constructed the inventor received as much blame as the manufacturer. The latter occasionally tried to alter the original model, with unfortunate results. The purchaser did not discriminate in his criticism when he found that his reaper would not operate. As soon as McCormick accumulated sufficient capital to concentrate production in a single factory, he ceased to sub-grant manufacturing rights. Hussey, on the other hand, continued to do so until his death, and often found it necessary to make awkward and hardly convincing explanations about badly constructed reapers which bore his name but which were not the output of his own shop.

Hussey conservatively limited production each season to the

number of orders he received in advance.[4] McCormick, with a keener appreciation of business psychology and of the extent to which a "spell of good weather" might completely alter a farmer's prospects, soon came to anticipate a larger demand than the early orders sent in, and built accordingly. He rarely made too many.[5] He displayed reapers in a grain region long enough before harvest-time so that a farmer, confronted with an unusually big crop and no labor, would be plagued by the sight of a mechanical solution for his dilemma sufficiently to buy.

In the McCormick-Hussey race for reaper supremacy during the forties, success was conditioned in greatest measure by the efficiency of the machine, but able generalship, energy, advertisements, skill with the pen, and fortuitous circumstances also helped to determine the final verdict. The conflict required talent and tactics akin to those which often decide the outcome upon a field of battle. The locale of the campaign depended upon the site of the factories of the opponents and the areas of greatest grain-production. Hussey at Baltimore and his brother at Auburn, New York, faced McCormick at Walnut Grove, Virginia, and soon at Brockport, in the Genesee Valley. New York and Virginia were two of the largest wheat States in the Union in 1840.[6] The army of each general con-

---

[4] "Cyrus H. McCormick, Complainant, vs. John H. Manny, Wait Talcott, Ralph Emerson, Jesse Blinn, and Sylvester Talcott, Defendants, in Equity, Circuit Court of the United States, Northern District of Illinois" (Washington, D. C., no date given). Defendant's testimony, p. 318. Hussey testified on Aug. 28, 1855, "I have heretofore depended upon orders; I don't pursue the system of employing traveling agents as other reaper builders do." This volume will be cited hereafter as *McCormick vs. Manny*, I.

[5] C. H. McCormick to Wm. Massie, Dec. 24, 1842: "We find no difficulty in selling as many machines as we can get made."

[6] According to the census of 1840, New York and Virginia were the third and fourth largest wheat States, respectively. Ohio and Pennsylvania led. The "Albany Cultivator," June, 1841, p. 94, gives the census grain statistics for all the States. See *post,* p. 201, ftn. 66, and p. 205, ftn. 5.

sisted of his selling agents and satisfied farmers. The weapon was the reaper. The campaign was confined to the summer season, while the rest of the year was spent in forging new and better weapons, and in searching for grain-growers who would use them. When spring came the call to arms and propaganda pleasing to each side appeared in the press; and in the autumn, after the yearly conflict was over, the battles of harvest-time were refought with the pen. The number of annual sales was the gage of the season's success, and a low price supplemented successful operation in winning the patronage of the farmers.

Realization of the fortune awaiting a successful reaper enlivened the rivalry between McCormick and Hussey and brought many other competitors into the field by 1850. By that date the original patents of each inventor had expired and other reaper-makers forced the two veterans to compete with their own ideas. But prior to the new decade, McCormick and Hussey feared no outside foe and fought it out in the East for the entertainment and instruction of the farmer.

In 1839, Cyrus McCormick could not have foreseen his ultimate victory. He faced the most discouraging situation of his whole career. His dream of success at Cotopaxi was shattered, his money was gone, his partner deserting, while debts grew larger every day, and the country was in the throes of one of the worst panics of its history. He turned to the reaper as a last resort, at a time when Hussey not far away was publicly boasting: "I consider myself alone successful. . . . Every previous attempt has totally failed . . . and . . . gone into oblivion." [7]

So far as is known by the writer, the McCormick reaper was not used beyond the limits of the home farm between 1836 and 1838. Improvements were added during these years, although work upon the machine was necessarily confined to the

[7] *Supra,* p. 169.

brief harvest season.[8] Joseph Smith, a farmer who lived near Staunton, heard in 1839 how successfully Cyrus McCormick reaped his father's grain and requested him to exhibit the machine publicly on the Smith farm. He accepted the invitation and announced in the local paper a trial for July 23, asserting that he thought the performance of his reaper was "now unexceptionable," and that it would cut one and a half or two acres of grain an hour.[9] The resulting exhibition in oats was sufficiently satisfactory to please a "large gathering," but as the inventor could not yet warrant the performance of his machine, only one of the spectators, a brother of the host, ordered one for the next harvest. Twelve of the onlookers signed a testimonial, and McCormick added this to an advertisement in the "Richmond Enquirer," in which he expressed his belief that his reaper was now ready for general use and stated that he would try to fill all orders he might receive. He was confident that the machine would pay for itself in one harvest on a large estate, since it wasted less grain than the cradle and was a fifty-per-cent labor-saver. Only two operators and five binders were necessary and the implement would harvest ten or fifteen acres of grain a day.[10]

[8] "Staunton Spectator and General Advertiser," July 18, 1839, adv. of C. H. McCormick. *McCormick vs. Manny,* II, pp. 192, 214, 215, 227-229, testimony of W. S. McCormick in 1855. *Seymour & Morgan vs. McCormick,* pp. 104, 186, testimony of W. S. McCormick, Oct. 18, 1851. *Hussey vs. McCormick,* 1857, pp. 14-17. Answer of C. H., L. J., and W. S. McCormick to O. Hussey's Bill of Complaint. McCormick had increased the length of the knife to six feet, and had improved the guard fingers. The divider now projected about six feet beyond the edge of the knife.
[9] C. H. McCormick to E. Burke, Commr. of Patents, Jan. 1, 1848, in "McCormick Extension Case, Patent of 1845," pp. 4, 5. "Staunton Spectator and General Advertiser," July 18, 1839. McCormick here writes that he has not done anything with his reaper for several years but has cut 75 acres of wheat and rye thus far in 1839.
[10] "Richmond Enquirer," Dec. 12, 14, 17, 1839, and Jan. 28, 1840, printing a letter of C. H. McCormick of Nov. 25, 1839. He hoped to have several reapers in operation during the next harvest and probably "in different

The publicity thus secured for the reaper brought two James River farmers to Walnut Grove. The son of Richard Sampson, of Goochland County, and a Mr. Scott, his neighbor, wished two machines and were ready to accept them without a guarantee. But Abraham Smith had already placed his order, and because McCormick wished to build another for home use, it was found that four reapers overtaxed the construction capacity of the blacksmith shop and required more attention than could be spared from the iron business. Three only were made —Robert, and probably Leander, McCormick assisting Cyrus in the building.[11] The Smith machine failed to operate well, due to a defective knife,[12] and the one made for Sampson gave even less satisfaction. Fifteen years later Richard Sampson recalled the arrival of Robert McCormick with the reaper in June, 1840. Three days were spent in vain endeavor to make it work, and then Sampson "sent it immediately out of the field and put it under an old shed at a tobacco house, where it stood until the shed blew down . . . and then placed it at the end of the house, where it stood, as a nuisance, until it was brought down here [for the Manny trial]." In 1844, Hussey said he saw it lying "in ruins."

Additional information about this same failure was given by another witness: "When we attempted to carry the machine to the wheat-patch, it was a very awkward thing to drive, and the negro . . . ran the machine against the gate-post and

sections of the country." *Ibid.*, Aug. 22, 1839, testimonial signed by five men, including N. M. Hitt, who believed "Mr. C. H. McCormick's Patent Reaping Machine" cut about "95 acres of wheat, rye and oats." "Staunton Spectator and General Advertiser," July 25, 1839; Aug. 1, 1839. *McCormick vs. Manny,* II, pp. 169 ff., testimony of Joseph Smith, Aug. 29, 1855, that about 200 were at the trial. "Farmer's Magazine" (London), Sept., 1839, p. 167, describing an American machine which is probably McCormick's.

[11] *McCormick vs. Manny,* II, pp. 192, 213-215, 851-855, testimony of W. S. McCormick and Richard Sampson, in 1855. See Phillips, p. 308.

[12] "Richmond Enquirer," Feb. 15, 1842, statement of A. Smith, of Rockingham County.

broke the hounds.[13] . . . I made a new pulley for the reel, the one on it being so small; the reel ran so fast that it threw the wheat over the canvas behind the machine, and scattered it over the field, and at the same time knocked the wheat out of the shuck as if it had been struck with a flail. . . . It worked mighty bad at best." In spite of this, Sampson paid McCormick ninety dollars for the reaper, but he decided to wait a few years for further improvements before he bought another one.[14]

The failure of the two machines sold in 1840 can be explained only on grounds of defective workmanship, for the reaper had worked successfully in 1839 and no important changes in construction had been made. Cyrus McCormick cut grain for his neighbors in 1840 and they wrote of the "admirable and satisfactory performance" of his implement.[15] He coarsened the teeth of the knife in the new machines and attached three blade-bearers to the front of the platform. He hoped that these would prevent the blade from sagging and biting into the wooden fingers. His cutter clogged in wet grain, because chaff wedged between the knife and the guards and also owing to the fact that the latter, being of wood, swelled and interfered with the vibration of the sickle.[16]

Since the machine of 1840 had not come up to expectations, Cyrus devoted the whole of the next season to experiment, and sold none.[17] The iron venture reached a climax of misfortune

[13] The hounds are side bars connecting the tongue with the framework of the vehicle.
[14] *McCormick vs. Manny,* II, pp. 198, 851-858, testimony of Richard Sampson and Alfred Cosby, who helped Robert set up the Sampson machine.
[15] "Valley Star" (Lexington, Va.), Aug. 31, 1840, testimonials of Wm. Taylor and John Alexander. Each stated that Cyrus McCormick's Patent Reaping Machine had cut fifteen acres of wheat for him that season.
[16] Pattison, II, a, C. H. McCormick to E. Burke, Commr. of Patents, Jan. 1, 1848.
[17] *Ibid.* Writing of the two reapers sold in 1840, McCormick stated: "*They* failed to operate *well.* . . . These gentlemen could of course say nothing in *favor* of the Reaper that year; they failing, and all that I could

in 1841, and this also probably contributed to the suspension of manufacture. The furnace was sold for a quantity of pig-iron, and the acceptance of the metal in lieu of cash indicates a determination to resume reaper-building as soon as improvements justified a greater confidence in the machines. Additional supports were applied to the clumsy reel so that it would not wabble as the reaper advanced over the rough field.[18] To prevent the scattering of the wheat as it was cut, a canvas strip two feet wide was added on top of the raised board at the back of the platform. The old grooved fingers were abandoned, and the knife now vibrated under guards shaped like spear-heads. Hitherto the serrations of the blade had all run in a single direction. In and after 1841 these were alternately reversed every one and one half inches along its entire length. This change proved to be most beneficial, because it permitted the knife to cut with equal certainty whether moving from right to left or from left to right and also greatly reduced the tendency of the cutter to clog.[19]

McCormick placed one of these improved sickles in Abraham Smith's machine in 1841, and it operated so well that the inventor announced for the first time that he was ready to warrant his reaper in every respect.[20] So pleased was he with its performance that he advertised that he had "triumphantly

do for the next harvest [1841] was to correct the defects in these two Machines." *McCormick vs. Manny,* II, pp. 192 ff., testimony of W. S. McCormick in 1855.

[18] *Ibid.,* II, pp. 192 ff., testimony of W. S. McCormick.

[19] Miller, *op. cit.,* p. 27. Swift, *op. cit.,* pp. 20-25. Here is shown a cut of a reverse-angled sickle. The new fingers were longer than the old ones and were placed at wider intervals. They were 2½ inches apart along the edge of the platform and projected from 6 to 8 inches in front of it. The knife had a 5-inch stroke in 1841. The sickle slid upon a curved support which held it close against the finger.

[20] Pattison, II, a, C. H. McCormick to E. Burke, Commr. of Patents, Jan. 1, 1848. "Richmond Enquirer," Feb. 15, 1842, statement of A. Smith, July 12, 1841. *Ibid.,* Oct. 3, and Nov. 2, 1841, advs. of McCormick.

succeeded in effecting his object with as much perfection as the principle admits of or is now desirable." [21] He unfortunately delayed for four years to patent his improvement, and was later forced to defend before the courts his right to the reverse-angled sickle.

As a result of the improved cutting effected by these altera-tions, the editor of the "Southern Planter" of Richmond stated in November, 1841, "We should be pleased to see Mr. McCor-mick and his reaper on this side of the mountains next sea-son."[22] This invitation, combined with the failure of Hussey to please the planters, must have cheered McCormick as he sat amid the wreck of his furnace venture at Walnut Grove that winter. The same editor had observed that his price of $100 was "extremely low," and as machines could be constructed for about $50, and seven were being made at the blacksmith shop in anticipation of a wider market in 1842, there seemed reason to hope that all debts would eventually be paid.[23]

Six machines were sold in 1842, and Cyrus McCormick later

[21] "Staunton Spectator," Sept. 23, 30, 1841: "Cyrus McCormick writes that he is prepared to offer his machine on terms that "cannot be unsafe to the public." It will cut on level or moderately hilly land; long or short, heavy or light, straight, tangled, or leaning grain. Eight Rockingham County farmers testified that they saw it work in oats at Bridgewater on July 23, 1841. In the "Richmond Enquirer," Feb. 15, 1842, the inventor states: "The undersigned having been admonished of the error of attempting to introduce a new machine prematurely into extensive use . . . and not having been fully satisfied until this year that its performance would in every respect challenge the closest scrutiny of the prejudiced . . . or was not susceptible of improvement, has been thus long delayed offering it extensively. He now expects to have a considerable number of these machines manufactured for the next harvest, and to introduce them in some of the most important grain-growing regions of the country, and proposes to warrant them. . . ."
[22] "Southern Planter," Nov., 1841, p. 217. "Richmond Enquirer," Oct. 3, and Nov. 2, 1841.
[23] *McCormick vs. Manny,* I, p. 207. In his contract with A. C. Brown of Cincinnati, on Sept. 19, 1844, McCormick stated that Walnut Grove reapers with extra blade and pinion cost about $43 to manufacture in 1844.

recalled that "they all gave satisfaction, allowance being made for defects which I had afterward to correct." [24] Early in the year he expected to make more for this harvest, but he finally "concluded to wait another year's experience, and additional testimony from different parts of the state, before hazarding a great deal." [25] McCormick's caution, probably necessary in any event on account of lack of funds, was complimented in the press as "patience and prudence in not hazarding its reputation in the hands of the public until the machine is perfected." [26]

One of the seven reapers was sold to William C. Peyton, a prominent planter of Roanoke, Virginia. Cyrus McCormick delivered the machine and stayed at the plantation long enough to teach the negro mechanic, Edmund, how to operate it. Peyton was much pleased with its work and wrote a letter for publication, expressing his satisfaction and assuring the readers of the "Southern Planter" that it would save at least a bushel of grain an acre, customarily lost when the cradle was used. For this reason, and because it dispensed with the labor of eight hands, it would pay for itself in one harvest if considerable grain was harvested.[27]

During the same season Robert McCormick took three reapers to Corbin Braxton of Chericoke, King William County, Virginia. Judging from Braxton's statement in the "Farmers' Register," the "worthy, intelligent old gentleman" must have finished his mission with a joy which went far to counteract the

[24] Pattison, II, a, C. H. McCormick to E. Burke, Jan. 1, 1848. The inventor writes that seven were sold in 1842.

[25] "Richmond Enquirer," Aug. 17, 24 and Sept. 30, 1842.

[26] "American Farmer," Aug. 17, 1842, p. 101.

[27] "Southern Planter," Aug., 1842, pp. 181, 182; Sept., 1842, p. 216. *Hussey vs. McCormick*, pp. 29-31, 34, 103, 111. The testimony of Peyton's overseer in this trial fifteen years later does not entirely support his employer's complimentary certificate of 1842. See also the "American Farmer" for Aug. 17, 1842, p. 101; Sept. 14, 1842, p. 134. "Richmond Enquirer," Aug. 24 and Sept. 30, 1842. *Supra*, Chap. III, pp. 72, 73.

humiliation of his similar visit to Richard Sampson's two years
before. One machine was started in heavy, green, and rusted
wheat on a wet day (most of the days were wet in the harvest
of 1842), and did "wonderfully." Fallen and tangled grain
was cut with equal ease.

During the first days of harvest we had each day quite a troop
of horsemen of the neighboring farmers following the reaper, all
expressing their admiration and entire satisfaction at its performance. . . . Farmers will wonder how they could have gotten on
before its invention. I believe it one of the most important agricultural improvements of the day, and I think that every farmer
cutting fifty acres of decent wheat would find it to his advantage
to have one.

Braxton believed that few alterations were needed to make the
machine mow as well as reap, and he ordered one for the harvest of 1843, so changed that it would cut grass.[28]

The harvest of 1842 was probably the first in which Cyrus
McCormick felt that his reaper had won a solid reputation
and had proved itself worthy of a wide sale. Over ten years
of intermittent experiment had been necessary to earn this
success, but the arrival of victory could not have been more
opportune. His machine was ready to retrieve his fallen fortunes at the moment when the returning prosperity of the
nation justified his hope that it would be profitable to exploit
it.[29] His only rival of consequence was temporarily weakened

[28] "Farmers' Register," Nov. 30, 1842, p. 503, letter of Corbin Braxton
of June 28, 1842. *Hussey vs. McCormick*, pp. 131 ff., testimony of H. B.
Tomlin, brother-in-law of Braxton, who used one of the three machines
delivered to the latter in 1842. *Ibid.*, p. 147, testimony of Wm. A. Braxton,
Corbin's son. *McCormick vs. Manny*, II, pp. 160 ff. T. B. Dunn, overseer
for Carter Braxton of Hanover, stated that he used a McCormick reaper
in 1842, on Mrs. Coulter's estate in King William County. It worked well,
"though delicate," and it choked in damp wheat. This contradicts Corbin
Braxton's letter of June, 1842, referred to above.

[29] See pp. 146, 147. Note that on Nov. 17, 1842, the home farm was transferred to A. McChesney as security for debts owed to Z. McChesney.

by the inferior machines which he had marketed in Virginia during the past three years. McCormick was now thirty-three years of age and had suffered a business experience which equipped him to meet with skill the difficult marketing problem attendant upon the introduction of a new implement to widely scattered and skeptical grain-growers. As the successful season of 1842 closed, the inventor announced that

for some time to come, he intends to devote his attention exclusively to introducing his machines in different parts of the country, by establishing agencies, selling rights (which he now offers for the first time), or otherwise; and will continue to have them *manufactured in the best manner,* on the same terms as heretofore . . . guaranteeing their performance in every respect; and if they perform as *warranted* to do, it will be seen, as stated also by others, that they will pay for themselves in one year's use . . . and if so, what *tolerable* farmer can hesitate to purchase? [30]

Prior to 1843, Hussey and McCormick had relied mainly upon non-competitive field trials, printed testimonials of satisfied buyers, and descriptive advertisements to effect their sales. Beginning in the summer of 1842, each competitor publicly admitted for the first time since 1834 that he was aware of the presence of his enemy. By tacit consent the lower James River region of Virginia was selected as the 1843 battle-field for the first reaper conflict in history. Both Hussey and McCormick had entered this area in 1840, but neither machine had worked well, and while McCormick retired for one season to ponder a better way Hussey continued to press sales and thus lessened his original popularity. McCormick reappeared in the harvest of 1842 with an implement which he could warrant, and eagerly accepted the challenge of Hussey in the spring of the following year.[31] In his public letter of June 28, 1842, Corbin Braxton

---

[30] "Richmond Enquirer," Sept. 30, 1842.
[31] See the close of the preceding chapter.

remarked that a neighbor who had two Hussey machines had told him they would not work in wet wheat and this gratuitous slap at a competitor probably hastened the inevitable contest.[32] McCormick wished to prove that his reaper merited a monopoly of the patronage of the planters, while Hussey was anxious to redeem his damaged reputation.

Judging from the emphasis in the McCormick correspondence of 1843, the question of lawsuits for debts arising from the iron business was far more important than reaper-building or the rivalry with Obed Hussey, but it is likely inaccurate to conclude that this was true. The letters which remain were chiefly exchanged with William Massie and lawyers, and the discharge of furnace obligations was naturally the chief theme of the writers. On the other hand, the advertisements in the papers of course gave the public no inkling of the fact that reapers were the main reliance to stave off bankruptcy. All of the McCormicks lived at Walnut Grove between 1839 and 1843, and they had no occasion to correspond on the subject of reaper-building. The machines were delivered in person by members of the family, and if letters were written to the purchasers they have probably long since been destroyed.

A seventy-five mile circle around Walnut Grove included most of the McCormick reaper territory at this time, and the short trips into this region from the home center made expensive letter-writing unnecessary. For this reason the story of the reaper rivalry of 1843 must be almost solely based upon two kinds of source material, newspaper advertisements (including public letters of the inventor or of his competitor and testimonials of satisfied purchasers), and recollections written in many cases long after the event. Advertisements and testimonials exaggerated the virtues of the machine, while the rival

---

[32] "Farmers' Register," Nov. 30, 1842, p. 503; the letter is a part of an advertisement of C. H. McCormick.

overemphasized its faults. It was not the custom at this time for one manufacturer to fight another by insinuation. The public was frankly told by Hussey that his machine was better than McCormick's and McCormick answered in kind. Consequently it is difficult, if not impossible, to write with the assurance that a just balance is being held between the two machines.

McCormick enlisted the powerful aid of Charles T. Botts, editor of the "Southern Planter" of Richmond, as the year 1842 closed.[33] Botts accepted an agency before he saw the reaper, although Cyrus took him a model for exhibition in his office. In the January issue of this publication the editor felt justified in taxing "the ingenuity of our readers . . . more than is our wont," with a cut and a detailed description of the reaper, because of its "universal popularity" and its "extreme importance to the grain growing community." [34] When the rye ripened in early June, Cyrus McCormick came over the mountains and pleased the crowd at the Henrico Agricultural and Horticultural Society Fair with a field exhibition of his implement. The president of the society purchased the machine forthwith and the inventor received several other orders the same day.[35] McCormick established his base of operations at the Rev. Jesse W. Turner's, near Richmond.[36] By the twentieth of the month, Hussey had forwarded two machines to the care of the editor of the "Southern Planter." He arrived several days later and hostilities immediately commenced.

It so happened that Ambrose Hutchinson, whose estate was

[33] There is a brief biography of Botts by A. O. Craven in Allen Johnson, ed., Dictionary of American Biography (N. Y., 1928 ff.), II, 472.
[34] "Southern Planter," Jan., Feb., and Mch., 1843. C. H. McCormick to Wm. Massie, Dec. 24, 1842: "I was at Richmond lately with my model, and found it was universally admired, made a good number of engagements."
[35] "Richmond Enquirer," June 6, 1843. "Lexington Gazette," June 15, 1843. "Southern Cultivator" (Augusta, Ga.), June 21, 1843, p. 100.
[36] For J. H. Turner see Craven, p. 145. Phillips, p. 173.

three miles northwest of the city on the Deep Run turnpike, had twenty-five acres of light wheat which he wished "Parson" Turner to cut with his reaper. The minister knew of the question which was agitating the neighborhood and, being somewhat of a sportsman himself, he persuaded Hutchinson to allow Hussey and McCormick to race their machines in his field for the entertainment of the country-side and for the best interests of agriculture. The contest was fixed for June 30. On June 24, McCormick wrote a letter, published three days later in the "Richmond Enquirer," challenging Hussey to the contest and inviting the attendance of the public:

"I have thought it due to myself, and to those gentlemen who have invested money in my machine, to avail myself of the earliest opportunity of accepting the proposition for a trial of the two machines upon the same ground." He added that he would "cheerfully submit . . . to the arbitrament of a disinterested tribunal of experienced farmers," and would start working at sunrise in order to prove that his reaper would cut damp wheat, and that it could harvest fifteen acres in a day, using two horses and two operators.

The editor prefaced this statement with the comment: "From the following challenge, we may look out for some 'rare fun'— not on the 'battle' but on the 'wheat' field. . . . Much good always follows such a struggle for superiority, conducted, as it will be, in the most friendly spirit." [37] Hussey had not waited to read the formal invitation in the press: as soon as he heard that Turner intended to harvest with the reaper he had requested Hutchinson to allow him to cut against McCormick. The course of Hussey during this summer poorly supports his common reputation for a lack of aggressiveness.

In the week that elapsed between McCormick's letter of the

[37] "Richmond Enquirer," June 27, 1843.

twenty-fourth and the day set for the trial, both inventors were busily working their machines in the vicinity of Richmond.[38] On the twenty-seventh Cyrus operated his reaper on the Tuckahoe plantation of E. L. Wight. He learned to his surprise that his rival had announced to the neighborhood that he would be on hand that afternoon to "give McCormick a go" in Wight's wheat. A small crowd gathered, and shortly after McCormick began cutting in the mid-afternoon a shower drenched the grain. Hussey could not cut the wet wheat and left McCormick master of the field, despite the fact that he had forced the fighting.[39]

After this skirmish on the twenty-seventh, Hussey, knowing of the contest arranged for the thirtieth, took his two machines up the James River to Carter's plantation. He worked his better reaper on an island in the stream. The bridge was swept away by the high water and he was unable to get the implement ashore in time for the Hutchinson trial. His smaller machine was on the bank of the canal, and, rather than not appear at all, he hauled it down to the contest field for the race with McCormick. The latter began to cut in Hutchinson's light grain at "sun-up," [40] and Hussey appeared with his reaper shortly before noon. The thirty or forty spectators appointed a committee of judges and the trial began. The names of the planters on this board of award suggest the importance with which the competition was regarded in the neighborhood. C. W. Gooch,

[38] *Ibid.*, July 11, 1843, letter of O. Hussey.
[39] "Southern Planter," Nov., 1844; Dec., 1844, pp. 271, 272; Mch., 1845, pp. 54-57.
[40] On June 22, Cyrus was at W. H. Temple's, of Cantfield, starting his machine and watching a Hussey reaper at work in the adjoining field of John Watkins of Ampthill. McCormick then returned to Turner's. On June 26 he was at W. D. Sims's (Westham), putting a reaper in operation. "Richmond Enquirer," June 30, July 11 and 14, 1843.

W. H. Roane, James Pae, Curtis Carter, and Francis Staples consented to give a verdict at the close of the trial.[41]

Although McCormick stopped work for two hours at noon, his reaper cut seventeen acres during the day. Hussey harvested but two acres and did poorly in tangled grain.[42] The contest was obviously unequal. Because Hussey's machine was smaller than McCormick's and his team was unaccustomed to the work, the outcome of the trial was unconvincing. Hussey argued that his larger machine was a much better one than the reaper he had been forced to use, and that he could defeat McCormick with it in heavy wheat. The jury of planters felt "great reluctance in deciding between them, but upon the whole, prefer McCormick's." Hussey's usual reaper, according to their report, was "heavier, stronger, and more efficient" than his rival's and would in all probability reap more in a day. Since McCormick's reaper used only two horses, while Hussey required three or four; since it cost sixty dollars less than Hussey's larger machine, had side delivery, and cut better in damp grain, it would probably be preferred by a majority of farmers. Both cut cleanly and both scattered less grain than the cradle. Either was worth more than its cost to any farmer with level land and much grain, but gullies, hillsides, and reaper breakdowns still made scythes indispensable.[43]

Because Hussey protested the award, W. H. Roane, one of the jurors, who had felt some scruples about voting for McCormick, invited a renewal of the contest during the following week in his own wheat at Tree Hill. Here some portions of his grain were so tangled and down that McCormick refused to try to cut them with his reaper, although he harvested twelve or

[41] W. H. Roane was an ex-Senator of the United States. The wealthy C. W. Gooch was a friend of Martin Van Buren and a former partner of Thos. Ritchie.

[42] *Ibid.*, July 4, 1843. "Southern Planter," Aug., 1843, pp. 183, 184.

[43] *Ibid.*, Aug., 1843, pp. 183, 184.

fourteen acres in other parts of the field. Hussey drove his heavy machine at a trot into the lodged wheat and broke his sickle and rake. Roane believed that Hussey's reaper was the better for use in the rank grain that grew on the James River bottom-lands, and ordered one for the next harvest.[44]

Nevertheless, McCormick had won the year's campaign, for a comparison of sales admits of no question that his reaper was the more popular. He sold twenty-nine machines and all save one proved satisfactory, while Hussey disposed of two and announced that as he had discovered his reaper could cut Kentucky hemp, he would probably devote his major attention to that territory in 1844.[45] He was temporarily driven to cover in Virginia and McCormick had gained the self-confidence he so much needed just at this time. It is more than a coincidence that he began the new year, 1844, with a trip through the North and West to introduce his reaper. Virginia had approved his machine, and he felt that he was ready to seek a market where broad, level prairies and great grain-fields made its use a necessity rather than a luxury.

The Wight-Hutchinson-Roane battle was refought in the columns of the "Southern Planter" for the next two years.[46] The monthly broadside of letters from each inventor continued so long that Editor Botts announced in March, 1845, as he

[44] *Ibid.,* Aug., 1843, pp. 183, 184; Mch., 1844; Nov., 1844. "Richmond Enquirer," July 4, 1843. "Albany Cultivator," Apr., 1844, p. 107; May, 1844, p. 168. These issues include letters of McCormick and Hussey.

[45] "Lynchburg Virginian" (Lynchburg, Va.), July 10, 1843. "American Agriculturist," Nov. 15, 1843, p. 300, letter of J. Lewis, Llangollen, Ky., Oct. 23, 1843. C. H. McCormick to E. Burke, Jan. 1, 1848. "Richmond Semi-Weekly Whig," Oct. 27, 1843, letter of C. H. McCormick, appending testimonials of 25 Virginian users of his reapers, including W. W. Gilmer, John H. Cocke, Wm. Poage, Mayo Cabell, W. R. Temple, E. L. Wight, Alex. Rives, C. J. Meriwether, and J. H. Turner.

[46] "Richmond Enquirer," July 11, 14, 1843, and Dec. 2, 1844. "Southern Planter," Mch., 1844, pp. 61, 62; Oct., 1844, pp. 237-239; Nov., 1844; Dec., 1844, pp. 271, 272. "Dollar Farmer" (Louisville, Ky.), Sept., 1843.

printed Hussey's latest defense, that "this thing must end some-
where, and this is the last of it. If these gentlemen desire to
continue this controversy they must seek some other arena.
. . . Our subscribers . . . are worn out and sick of the whole
matter." [47] In spite of this ultimatum McCormick replied again
to Hussey, and Botts refused to publish the letter, stating that
the argument had "degenerated into a personal matter." If any
readers were interested, McCormick's reply could be read at
Botts's office.[48]

As late as 1848, Hussey wrote the Commissioner of Patents
that his rival's patent should not be renewed, because, among
other reasons, McCormick had gained an unmerited advantage
in the Hutchinson trial over "the best Reaping Machine which
was ever offered to the world." [49] This statement is humorous
in view of the fact that McCormick was selling fifteen hundred
machines a year in all parts of the North and West in 1849,
while Hussey marketed but one hundred. If Hussey's reaper
had been the better, the choice of the farmers would have been
unaffected by the decision of four or five Virginian planters
five years before.

As a result of his victory in the harvest of 1843, Cyrus Mc-
Cormick sought to extend his business for the next season. "As
it is not at all probable that I can always manufacture the
reaper to supply the wants of the country," he announced in
the "Richmond Semi-Weekly Whig" of October 27, 1843,

[47] "Southern Planter," Mch., 1845, pp. 54-57. As early as Nov., 1844,
Cyrus McCormick had written to this publication (Dec., 1844, pp. 271,
272), "And feeling no apprehension from Mr. H's competition, I have no
time to spare from making machines to meet the public demand for next
harvest, to be wasted in this idle tournament."
[48] *Ibid.*, June, 1845, p. 144. C. H. to W. S. McCormick, May 15, 1845:
"I have written an answer to his [Hussey's] piece at Botts, but doubt
whether he will insert it in the June no. Think him a little fishy at any rate,
neither flesh nor fowl."
[49] *Obed Hussey vs. U. S.*, O. Hussey to the Commr. of Patents, Feb. 21,
1848.

"I propose to form partnerships for their manufacture and also to sell patent rights." By the new year James M. Hite of Clarke County, Virginia, had bought the exclusive privilege of making and selling reapers for eight counties in the Valley of Virginia and along the Potomac River; Colonel M. Tutwiler, of Fluvanna County, of furnishing the machine to purchasers in Virginia south of the James River and the Blue Ridge Mountains; and Jabez Parker, of Richmond, of supplying five counties around that city. Monopolies of Washington County, Maryland, and of Monroe County, Michigan, also were sold.[50] In each case the contract was to continue until the expiration of the 1834 patent, in 1848. About fifty machines were constructed at Walnut Grove for 1844, and all save seven or eight of them were sold in Virginia. Hite marketed fourteen or fifteen of his own manufacture, and Parker at least ten. The output of the other licensees is unknown, but at least seventy-five McCormick reapers were sold in Virginia in this harvest. As Hussey claimed to have found purchasers for only eleven of his reapers that year, the tide of public favor in the East was still running strongly for his competitor.

Nevertheless, the number of sales does not tell the whole story. Although Hussey did not come to the Old Dominion that season, a few of his machines were sold there, and when they worked beside the reapers constructed by Hite, in western Virginia, they gained the preference. In fact, the sale of manufacturing rights, although probably necessary for the sake of the income, taught McCormick a valuable lesson. The machines built by Parker at Richmond gave satisfaction, but in several instances the Hite-McCormicks were defectively made and the reputation which the inventor had gained during the previous harvest was in a few quarters not maintained. This was even

[50] C. H. McCormick to E. Burke, Jan. 1, 1848, in Pattison, II, a. C. H. McCormick to Wm. Massie, Jan. 2, 1844.

more true during the next three harvests, and Hussey rewon the patronage of the Virginia planters.

Both inventors took their reapers to the West during the harvest of 1844. In the case of Hussey, this was a return to the area of his first experiments between 1833 and 1836, although in 1844 he seems to have been interested primarily in demonstrating that his machine could cut Kentucky hemp. He stated after the harvest that the endeavor was completely successful, although because his reaper was not used for this purpose in the future, the accuracy of his assertion may be questioned. Two of his reapers were exhibited in Illinois, and H. L. Ellsworth, Commissioner of Patents, wrote a congratulatory testimonial after witnessing its use in Indiana.[51] Hussey apparently did not visit Ohio, where his original machine of 1833 was constructed, nor did he and his rival meet in the West during the harvest.

The relative decline of McCormick's Virginian market after 1845 was not in accord with the inventor's wish. He tried to maintain the quality of the Walnut Grove output and to persuade his brother William to continue manufacture there after his own removal to Chicago. During his long absences in the West he found it necessary to direct the Eastern campaigns against Hussey by mail. Besides replying to his competitor publicly in the "Southern Planter," he coached his father and brothers in the proper tactics to pursue in the struggle. His letters reveal the inventor's private opinion of his own machine, its defects as well as its merits, and his judgment of the strength of the competition he had to face. He was not one who would hide either his successes or his failures from his family. The content of his last letter to Editor Botts on the subject of the

[51] An Ellsworth of Lafayette County, Indiana, also acted as an agent for McCormick, although it is not certain that he was the same man. See letter of C. H. to W. S. McCormick, Aug. 6, 1845, in which it is stated that Ellsworth had sold the "old machine" for $110 and transportation cost.

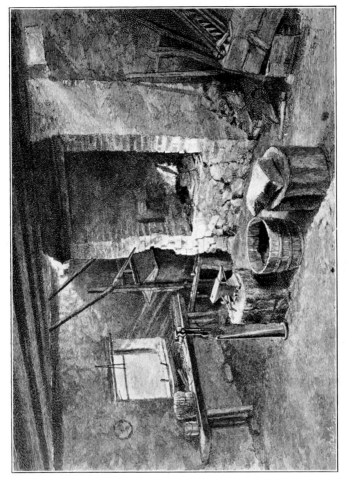

The Walnut Grove Blacksmith Shop

The birthplace of the McCormick reaper

Hutchinson trial of 1843, which the latter refused to publish in the spring of 1845, is in part revealed in a note which Cyrus McCormick wrote to his brother at the same time:

I propose in my piece to cut against Hussey in N. Y. or Pa. under direction of a Committee through harvest, and the owner of least approved machine to purchase the right of state for the other at $10,000 to end of old patent . . . as he proposes to warrant his *little* machine to cut ⅓ more than ours. This he won't try. . . . Hussey ought to be beaten in Virginia, in Md. and in N. Y. if it can be done. . . . Don't try Hussey by a flirt but by a day or more if machine good and it be required.[52]

This was bold language for a man to use who had just skirted the edge of bankruptcy and whose father's farm was still in the possession of a trustee who was holding it as security for the payment of debts. He did not have $10,000 to wager, but he was aware that his competitor had no larger resources and that Hussey had been rash to guarantee that his smaller-size reaper would cut one third more than McCormick's. About the same time McCormick wrote to his father: "Hussey must be watched with caution about Richmond and in Frederick. A complete machine should be kept for him at Richmond. . . . For him to get a preference would do a great harm. His swell will not affect much if he gets no advantage in harvest." [53]

In 1845, Hussey reapers were used not only in the middle seaboard States but also in New York, Michigan, Illinois, Wisconsin, and probably in Ohio and Kentucky.[54] He received

[52] C. H. to W. S. McCormick, May 15, 1845. *Ibid.* to *ibid.*, Apr. 2 and Aug. 6, 1845. On the latter date he wrote: "It is a glorious thing that Hussey has been twice beaten as you say, and once by Mr. Hite. I hear nothing of him in this country." Cyrus was then in New York State.
[53] C. H. to R. McCormick, May 3, 1845.
[54] "Genesee Farmer," Sept., 1845, pp. 134, 135. "Prairie Farmer," Nov., 1845, p. 258; Mch., 1846, p. 103; Feb., 1846, p. 69. "Ohio Cultivator," Jan., 1845, p. 40. These references tell of the work of the Hussey reaper near Seneca, N. Y., Prairie Ronde, Mich., Dixon, Ill., and Janesville, Wis.

a fifteen-dollar premium at the fifth annual fair of the New York State Agricultural Society at Utica and also exhibited at the yearly show of the American Institute at Niblo's Garden in New York City.[55] The editor of the "Ohio Cultivator" conceded that McCormick's was a slightly better machine, although Hussey's was smaller and not so complicated, while the "Prairie Farmer" of Chicago called the McCormick and Hussey reapers the best on the market.[56] Hussey with doubtful accuracy advertised that McCormick had failed in Kentucky that season and made much of the imperfection of the reapers which his rival was having manufactured at Cincinnati.[57]

The pronounced failure of the McCormick reapers made at Walnut Grove for the harvest of 1846 once again worked to Hussey's advantage in the East. Cyrus McCormick spent the entire year, save January, in New York and the West, and his prolonged absence, together with the long illness and death of his father, unfavorably affected both the workmanship and the performance of the machines which were made at the blacksmith shop. Although the editor of the "Southern Planter" acted as an agent for the reaper, he felt impelled at the close of the harvest to inform his subscribers that there had been "great complaint of the manner in which it was gotten up." He retained his agency in spite of this defection, but Cyrus McCormick could never rely upon his loyalty.

Perhaps the worst blow the reputation of the McCormick reaper suffered in the East during that season was struck by T. Pollock Burgwyn, an influential planter of Halifax, North Carolina, who with his father and brother devoted a part of their large estates to grain-culture. McCormick had introduced

[55] "Genesee Farmer," Oct., 1845, p. 154. "American Agriculturist," Oct., 1845, p. 301; Nov., 1845, p. 33. "Southern Planter," Nov., 1845, pp. 256-258.
[56] "Ohio Cultivator," Apr. 1, 1845, p. 55. "Prairie Farmer," Nov., 1845, p. 257.
[57] "American Farmer," Sept., 1845, p. 91.

a few reapers into North Carolina during the previous harvest, but they had not given satisfaction. Burgwyn capped the discontent in 1846 by writing to the "Southern Planter" that he had used one McCormick and one Hussey reaper to cut his two hundred acres of wheat, and was "candidly and decidedly of the opinion that Hussey's machine is vastly superior in execution and durability." Mr. Botts, the editor, prefaced the publication of this letter by writing:

We shall express no *opinion* ourself in the discussion which must necessarily follow . . . and we would greatly prefer that neither of the gentlemen more particularly interested in the subject would appear in our columns. We will publish statements of facts for either, provided they are made over responsible names, and are short and pertinent.[58]

Apparently he desired to amuse his readers with a sequel of the verbal battle between Hussey and McCormick over the Hutchinson trial. If this was his wish, he was disappointed. William S. McCormick sent a copy of the article to his brother in the West, and the latter replied in October, 1846:

The Burgwyn matter was all I doubt not, of his own [Botts's] procuring . . . and the beauty is, neither Botts nor Burgw. has been noticed in other papers. I am glad you sent me the piece. I don't fear it at all. His paper will have no influence after the manner of its conduct, etc. He locked me out before (refused my piece), and now invites me into his columns again. I have sent out my circulars for certificates as you have seen I suppose, and I'll be up to Botts, I *guess*. I'll give him a *dig in time* . . .[59]

[58] "Southern Planter," July, 1846, pp. 150-152. For other letters of North Carolinians puffing Hussey at McCormick's expense see the "American Farmer," Oct., 1847, p. 104; Mch., 1848, p. 284, letters of Josiah Collins of Washington County and of Thos. D. Warren of Edenton, N. C. On the Burgwyns see Phillips, pp. 253, 254.
[59] C. H. to W. S. McCormick, from Brockport, N. Y., Oct. 13, 1846.

McCormick was correct in judging that his loss of favor in Virginia and North Carolina would not affect him in the West, but there is no doubt that he underestimated the extent of his temporary eclipse in his own State. Hussey used the letter as advertising material for his own machine as late as 1848 [60] and Burgwyn arose repeatedly during the next decade to trouble the agents of the McCormick reaper.[61]

During the harvest of 1846, Hussey for the first time introduced his reapers in Champaign County, Ohio, and at the close of the season arranged with the firm of Minturn & Allen, of Urbana, to manufacture them for the local market. Therefore for 1847 he would have a factory to check A. C. Brown, who was making McCormick reapers at Cincinnati. Hussey's brother at Auburn, New York, was endeavoring to stem the output of machines made at Brockport by McCormick licensees. A few Hussey machines were also used in Illinois in 1846.[62]

While McCormick was winning a premium at the New York State Agricultural Fair at Auburn, over T. R. Hussey, in September, 1846,[63] Obed Hussey attended the fall exhibition of the New Castle, Delaware, Agricultural Society. He and Moses Pennock, the inventor of the horse-rake, were the guests of honor. Hussey had the pleasure of hearing that his reaper,

[60] The letter of Burgwyn is reprinted in the "American Farmer," Sept., 1846, p. 79. "Ohio Cultivator," Apr. 15, 1848, p. 64.

[61] *Post,* pp. 370 ff.

[62] "First Annual Report of the Ohio State Board of Agriculture, 1846" (Columbus, 1847), p. 27. "Albany Cultivator," June, 1847, p. 170. "Ohio Cultivator," Oct. 1, 1846, p. 147. "Prairie Farmer," Sept., 1846, p. 285. "Monthly Journal of Agriculture" (N. Y.), May, 1847, p. 486. Patent Office Records, "Hussey Extension Case, Patent of 1847," p. 127, statement of Jacob Minturn of Urbana that he and Allen made 24 Hussey reapers in 1847, perhaps 50 in 1848, and a like number annually thereafter. They paid Hussey a fee of $10 per machine. Pattison, Sec. IX, letters of S. M. Hitt, Mt. Morris, Ill., to O. Hussey, Jan. 1 and Aug. 31, 1847. "Scientific American," Oct. 31, 1846, p. 44.

[63] C. H. to W. S. McCormick, from Brockport, N. Y., Oct. 13, 1846. "Ohio Cultivator," Apr. 15, 1847, p. 64.

"one of the greatest, the very greatest improvements ever made in farming implements after the Horse Rake, was constructed twelve years ago, yet it is only now beginning to be *known*. Had there been spirited and well conducted Agricultural Societies in every County of the Union, it would have been generally introduced ten years since, saving or earning the agricultural community probably ten millions of dollars to this time." [64] During the same autumn, McCormick was happy because of his successes in New York and in the West, and Hussey was experimenting with his famous open-back guard finger.[65]

As the New York and the Western markets opened up with amazing rapidity after 1844, Cyrus McCormick gave less and less personal attention to sales in his native State. The demand of the Genesee Valley [66] and the prairie belt so overshadowed that of the limited wheat areas of the East that he naturally turned toward the places of most profits. The waning of his popularity along the seaboard parallels the rise of the fortunes of Hussey in the same region. He made no serious effort to rewin the patronage of the East until 1850, when he was firmly established in Chicago.

Hussey made only half-hearted attempts to rival McCormick in the West, and except for his brother's small plant at Auburn, New York, and Minturn & Allen, at Urbana, Ohio, he confined production to his inadequate Baltimore factory prior to 1850. Here he broadened his output to include corn- and cob-grinders, turnip-cutters, and steam-engines, while the few

[64] "American Farmer," Feb., 1847, pp. 247, 248.

[65] *Hussey vs. McCormick,* pp. 23, 24. His patent on this improvement was issued on Aug. 7, 1847.

[66] "Genesee Farmer," Sept., 1853, p. 289. In 1849, Monroe County, of which Rochester was the county-seat, produced 1,441,653 bushels of wheat, and the six New England States, 1,039,112 bushels. Livingston County, N. Y., grew 1,111,986 bushels in 1849, and Ontario and Niagara counties a little less than a million bushels each. See Chap. IX, p. 204, ftn. 2.

reapers he sold each year, numbering fifty or sixty in 1850, were well constructed and were received with favor from Pennsylvania south to North Carolina.[67] This seaboard area regarded him as its own, and its press boosted his reaper with a will. Cyrus McCormick on the contrary was a target for criticism, since he was a resident of Chicago after 1847, and apparently believed that the prairie market alone merited his serious attention. Furthermore, many Eastern farmers needed mowers even more than reapers, and while Hussey found that his machine, slightly altered, cut grass well, his rival's mower, first tried in 1849, did not work satisfactorily until 1854.

Between 1844 and 1850 there was no recorded formal field contest between Hussey and McCormick in the East. Honors received at agricultural fairs and at kindred exhibitions were about equally shared. Their rivalry assumed a new form in 1848, because both inventors endeavored in that year and for the next decade to secure an extension of their original patents. Consequently, the battle-ground was widened to embrace the lobbies of Congress and the Patent Office, as well as the grain-fields and the newspapers of the land. The expiration of their monopolies invited new competitors to enter the arena, and the duel of the years 1839 to 1847 rapidly became thereafter a general mêlée, in which Hussey remained one of the most persistent but one of the least formidable of McCormick's opponents.

[67] Certified copy, "Court of Claims Record, No. 1654, Obed Hussey vs. U. S.," deposition of Hussey, Apr. 18, 1848. Hussey claims to have made 248 reapers from 1839 to 1847 (both inclusive). His yearly sales in this period were, respectively, 16, 36, 22, 10, 2, 11, 33, 58, and 60. His total profits since 1833 were only $7,300. On Feb. 2, 1848, he thought he was worth $500. "Hussey Extension Case, Patent of 1847," p. 84. In 1845, Hussey associated with Thos. J. Lovegrove, a former agent. Lovegrove was to build engines while his partner manufactured reapers. Greeno, p. 33, E. Stabler to J. A. Pierce, Feb. 5, 1854: "His [Hussey's] shops . . . are for the most part dilapidated sheds . . . too confined and cramped up to do any part of his work to the best advantage."

CHAPTER IX

THE FIRST INVASION OF THE WEST, 1844-45

WHILE Obed Hussey and Cyrus McCormick were battling for the relatively small patronage of the Eastern grain-growers, the Virginian, with more foresight than his rival, also entered the level trans-Allegheny country and sought the richest prize that America could then offer to the inventor of a reaper. It need not be presumed that he deliberately kept his competitor occupied along the seaboard while he gained his first foothold on the prairies. In fact, Hussey had cut grain in Ohio as early as 1833, and had journeyed West again during the same harvest in which Cyrus McCormick made his first trip through that region to promote the sale of his machine.

Hussey must have realized that the Mississippi Valley furnished a far larger market than the East. The agricultural papers had often called attention to that area as the future realm of the reaper. Why he did not return in force to the scenes of his first experiments is not clear, but he was almost twenty years older than his rival, and age, combined with his natural conservatism, possibly restrained him from risking a new venture. He had formed a partnership in Baltimore and his slowly increasing yearly sales kept his little factory busy. His machine was gaining favor as a mower, and the East turned more and more to grass-growing as the fertility of the soil declined and as the grain competition of the West became harder to combat.[1]

[1] Easterners were aware that the art of reaping had forged ahead of mowing and that a good grass-cutter was needed. "American Agriculturist," VI (1847), pp. 46, 314, 341, 342. "Albany Cultivator," June, 1845, pp. 181, 182; Dec., 1846, p. 387. "Ohio Cultivator," Sept. 1, 1847, p. 130.

As railroads and canals pushed across the Appalachians, and freight rates to Eastern ports were reduced, the farmers of the middle States found it annually more difficult to raise grain with profit. Wheat and other cereals sharply declined in price during the early 1840's. Under such circumstances a Virginian or Pennsylvanian farmer who grew but fifteen bushels of wheat per acre could not compete with a Wabash Valley yield of twice that amount.[2] Short harvests in Europe increased the demand, but the grain surplus flooded even the larger market, and farmers were forced to grow bigger crops in order to make a profit equivalent to the return from less acreage and higher prices ten years before.[3] New York agricultural papers advised their subscribers to surrender in the unequal contest with the West and to use their lands for orchards, vegetables, and stock-

[2] "American Agriculturist," Aug., 1844, pp. 238-240: Since grain prices are low, every effort must be made to produce cheaply for export so that the European producer can be undersold in his own market. For similar advice see the "New Genesee Farmer," Sept. 1844, pp. 76, 77; "Farmer and Mechanic," Jan. 14 and 21, 1847, pp. 30, 42. In 1844 and 1845 the farmers of the United States harvested 95,607,000 and 106,584,000 bushels of wheat respectively, and 421,953,000 and 417,809,000 bushels of corn. In 1845, New York led in wheat-production, with 16,200,000 bushels, and Ohio and Pennsylvania followed with 13,573,000 and 12,580,000 bushels, respectively. Ohio and Kentucky were the bumper corn States. Soil-exhaustion in New York is discussed in the "Genesee Farmer," Sept., 1853, p. 299. This account states that Albany County, which averaged from 20 to 40 bushels of wheat per acre in 1775, now [1845] averages a yield of 7½ bushels. Similar conditions prevailed in Dutchess, Rensselaer, Columbia, and Westchester counties. The Western yield did not average 30 bushels an acre. Illinois statisticians did not claim over 22 and those in Ohio estimated 20 or less for that State. Some Midwestern farmers were already complaining of soil-exhaustion, and debating the advisability of substituting stock-raising for grain-culture. See "Ohio Cultivator" for Apr. 1, 1856, p. 98, and "Monthly Journal of Agriculture," May, 1847, p. 487.

[3] The repeal of the English corn laws and famine in Ireland stimulated American grain exports to England. "American Farmer," Nov., 1846, p. 145.

raising.[4] In the late 1820's, the Erie Canal brought prosperity to the grain-growers along its banks, who had largely contributed to the cost of its construction, but by 1845 it was chiefly a highway for the benefit of the Ohio country, and of the rising cities of Buffalo and New York, which handled the cereal wealth of the West on its way to the sea. While Eastern landowners were complaining that the cost of raising a bushel of wheat varied from fifty cents to one dollar, a prairie farmer living near Alton, Illinois, boasted that he could sell most profitably at New Orleans for seventy-five cents a bushel, because the expense of production was but thirty cents, and twelve cents more would pay the freight to that market.[5]

The Western farmer would derive little benefit from increased transportation facilities unless more laborers were avail-

[4] "Farmers' Cabinet," Sept. 15, 1846, pp. 62, 63. Estimating that a 100-acre wheat farm in the West would yield an annual profit of $2,365, a Hudson Valley wheat farm of equal size would show only a yearly net profit of $1,250. "American Agriculturist," Feb., 1846, pp. 42, 43: Farmers will be prosperous for some years to come. Since foreign tariffs are falling, and the population of Europe is increasing due to universal peace, we can export grain profitably in large amounts. Because of the growth of manufacturing in the United States, there are more consumers for the farmers to feed, and internal improvements reduce freight rates on commodities moving to the East. The balance of power is with the farmer. *Ibid.*, Aug., 1848, pp. 241-244. "Southern Planter," Jan., 1847, p. 32. "Ohio Cultivator," Aug. 15, 1848, p. 122.

[5] "N. Y. Farmer and Mechanic," Apr., 1846, p. 138. "American Agriculturist," July, 1848, p. 231; Aug., 1848, pp. 241-244; Jan., 1848, p. 221. Western estimates of the cost of raising one bushel of wheat varied from thirty to sixty-five cents. In 1840 the wheat export of the United States for the first time surpassed the 1793 record of 1,450,575 bushels, but this total was not again equaled until 1846. During the period from 1840 to 1846, the annual export of flour varied from approximately 840,000 barrels to 2¼ million barrels. In 1847 the United States produced 114,245,500 bushels of wheat worth $137,094,600. See the "Prairie Farmer" for May, 1849, p. 159; the "Southern Planter" for Aug., 1848, p. 233, and the "Ohio Cultivator" for Aug. 15, 1848, pp. 122, 123.

able for the harvest.[6] Unrest in Germany and Ireland brought thousands from those countries to America in the late 1840's, and while most of the Irish stayed in the cities of the seaboard, many Germans sought the soil of Illinois, Wisconsin, Iowa, and Missouri. Land was cheap and plentiful, and very often the immigrant settled down as a freeholder, soon needing hired men of his own. The wages of agricultural laborers tended to mount rather than to decline,[7] and there was a prejudice, whether justified or not, against a workman who could not speak English and who had been accustomed to methods of farming quite different from those employed in the United States. A farmer of Seneca Lake, New York, illustrated this antipathy when he wrote in the "Genesee Farmer":

Many a farmer with an excited woe begone face, have I seen this season, riding about in search of cradlers; 'tis true he could find plenty of wild Irish and others, who like Highland Willie, 'could neither say nor do', but experienced cradlers were few indeed; and when found, *only to think,* the price of two bushels of wheat for a single day's work.[8]

[6] *Ibid.,* Oct. 1, 1846, p. 147: The recent abundant wheat crop and the high price of labor have turned the attention of Ohio farmers to reapers. "Prairie Farmer," Sept., 1846, p. 284. "Genesee Farmer," Nov., 1847, p. 261.

[7] "Albany Cultivator," Sept., 1847, p. 286. According to the report of the Commr. of Patents, wages in New England ranged from $11 to $15 per month; in New York, $10 to $12 per month; in New Jersey, $15 per month, without board; in Pennsylvania, $10 to $12 per month; in Maryland, $8 to $10 per month; in the Old South, $5 to $10 per month, and higher where slave labor did not compete; in the Middle West, $8 to $10 per month, save northern Illinois, Michigan, and Iowa, where it varied from $11, to $15. This, of course, was by the year. Extra laborers in harvest-time were frequently paid $1.25 or more a day. "Prairie Farmer," Oct., 1847, p. 324; Jan., 1848, pp. 26, 27. A Wisconsin farmer states that he had often vainly offered $1.50 to $2.00 a day during harvest.

[8] "Genesee Farmer," Sept., 1845, p. 134. "Prairie Farmer," Oct., 1847, p. 324; Sept., 1847, p. 231: Barn space is too small to house the crop in the Middle West. Farmers are accustomed to stack their grain in the open

This aversion entered politics, and the American or Nativist movement, evident as early as President Jackson's day, received great impetus after 1845. Religious intolerance was a large factor in the Eastern phase of this hostility to the Irish, but economic and racial rivalry was at its roots as well. Although the American farmer had been handicapped for many years by the high price of labor, he was told that he should aid in warding off the foreign menace. Even Elihu Burritt, "blacksmith philosopher," and advocate of world brotherhood, exclaimed in 1847:

Western Farmer! what are you going to do for the Old World next year? Are you going to feed them, or let them die of hunger? If you cannot engage to grow *one thousand millions* of bushels of Indian corn for them the coming season, and send it over in season, they will come after it themselves, and your prairies will swarm with them, as with an ocean of bull frogs. So be up now and at it. There will be no potatoes raised here this season, and you must plant corn for half the world.[9]

It is probable that few farmers in the West raised more grain in order to stave off immigration from Europe. They expanded their acreage as the demand grew, and the reaper was ready to make this possible. In 1842 the "Union Agriculturist and Western Prairie Farmer" of Chicago extended the following invitation to men of science:

We therefore say to inventors—here is, a field for you to operate in; anything that you wish to have introduced into extensive use, which you know to be really valuable, you can bring here with a

field rather than shock it, and later move it to cover. "McCormick Extension Case, Patent of 1845," pro testimony, pp. 48, 49. Wm. Marshall of Cordova, Ill., testified that many laborers did not know how to use a cradle. See also *ibid.*, pp. 56, 57.

[9] "Farmers' Cabinet," July 15, 1847, p. 365, copying from the "Christian Citizen" (Worcester, Mass.). Burritt was writing from England.

good prospect of success. Bring along your machines, and also give us a chance to advertise them.[10]

Many explanations have been given for the journey of Cyrus McCormick to the West in 1844. Those of his enemies who later wished to be particularly invidious charged that he deserted Walnut Grove in order to escape his furnace debts and to leave his father and brothers with the burden of their payment. This thesis is untenable in view of the fact that he did not permanently settle in the West until 1848, and by then all obligations were discharged, his father was dead, and the home farm had been returned by the one who for four years had held it as security. The attainment of solvency had been in large measure due to his energy in marketing his reaper between 1842 and 1846.

The economic motive for his move across the mountains was doubtless the most important one, although it need not be expressed so baldly as William S. McCormick wrote in 1857: "Much as I love old Virginia, we should have starved in our business had we remained there. . . . Now she will have to adopt labor-saving machines." [11] While on his trips to the Ohio Valley, Cyrus wrote home of crops wasting for lack of labor

[10] "Union Agriculturist and Western Prairie Farmer," Jan., 1842, p. 3. "Chicago Daily Journal," July 21, 1848: "They [reapers] are just the things for our prairies, where more grain is sown than can possibly be gathered in the ordinary way, and their comparative cheapness puts them within the reach of every tiller of the soil. So indispensable will be their use that hereafter the sickle, the scythe, and the cradle may as well hang themselves 'upon the willow.'" "Albany Cultivator," Aug., 1849, p. 257, copying from the "Prairie Farmer": Each reaper is equivalent to 4½ men and since 2,900 [2,800 of McCormick's] have been sold in the past three years, they do the work of 13,050 men. The 180 reaper-threshers in use equal 3,600 laborers. Ibid., Sept., 1850, p. 313. "Genesee Farmer," Nov., 1849, p. 255. "McCormick Extension Case, Patent of 1845," pp. 21 ff.

[11] W. S. McCormick to Thornton Berry, Cline's Mills, Va., Mch. 25, 1857, L.P.C.B., No. 5, p. 801.

to harvest them.[12] He pictured himself as an ambassador of prosperity, and a generation later said with much truth that he had saved the farmer one hundred dollars for every dollar that he had pocketed. There was a strong strain of idealism in his nature, and although profits were his chief aim in 1844 and the years which followed, it would be incorrect to discount altogether his intense belief in his reaper as an instrument which would lead to happier days upon the farm. He liked to believe that his machine would enable the American farmer to "beat the world growing wheat." [13]

During the winter of 1843-44, Cyrus carefully planned his trip to the West.[14] Either Robert McCormick refused to join in the venture, or his son resolved to carry it through without his aid. Whatever the cause, an exception was made in their normal business arrangement, and the eight or nine machines constructed at Walnut Grove for the trans-Allegheny market were bought outright by Cyrus from his father for $50 apiece. One each was designed for exhibition and sale in the Genesee Valley, New York; Southport, Wisconsin; Monroe County, Michigan; Cooper County, Missouri; Cincinnati, Ohio; Indiana, Illinois, Kentucky, and Tennessee. The problem of trans-

[12] "Ohio Cultivator," Apr. 15, 1847. Testimonials are here printed in which farmers express their opinion that if it had not been for the reaper much grain would have been lost in the harvest of 1846.

[13] "Chicago Times," July 5, 1866, letter of C. H. McCormick. "Chicago Daily Democrat," Oct. 19, 1848. In a letter in this issue he writes, "The concurrent and universal opinion of the farmers of the prairies now being that the quantity of wheat grown has already been, and will continue to be, greatly increased by the facilities for harvesting afforded by the Reaper . . . and if they can get enough of McCormick's Reapers, they can beat the world . . . growing wheat." "Prairie Farmer," Oct., 1849, p. 317, letter of "Silex," of Dubuque County, Ia. For a paragraph from this letter see post, p. 467, ftn. 32.

[14] In a letter of Sept. 13, 1843, published in the "Richmond Semi-Weekly Whig" of Oct. 27, 1843, C. H. McCormick states that he wants partners in the Northern and Western States, and particularly at Pittsburgh and Cincinnati.

portation was a serious one. Because the Ohio, Indiana, Kentucky, and Tennessee reapers were carted to Scottsville, Virginia, transported to Richmond by canal, and freighted by sea to New Orleans and so up the Mississippi, they arrived at their destinations too late for the harvest of 1844.[15] Three of these were finally sold at reduced prices and the financial return from the eight sent to the West merely paid the expenses attendant upon their introduction there. But Cyrus McCormick did not gage the success of this first adventure with his reaper, far from home, by his cash on hand at the close of the season. This was pioneer work which would bear rich fruit in the near future.

In late June, 1844, after the Virginia harvest was over, McCormick started for the Genesee Valley, and on July 17 six farmers near Rochester wrote for publication that they had witnessed a field trial of his machine and that it had performed well.[16] McCormick sold the one he had designed for this market, and made arrangements with Backus, Fitch & Co. of Brockport to construct machines for 1845.[17] From New York

[15] Pattison, II, a, C. H. McCormick to E. Burke, Jan. 1, 1848. "Albany Cultivator," May, 1845, pp. 181, 182. C. H. McCormick in the "Richmond Enquirer," Nov. 19, 1844. "Southern Planter," Dec., 1844, pp. 271, 272. C. H. to W. S. McCormick, Aug. 6, 1845. Photostat of letter from John Ornsdorff, of Adairsville, Ky., to Esau Ornsdorff, of Delevan, Ill., Sept. 26, 1845. The latter had received his McCormick reaper and it worked well. The former had ordered one, but it was still at Clarksville, awaiting transportation. The original letter is in the possession of Miss Julia A. Drake, of the University of Texas.

[16] "New Genesee Farmer," Aug., 1844, p. 68. "American Agriculturist," Aug., 1844, pp. 238-240. "Ohio Cultivator," Jan. 1, 1845, p. 8.

[17] "New Genesee Farmer," Sept., 1844, pp. 76, 77, 80. Here is a testimonial signed by twelve men, and the statement that Ansel Chappell bought the first McCormick Reaper "ever offered for inspection in this vicinity." "McCormick Extension Case, Patent of 1845," pp. 14-16, testimony of Ansel Chappell. *McCormick vs. Manny,* II, p. 409, testimony of Jeremiah Sheppard of Brockport, N. Y. Backus, Fitch & Co. owned a furnace and a machine-shop. They purchased manufacturing rights for six New York counties.

the inventor journeyed into Ohio, but the machine he had previously freighted by way of New Orleans and Cincinnati arrived too late for use that summer. Nevertheless it was exhibited at the Hamilton County Agricultural Fair at Mt. Pleasant in the autumn, and the judges, relying upon testimonials from Virginia and New York, "confidently recommend it to the patronage of our brother farmers, and the West generally" and awarded it a certificate of merit.[18] Thus the inventor won his first trophy in the Mississippi Valley.

Leaving Ohio, Cyrus McCormick moved north to Michigan, where he superintended the operation of a reaper which had already been delivered to a farmer of Raisinville in Monroe County.[19] Thence he traveled by way of Chicago [20] to Beloit and Southport, Wisconsin, and here, after watching one of his machines reap satisfactorily, he was persuaded, for the only time in his life, to go gunning—on this occasion for prairie chickens.[21] After a similar success with a reaper in Missouri, he turned toward Virginia, stopping at Cincinnati to arrange with A. C. Brown of that city for the manufacture of machines

[18] "Western Farmer and Gardener" (Cincinnati), Nov., 1844, p. 82. "Albany Cultivator," June, 1845, pp. 181, 182, letter of W. H. H. Taylor, of Cincinnati, O. "Cincinnati Enquirer," Jan. 19, 1898, reminiscences of Christian Speicher, formerly a tailor of Millersburg, O.

[19] Jacob Bender brought a McCormick reaper from Maryland to Michigan in June, 1844, and sold it to Thos. Caldwell of Raisinville. "Richmond Enquirer," Nov. 19, 1844.

[20] McCormick probably exhibited a reaper in Illinois in 1844, but no certain information confirming this has been found. A brief unsigned memorandum, written after 1884, and in the handwriting of Cyrus McCormick's daughter, states that he visited Rockford, Keokuk, and Peoria on his way south from Wisconsin to St. Louis.

[21] Letters of C. H. McCormick in the "Chicago Times," July 5, 1866, and in the "Richmond Enquirer," Nov. 19, 1844. C. H. McCormick, Jr., was told by his father that a real-estate promoter of Beloit, who wished to induce the inventor to locate his factory in that town, was the host on the shooting trip. McCormick brought down two birds with three shots, and decided to rest upon the laurels of that record for the rest of his life.

for the harvest of 1845.[22] Home once more, he announced that his machines, "diffused" through ten States during the recent harvest, had performed "without a failure and with the most perfect success." [23]

At the same time the editor of the "Southern Planter" graciously informed his subscribers that he now preferred McCormick's reaper to Hussey's, as it "wins golden opinions wherever it goes." In fact, the outcome of the Virginia season had been most encouraging. The demand for the reapers had outrun the supply, and such well-known plantation-owners as Corbin Warwick, Robert Rives, and Robert Stannard added their public approval to those testimonials which had been given during the previous years.[24] Hussey's emphasis upon his rival's failure in Jefferson County, Virginia, where several of Hite's machines failed to perform well, could not detract from the general satisfaction felt by McCormick at the close of this successful year.[25] Unfortunately he found it impossible to devote enough attention to the home market during the next few

[22] Memo. of Miss McCormick, mentioned in ftn. 20, p. 211. According to this account, McCormick journeyed up the Missouri River as far as Boonesville. "Richmond Enquirer," Nov. 19, 1844. The Brown contract, dated Sept. 19, 1844, will be found in *McCormick vs. Manny*, II., 596 ff.

[23] "Richmond Enquirer," Nov. 19, 1844, advertisement of C. H. McCormick. "Southern Planter," Dec., 1844, pp. 271, 272. Here McCormick lists the States (Maryland, Kentucky, Ohio, Indiana, Tennessee, Illinois, Missouri, Wisconsin, Michigan, and New York) which his machine entered in 1844.

[24] "Lynchburg Virginian," May 8, 15, 19, and 29, 1845. "Richmond [Va.] Compiler," June 21, 1844. "Ohio Cultivator," Mch. 15, 1845, p. 47. "Richmond Enquirer," July 4, 1844.

[25] "Southern Planter," Nov., 1844. McCormick states that in general Hite's output gave great satisfaction. In proof of this fact he announces that Hite will make a considerable number for 1845 and has ordered 100 blades from Walnut Grove. Pattison, Sec. IX., testimony of J. M. Hite, Mch. 16, 1848. *McCormick vs. Manny*, II., pp. 105, 144. "Albany Cultivator," Feb., 1845, p. 59; May, 1845, pp. 181, 182. "Southern Planter," Oct., 1844, pp. 237-239; Dec., 1844, pp. 271, 272; Mch. 1845, pp. 54, 55.

seasons to preserve the popularity he had won there between 1842 and 1844.

In the autumn of 1844, as he reviewed his preparations for the harvest of the next year, he must have pictured four or five hundred reapers ready for the market by the time the grain crop began to ripen. As not more than seventy-five had been sold the previous summer, the prospect of six or seven times that number in process of construction was most heartening. Hite, in Clarke County, Virginia, was apparently going ahead with fifty or more,[26] the home blacksmith shop would turn out as many, Parker at Richmond would probably build half that number,[27] and Tutwiler in Fluvanna County would add a few to the Eastern total.[28] One hundred and fifty or more machines, including the few which Brown at Cincinnati would ship East, would surely swamp Hussey, when added to the several McCormicks already sold in North Carolina and Maryland.

North in New York State, Backus, Fitch & Co. had contracted to make forty for four counties and to pay McCormick $20 for each one sold, not to mention the number they might manufacture for the two other counties, which they had purchased from him for $100 apiece. John W. McCoy & Son of Southport, Wisconsin, had promised $1,000 for the privilege of supplying four counties in their own State, and Henry Bear, far west in Cooper County, Missouri, had agreed to pay $20 for each of about thirty machines he planned to make and sell. The monopoly right to Lafayette County, Indiana, had also been sold for $100; and, above all, A. C. Brown at Cincinnati

---

[26] *Ibid.*, Nov., 1844, letter of C. H. McCormick, Nov. 8, 1844.

[27] *Hussey vs. McCormick*, pp. 209-212. "Richmond Enquirer," May 16, 1845, and Jan. 16, 1846.

[28] "Lynchburg Virginian," May 8, 15, 19, 29, 1845.

was going ahead with approximately two hundred machines and guaranteed the inventor a $20 royalty for each.[29]

If all went well, the McCormick reaper would be known from the Potomac to the Missouri River within a year, and all of the long-due furnace debts could be paid with the $10,000 in prospect. It must have been a happy Christmas at Walnut Grove in 1844, with a good Democrat soon to occupy the White House, the iron-venture troubles gradually clearing away, reaper hopes ever higher, the country in a new boom cycle, and the family rejoicing over Amanda's approaching marriage to the son of a prosperous farmer of the neighborhood.[30] Hussey had seemingly been decisively defeated and as the new year opened McCormick received a second patent for certain improvements on his reaper which he later considered to be largely responsible for making it an assured success.[31]

Although McCormick publicly faced the approaching summer of 1845 with optimism, he was aware of one improvement, above all others, that was needed to win for his reaper the unqualified approval of the farmers and to supplant Hussey in the harvest field. His machine cut well, but the laborer who walked rapidly beside it on a hot day, striving to keep pace with the inexorable knife and reel which piled grain on the platform for him to rake to the ground in orderly gavels, had a killing task in heavy wheat. If a seat were placed upon the machine, so that the rakeman could sit while he worked, the chief objection to the reaper would be met. But the reel revolved through the space where such a seat would find its natural

[29] A summary statement of his arrangements for the 1845 harvest may be found in his letter to E. Burke, Jan. 1, 1848. "Richmond Enquirer," Nov. 19, 1844. "Ohio Cultivator," Jan. 1, 1845, p. 8; Mch. 15, 1845, p. 47. "Southern Planter," Dec., 1844, pp. 271, 272. "Western Farmer and Gardener," Oct., 1844, p. 57; Nov., 1844, p. 82.

[30] Amanda J. McCormick and Hugh Adams were married on May 8, 1845. L. J. McCormick, pp. 326, 327.

[31] Post, p. 276.

place; and even if this difficulty could be surmounted, considerable readjustment of the balance of the reaper would be necessary in order to counteract the addition of a man's weight on one portion of the framework.

McCormick had long before realized the need of a raker's seat, and now his experience in the heavy wheat of the West convinced him that it was imperative to remedy the fault immediately. Upon his arrival at Walnut Grove in the autumn of 1844 the thought of both father and son was directed toward a solution of the problem, as they made machines in the blacksmith shop that winter for the coming harvest. Finally Robert McCormick discovered a position for the seat which seemed practicable, if certain changes were made in the arrangement of the reel and in the construction of the framework. Only an actual test in the ensuing harvest could determine the value of his plan, but Cyrus left for the West in February [32] sufficiently convinced of its feasibility to consent to its incorporation in the reapers made at Walnut Grove for that harvest. He urged his father to take out the patent, but as soon as the grain was ripe in Virginia, field tests demonstrated that the rakeman could not operate from the seat he had invented.[33] The forty-eight

[32] C. H. McCormick to J. D. Davidson, of Lexington, Va., Feb. 17, 1845. "Richmond Enquirer," Feb. 26, 1845: Robert and Cyrus McCormick announce that a raker's seat will be attached to the machines for 1845 without extra charge. It can be added to the old machines at small cost.

[33] C. H. to W. S. McCormick, from Cincinnati, Apr. 2, 1845, "I think that the seat can be patented, and father can take it in his name as he first thought of it." There is some evidence that the first seat was added early in the autumn of 1844, even before Cyrus returned from the West, to Walnut Grove. In "McCormick Extension Case, Patent of 1847," pp. 85-96, John Magness, one of the sub-manufacturers of A. C. Brown at Cincinnati, testified that when the model machine arrived at Brown's shop from Walnut Grove, in Sept. or Oct., 1844, it had a seat. A. C. Brown stated that when he made the contract of Sept. 19, 1844, with McCormick, the latter left a reaper as a model, with a raker's seat. Was this possibly a reaper which Cyrus had experimented with in the West in 1844, or had it been sent from Walnut Grove?

farmers who bought Walnut Grove reapers that season removed the worthless device and continued to rake the grain
from the platform in the same old arduous fashion.

A year before, J. M. Hite's son in Clarke County had constructed a horizontal frame on wheels and attached it to the
rear of his father's reaper so that a raker could stand upon it
and ride as he removed the grain from the platform in front
of him. This too simple solution of a difficult problem proved
impractical because of the rough field and the necessity of
frequently turning the machine. It found little favor save with
its inventor, and he was refused a patent upon it in 1844.
Nevertheless it became a factor of some importance in Cyrus
McCormick's suit against J. H. Manny, about ten years
later.[34]

Either before or after Cyrus heard of the failure of his
father's invention, he experimented again in Brown's shops in
Cincinnati and by midsummer, 1845, discovered a position
for the raker's seat which worked well when it was tested in
a Kentucky grain-field.[35] He then carried this improved machine to Buffalo and staged an exhibition in August on the
estate of General Samuel J. Mills of Mount Morris, New York.
This influential farmer was highly pleased with the new arrangement and sent a letter of strong commendation to the

[34] I. I. Hite's application for a patent was rejected on Nov. 1, 1844.
U. S. Patent Office Records, "C. H. McCormick-I. I. Hite Interference,
1855."
[35] "Ohio Cultivator," July 15, 1845, p. 108. "Dollar Farmer," July, 1845,
p. 7. "Staunton Spectator," Dec. 16, 1845, letter of C. H. McCormick.
"Southern Planter," Jan., 1846, pp. 5-8. Here is shown a cut of the
1845 machine with a raker's seat, and a statement by C. H. McCormick
that it had been added during the last harvest at Cincinnati. He then
describes its success at Mt. Morris, N. Y., later in the summer. "Richmond Enquirer," Dec. 23, 1845, statement of C. H. McCormick regarding
his invention of the seat at Cincinnati. Pattison, II, a.
[36] C. H. to W. S. McCormick, Aug. 9, 1845. "Albany Cultivator," May,
1846, p. 165.

editor of the "Albany Cultivator." [36] In the meantime Robert and Leander McCormick were again seeking to find a better way at Walnut Grove, and Leander finally wrote his eldest brother, describing a method of attaching the seat which somewhat resembled the solution already reached by Cyrus. Cyrus replied to Leander that he preferred his own arrangement and subsequently patented it in 1847.[37]

The story of the invention of the raker's seat illustrates the obstacles to be surmounted when changes in the construction of the reaper were necessary or a new appliance had to be added to its carefully balanced framework. The general form of seat desired and the most advantageous position for the riding rakeman could be readily determined, but a year of study was required with experimental construction work in the shops of Walnut Grove and Cincinnati, and trials in the grain of four States, before Cyrus McCormick finally discovered how this device could be utilized in the most convenient location without sacrificing the efficient operation of the other elements of the reaper.

For a large part of the time while this problem commanded the attention of those engaged in the manufacture of the Virginia Reaper, Cyrus McCormick was away from Walnut Grove. The efforts of those working toward a common end required coördination, and the progress made at the homestead or across the mountains had to be frequently explained by letter. If this were not done, time-consuming and futile ex-

<hr>

[37] *McCormick vs. Manny,* II, pp. 195, 196, 205-208, testimony of W. S. McCormick in 1855. He testified that C. H. McCormick first suggested the raker's seat from Cincinnati. A temporary one was made at Walnut Grove. It was there discovered that the reel was in the way, so it was moved a little forward. "I do not know whether the complainant [Cyrus] had done so when he constructed the machine with a seat or not." This somewhat differs from the contemporary evidence. *Post,* pp. 276 ff.

periments would be duplicated and time was an important factor
in view of the approaching harvest. Nor was it easy to satisfy
the several builders of the McCormick reapers of 1845, who
believed that their plans for adding a raker's seat were unquestionably the best.[38]

To steer a straight course through a maze of conflicting
advice toward a goal which should be reached quickly, made
the task even more difficult. The inventor doubtless felt a sense
of relief on August 9, 1845, when he wrote to his brother
William, from Buffalo, minutely describing the new raker's
seat and other mechanical changes he proposed to make.[39] About
one month later, he still further elaborated the matter in these
words:

I will forward the enclosed drawings of the machine without
further delay, and have written nothing on the sheet which would
prevent its being used in any way (to work from etc.). Now,
after having thought much and indeed laboriously, as you will
readily imagine when you trace my course since the first trial and
failure of the first seat, giving my first ideas of the plan of raking
and desiring the attention of you all to the subject, and again the
result of my first experiment with suggestions and alterations etc.
Although the plan described by you and Leander is such that L.
thinks he could be pleased with nothing else, is certainly worthy of

[38] *Post,* p. 220, ftn. 44.
[39] "McCormick Extension Case, Patent of 1847," pp. 85-96, 107-112, 113-
117: John Magness stated that he made machines in Cincinnati for A. C.
Brown with a raker's seat "fastened to the outside hounds and extending
back to the reel post, with no cross piece to keep the raker secure." This
was in 1845. Then Cyrus McCormick decided in early June that the seat
should be higher so that the raker could work in a more erect position
and have a crosspiece to lean against. He tried this out in Kentucky early
in July, 1845, and then took it to New York. *Ibid.,* pp. 85-90: A. C. Brown
testified that it was in early June, 1845, after the first seat did not work,
that Cyrus McCormick directed him to make a higher seat, extending nearly
over the main driving wheel. This brought the raker nearer to the end of
the reel and gave him a crosspiece to lean against. *McCormick vs. Manny,*
II, pp. 195, 196, testimony of W. S. McCormick.

consideration and deserving credit, and, as you say, is in the operation of raking very much like mine I suppose; still I think the
construction of my last improvement decidedly best. It is now
braced in the strongest possible manner, is simple, the wheels put
out of the way of straw and sand, variations in the height of cutting effected more completely, balance and strength of the machine much improved, and position of the raker as I think better.
These are advantages that strike my mind without a single counterbalancing advantage [disadvantage?].[40]

Notwithstanding his confidence that the best way had been
found, he characteristically refused to hurry his application for
a patent. The success in the harvest of 1845 was confirmed by
further tests during two more seasons and by the testimonials
of many farmers before he was ready to seek protection from
the Government for his invention.[41] As he had waited until
1834 to patent his first reaper, and even longer following the
improvements of 1841,[42] so now for a third time he moved
with a caution which contrasts significantly with his aggressiveness in situations where he had no doubt of the rightness of his
course. But in the harvest when the raker's seat was evolved,
other matters simultaneously demanded his supervision and
tested his ability to control a complex business situation.

By early March, 1845, Cyrus was once more in Cincinnati,
supervising the building of the machines Brown had contracted to make. His first conversation with the manufacturer
cast a shadow over the happy prospects which had seemed so
warranted when he started out on horseback from Walnut
Grove.[43] Brown was far behind with his work, had sublet

[40] C. H. to W. S. McCormick, from Cincinnati, O., Sept. 6, 1845.
[41] "Albany Cultivator," May, 1846, p. 165.
[42] *Post,* Chapter XII.
[43] C. H. McCormick wrote to J. D. Davidson of Lexington, Va., on
Feb. 17, 1845, telling him that he intended to start West "in a few days."
On Mch. 10, 1845, Corbin Braxton wrote to Cyrus at Cincinnati.

rights of manufacture to less competent mechanics, and was disposed to make "improvements" upon the model furnished by McCormick for his guidance.[44] It would be fortunate if one hundred and fifty rather than two hundred Cincinnati machines could be completed in time for the harvest. Notwithstanding this discouragement, Cyrus wrote home with confidence, urging his father and two brothers to make every effort in Virginia, and expressing the hope of his own success in the Ohio Valley:

Bear has written me he will have his 30 machines ready for harvest. . . . McCoy and Son of Wisconsin have written that they will have 15 or 20 machines for harvest, and will execute bonds for the $1000 (for the 4 counties). . . . John Cameron of Iowa offered $1000 for 6 counties, the whole time [of the patent]. . . . I offered 4 choice for 8 years for same and think it *probable* that he may accept it. . . .

Now very extensive publicity will be given to the reaper in all the West, and its salvation in a manner depends upon its success in the next harvest. . . . Instead of my being able to return home it would now be a great thing if Leander could assist in some of these places, which, however, can not be done this season. I know.[45]

McCormick made a hurried trip to Missouri and reported on his return:

I found Mr. Bear behind with his 30 machines. . . . I now only expect him to build 20 . . . which I think will be pretty well done. . . . He has no doubts as to selling them. . . . I have received a letter from Mr. John Cameron accepting my offer. . . . J. M.

[44] As a possible offset to this see "McCormick Extension Case, Patent of 1847," pp. 95, 96, where John Magness testified that "we concluded that Cyrus McCormick had a principle to object to all suggestions, even if he did adopt them afterwards. He did object to any suggestions we made." Magness leaves the impression that he was mainly responsible for the final arrangement of the raker's seat.

[45] C. H. to W. S. McCormick, from Cincinnati, Apr. 2, 1845.

Hite, Jr. has sent in 18 or 20 orders recently from N. Indiana, and many others expected. Mr. B.[rown] sent another smart agt. to Ill. 2 or 3 wks. ago, where many can be sold. No doubt about disposing of all that can yet be made here this year.[46]

In spite of the failure of the raker's seat added at Walnut Grove, Robert and William S. McCormick evidently wrote to Cyrus more glowing accounts of the Eastern sales than were warranted by the actual facts. In early August the inventor was on a packet-boat in the Erie Canal, returning to Cincinnati from Brockport by way of Buffalo, and used his leisure moments to send his brother a summary of the season's business in the West:

I am glad to learn that . . . the machines have succeeded so well in Va. and Md. . . . The Cincinnati business . . . seems not likely to result very well. I have before explained the sort of (indifferent) wood and the sort of contracts Brown had made with *other shops* that I considered both incompetent and indisposed to do good work. . . . Some [of Brown's] machines have been rejected, some finally approved, all defective in some way or other, while the performance generally pleased and often delighted all who saw it.[47] Moreover, in addition to the delay in getting out the machines, the press and confusion consequent thereto, a breach in the Beaver and Cleveland canal caused a further delay, so that the machines for North Indiana (30 or more) would not reach their destination until after the close of the wheat harvest. . . .

[46] C. H. to R. McCormick, May 3, 1845. The number of orders procured by Hite had grown to 25 by May 15. See C. H. to W. S. McCormick on that date, and the "Albany Cultivator" for May, 1845, pp. 181, 182.

[47] "Ohio Cultivator," June 1, 1845, p. 81, Brown had promised to exhibit the McCormick reaper at the Columbus Agricultural Fair on June 25 and 26, but was prevented by delays at the factory. See *ibid.*, July 1, 1845, p. 97; July 15, 1845, p. 108. The editor reported that there were no McCormick reapers around Columbus, although one was tried in Clark County and did not work well, possibly owing to inexperienced operators and poor construction.

Brown . . . still hoped . . . to get them sold on some terms, if successful in getting them to operate well on oats, to those who had ordered and whose orders I hold. . . . Cameron of Iowa is said to be worthless and did not get the machine. . . . You will be surprised when you read that not the first motion was made by Backus, Fitch and Co. [of Brockport, N. Y.] to build a machine! It is even so, and better so than to have built machines as Brown did, I suppose. . . . Without anything like a reasonable excuse . . . B. F. and Co. just neglected the business . . . and without ever giving me any intimation of the same until I reached Brockport, did nothing. Backus was blamed and took the responsibility.[48]

The McCoys in Wisconsin did not fulfil their contract, and McCormick was unable to collect damages. Bear in Missouri built and sold twenty, of which only four performed well, and McCormick received nothing even from the few which succeeded. The Cincinnati business finally yielded him $1,945, paid by a subsequent agreement in which Brown promised to build one hundred reapers for $60 each.[49]

The exact number of McCormick machines in successful use west of the mountains in 1845 cannot be stated with assurance. If Bear of Missouri eventually placed four in the field, and Brown of Cincinnati was behindhand with many of his one hundred and fifty, the total Western output of the season probably did not exceed seventy-five.[50] It was a poor start at the best, especially as so many farmers who had ordered in the spring were disappointed by the failure of their reapers to arrive when their grain was ripe. Doubtless most of the one hundred and fifty Cincinnati reapers were sold in subsequent har-

[48] C. H. to W. S. McCormick, Aug. 6-9, 1845. Salem G. Pattison states in "The McCormick Harvesting Machine Company," pp. 2-4, that 50 of the 150 made by Brown were sold.

[49] C. H. McCormick to E. Burke, Jan. 1, 1848. "Richmond Enquirer," Mch. 19, 1847.

[50] "Prairie Farmer," Oct., 1845, p. 242; Feb., 1846, p. 70. "Richmond Enquirer," Dec. 9, 1845. *Seymour & Morgan vs. McCormick,* pp. 132-137, testimony of Jonathan Read of Williamsburg, N. Y.

vests, but this could not dispel Cyrus McCormick's discouragement as he turned eastward in the early autumn of 1845. He knew that in Missouri fields there were reapers abandoned by farmers who could not make them operate, and that others were stored unsold in Ohio, Illinois, and Indiana at various canal towns because they had reached their destination after the wheat was cut. His springtime vision of four hundred Virginia Reapers at work along the Genesee and on the prairies was rudely shattered.[51]

Furthermore, the situation in the East upon his return was not calculated to restore his hopes. Walnut Grove had manufactured and sold forty-eight reapers, and although Cyrus McCormick publicly declared in the autumn that he had not heard a single complaint,[52] other evidence indicates that public opinion in his native State was swinging back in favor of Hussey's machine. His rival made the most of McCormick's long absences, and found that McCormick reapers so-called, made by Hite, were easy to conquer. Jabez Parker of Richmond, a faithful supporter of Cyrus and an efficient maker of his reapers, was dead, and his son showed no disposition to continue production.[53] Robert McCormick was in poor health,[54] and Leander, who was invaluable in the Walnut Grove blacksmith shop because of his mechanical skill, married in late October and was anxious to settle down upon a farm of his own. To be sure, the monetary return of the season had gone

[51] "Southern Planter," of Jan., 1846, p. 6.

[52] "Richmond Enquirer," Dec. 19, 1845. "Albany Cultivator," May, 1846, p. 165. See also the "Southern Planter" of Jan., 1846, pp. 5, 6, which prints certificates of fifteen farmers praising the machine. Among these is one of Richard Sampson, who later testified in *McCormick vs. Manny*, II, pp. 851-855, that the 1845 reaper did not perform well.

[53] McCormick had purchased back this right of Parker to manufacture for five Virginian counties, save that Parker's son and the son's partner reserved the privilege of selling five reapers in this territory in 1846. "Southern Planter," Jan., 1846, pp. 5, 6.

[54] C. H. to R. McCormick, May 3, 1845.

far toward paying all of the remaining furnace debts, but the net profit fell short by more than one half of the total Mc-Cormick had had reason to expect, even granting that his business rival's figure of $4,615 is accurate.[55]

Cyrus McCormick learned a costly lesson from the disappointments of the 1845 harvest, but more resources than he could then command were required before he could profit from his experience. Neither errors in his plan of campaign nor defects in the principles of his implement could be fairly charged with the collapse of his hopes. His agents had canvassed enough orders, the press had usually been friendly and generous with its space, and self-reproach on the score of lack of energy was unwarranted. The failure of his manufacturers to fulfil their contracts, the poor construction of the machines they had succeeded in building, and the tardiness with which this defective output was placed upon the market, summed up the causes of the season's discontent.

Reaper-building in the chief grain areas of the United States was not enough to persuade farmers to lay aside their cradle-scythes, and dependence upon machine-shops to copy a perfect model faithfully was visionary. Before the McCormick reaper could become as familiar as the plow on every grain-growing farm in the land, it would be necessary to erect a big factory at a spot where grain, transportation facilities, and building materials met, and personally guarantee both the quality of the product and the timeliness of its delivery. Cincinnati, Brockport, or Pittsburgh seemed the appropriate location for such a plant in 1845, but unless Cyrus were willing to put most of the financial control and profits of such an enterprise in the

[55] "McCormick Extension Case, Patent of 1845," section of the book entitled, "In the matter of the Application of C. H. McCormick of Chicago for an extension of his Patent," etc., p. 11. McCormick's opponents naturally exaggerated his yearly income under the 1834 and 1845 patents.

hands of others, such an ambitious project must remain for the time a splendid dream.

The matter of personal supervision of manufacture and harvest tactics was an especial problem during 1845. Cyrus tried from early spring until late summer to guide affairs at Walnut Grove by long letters written from the West. Although Cincinnati is not very far in a straight line from Rockbridge County, Virginia, Walnut Grove was off the main highways of the nation's business, and mail traveled slowly and infrequently. The telegraph, which within a few years would so much help to speed up commerce, had been first tried during the previous summer between Washington and Baltimore, but it would be long before its wires traversed the Valley of Virginia. Walnut Grove is now nearer by mail to San Francisco than it was to Cincinnati in 1845. During the brief harvest-time, rapid and radical revisions of the original plan are often necessary. These can be carried out to-day with a minimum of inconvenience, but in the forties the manufacturer was compelled to stand by helplessly and see machines unsold or competitors gain an unmerited advantage because unlooked-for changes in the weather rendered unwise the original allocation of the reapers.

A few quotations from Cyrus's letters to his family and friends in Virginia will illustrate the manner in which the inventor tried to superintend Eastern business in 1845 in spite of this handicap of distance. Before he started for Cincinnati in February he made arrangements with Corbin Braxton to keep him in touch with the situation along the lower James River. Braxton wrote him in early March to send an extra blade for each of the six old machines in his neighborhood and assured him that his plantation carpenter would add the raker's seat improvement to those reapers if their owners requested it.

I think it would be well to refer persons in the vicinity of Richmond to Mr. Parker for repairs. . . . It is desirable to give satisfaction to all if possible, for now in the infancy of the reaper's existence a few dissatisfied persons might do you serious injury. The next time I go to Richmond I will see Parker. . . . If we are to make alterations . . . they [patterns] must be here in time. . . . The forward wheat bids fair to be in by the middle of May unless it is cut off by frosts.[56]

Early the next month Cyrus sought from his brother information about the Virginia outlook:

If you all knew my uneasiness here by myself for your welfare as well as for the success of the business, you would not delay writing so long, whether you have anything of importance to communicate or not. . . . I hardly think it possible that I can return to Augusta [Walnut Grove] this side of June. I have written to New York proposing to go there. . . . Has Leander gone to Roanoke? I thought he ought to take 3 or 4 there. . . . Then Leander was to go over mountains, round by Fredericksburg, up valley, etc. 2 or 3 suggested neighborhood Harrisonburg. Then I thought you were to make a trip down valley, perhaps South Branch Potomac, Pa., etc. Leander ought to see Middlekauff if he could. . . . Suggested a lot to be taken to Md. Calvin Page, Fredericktown, would interest himself, machine builder. I left some names, I think. Great opposition by day laborers. Care to be taken. . . . [then follows suggestions about exchanging new blades for old ones]. . . Advise Parker to attend all machines below Richmond, for pay, etc. . . . Father thought if well he could go to Roanoke. Sampson and that whole east should be well attended to. . . . Hussey will be in that quarter. It will surely not be necessary to say that no necessary attention should be spared in attending to all points this year, above everything else.[57]

Probably some of his letters to Walnut Grove have been lost, and after April 2, 1845, a month passed before he was

[56] Corbin Braxton to C. H. McCormick, Mch. 10, 1845.
[57] C. H. to W. S. McCormick, Apr. 2, 1845, from Cincinnati. "Middlekauff" was probably Daniel S. Middlekauff of Hagerstown, Md., who patented his own mower on Mch. 14, 1854.

heard from again. This time his father was the person addressed:

William or Leander could attend to the machine in eastern part of State I think in time also to attend in Md. It is so important to have the old machines to perform well that I thought Leander would attend to that—to see as he passed too how many and where blades were wanted as the owners may not always know without examining, etc. I advised to put a machine in every good situation on trial, putting together, explaining and having printed directions, which I think have been sent to you. . . . It would be well at the right time for Wm. and L. to meet in Md. . . . after getting a trial with success there will be plenty of places. I think I gave a list of some names I had spoken to, who agreed to try them, etc. all around F. town, up toward Harp. Ferry, etc. I think two ought to be there on acct. of the heavy wheat, opposition of hands, etc. Hussey will probably be there. . . . It will be important that I should be well advised of first and all trials in Va. that I may know here before harvest. . . . I have given the best advice I could, and must leave the matter with you all to do the best you can.[58]

This is business, not literature. It leaves a picture of the inventor, worried by the Cincinnati situation, trying to make his pen keep pace with his thoughts. He usually wrote like this. During his whole life his letters mirror his restless energy. Business was his usual theme, with sentiment squeezed tight in a last racing paragraph. His letters skip along from one topic to the next, his meaning often conveyed by a series of almost uncoördinated phrases, the details left to the reader's imagina-

[58] C. H. to R. McCormick, May 3, 1845, from Cincinnati. On May 15 he wrote to W. S.: "It would be well for one of you to call on Dr. Braxton if convenient, just to see how machines in his neighborhood are doing, etc. I think it would be better, and perhaps very well, to ship the machines at Norfolk to New York to care of Fuller, Waller and Co., and let me make some arrangement for them if they will do well, which can be tried in old Va. . . . Mr. Hite wished to take a machine into Pa. If you dont like him to do so, ?? but to be careful to take a good one. He is of course to pay a fee."

tion, and the main subjects sketched in with broad strokes. He seemed always to write under pressure, striving to finish before the last mail closed, compressing a maximum of information within a minimum of space by the use of a few key-words, a sort of McCormick shorthand sometimes unintelligible to the reader to-day. And yet when he composed a letter for publication, with the purpose of advertising his reaper or replying to an opponent, the subject was carefully and forcibly presented, with words well chosen, and with lawyer-like attention to the logical development of his argument. Few cared to meet him in such a contest, for he seemed as formidable with his pen as in the harvest field.

Those who knew Cyrus McCormick recall his love of good music and of the old-fashioned flowers which grew in the garden at Walnut Grove. His letters hide this side of his nature, although the death of his father awakened unsuspected emotion, and matters religious always struck a responsive chord. They reveal a strong man with a will to power, wrapped up in his business, firmly believing in the rectitude and importance of his course and in his right to dominate his associates because he had the ability to do so. These letters make clear the long road that the inventor had traveled since the troublous days, four or five years before, when he leaned so heavily for guidance upon his father and William Massie.

The grain area of the United States was too far flung and the harvest arrived at the same moment in too many places, for the stage-coach, horse, or railroad to carry Cyrus McCormick on time to the spot where his supervision was most needed. If he had lived in England, where the harvest moved from the south to the north of a narrow country with some regularity, it might have been satisfactorily managed, but in the United States, with its mighty girth from east to west, simultaneous wheat-cutting on a thousand-mile front was far too stupendous for the personal attention of one man. Nevertheless for two more seasons the inventor sought to control his growing enterprise by long journeys and much correspondence.

CHAPTER X

LAST DAYS AT WALNUT GROVE, 1846-47

IN May, 1846, while the workmen at Walnut Grove were making every effort to finish the season's supply of McCormick reapers in time for the Virginia harvest, President Polk called for volunteers to repel the Mexican "invasion." Public attention was focused upon the Rio Grande. Fifty thousand men, many of them from the farms of the land, were donning uniforms and marching south. This army must be fed, and reapers were needed to replace the soldiers who had hitherto worked in the harvest fields. News from Europe told of bad weather, blight, and short crops, while lower tariffs both at home and abroad encouraged the export of American farm products. Fewer laborers and a greater demand for grain signified a larger market for machines and a higher price for wheat. It is little wonder that Cyrus McCormick counseled his twenty-six-year-old brother Leander to stay by the reaper and not to volunteer for service against the Mexicans.[1]

About four hundred reapers were planned for the 1846 harvest—one hundred by the Brown factory at Cincinnati; two hundred by the two Brockport firms, and perhaps one hundred by the three producers in Virginia. During the autumn of 1845 the inventor once again visited Illinois and found the editor of the "Prairie Farmer" ready to promote any machine that would aid in saving the grain wasted yearly because of the scarcity

[1] *Post*, p. 242.

of labor.[2] In short, pre-season hopes seemed as justifiable as in the spring of 1845. Added confidence could be placed in a reaper which was now "perfected" by the addition of a raker's seat, and in his many advertisements McCormick emphasized this improvement.[3]

In the late winter or early spring of 1846 he left Walnut Grove, to canvass for orders through New York and the West and to push forward the work of his sub-manufacturers.[4] All of his letters written between the time of his departure and the next October are lost. As in the early days, advertisements in newspapers and periodicals, together with testimony given in subsequent lawsuits, necessarily form the chief source material for this harvest. Doubtless the costly lessons of 1845 had been well learned, and he used every precaution during the spring to prevent his lessees from again breaking faith. But now, when both McCormick and the farmers wished large crops in order to profit from the European shortage and the war demand, scab, rust, and Hessian fly ruined much of the Eastern wheat.[5]

[2] "Prairie Farmer," Nov., 1845, p. 275; Jan., 1846, p. 22. The editor complains of the few agricultural machines for sale in the West. There is not a horse-rake, a straw-cutter, or a corn-crusher on the market. *Ibid.*, Feb., 1846, pp. 69, 70: "We may add that from the great number of enquiries made at our office this winter, some machine or machines to out grain will be in great demand in the Western States for a few years to come, and those who wish to make sales will do well to be on hand."

[3] "Southern Planter," Jan., 1846, pp. 5-8. "Richmond Enquirer," Dec. 19, 1845. McCormick believed that his raker's seat improvement would make at least $30 difference in the cost of the average harvest. One man could be replaced by a boy, and since the machine could go faster, two or three acres more than formerly could be reaped in a day.

[4] He was at Walnut Grove as late as Feb. 3, 1846, for on that day he made a settlement with his father for all reapers sold from Robert's shops since 1840. *McCormick vs. Manny*, II, pp. 198, 284.

[5] "American Farmer," July, 1846, p. 30. Scab was thought to be more serious in some sections than in any year since 1814, but the Pennsylvania wheat was generally good.

Nor did his contracts, as a whole, turn out much more satisfactorily than in the preceding year. After the season was over, the "Ohio Cultivator" challenged its readers, "If any farmer in Ohio used it [the McCormick reaper] successfully the past year, we should like to be informed of it." [6] The full implication of this inquiry was undeserved, but Brown had once more failed to build machines well enough to give universal satisfaction. Cyrus McCormick felt that his reapers must be made at Cincinnati, and as Brown had the only shop adequate for the purpose, he could not be lightly dropped because of his poor workmanship for the past two seasons.[7] Leander must be induced to come to Cincinnati and supervise manufacturing.

Twelve of the reapers made at the home farm arrived too late in the West for the harvest and were stored for sale the next season, while the other sixty or more constructed there, fell even below the standard of 1845.[8] Robert McCormick was bedridden from about May 1 until his death nine weeks later, and William and Leander sorely missed his expert direction in the shop. As late as 1848, Cyrus was still owed the fifteen-dollar patent fee on each machine which had been made and sold at Walnut Grove in 1846.[9] Obed Hussey rejoiced at his rival's

[6] "Ohio Cultivator," Feb. 15, 1847, p. 29.
[7] McCormick sold A. C. Brown on May 15, 1845, for $1,900, the right to supply reapers to sixteen Ohio counties for four years from Aug. 1, 1845. Brown should pay the first of three equal instalments on Sept. 1, 1846. On Oct. 13, 1846, Cyrus wrote to W. S. McCormick that he had not heard from Brown and doubted that he would receive the whole sum due. See also C. H. to W. S. McCormick, May 15 and Aug. 9, 1845.
[8] C. H. McCormick to E. Burke, Jan. 1, 1848.
[9] *Ibid.* W. S. McCormick made a Southern trip in a vain endeavor to restore the popularity of the reaper in North Carolina. See his letter to W. A. Braxton, Feb. 5, 1859, L.P.C.B., No. 18, p. 238. "Southern Planter," July, 1846, pp. 150 ff. "Ohio Cultivator," Apr. 15, 1848, p. 64. "American Farmer," Sept., 1846, Supplement. In some manner a McCormick reaper found its way to an agricultural school in Georgia before the season was over and was probably the first implement of its kind to work in that State. "Southern Cultivator," Mch., 1848, p. 41.

discomfiture in the East. McCormick's agent, the editor of the "Southern Planter," after unctuously informing his subscribers that "it is very painful to be compelled to inflict a private injury in the discharge of a public duty," added that since Virginia planters had spent $15,000 for reapers during the recent harvest, he must tell them that the McCormick machine had caused much complaint.[10]

Genesee Valley grain particularly suffered from the blight. Backus, Fitch & Co., of Brockport, made one hundred reapers for the New York market, and sold thirty. Cyrus McCormick blamed this poor showing upon the short crop, prejudice among the farmers, and "some bad sickles." [11] Later testimony reveals that the dividers were at fault, and a few machines were returned to the factory in order that this defect might be corrected.[12] Even by 1848, McCormick had gained no financial return from this contract, save that he took twenty-three of the unsold reapers to Indiana in 1847 and disposed of them there.[13]

Seymour, Chappell & Co. (Seymour, Morgan & Co.), also of Brockport, alone did well in this harvest.[14] Most of the hundred machines they manufactured for the prairie market were taken, by steamboat, from Buffalo to Chicago, where at least

[10] C. H. McCormick to E. Burke, Jan. 1, 1848. The inventor writes that 15 of the 75 Walnut Grove reapers were still unsold, and that others had been released for reduced prices. "Southern Planter," Jan., 1846, pp. 5-8. "Richmond Enquirer," Jan. 16, 1846. Tutwiler and Hite still constructed a few reapers for 1846. "Albany Cultivator," May, 1846, pp. 161, 165. "Genesee Farmer," Apr., 1846, pp. 91, 100.

[11] *McCormick vs. Manny,* II, pp. 409, 411, testimony of Jeremiah Sheppard and Geo. Barnett. "McCormick Extension Case, Patent of 1845," p. 17. Jos. Ganson stated that when McCormick closed the Backus, Fitch & Co. contract in 1845, he told him (Ganson) that he owned slaves and was worth between $8,000 and $12,000.

[12] *Seymour & Morgan vs. McCormick,* pp. 37, 40.

[13] C. H. McCormick to E. Burke, Jan. 1, 1848. C. H. to W. S. McCormick, Oct. 13 and Nov. 15, 1846.

[14] "McCormick Extension Case, Patent of 1845," pp. 14-16, testimony of Ansel Chappell. C. H. McCormick to E. Burke, Jan. 1, 1848.

ninety of them were sold by Cyrus McCormick.[15] These reapers gave general satisfaction, and the inventor was pleased to discover that the Western farmer paid his bills as promptly as did his neighbors in the East, in spite of the common report to the contrary.[16] The evident surprise with which McCormick informed his brother of this fact unconsciously reveals the provincialism the Virginian was shaking off as his experience broadened.

Although the harvest had not fulfilled the hopes of the inventor, the Western press indicates for the first time that prairie farmers were awakening to the possibilities of machine harvesting. The twenty-seven hundred cradles made and sold by Charles M. Warner of Chicago during this harvest [17] loom very large beside the ninety McCormick reapers distributed through the same sales territory. Nevertheless both the "Prairie Farmer" and the "Ohio Cultivator," the two most influential agricultural papers of the West, concur concerning the extraordinary interest in reapers which had been aroused. The editor of the former magazine wrote in his September, 1846, issue:

We have received an incredible number of letters during the present season, asking questions about Harvesting Machines; and the conversations we have had with farmers from the country,

[15] "Prairie Farmer," Aug., 1846, p. 262. The editor remarks that about thirty McCormick reapers were landed at Chicago wharves early in July. They were snatched up at once and many would-be purchasers were disappointed. *Ibid.*, Sept., 1846, p. 285. Many McCormick reapers were used here this season and they gave a "good degree of satisfaction." No farmer should purchase, however, who has not at least fifty acres of grain. "Ohio Cultivator," Oct. 1, 1846, p. 147; Apr. 15, 1847, p. 64. "Chicago Daily Journal," July 2, 24, 28, 30, and Aug. 15, 1846. Most of the 90 machines were sold in Kendall, Du Page, and La Salle counties, Ill. "Chicago Daily Democrat," June 30, 1847; Oct. 13, 19, 1848. "Richmond Enquirer," Mch. 19, 1847.

[16] C. H. to W. S. McCormick, Oct. 13, 1846.

[17] This is the number given by Cyrus McCormick in his letter of Feb. 8, 1847, published in the "Richmond Enquirer" of Mch. 19, 1847.

show that there exists quite a fever of excitement on the subject. The number of new patents, too, offered for sale, show that invention is on the alert to supply the demand. All this is well within certain bounds. But there is danger here, as on all similar subjects, that the farmer especially may be too eager. It becomes him not to forget the days of Rohan potatoes, Morus Multicaulis, and Berkshire pigs; but while he keeps an eye out for real improvements to beware of getting crazy, even about a good thing.[18]

This was a new rôle for an agricultural editor. His customary problem had been to prod conservative farmers to adopt improved methods.

Some wheat-growers saw clearly the significance of the reaper in their occupation. "For my own part," exclaimed H. E. Towner of Will County, Illinois, in July, 1846, "I consider it [the McCormick reaper] to the Western country the most important invention of the age, and that it will greatly increase the product of the country, not being able without it to reap so much as can be sown." [19] Nor was such praise confined to the farmer who had used the reaper. In the same month of July, 1846, the editor of the "Chicago Daily Journal" stated that the McCormick machine "will cut from 15 to 20 acres per day, which is as decided an advance upon the old method of 'cradling' as the Magnetic Telegraph is on steam. These machines are highly useful in this State, where the harvest is large, while the means of saving it is disproportionally small." [20]

Because Cyrus McCormick doubtless read more complimentary notices about his machine in Illinois during the harvest

---

[18] "Prairie Farmer," Sept., 1846, p. 284. "Scientific American," Oct. 31, 1846, p. 421.

[19] "Chicago Daily Democrat," June 30, 1847.

[20] "Chicago Daily Journal," May 20, and July 2, 1846: Writing of the Darling harvester, the editor remarked, "Here is a field for their operations where in many cases hundreds, nay thousands, of acres are enclosed by one fence, forming a campania of waving grain the like of which one may search the rest of the world in vain to find."

of 1846 than at any previous time in his career, it is small wonder that he at once made arrangements with C. M. Gray and S. R. Warner of Chicago to build one hundred reapers for three counties of that State for the next harvest, and also sold to D. J. Townsend of Au Sable Grove, Illinois, the right to supply four counties in his vicinity.[21] It was shrewd business to occupy Mr. Gray with reaper-building so that he could not devote so much attention to the manufacture of grain cradles. McCormick's contracts with Brockport firms were equally ambitious. Seymour, Chappell & Co., and Fitch, Barry & Co. were to construct reapers for the Illinois market,[22] and Leander was expected to teach the Cincinnati workmen how to make one hundred good machines. Hussey had arranged for Minturn & Allen to build his reapers at Urbana, Ohio, but Brown at Cincinnati should be able to check McCormick's rival in that State without difficulty.[23]

With these contracts closed by the end of the year, Cyrus turned again toward Walnut Grove, observing with pleasure the fine appearance of the winter wheat along his road.[24] His reaper received a premium over a T. R. Hussey machine at the autumn fair of the New York State Agricultural Society at

[21] *Ibid.*, July 28 and 30, 1846. "Ohio Cultivator," Jan. 15, 1850, p. 31. "Prairie Farmer," Dec., 1846, p. 372, letter of C. H. McCormick, dated at Chicago, Nov. 9, 1846. C. M. Gray was experimenting with a reaper of his own in 1846. See *ibid.*, Mch., 1846, p. 103. "Chicago Daily Democrat," June 30, 1847, Oct. 13, 19, 1848. For the terms of the contract with Gray & Warner, see *post*, pp. 306, 307.

[22] C. H. to L. J. McCormick, from Cincinnati, Jan. 8, 1847: "Seymour and Co. are going ahead with the 200 and will have them out in good season, and well done, paying me $35 patent fee, and commission for getting the orders, you know, and *they shipping*. No responsibility on our part."

[23] Minturn & Allen possibly made no Hussey machines for the 1847 harvest. See their advertisement in the "Ohio Cultivator" of Apr. 15, 1848, p. 64.

[24] C. H. to W. S. McCormick, Oct. 13, 1846. Wheat was selling at $1.05 to $1.20 per bushel in Dec., 1846. "American Agriculturist," V, p. 383.

Robert McCormick

Auburn.[25] Horace Greeley, the champion of the farmer, commended McCormick's implement, in the "New York Tribune,[26] and henceforward was the inventor's friend, although the two men radically disagreed on questions of politics and slavery.

The year had been an especially arduous one for Cyrus McCormick. So far as is known, he was away from Walnut Grove for the twelve months following January, 1846, and during this period crossed and recrossed the country between Chicago, Cincinnati, and Brockport several times. Besides the constant worries occasioned by the faulty construction of his reapers and by the failure of the wheat crop in the Genesee Valley, a skin infection forced him to seek the healing waters of Avon Springs, New York, in the early autumn.[27] Here he learned to love the lake region of that State, and in later years sought it almost annually for his vacations.

But the death of Robert McCormick on July 4, 1846, overshadowed all else in his son's mind during the harvest. The

[25] *Ibid.*, V (1846), p. 308: The editor did not see anything new or worthy of record at the fair "except a flaxpuller." *Ibid.*, V, pp. 357, 358. It is interesting to note that although the reaper premium was $5, an Oneida County farmer was awarded $25 for a butter display, and Nicholas Longworth of Cincinnati received a loving-cup and $10 for an exhibit of ladies' wine. "Genesee Farmer," Oct., 1846, p. 238. "Ohio Cultivator," Apr. 15, 1847, p. 64. "Transactions of the New York State Agricultural Society" (Albany), VI (1846), p. 97.

[26] In the "New York Tribune" for Sept. 19, 1846, p. 2, Greeley wrote: "Mental indolence is the chief danger of the Farmer's condition. It is possible to exist in his vocation with very little thought. . . . The Farmer is in danger of falling into the habit of doing just as his father did, and for the reason that his father did it. . . . The moral of the Fair is *Improvement*. . . . One such Fair as this is worth more to the People of a State than a dozen 'glorious victories' in the field of human slaughter."

[27] On Oct. 13, 1846, Cyrus McCormick wrote to William S. that he had been at Avon Springs for twenty-three days. He had written to his brother as early as May 15, 1845, "I have been greatly troubled at times by the disease of my skin—have been taking the warm bath, and washing with salt and water for awhile—think it promises to relieve me soon with a little medicine."

father had ever been Cyrus's best friend and counselor, and the two men had worked together in close companionship for at least fifteen years. Inspired by the same purpose, they toiled side by side in field and shop. Victory and defeat were mutually shared, and each found in his association with the other a sympathy which made them more than business partners, and even more than father and son.

Cyrus McCormick, for the first time in his life, experienced a great personal loss—a sense of aloneness, as well as sorrow, that occasionally impelled him to throw aside the mask of business behind which he customarily hid, and to reveal a capacity for affection and deep feeling unsuspected save by his few close friends. As he wrote of his reaper and his plans for the next harvest, to his brother William in the late summer of 1846, memories of his father often arose to crowd out all other thoughts:

I often wonder whether you who have been present throughout the illness and at the death of our *lost* father, could have been and continue to be so deeply affected by it as I have. I should think not, as in all my reflections, it seems but a little while since I saw him and left him well,—and my returning and not again meeting him often shocks me.[28]

From the winter's night when Robert McCormick, inadequately clothed, rushed from the house to extinguish a fire in one of his shops, until his death about five months later, Dr. Estel and the Rev. James Morrison called frequently at Walnut Grove.[29] Although he had mastered a severe cold before Cyrus McCormick left for the West in late February or early March,

[28] C. H. to W. S. McCormick, from Schoolcraft, Prairie Roads, Mich., Nov. 15, 1846. Cyrus continued: "I hope we shall meet before very long and have an opportunity of talking and sympathizing with each other. . . . I see a great deal of profanity and infidelity in this country, enough to make the heart sick." See also C. H. to W. S. McCormick, Oct. 13 and Dec. 11, 1846.

[29] L. J. McCormick, pp. 340, 341, statement of Mary Caroline Shields.

1846, the effort had sapped his strength, and other more serious ills quickly followed. After stubbornly driving himself to his daily work during the early spring, by May he was no longer able to resist the advice of his physician. Almost two months of hope and despair ensued, with the pastor sending to Robert's anxious son in the West such comfort as the desperate situation permitted:

You well know that every attention that human kindness can bestow he receives. Every member of his kind family takes pleasure in doing everything they can for his comfort. . . . He is calm, composed . . . perfectly resigned to the will of God. You well know that he is well instructed in the truths of the Bible. . . . I have discovered no fear of death in him. . . . God has indeed been very kind to you. Your privileges have been very great. You have had parents such as are equalled by few.[30]

To a people so secure in their faith, the text of the funeral sermon preached by the Rev. James Morrison, "The righteous hath hope in his death," was the highest tribute that could be paid to an old neighbor. The service was soon over, as the graveyard of Old Providence was just outside the church door.[31]

By the time Cyrus McCormick arrived home in early February, 1847, Leander was about ready to set out for Cincinnati, to supervise the building of reapers at A. C. Brown's factory.

[30] The Rev. James Morrison to C. H. McCormick, May 30, 1846. Cyrus McCormick wrote to his brother William on Oct. 13, 1846: "It is probable our dear father fell a victim to his great anxiety for us all and consequent want of sufficient care and prudence, of which I was often much afraid and warned him. I have also queried whether the increase of medicine last advised and given him by Dr. Estel did not hurry his death; still it was the will of the Lord, and as well as for his own good, was I hope designedly to be sanctified to the good of us all by weaning us from the world and fixing our thoughts more upon the world to come . . . that we may lay up treasures in heaven."

[31] L. J. McCormick, pp. 340, 351. "Staunton Spectator," July 23, 1846. Proverbs, xiv, 32. Robert had rejoined Old Providence in 1836.

For two years Cyrus had endeavored to persuade him to leave
Rockbridge County and be his partner in charge of reaper-
manufacturing either at Cincinnati or Brockport. Even the elder
brother's promise in August, 1845, that Leander would have
"regular and *good* Presbyterian preaching [at Brockport] and
he would see Niagara Falls" did not stir him.[32] Leander Mc-
Cormick's unwillingness to leave the Valley at this time is
sufficiently explained by his marriage to the daughter of a
prosperous landowner of the neighborhood.[33] Following that
event, he purchased the South River farm of over five hundred
acres from Cyrus McCormick,[34] and seemed far more disposed
to settle down as a gentleman farmer than to cross the mountains and "go into trade." After helping with the building of
seventy-five machines at Walnut Grove in 1846—probably directing the work because of the illness of his father and the
absence of Cyrus—he and his bride moved from Walnut Grove
to their new home.[35] The inventor continued to urge him to
oversee reaper-building in the West, but as late as December
of that year Leander hesitated to accept. On the eleventh of that
month Cyrus wrote to William:

I . . . have come to the conclusion that 100 or 150 Reapers
should be made at Cincinn. or some other point in the West, 100
at least, and I think a favorable arrangement can be made at A. C.
Brown's shop, as I think there will be sufficient room, and being in
debt to me I think an arrangement can be made; and if so I should

[32] C. H. to W. S. McCormick, Aug. 9, 1845.
[33] Leander married Henrietta Hamilton at Locust Hill, Va., Oct. 22,
1845. They had first met in May of that year, when she was a bridesmaid at
the wedding of Leander's Sister, Amanda. "Memorial," p. 16. C. H. to
W. S. McCormick, May 3, 15 and Sept. 6, 1845. Cyrus was much pleased
with Leander's choice.
[34] Rockbridge County Records, Deed Book, "Z," p. 29. Deed of C. H. Mc-
Cormick to L. J. McCormick, Jan. 26, 1846. Cyrus sold to his brother 573¼
acres of land in Rockbridge County for $5,500 cash. *Supra*, p. 147, ftn. 78.
[35] This was on Aug. 10, 1846. "Chicago Tribune," Feb. 21, 1900.

like to get an arrangement for Leander to come out and attend to the business, as you and he do not seem inclined to unite, and as one shop I should think sufficient to do the business of that direction. It seems wrong to pay $20 or $25 freight . . . when they might be made in the west—considering too the greater uncertainty of shipping, and I will give Leander such wages or such an interest in the business, one way or the other, as will present an inducement to come; and you can go ahead and supply the home demand—and they should be sent into Pa. . . .[36]

Finally, in January, when Cyrus was in Cincinnati starting A. C. Brown on the season's building, Leander agreed to come to that city "if the inducements should be sufficient." [37]

In accordance with the McCormick-Brown contract of January, 1847, Cyrus proposed that his brother should be a one-third partner in the venture of making one hundred or more machines. Leander was to raise from $1,000 to $1,500 in Virginia before he reported for duty at the factory on February 15, and, if all went well, a clear profit of about $1,550 on his investment was in prospect. This sum included a weekly wage of $15 for supervising reaper construction at Cincinnati and attending the harvest in the Ohio Valley. He was empowered to

[36] As early as Oct. 13, 1846, Cyrus had written to W. S. about the building program for 1847. He stated that he needed 100 or 150 reapers for the "southwestern demand" and would like to unite with his two brothers in making these. They could build and he would pay them a cash price for all they made, or else he was willing to be a one-third or one-half partner with them, as they preferred. If such an agreement could be reached, he would not look further for manufacturers along the Ohio River, since that territory could be supplied from Walnut Grove. On Nov. 15 he again wrote William, emphasizing that he did not wish to appear to urge his brothers to join with him, for if they did not care to do so he could make other arrangements, even more profitable to himself. In the latter case they could continue to build at the homestead for the Southeastern market, including Maryland and Pennsylvania. "We will not differ as to terms." Leander could supervise building, while William could manage the office and sales.
[37] C. H. to L. J. McCormick, from a steamboat in the Ohio River, Jan. 8-18, 1847.

discharge and employ laborers, reject bad materials, and correct
defects in workmanship. Brown promised to have the reapers
ready for shipment by May 15, and Cyrus McCormick hoped
that his brother would consent to spend at least six weeks
among the farmers of the West, putting the machines in
operation.

I presume that this will be to you a desirable little enterprise
and possibly as honourable, more profitable and every way a more
justifiable separation from *Henrietta* (if so by the bye) than to go
to Mexico to be shot *at,* if not shot down—not *faulting* that either,
in those who have a taste for that particular sport.

In the early spring of 1847, Cyrus McCormick once again
left Walnut Grove for the West. Since he delayed in Washington for several weeks in order to prepare drawings and a
model to accompany his application for a patent on his raker's
seat, he did not reach Cincinnati until April.[38] Here he in-
augurated a campaign of advertisement, spurred on his agents,
and conferred with A. C. Brown and Leander McCormick on
matters of business.[39] Soon he was on his way North to urge
forward the work of his two sub-manufacturers in Brockport,
New York. Publicity was given to the reaper in the Mohawk
Valley, and the editor of the "Genesee Farmer," "without the
knowledge or solicitation of any one," recommended its use
to his subscribers.[40] Far out in Chicago, Gray & Warner had

[38] The patent-application was filed by C. H. McCormick at Washington
on Apr. 3, 1847. He wrote from that city on Mch. 19, 1847, to Seymour,
Chappell & Co., telling them to prod their agents, and planning for 1848.
This letter is in the "Farm Implement News" (Chicago), Vol. XXIII,
1902, pt. 1. "Richmond Enquirer," Mch. 19, 1847. C. H. to W. S. Mc-
Cormick, Mch. 31, 1847.
[39] "Ohio Cultivator," Apr. 15, 1847, pp. 57, 64. In this issue, as well as
in a letter to Leander on Jan. 8, 1847, he mentions 600 handbills and 150
order blanks he had prepared for distribution.
[40] "Genesee Farmer," June, 1847, p. 140. "Monthly Journal of Agriculture," June, 1847.

already announced in the "Prairie Farmer" that they would
have one hundred McCormick machines ready for the northern
Illinois harvest, and D. J. Townsend of Kendall County in the
same State was constructing forty or more for the use of his
own neighbors.[41] Forecasts of a bountiful harvest gave warrant
for this ambitious program.

The demand for the reaper exceeded the expectations of the
builders. The Illinois output was too small, while Seymour,
Chappell & Co. of Brockport learned that the two hundred
and fifteen which they forwarded to the West were not suf-
ficient to meet the requirements of the market. Fitch, Barry &
Co. of the same town sold about twenty-five in New York
State [42] and J. M. Hite found a few purchasers along the
Potomac.[43] Despite Leander's supervision of manufacturing at
Cincinnati, the one hundred Brown-McCormick machines
caused some complaint and twelve or fifteen of them remained
unsold, while others were released at reduced prices.[44] Cyrus
McCormick spent most of the harvest in the Wabash Valley,

[41] "Prairie Farmer," Feb., 1847, p. 71. "Chicago Daily Democrat," June
30, 1847.

[42] Pattison, II, a, C. H. McCormick to E. Burke, Jan. 1, 1848. "Genesee
Farmer," Nov., 1847, p. 261 ; adv. section, p. 5. "Chicago Weekly Journal,"
Sept. 6, 1847, letter of C. H. McCormick of Sept. 1. He asserts that of
the 213 reapers made at Brockport and sold in the West, all save one
gave satisfaction and all but a very few had been paid for. This was true
in spite of the failure of the winter wheat crop. "Chicago Daily Democrat," Oct. 13, 19, 1848.

[43] Pattison, Sec. IX, letter of Cuthbert Powell to J. M. Hite, June 12,
1847. Contrast the favorable notices of the McCormick reapers in the
West and New York, as given above, with the caustic letters of Josiah
Collins, of Washington County, N. C., and of T. D. Warren, of Edenton,
N. C., in the "American Farmer," of Oct., 1847, p. 104, and Mch., 1848,
p. 284.

[44] Pattison, II, a, letter of C. H. McCormick to E. Burke, Jan. 1, 1848.
McCormick believed that his net profits from the Brown contract would
not exceed $1,500.

although he also found the time to visit the wheat lands of Wisconsin.[45]

While Leander was busy at Cincinnati in 1847, William McCormick, who was now left alone at the Walnut Grove factory, joined with his elder brother in building a few reapers there for the Eastern market.[46] The pressure of farm work, the absence of his brothers, and William's own lack of mechanical talent, combined to render unsalable the thirty-five machines finally completed.[47] These were the last reapers produced in the blacksmith shop, and the old forge and anvil once more assumed the humbler rôles from which they had been elevated in 1831. This birthplace of the McCormick reaper stands to-day, and the visitor wonders how such limited facilities could have permitted the building of fifty or seventy-five machines annually for a number of harvests in the mid-forties. William McCormick continued to farm on the old homestead and to dispose of Cotopaxi iron and rejected reapers until he was summoned in 1850 to Chicago to assist his brother at the reaper factory in that city.

Over five hundred more McCormick reapers had been placed on the farms of the United States during the harvest of 1847. The failure of the home-built machines was the only serious check the inventor experienced, and he could look back upon the season as the most satisfactory of his career up to that time. The news of his invention had reached the western boundary of the Union and almost $9,000 in profits was a most gratifying evidence of his success.[48] Wheat sold for about $1.20 a

[45] "Chicago Weekly Journal," Sept. 6, 1847. "Genesee Farmer," Nov., 1847, p. 261. "Ohio Cultivator," Sept. 1, 1847, pp. 129, 130. "Prairie Farmer," Nov., 1847, p. 357; Feb., 1848, p. 43; Sept., 1847, p. 281.
[46] "Richmond Enquirer," Mch. 19, 1847, letter of C. H. McCormick.
[47] C. H. McCormick to E. Burke, Jan. 1, 1848.
[48] "McCormick Extension Case, Patent of 1845," section of the volume entitled, "In the Matter of the Application of Cyrus H. McCormick of Chicago for an extension of his patent dated January 31, 1845," etc., p. 11.

bushel in March and April, and at that time there were 700,000 bushels in Chicago warehouses awaiting the opening of lake navigation for shipment east. On March 22, Milwaukee dealers had 160,000 bushels in store and the amount was increasing 1,500 to 2,000 bushels daily.[49] At the close of the year the Commissioner of Patents estimated that the grain crop of the country had been worth about $205,000,000, notwithstanding the blight and considerable winter-killed wheat.[50] Editors of agricultural papers generally favored the McCormick reaper and sought to convince the farmers that its use would solve their labor problem without yoking them in bondage to capital. The hired man was assured that machinery was not his enemy, and that his fear of unemployment was groundless.[51]

Glorious news from the armies in Mexico added to the dominant optimism in 1847, and even the busy Cyrus McCormick found time while in Washington on patent business to add a postscript to a letter to his brother relaying to him the news of Taylor's victory at Buena Vista.[52] Abraham Lincoln, an obscure member of the House of Representatives, and

Here McCormick's rivals contend that he cleared $4,615 in 1845; $7,625 in 1846, and $10,455 in 1847. Comparing the last amount with the inventor's own statement in his letter to E. Burke, Jan. 1, 1848 (Pattison, II, a.), and with the contracts made by him for 1847, it would seem that $9,000 is a more accurate figure for that harvest.

[49] "N. Y. Farmer and Mechanic," May 6, 1847, p. 228; Apr. 15, 1847, p. 192.

[50] "American Agriculturist," Jan., 1848, p. 1; June, 1848, p. 221.

[51] The editors of the "Southern Planter" and the "Ohio Cultivator" were McCormick agents and the "Genesee Farmer" and the "Prairie Farmer" were favorably disposed, although the editor of the latter was soon to be an enemy. The "American Farmer" of Baltimore, and the "Albany Cultivator," were the only two farm papers of note which praised Hussey's reapers with the apparent intention of injuring McCormick's sales. "Ohio Cultivator," Sept. 1, 1847, p. 130: "The greatest amount of labor that can be done with the smallest number of hands, will give the greatest product to be divided between employer and employed. . . . Savages alone live without machinery."

[52] C. H. to W. S. McCormick, from Washington, D. C., Mch. 31, 1847. The battle was fought on Feb. 22, 23, 1847.

a few other Congressmen equally hard to please, were determined to worry the administration with their "spot" resolutions, but all in all it was a wonderful year for soldier, politician, and business man.

When Cyrus McCormick again reached his native county in mid-December, for a brief period of relaxation, he must have realized that this was the last winter when he could call Walnut Grove his home.[53] He had made a partnership agreement with Charles M. Gray of Chicago early in the autumn which probably meant a permanent removal of his residence to the West.[54] The homestead had greatly changed since the spring of 1844 when he first left it, to introduce his reaper to the prairies. At that time the farm was pledged as security for the iron-furnace debt, and Robert McCormick, assisted by Leander and William, were building a few reapers for Cyrus to market. By 1847 the McCormicks were debt-free, Robert was dead, Leander, Mary Caroline, and Amanda married, and Walnut Grove was now the property of William McCormick, who purposed to make a home there for his mother during the rest of her life.[55] The blacksmith shop had outlived its usefulness and its presiding genii were gone. It remains a monument to the McCormick reaper and a symbol of the rapidity with which business grew in America when machinery was introduced to speed up the work of production.

[53] John P. McCormick to Wm. Massie, Dec. 18, 1847.
[54] For the contract with Gray see the next chapter. "Chicago Weekly Journal," Sept. 6, 1847.
[55] The farm routine at Walnut Grove at this time is the subject of letters from W. S. McCormick to Wm. Massie, Jan. 30, Feb. 10, Mch. 27, July 25, and Aug. 9, 1849. W. S. was hiring and buying negroes, exchanging rye for seed wheat, and paying a doctor for Elixir Vitriol for his wife. L. J. McCormick, pp. 302, 326, 327, 314, 315. Mary Caroline McCormick married the Rev. James Shields on May 11, 1847, and W. S. McCormick married Mary Ann Grigsby on July 11, 1848. Mr. and Mrs. Shields soon moved to Mexico, Pa.

The harvest of 1847 closes the preparatory period in the history of the McCormick reaper. Over one thousand machines were then working on as many farms, in almost every State of the North and West. Less than three years later the editor of the "Prairie Farmer" listed fifteen different inventors and manufacturers of reapers, mostly in Illinois.[56] He judged that "the work, so far as success is concerned, is accomplished," and that within five years "very little [wheat] will be cut otherwise [than by machinery] on the smooth lands of the West."

While Congress was listening to the supporters of a Homestead Bill voice their land hunger in verse—

> The land is the gift of a bounteous God,
>   And to labor his word commands;
> Yet millions of hands want acres,
>   While millions of acres want hands.
>
> * * *
>
> Who hath ordained that a parchment scroll,
>   Should fence round miles of lands? etc.,[57]

a rustic poet of the West was moved by the new order of things to write:

> But hark! the rattling "Reaper,"
>   Here it comes, with noisy din,
> And the grain shrinks before it
>   Like good intentions before sin.
> One rides upon the "Reaper,"
>   Waving oft the reaper's wand,
> And every pass he makes
>   Lays a sheaf upon the land; . . .
> O band of strong cradlers, with regular sweep,
> Your vocation is gone!—'tis the "Reaper" must reap![58]

[56] "Prairie Farmer," Jan., 1850, p. 30.
[57] "Congressional Globe," 32d Cong., 1st Sess., May 10, 1852, p. 1319.
[58] "Michigan Farmer," Sept., 1850, p. 297.

Here were cause and effect working hand in hand at Washington and the West.[59] The country was growing, and the settler pressed for free land and railroads in some measure because he now had the tools with which to gather large harvests of grain.

With such forces at work, it was high time for Cyrus McCormick to change his base of operations from Walnut Grove to the West and concentrate production in one spot where he could closely supervise it. He had served a long and valuable apprenticeship in the harvest fields, and could now bring an unrivaled knowledge of actual field conditions to the business of manufacturing. Costly experience with reapers poorly made by sub-manufacturers made such a centralization of output advisable, and the small amount of money he had saved permitted its realization. If his original patent of 1834 were not renewed in 1848, profitable manufacturing agreements could no longer be made with other firms.[60] With his own factory, the inventor could produce a good reaper at a cost of $50, and sell

[59] Another rhymester in the "Ohio Cultivator" for Feb. 1, 1853, p. 39, wrote:

> Our father's sickles long have hung,
>   Unthought of in the loft,
> And soon the cradles that they swung,
>   And boasted of so oft,
> We'll hang there too, without remorse,
>   As relics, and we'll show,
> How fast, and well, the noble horse,
>   Can reap for us and mow.

[60] U. S. Patent Office Records, "McCormick Extension Case, Patent of 1847." Paper No. 4. Statement of C. H. McCormick, under oath, Dec. 7, 1858: "After this invention [1845] was made, I soon discovered that the difficulties of enforcing my rights under it against infringers were so great, that I was endangered of losing all benefit whatever from my invention, besides incurring losses in prosecuting infringers. I then determined to go into the manufacture of reaping machines myself. For this purpose I set up a factory at Chicago, Illinois, and the result has proved that but for it I should have been entirely ruined by the expense of litigating my patents."

it for more than twice that amount.[61] The situation at Walnut Grove, the approaching expiration of his 1834 patent, the poor workmanship of many who had hitherto built his reapers, the rapid increase in population, transportation facilities, and grain crops, and the hope of making larger profits by the operation of his own factory, combined in 1848 to direct Cyrus McCormick once and for all time to the West.

[61] "McCormick Extension Case, Patent of 1845," adverse testimony, pp. 41, 42, deposition of Harvey A. Blakesley, a bookkeeper of C. H. McCormick & Co., Dec. 25, 1850. He states that profits per machine are estimated at $74, of which $44 goes to the firm and $30 to McCormick as patentee. *Post*, p. 317, ftn. 54; p. 426, ftn. 61.

CHAPTER XI

THE NEW HOME OF THE McCORMICK REAPER

A LTHOUGH the farewell of Cyrus McCormick to Virginia in 1848 was necessary, the reasons which led him to choose Chicago for the new home of his reaper are not at once apparent. Brockport, Rochester, Pittsburgh, and Cincinnati had seemed desirable to him before this time, and it would have been more in accord with his long expressed preference if he had selected one of these cities for his factory.[1] While he did not spare himself in his work, he always placed great emphasis upon considerations of health. One of his letters in 1846 reveals his belief that Chicago, because of Lake Michigan, did not share the sickly season of late summer with other Western towns.[2]

As manufacturing agreements were continued in 1848 with the two Brockport firms, each consisting of a number of partners, McCormick may have felt that they could supply the Eastern demand, and that they would be unwilling to give him a directing part in the business with the small capital that he had to invest. He always preferred to play a lone hand. To pool his energy and money with associates did not greatly attract

[1] "Richmond Semi-Weekly Whig," Oct. 27, 1843. C. H. to W. S. McCormick, Aug. 9, 1845: "Cincinnati and New York [Brockport] are the two most important points for manufacturing."

[2] C. H. to W. S. McCormick, Nov. 15, 1846. He notes the sickness prevalent in the West, and adds: "It has given me a bad opinion of the western country—to live in. Chicago was much less affected, protected by the lake breezes. I consider it a healthy place for a western place." See also *idem* to *idem*, Dec. 11, 1846.

him. The wheat center of the United States had been just south of Rochester when his reaper was invented, but had recently moved westward very rapidly. New York farms could not compete with the prairie grain output, in quality, quantity, or price. For this reason, combined with the increase of manufacturing in the East, New York farmers were turning more and more to the growth of hay and stock, and needed mowers, but the McCormick machine did not perform well in grass. The inventor found it difficult to sell his machines in the South, and, while Cincinnati was conveniently situated for the supply of Ohio and Kentucky, it was not central for the Middle West. If he located at Cincinnati he would probably find it necessary to unite again with A. C. Brown, who had produced few satisfactory machines since the beginning of business relations with him.

The people of Illinois and Wisconsin had given the reaper a more cordial reception than those of any other section. The farmers of a single county in the latter State had purchased forty in one season. Furthermore, Illinois was an isthmus between the Great Lakes, which could carry machines eastward, and the Mississippi, which could float them to almost any part of the Middle West, far West, and South. The name of Charles M. Gray was well known among farmers and the stamp of his workmanship gave reputation to any commodity. He had made one hundred good reapers in 1847 and was now ready to join McCormick in a still larger building program. Except in the small territory allotted to D. J. Townsend of Kendall County, Illinois, Chicago-made reapers might be marketed throughout the West without invading any other contract. Brockport sales could be confined hereafter to the seaboard States and construction at Cincinnati was discontinued at the close of the 1847 harvest.

When, in 1847, Cyrus McCormick chose Chicago as the home of his reaper, he could not foresee that it was to be the railroad center of the United States, and a grain focus for both the United States and Canada. He did appreciate the water facilities, at a time when the steamboat was his main reliance for transportation. Lacking sufficient capital to be wholly independent in his choice of a factory site, by rare good fortune he had found the right man in the right place and had closed the contract for 1848 with Gray late in the previous summer.

If it is true that Chicago had less than seventeen thousand people in 1847, the next three years witnessed the coming of over ten thousand more. In spite of the food and money raised by its citizens to relieve the starving in Europe,[3] immigrants from Ireland and Germany came in large numbers and real-estate values soared skyward.[4] McCormick reached Chicago at the beginning of its rapid rise to great consequence. William B. Ogden and Stephen A. Douglas, a new-comer in the city, were planning a system of railways and canals which would make Chicago both the gateway of the West and a seaport as well.[5] Before 1850 the Illinois and Michigan Canal was finished and direct water communication was already opened with Liverpool.[6] Railway cars brought the first load of wheat to the harbor-front in 1848,[7] and, for all that the conservative might

[3] "Prairie Farmer," Jan., 1849, p. 39. Alfred T. Andreas, "History of Chicago from the Earliest Period to the Present Time" (3 vols., Chicago, 1885), I, pp. 154 ff.

[4] Ibid., I, p. 183. In 1847, Chicago had a property valuation of $5,849,170; a population of 16,859; a debt of $13,179, and a yearly tax income of $18,159. In 1850 the property value was $7,220,249; debt, $93,395; population, 28,269, and annual income from taxes, $25,270.

[5] Ibid., I, pp. 252, 608, 616, 617.

[6] The first ship, the General Frye, locked through the Illinois and Michigan Canal on Apr. 10, 1848. By the end of June the arrival of the English propeller Ireland signified that Chicago could now freight to Europe without transshipment. Ibid., I, p. 155.

[7] Ibid., I, p. 248. This was on Nov. 20, 1848, on the Galena and Chicago Union R. R., which then extended ten miles from the city to the Des Plaines River. The rolling-stock of the company consisted of one engine and six old freight-cars. During 1849 the road earned $23,763.74, and during 1850,

say to champion plank roads at the expense of iron rails, politics, excess capital, and sound judgment combined to make Chicago a chief beneficiary of the railway boom of the early fifties.[8] By 1847, when Cyrus McCormick concluded his partnership agreement with Gray, the city imported goods worth about $2,225,000 annually and exported commodities valued at slightly over that sum. Among these latter were 1,974,304 bushels of wheat, 32,538 barrels of flour, 48,920 barrels of beef and pork, 411,088 pounds of wool, 60 bales of buffalo robes, and 28,259 pounds of deerskins.[9] The first telegram was received in Chicago in January, 1848, and three months later almost instantaneous communication with the East was possible, thanks to this prerequisite of the age of big business.[10]

Railways and ocean vessels could aid Chicago little unless she kept step with the new industrialism. Bitterly its leading citizens saw President Polk veto the Rivers and Harbors Bill of 1846, providing for an appropriation of money to dredge

now extended to Elgin, $104,359.62. Wm. B. Ogden was president of the board of directors.

[8] Beginnings had been made in 1846 and 1847, on the Alton and Springfield R. R., the Alton and Sangamon, and the Rock Island and LaSalle. In the "Chicago Democrat" of Feb. 16, 1848, it is argued that plank roads are cheaper and safer than railways. The editor noted that 70,000 teams had arrived in Chicago over plank roads during the past year.

[9] Andreas, I, pp. 557-559.

Year	Wheat Exported from Chicago	Price per Bu.
1848	2,160,800 bushels	$ .75
1849	1,936,264	.74
1850	883,644	.83
1851	437,660	.63
1852	635,496	.54
1853	1,206,163	.73
1854	2,306,925	1.20
1855	6,298,155	1.43
1856	8,364,420	1.16
1857	9,846,052	1.05

For somewhat different amounts see the "Prairie Farmer" of Jan., 1849, p. 35.

[10] Andreas, I, p. 263.

an adequate harbor at the mouth of the stream along which their trade centered. In protest, a convention was held in the city in July, 1847, to remind the President that the Middle West should be brought within the scope of his policy, and that his political party included many Democrats who did not live in the South.[11] A Chicago Board of Trade was organized,[12] and Douglas and Ogden were relied upon to secure the federal aid and the funds necessary to join the city, by rail, in happy economic and political union with the Gulf of Mexico and the far West. Bridge after bridge was thrown across the Chicago River, and distressing was the disaster when a tremendous wall of ice and water swept down the stream in 1849 and in the twinkling of an eye destroyed the work of years.[13]

At this time the Chicago River and the streets and drinking water of the city were menaces to health. Smallpox and cholera epidemics took heavy toll between 1847 and 1850.[14] Despite the new county hospital, the Rush Medical College, and the Alms House, accommodations for the sick were less than adequate. As early as 1845 it was noted that the tideless, sluggish stream was unsightly and malodorous because of the refuse from the rising packing-houses along its banks.[15] Vaccination could hardly be a sufficient shield against all disease when the Hy-

[11] *Ibid.,* I, pp. 235-238, 242. Men from eighteen States were present during the three-day session. Chicago received no adequate aid from the United States for harbor-development until 1852. In 1847-48, Congress voted money for a lighthouse and a marine hospital. In 1847 the citizens owned 19 schooners, 1 propeller, and 1 brig.

[12] *Ibid.,* I, p. 581. The Chicago Board of Trade was organized in 1848. Cyrus McCormick was not one of the 82 charter members.

[13] *Ibid.,* I, pp. 155, 199-201. This flood was on Mch. 12, 1849. Besides the destruction of the bridges, 40 water craft were wrecked. The money loss was estimated at over $100,000.

[14] *Ibid.,* I, p. 595. The immigrant ship *John Drew* was blamed for the cholera epidemic of 1849. The county hospital was opened in Old Tippecanoe Hall, Mch. 30, 1847. Most of the charity patients were treated in the almshouse.   [15] *Ibid.,* I, p. 191.

draulic Mills were pumping drinking water through their
leaky wooden pipes from such a short distance out in Lake
Michigan that the supply was tainted by the effluvium of the
city. It was 1853 before this was remedied.[16] Moreover, a
deadly miasma arose from the very streets of this low-lying
metropolis, according to a local paper. In August, 1850, the
"Gem of the Prairie" complained:

Many of the populous localities are noisome quagmires, the
gutters running with filth at which the very swine turn up their
noses in supreme disgust. Even some portions of the planked
streets, say, for instance, Lake between Clark and LaSalle, are
scarcely in better sanitary condition than those which are not
planked. The gutters at the crossings are clogged up, leaving standing pools of an indescribable liquid, there to salute the noses of
passers-by. . . . During the hot weather of the last few weeks,
the whole reeking mass of abominations has steamed up through
every opening, and the miasma thus elaborated has been wafted
into the neighboring shops and dwellings, to poison their inmates.
. . . Lime has been distributed to some extent, but in insignificant
quantities. . . . Here is a long bill of complaints to prefer in the
ears of the city fathers. . . . The only condition of health and
decency is a regular, thorough system of drainage. Such a system
is feasible, and must be adopted if the "Garden City" is to be
habitable.[17]

The mayor and Common Council, in session in their new
municipal building on North State Street, decided that the lake
breezes and the approaching cold weather were the best remedies which could be prescribed at the moment.[18] In view of

[16] *Ibid.*, I, pp. 186, 187.
[17] *Ibid.*, I, pp. 190, 192. Road surfaces had been made with stone, but
these sank after a year or two of use. Then plank streets and roads came
into vogue in the late forties. Heavy wagons quickly wore through the
timber, and as Andreas writes, "the pavement was a dangerous and active
weapon, flying up into horses' faces and dashing foot-passengers with mud."
[18] *Ibid.*, I, p. 180. In Jan., 1848, the Market Building, on State Street, was
erected by the city and was the first municipal structure.

such conditions, even worse in most of the towns of the West at that time, it is small wonder that Cyrus McCormick, accustomed to the bracing air of the Blue Ridge, should emphasize considerations of health when selecting the new home of his reaper.

The citizens of Chicago were too busy making money, between 1847 and 1850, to give much thought to education and recreation.[19] A proposal to open a high school was frowned upon by members of the City Council in 1849 and had to await realization until 1856. But before 1849 there were nearly two thousand children in the elementary schools, "two-thirds of whom are in daily attendance in spacious, ventilated, well regulated school rooms, where they are taught by those whose duty is their pleasure." [20] In 1847 and 1848, Shaksperean drama was played in Chicago by such notables as Forrest, Booth, Murdock, Marble, and Mrs. Hunt (Mrs. John Drew) at Rice's New Theater. A moving diorama of the burning of Moscow delighted the patrons of the Saloon Building, and Tom Thumb at the Court House received the homage of the crowd. Minstrels at Mooney's Museum also were applauded in 1848, although many visited this amusement palace merely to see its venerable manager, David Kennison, reputed to be the sole surviving participant in the Boston Tea Party.[21]

The Mexican War and the California gold rush furnished excitement enough during these years,[22] but one paper of the

[19] *Ibid.*, I, p. 155. On Jan. 17, 1848, merchants protested against the State law which limited the rate of interest to 6%. They complained that this statute made capital shun Illinois. Thus the city-country conflict had already begun.

[20] *Ibid.*, I, pp. 212, 213, 218. In 1847 the City Council Committee on Schools were "of the opinion that there are insuperable objections to the establishment of such a [high] school, independent of the inability of the city at the present time to build one."

[21] *Ibid.*, I, pp. 484-486.

[22] *Ibid.*, I, pp. 155, 279.

city felt ashamed in 1847 at the lack of enthusiasm aroused by the Fourth of July. "The Montgomery Guards, under Captain Snowhook, did themselves great honor on the 4th. . . . It is a strong argument against Native Americanism when we see the Sons of Erin were the only military company that turned out to celebrate the Declaration of Independence." [23]

It is doubtful whether Cyrus McCormick was primarily interested in Chicago's parading soldiers, her theater, or her lack of high schools, during his first years in the city.[24] Railways, steamboats, telegraph lines, bridges, and better streets were more or less directly connected with his immediate purpose,[25] while the prevalence of Presbyterianism in Chicago keenly interested him. In 1845 he had noted the good preaching at Cincinnati and Brockport as strong points of attraction to draw him to those cities. By the autumn of 1848 the five hundred members of the First Presbyterian Church of Chicago, founded in 1833, had progressed far enough with their new $28,000 brick edifice, at the corner of Clark and Washington streets, to hold services in the basement.[26] But the same year a group of less than thirty persons, soon including Cyrus McCormick himself, organized the North Presbyterian Church and called the Rev. R. H. Richardson to be their pastor. Before winter came the congregation had moved from its temporary quarters in Rush Medical College to a small new church at the corner of North Clark and Michigan streets.[27] This tiny beginning expanded into a large brick building at the junction of Cass and

[23] "Chicago Democrat," July 13, 1847.

[24] Gas was first used for illumination in Chicago on Sept. 4, 1850. During the next five years much was done to improve the city police and fire departments. Andreas, I, pp. 155, 179, 202, 224.

[25] As late as Apr. 6, 1857 (L.P.C.B. No. 6, p. 89), W. J. Hanna wrote from the factory office, "The streets here are in such a shocking condition that it is almost impossible to get hauling done to the Rock Island R.R. Depot, or your machines would have been all off long ago."

[26] Andreas, I, p. 301.   [27] Ibid., I, p. 310.

Indiana streets by 1861. During its early years Orloff M. Dorman and Charles A. Spring, Sr., were prominent members, and the church bond was probably either the cause or the effect of their close association with McCormick and his reaper factory in Chicago.[28]

Cyrus McCormick had stopped in Chicago several times between 1844 and 1848, when he began his permanent residence in that city. These earlier visits, however, had been occasioned by his wish to find some one to manufacture his machines there, or merely by the fact that Chicago was a natural "port of call" for any traveler to the Northwest. But when he formed his partnership with C. M. Gray for the harvest of 1848, it was important to know others in Chicago besides the manufacturers of agricultural machinery and potential reaper agents. Lawyers to draw up a partnership agreement which would protect his rights, and men of wealth who would loan him money to meet his obligations under the contract, were needed. Therefore it is not strange that he brought to Chicago in 1848 a letter directed by Stephen A. Douglas to two lawyer friends, Ebenezer Peck and James A. McDougall.[29]

The inventor had been presented to Douglas by Congressman McDowell of Virginia. Close friendship need not be pre-

[28] *Post*, p. 267.

[29] McCormick's letter of introduction is in the possession of Mr. Oliver R. Barrett, of Kenilworth, Ill. Douglas wrote that Cyrus McCormick came to him warmly recommended by Gov. McDowell of Virginia "as a highly respectable and worthy gentleman." "He is the inventor of a machine known as the Virginia Reaper, and wishes to introduce it into use in Illinois. Any assistance you may render him will be duly acknowledged by your friend, S. A. Douglas." Andreas, I, pp. 428, 429. The law firm of Peck & McDougall was one of the best known in Chicago at this time. Both men were prominent Democrats. McDougall was soon to be Attorney General of Illinois, but moved to California in 1849. Peck deserted Douglas after the Kansas-Nebraska Act, and Lincoln later appointed him a judge of the Court of Claims at Washington.

sumed at this early date, but ten years later the statesman was a frequent visitor in the McCormick home. Both were men of large vision, both were ardent Democrats, one was a fighter in politics and the other was equally aggressive in business. These two Chicagoans had much in common, although Douglas refused to support his friend's decade-long effort to win from Congress an extension of his original patent. One sponsored the reaper and the other placed his faith in the railroad. The reaper and the railroad were to go hand in hand. Both discerned their own advantage in the implements they championed, but both saw also the greater and happier America which would come from their use. Both dreamed of the day when the vast region west of the Mississippi would be brought under cultivation. If the railroads of the one permitted settlers to go into Nebraska, so the reaper of the other furnished freight for those roads to carry and contributed to the prosperity of the farmer. Douglas wished to unite the Old Northwest and the New South economically and politically. Nothing would have better satisfied the Southern-born McCormick. It was most appropriate that the inventor should come to make his home in Chicago armed with a testimonial of good character from Douglas.

At the close of the harvest of 1847, when the partnership of Charles M. Gray and Seth Warner of Chicago dissolved, the firm owed Cyrus McCormick over $2,500 in patent fees on the reapers, to the number of almost one hundred, which they had built and sold. This debt might be discharged before the new year if the agents were urgent, and if the price of corn and pork allowed the farmers to pay for their machines. Under such circumstances the inventor entered a partnership with Gray on August 30, 1847. Excepting the arrangement with Leander McCormick for the manufacture of machines at the Brown factory at Cincinnati for 1847 and a possible similar agreement with his father at Walnut Grove eight years before, this was the first time that Cyrus McCormick had ventured to unite in business with another since the unfortunate furnace partnership of 1836. As that had led to the estrangement of McCormick and Black, so this association with Gray, while yielding over $30,000 profits in one year, was to result in bitter disagreement, suits at law, and personal enmity, which at least on Gray's part was still evident as late as 1857.[30] Because McCormick customarily found harmony impossible with his partners, it is natural to conclude that the whole fault did not always rest with them.

The contract with Gray is long and involved, and yet the subsequent misunderstanding is meaningless unless its most important terms are known. On the same day that it was made, the partners purchased from William B. Ogden three lots situated near the pier "a few rods west of the Lake House." Here a factory was to be started at once, equipped with modern machinery, including a ten-horse-power steam-engine. The construction work, the purchase and installation of the equipment, the supervision of reaper-building, and the keeping of accounts were to be under Gray's management, although always subject to his partner's advice. Gray was to buy all necessary building materials for factory and reapers, "with his own individual means." He was required to "keep regular and correct accounts subject to Cyrus H. McCormick's inspection at all times," and

[30] David Zimmerman, from Urbana, O., to C. H. McCormick, Jan. 5, 1857. Gray told Zimmerman that he had built the first McCormick machine which worked successfully. Andreas, I, p. 621. Gray was Mayor of Chicago in 1853. He was a wholesale grocer, a cradle-manufacturer, and later a reaper agent in Ohio. In his old age he was asst. gen'l freight agent for the Lake Shore and Michigan Southern R.R. One other reason for the breach between McCormick and Gray in 1848 was that the latter produced a reaper on his own account which he contended was better than McCormick's. He exhibited it at the Chicago Mechanics' Institute and the board of judges was inclined to agree with his opinion of its merits. However, he soon abandoned it.

to furnish monthly financial statements showing the capital outlay and the amounts likely to be required for running the business. When it was necessary to buy supplies on credit, the seller should understand that they were for the use of Mc-Cormick & Gray, and the title should be in that firm, but Gray alone was to be held responsible for payment of all bills for such supplies. For this work he would be paid $1,000 a year by the company.

Cyrus McCormick was to receive from the firm a thirty-dollar patent fee by December 1, 1848, for each of the five hundred machines which were to be made and sold. He should also be paid $2.00 a day for the time that he spent in the harvest field on company business. The net profits, as well as the whole cost of manufacturing, were to be divided equally between the partners. The field of sale was designated as Wisconsin and all of Illinois, save for the four counties supplied by Townsend, although their territory was to be broadened if need should arise. Of course Gray would contribute much of his half of the capital by purchasing the necessary supplies and machinery, and on August 30, 1847, each partner agreed to advance $2,000 at once for company use. Before the close of the year McCormick was to furnish another $2,000, and on January 1, 1848, "and monthly thereafter, to deposit in like manner whatever sum is required to make up his half of the capital required for the business." Although it was not stated in the contract, McCormick later contended that Gray very well understood that the sum of $2,500 or more, owed to him by Gray & Warner, was to be considered a part of his investment.

Elaborate provisions were included in the agreement detailing the terms of sale of the machine, the distribution of the monies collected, and the payment of agents. If either party failed to fulfil his part of the contract, he could be held responsible for the consequent money loss, and all of the company's property was security for the payment of this loss to the aggrieved partner. It is unsatisfactory, and probably unjust to Gray, to base the story of this discordant partnership solely upon the Bill of Complaint of Cyrus McCormick in the lawsuit which followed. Nevertheless, no other document remains, and Gray's defense can only be hypothecated from the statement of his opponent.

The erection of the factory was started at once, and soon five hundred reapers were under way for the coming harvest. Meanwhile Cyrus McCormick was in the East, attending to his patent-extension case, and this, as well as Brockport business, fully occupied his time on the seaboard until June, 1848.[31] The winter in the West was unfavorable for wheat and, if McCormick can be believed, Gray was extravagant; did not send him the monthly financial statements agreed upon, and, without McCormick's knowledge, sold one half of his interest in the firm because of the poor prospects for the harvest. Perhaps Gray was driven by financial necessity to seek aid—an extremity, as he contended, occasioned by McCormick's failure to advance his share of the capital.

The inventor countered this charge by declaring that he would have paid in more than his moiety if the debt owed by Gray & Warner had been credited to his account when it fell due on December 1, 1847.[32] At that time, the Virginian, without word to the contrary, assumed that this obligation had been met. On his part, Gray apparently believed that he was free to go for help to William B. Ogden, since McCormick had not

[31] "C. H. McCormick vs. Gray and Ogden, Supreme Court of the United States," No. 176, p. 8, McCormick's Bill of Complaint, in which he states that he was absent from Chicago from Sept. 10, 1847, to June 1, 1848.

[32] *Ibid.*, pp. 7-9. McCormick stated that he paid in $3,977 by Dec. 28, 1847, and this plus the [cir.] $2,500 which was owed to him by Gray & Warner, totaled all that was due from him by that date. About May 22, 1848, he sent another draft for $1,200, and at various times between January and May, 1848, as his agents sent in collections, he forwarded additional sums.

contributed the sums stipulated, while McCormick judged that his partner had broken the contract by not sending him regular statements of the financial condition of the firm.

However that may be, Gray sought out William B. Ogden, the Crœsus of Chicago, and William E. Jones, about mid-January, 1848, and, "pretending to be in great need of capital to carry on the business," secured a promise of a $7,000 loan to the company in exchange for one half of his interest in the venture. In the agreement of Gray with Ogden and Jones, it was noted that this arrangement was necessary in order to prevent the closing of the factory due to McCormick's neglect in furnishing his portion of the capital. The inventor answered that he knew nothing of this deal until late July, 1848, that the charge was "untrue and false," and that Gray, who could have borrowed money at a reasonable rate of interest, would never have released any part of his partnership interest if he had believed that the business was going to be profitable. All but thirteen of the five hundred reapers were sold that season; about $21,000 was collected by the close of the harvest, and Gray, after paying $10,000 of the company debts, reserved the balance. So charged his partner, who also declared that Gray had caused him "great loss and embarrassment" by refusing to continue the agreement for another year, and by hesitating to state the sum for which he would sell his remaining one-quarter interest.

Since Gray held the money which had been collected during the summer, and demanded damages from McCormick for breach of contract, and since the latter charged Gray with corresponding violations of the agreement, the two discordant associates finally agreed to assign to Ogden for collection all of the firm's assets of indebtedness (about $36,000) and to submit their differences to Judge H. J. Dickey for arbitration. This resolution was reached on September 25, 1848, but six months of effort under this arrangement failed to bring a settlement satisfactory to the partners.[33]

Cyrus McCormick protested that Judge Dickey's award of March 30, 1849, violated the terms agreed upon in the assignment of the firm's assets to Ogden. In short, according to this agreement, after Ogden had collected all money due, he was to pay McCormick at once the patent fees totaling $14,610 which the firm owed him for the four hundred and eighty-seven reapers made and sold. The judge disregarded this stipulation in his award. Consequently, on June 16, 1849, the inventor filed a Bill of Complaint, praying the court to annul the arbitrator's decision, to enjoin Ogden from paying any money to Gray, and to restrain the latter from collecting any of the company's money in violation of the assignment of that right to Ogden. Thereupon Gray, with Ogden and Jones, entered a demurrer, charging that "the said bill is argumentative, and in other respects erroneous, defective and insufficient."

The Circuit Court of the United States,[34] sitting at Springfield, Illinois, upheld the demurrer, and before the close of the year McCormick appealed to the Supreme Court. Reverdy Johnson, a distinguished lawyer, was McCormick's counsel, and late in 1851 Justice Curtis delivered the opinion of the court in favor of the inventor. By the decision the arbitrator was declared to be bound by the terms of the McCormick & Gray assignment to William B. Ogden. Consequently "the decree

[33] Under date of Dec. 20, 1848, Gray declared himself bound to McCormick for $10,000. On Jan. 14, 1848, when the partners came before Judge Dickey for a hearing, the assets of the firm were: real estate, $9,406.06; machinery, $3,637.17; due from sales, $36,853.15; value of materials and 13 unsold reapers, $3,021.14. Total, $52,917.52. The liabilities were estimated at $21,710.09 (including $14,610 due in patent fees to McCormick), leaving a year's profit of over $31,000 to be divided, half to McCormick, and one quarter each to Gray, and to Ogden and Jones.

[34] The federal court had jurisdiction, because McCormick still claimed Rockbridge County, Va., as his legal residence.

of the Circuit Court must be reversed, and the case remanded with directions to that court to overrule the demurrer, and order the defendants to answer the bill." Presumably the ultimate division of the firm's assets was in accord with McCormick's contention, but records fail from this point on and nothing is known of the final settlement with Gray.[35]

The lack of harmony between the partners should not obscure the fact that it had been a most profitable year. McCormick's net return from the Chicago enterprise seems to have exceeded $30,000, not to mention his patent fees from Townsend, the Brockport manufacturers, Hite, and perhaps others in Virginia. The dark spot of the season was his failure to secure a patent-extension, but if so much money could be made by the manufacture and sale of his reapers the future could not have seemed very gloomy. Gray sold his remaining quarter-interest to Ogden, and the expiration of McCormick's patent brought most of his other contracts to a close. He arranged for reaper-construction at Brockport and by Townsend at Au Sable Grove, Illinois, but his patent fee was necessarily reduced.[36]

On October 7, 1848, the "Gem of the Prairie" announced that Cyrus H. McCormick, William B. Ogden, and William E. Jones had formed a partnership. The style of the firm was McCormick, Ogden & Co., and fifteen hundred reapers were to be made for the harvest of 1849, to supply the demand of the entire Northwest and Southwest save the four Illinois counties which Townsend still controlled.[37] The story of the

[35] "Scientific American," Mch. 13, 1852. "Richmond Whig," Mch. 2, 1852. The partnership was a subject of discussion as late as 1855. See C. H. McCormick to J. L. Wilson, Aug. 11, 1855. 13 Howard 33 ff.

[36] Townsend stopped manufacturing McCormick reapers after the harvest of 1849. "Ohio Cultivator," Jan. 15, 1850, p. 31.

[37] The contract for 1849 with Ogden and Jones was concluded on September 25, 1848, when Gray relinquished his interest in the firm, and when McCormick and he agreed to entrust Ogden with their assets.

firm of McCormick & Gray, which has just been told, reveals the origin of this new partnership; the share of each associate in the business, and the circumstances beyond the inventor's control that made this new arrangement necessary. The tradition that Ogden welcomed the inventor to Chicago and that the latter sought a partnership with him, has no basis of fact.[38] The magnate's first connection with the reaper was contrary to McCormick's knowledge and wish, and constituted one grievance against Gray.

During the year of his partnership with Ogden, there was a suit before the courts in which McCormick was the plaintiff and his associate one of the defendants. Notwithstanding this fact, the relations of McCormick and Ogden were cordial, and the latter, in the autumn of 1849, after his year with McCormick had ended, certified that his friend's reaper was the best on the market.[39]

By this time the harvest was over and the season had been more profitable than ever before. On September 10, 1849, Ogden and Jones sold out to McCormick for $65,000, a sum which about equaled the inventor's share of the profits, together with his patent fees, from the sale of fifteen hundred reapers.[40] This profit embraced all outstanding assets of indebtedness and did not take into account those farmers who never paid for their machines, including those who skipped to the California gold-fields, leaving their creditors unsatisfied. Even in 1858 there were nearly $3,000 in 1849 reaper notes unpaid.

[38] For this tradition see W. L. Stevens in the "Rockbridge County News" of Feb. 18, 1909, and J. L. Jones, "The Harvest Field," in "Unity" (Chicago), LXVI, pp. 89-91.

[39] There is a McCormick advertisement in the "Genesee Farmer" of July, 1850, p. 173, with a testimonial of Wm. B. Ogden, dated Oct. 3, 1849, attached.

[40] MS. agreement of Sept. 10, 1849, between the partners. "Gem of the Prairie" (Chicago), Dec. 1, 1849.

Late in 1848, Leander McCormick arrived in Chicago to assist his brother in the construction work at the factory. His wife wrote to her Virginia home in early December of their long trip by way of Lake Erie, and of their temporary residence at the Sherman Hotel until their new home was completed. Here Cyrus McCormick had a room "finely furnished," and his sister-in-law, homesick among the Yankees, marveled at the life of the metropolis, proud of her new cherry-colored bonnet with its big plume, and pleased to discover that white servants worked harder than slaves.[41] About one year later Cyrus McCormick's other brother, William, reluctantly held an auction sale at the old homestead of Walnut Grove, bade good-by to his aged mother, and reported for duty in Chicago. Thus the brothers were once again united around the reaper.[42]

In the meantime the partnership with Ogden and Jones had been immediately followed by an agreement for one year with Orloff M. Dorman.[43] By this contract of September 22, 1849, the factory with its machinery was leased by McCormick to the new firm of C. H. McCormick & Co. for $5,000. After deducting this sum from the net profits of the year's business, as well as a patent fee of $30 for each reaper and $20 for each mower made and sold, McCormick was to receive three quarters of the balance and Dorman one quarter. Dorman invested about $12,000, and largely confined his superintendence to the company office and to the agents. The terms of the contract

[41] Caroline Kirkland, "Chicago Yesterdays, a Sheaf of Reminiscences" (Chicago, 1919), Chap. III. Letters of Mrs. L. J. McCormick, dated Dec. 3, and 10, 1838, to Martha Hamilton of Covington, Va. The date should surely be 1848.

[42] W. S. McCormick to ?, Sept. 4, 1850. He wrote that he would leave for Chicago on September 20. McCormick vs. Manny, II, 202.

[43] MS. agreement of September 22, 1849, between C. H. McCormick and O. M. Dorman. "McCormick Extension Case, Patent of 1845," pp. 37-40, deposition of O. M. Dorman, Sept. 26, 1850. "Prairie Farmer," Dec. 4, 1849. "Ohio Cultivator," Jan. 15, 1850, p. 31, Feb. 15, 1850, p. 3. "Wisconsin Farmer and Northwestern Cultivator" (Racine), Feb., 1850, p. 42.

also stipulated that Leander McCormick should be employed
for $750 a year as an assistant of his brother in the work of
building reapers and mowers. William McCormick began his
fifteen years of service in the office of the firm as Dorman's
aid.[44]

About sixteen hundred reapers were made for the harvest
of 1850 and all but fifty were sold.[45] The McCormick-Dorman
partnership was harmonious, but at the close of the season the
inventor decided that he was ready to strike out alone, and,
despite Dorman's wishes, refused to renew the agreement for
another harvest.[46] For the next nine years Cyrus McCormick
conducted his business without partners.

Between 1848 and 1851 the erection of the new home of the
McCormick reaper went steadily forward. On January 18,
1849, the "Chicago Weekly Democrat" reported in the following paragraphs the progress which had been made:

This is truly a mechanical age, and probably nothing so dis-
tinctively marks the civilization of the present day as the state of
perfection to which machinery is being brought. . . .
These remarks were suggested by a visit yesterday to the Reaping Machine Factory of Messrs. McCormick and Gray. It is situ-

[44] *McCormick vs. Manny*, II, pp. 202, 206. *Hussey vs. McCormick*, pp.
10, 11. L. J. McCormick stated that "for two years next after the year
1848 or 1849 [I] received a salary, the amount of which was determined
by the profits of the business of making and selling reaping machines."
He also testified that in 1849 and 1850 he was a partner to the extent of
one-sixth interest. See also L. J. McCormick's testimony in *Cyrenus
Wheeler vs. C. H. and L. J. McCormick* (1870), p. 852.

[45] *Hussey vs. McCormick*, pp. 228-232. However, in *Seymour & Morgan
vs. McCormick*, pp. 103, 104, William S. McCormick stated that 481 reapers
were still on hand at the close of the season. It was to McCormick's
advantage in this case to demonstrate the extent to which Seymour &
Morgan had injured his sales, since patent infringement was charged.
A summary of McCormick's business from 1849 to 1858 is on page 197,
pro-testimony section, "McCormick Extension Case, Patent of 1845." This
shows that 1,603 machines were made in 1850.

[46] *McCormick vs. Gray and Ogden, op. cit.,* p. 8.

ated on the north side of the river near the piers; and is a well finished brick building, 100 feet by 30 or over and three stories high. Attached to the main building is a building containing the steam engine, lathes for turning iron, and also a building containing six forges. There are 33 hands employed in the factory, ten of whom are blacksmiths.

The steam engine particularly attracted our attention. . . . This engine drives some fourteen or fifteen machines; viz. a planing machine, two circular saws, a tenent saw, a lathe for turning handles for rakes, pitch forks, etc.; also two lathes for turning iron, a gage's patent die, two morticing machines and two grind stones. Machines are being set up for various other uses in several branches of carpenter's work.

The smithy contains 10 forges in all. . . . We understand the proprietors design enlarging this portion of the establishment as it is at present too contracted for the wants of the factory.

When Ogden and Jones retired from their partnership with McCormick in September, 1849, the factory consisted of a brick building, partly two stories and partly three stories high, 40 by 190 feet in size. This structure housed three planing machines, six saws, two wood lathes, seven iron lathes, three boring machines, and a fan for blowing the sixteen blacksmiths' fires. Most of this machinery was driven by a thirty-horse-power engine which was one of the wonders of industrial Chicago at that time. There were wood-working and iron-working departments, and by 1850 about one hundred and twenty men were employed.[47] McCormick was sole owner of this establishment in the autumn of 1849, together with a long river frontage which permitted reapers to be loaded at his own

[47] "American Agriculturist," Sept., 1849, p. 292. "Wisconsin Farmer and Northwestern Cultivator," Dec., 1849, p. 274. "Chicago Daily Democrat," Jan. 5, 1849. A new addition had just been finished. It was 80 ft. x 40 ft. in size and three stories high. A blacksmith shop 40 ft. x 50 ft., containing 10 forges, also was completed, and the new 30-horse-power steam-engine recently installed. "Chicago Daily Journal," June 16, 21, 1849; Jan. 4, 1850. "Gem of the Prairie," Apr. 24, 1849.

dock, and consignments of wood, coal, and iron to reach him without his having to pay high transfer charges across the city.

During the noon hour of March 25, 1851, a fire of undetermined origin started in the paint shop and destroyed the entire south wing of the main factory building. A high wind was blowing, and, although "the noble exertions of the Firemen, and others of our citizens" were duly extolled in the press by the factory manager, Leander McCormick, the fireproof engine-room in the center of the structure seems to have deserved the major credit for preventing the total destruction of the plant. A loss of $7,000, not covered by insurance, resulted.[48] This disaster occurred in the midst of the spring rush of reaper-building, but reconstruction was begun immediately and the annual output was ready by harvest-time. Cisterns were now sunk in the factory yard; day- and night-watchmen were employed, and a force-pump and enough hose were provided to throw a stream of water upon the roof of any building in case of need. When the wing was rebuilt, larger than before, the roof was covered with tin, and all windows were equipped with fireproof shutters.

Within a week after the fire a reporter of the "Chicago

[48] "Chicago Daily Journal," Mch. 26 and Dec. 23, 1851. The fire was variously attributed to spontaneous combustion, an incendiary, and a spark from a passing steamboat. The rebuilt wing was of brick, 80 ft. x 40 ft., and four stories high. New machines "of the latest design," for cutting out the different parts of the reaper, were installed by December, 1851. These included mortising machines, screw and nut-cutting dies, boring machines, and a powerful press for making nuts and sickle parts. The largest planing machine in the city was added. "Chicago Weekly Democrat," Mch. 29, 1851. "Gem of the Prairie," Mch. 29, 1851. Another fire on Sunday, July 6, 1856, destroyed a partially finished building and did much damage to the files in the company office. Incendiarism was suspected and the loss was about $2,500. W. J. Hanna to W. S. McCormick, July 17, 1856, L.P.C.B. No. 2, p. 638. *Ibid.,* No. 2, pp. 501, 511, 525, 661; No. 3, pp. 1, 4, 320. On this occasion Cyrus McCormick gave $500 to the Chicago Firemen's Benevolent Association.

Daily Journal," rendered eloquent by the new sounds of a machine age, wrote for his paper:

An angry whirr, a dronish hum, a prolonged whistle, a shrill buzz and a panting breath—such is the music of the place. You enter—little wheels of steel attached to horizontal, upright and oblique shafts, are on every hand. They seem motionless. Rude pieces of wood without form or comeliness are hourly approaching them upon little railways, as if drawn thither by some mysterious attraction. They touch them, and *presto,* grooved, scallopped, rounded, on they go, with a little help from an attendant, who seems to have an easy time of it, and transferred to another railway, when down comes a guillotine-like contrivance,—they are morticed, bored, and whirled away, where the tireless planes without hands, like a boatswain, whistle the rough plank into polish, and it is turned out smoothed, shaped, and fitted for its place in the Reaper or the Harvester. The saw and the cylinder are the genii of the establishment. They work its wonders, and accomplish its drudgery. But there is a greater than they. Below, glistering like a knight in armor, the engine of forty-horse power works as silently as the "little wheel" of the matron; but shafts plunge, cylinders revolve, bellows heave, iron is twisted into screws like wax, and saws dash off at the rate of forty rounds a second, at one movement of its mighty muscles. But there is a greater still than this. There by the furnace fire, begrimed with coal and dust, decorated with an apron of leather, instead of a ribbon of satin, stands the one who controls—nay, who can create the whole.[49]

Additions were made to the factory building, new machinery was purchased, and more workmen were employed almost every year. By the close of 1851, Chicago papers were boasting that it was the largest factory of its kind in the world, that Western-made reapers could undersell those of the East, and that McCormick "conquers nature to the benign end of civilization and brings bread to the mouths of the poor." [50]

[49] "Chicago Daily Journal," Mch. 31, 1851. The account is entitled "The Magic of Machinery."
[50] "Chicago Daily Democrat," Dec. 23, 1851.

The move from Walnut Grove was completed and the Mc-
Cormick reaper had a new and permanent home. Mary Ann
McCormick, the mother, died of typhoid fever on June 1,
1853, at the home of her daughter Amanda Adams, who alone
of her children still lived in the Valley of Virginia. Before the
close of the decade the Adams family also moved to Chicago
and, with the aid of Cyrus McCormick's money and the repute
of his name, Hugh Adams was successfully established in a
wholesale grocery and commission merchant business.[51] Both
Leander and William McCormick learned, shortly after their
arrival in Chicago, that the modest salaries paid by their elder
brother could be most profitably invested in city houses and
lots.[52]

The old homestead, still owned by William McCormick, was
leased to a farmer, and several efforts were made to sell it
before 1860.[53] In 1858, William wrote to his brother-in-law,
the Rev. James H. Shields:

[51] Prior to Oct., 1857, when he moved to Chicago, Hugh Adams was a
grocer at Kerr's Creek, Va., and was clearing a profit of about $1,500
annually. He invested his surplus in Chicago real estate under W. S.
McCormick's direction. He owned a few slaves, and in 1856, estimated
that he was worth $22,000. Hugh Adams to W. S. McCormick, Mch. 10,
1855, Feb. 9 and Sept. 4, 1856. W. S. McCormick to H. Adams, Aug. 21,
1857, L.P.C.B. No. 8, p. 534. At the same time, C. H. and W. S. Mc-
Cormick were urging their sister Mary C. Shields and her husband to
move to Chicago. Cyrus promised to furnish capital for the Rev. Jas.
Shields to enter the lumber business and would guarantee him against loss.
W. S. McCormick to Mary C. Shields, Aug. 21, 1857, L.P.C.B. No. 8,
p. 521. L. J. McCormick, pp. 325, 326.

[52] L.P.C.B. No. 1, pp. 393, 398, letters of W. S. McCormick, May 9,
1856, to J. B. McCormick and to A. D. Hager. Money invested in Chicago
real estate would earn 25% a year. C. H. to W. S. McCormick, Oct. 1,
1856. He suggested buying land in the West along railroad lines. *McCormick vs. Manny*, II, pp. 202-206, 236, testimony of W. S. McCormick
that his salary was $3,000 a year in 1854.

[53] W. T. Rush to W. S. McCormick, Dec. 29, 1855. Jas. Campbell to
W. S. McCormick, May 19, 1855. C. H. to W. S. McCormick, Feb. 7,
1857. The latter had urged his brother to buy it, but Cyrus replied that
he had no use for it at that time. W. S. McCormick's desire for money

Walnut Grove

Will you and Sister C. [Caroline] remove to Walnut Grove and keep it as long as you live, and let us all occasionally resort to it as a sacred spot? If we *enable* you to do so you might help to civilize and Christianize that barbarous people. . . . I ask you this question about W. Grove *seriously*. C. H. ever talks of buying it and keeping it up as a sacred spot even at a loss to him. *He* could afford now to do it. *I* should love to make my home again at Walnut Grove if pecuniary interest were not in the way of it. . . . What says Caroline? You could have Hannah to cook and Anthony to drive your carriage and couldn't you splurge.[54]

Hannah and Anthony were slaves, and they, together with Eunice, Emily, and Joe, owned by Cyrus McCormick, were hired out by the year to friends in the Valley who would treat them kindly. In 1856 the inventor thought of selling Eunice— or of bringing her to Chicago and freeing her. He received about $40 as the yearly wage of Emily and $70 for Joe.[55]

The contrast between the Cyrus McCormick of 1845 and that of 1851 is most striking. In the former year he traveled as best he could from farm to farm in the Ohio Valley, searching out purchasers to keep his father's little shop busy at Walnut Grove. Six years later his own factory, one of the largest in Chicago, was yielding him a handsome annual income.[56] Up to the season of 1848, when the inventor first settled in Chicago, about 1,278 McCormick reapers were made and sold. In the

to invest in Chicago real estate was a chief reason for his wish to sell Walnut Grove, and by 1858 he sought to borrow $15,000, using it as security.

[54] The offer, made also three years before, was not accepted, and that autumn the owner tried again to sell it for $18,000. J. Shields to W. S. McCormick, Feb. 15, 1855. W. S. McCormick to J. Shields, Oct. 5, 1858; to Jas. Campbell, Oct. 18, 1858, in L.P.C.B. No. 16, pp. 24, 193.

[55] C. H. McCormick to W. T. Rush, Feb. 20, 1852; Jan. 12 and 20 and Sept. 13, 1855. Rush hired Emily and Joe during these years. C. H. to W. S. McCormick, Dec. 1, 1856. He suggests the possibility of persuading the aged Eunice to go to Liberia, but she died in Virginia in 1858.

[56] "McCormick Extension Case, Patent of 1845," adverse testimony, pp. 37-40. The factory was valued at about $40,000 in 1850.

three-year period of partnerships between 1848 and 1850, approximately 4,000 more were marketed.

The inventor had achieved several of his initial objectives by the close of 1850. He was financially able to dispense with partners, and almost a decade was to pass before he invited his two brothers to join him in the firm. As employees, William and Leander McCormick could be relied upon to render him expert and devoted service in the office, machine-shop, and harvest field.[57] They had grown to manhood with the reaper, and henceforward Cyrus was able to spend many months each year away from Chicago, with the assurance that his rapidly growing interests in that city would be capably managed. The new arrangement was most opportune. Lawsuits, patent-extension business, and the introduction of his reaper overseas increasingly demanded his presence in the East and in Europe.

Manufacturing rights, which had been granted to independent builders in the period from 1844 to 1848, expired one by one and were not renewed. By 1851 Cyrus McCormick possessed a factory in the heart of the future wheat belt of the United States and, for the first time since the early days of reaper-making, all of his machines were produced under one roof. Thus was realized a second objective toward which the inventor had been striving since his first unfortunate experience with sub-manufacturers seven or eight years before. In short, the season of 1851 marks the consummation of his early hopes, and his victory during that year at the great World's Fair in London was the crown upon a decade of achievement.

His progress had been phenomenal, but it had not been unbroken by discouragement. The poor quality of the machines made by the Brockport and Cincinnati firms, and the temporary loss of his Eastern market were but two of the outstanding

[57] "Albany Evening Journal," Oct. 17, 1850: C. H. McCormick states that his business will be under the immediate superintendence of W. S. and L. J. McCormick.

checks which marked his rise. The failure of his efforts to secure an extension of his 1834 patent, coinciding in time with the events just described, will be considered in the next chapter. The editor of the "Richmond Whig" wrote in his paper on March 2, 1852, that Cyrus McCormick "is quite as lucky as Cæsar. Everything he undertakes succeeds. It would not be a bad idea for him to set up for the Presidency." Quite on the contrary, it had been an uphill fight all of the way. Lack of money and of influential friends, strong competition, conservative farmers, and poor transportation facilities were some of the barriers which had had to be surmounted. McCormick had earned his prosperity of 1850, but he was not content with his measure of success.

CHAPTER XII

THE PATENT-EXTENSION BATTLE

BETWEEN 1845 and the close of 1847, Cyrus McCormick patented improvements which, in his opinion, perfected the reaper and made it of practical value under almost any harvest conditions. On January 31, 1845, he received a patent for several alterations in construction, including a blade-supporter so curved or "angled downward" that straw could not easily clog the action of the knife; sickle-teeth with alternately reversed serrations; single spear-shaped iron fingers attached to the platform above the blade—"humped" so that choking would be almost impossible, and so shaped that the shoulder of each formed an acute angle (an effective draw-cut) with the teeth of the moving blade; an improved divider with dividing iron and bow, and a better method of bracing the reel.[1] Several of these changes had been used in the McCormick reaper for a number of years prior to the date of the patent. The reverse-angled sickle was employed as early as 1841, and experiments with the spear-shaped fingers were probably also made in that season.

During the harvest of 1845 a raker's seat was at last successfully placed upon the machine by the inventor,[2] but it was October 23, 1847, before he protected his right to this improvement

---

[1] Cyrus petitioned for the patent, filed an affidavit and specification, and paid the required $30 on Dec. 24, 1844. "Journal of Franklin Institute," 1845, p. 247. U. S. Patent Office, "Specification of Cyrus H. McCormick of Rockbridge County, Virginia, for an Improvement in Reaping Machines, forming Part of Letters Patent, No. 3895, dated Jan. 31, 1845."

[2] *Supra,* pp. 214 ff.

by a patent.[3] The use of the seat necessitated a new arrangement of certain parts of the machine, in order to readjust the balance because of the added weight of a second man on the reaper, and also to move the reel-supports so that the worker could freely wield his rake. These two alterations were covered in this patent by placing the gearing and sickle-crank in front of the driving wheel, where they were better protected from dirt, by moving the reel farther forward and making it shorter, and by counterbalancing this reduction of width by adding a wheel-board or guide to prevent the grain from passing uncut under the machine or into the gearing.[4] Hussey and other less prominent inventors had found a place for a rakeman on their implements long before 1845. But this was the first time that those mechanical elements, so combined in 1831 as to warrant the 1834 patent, had been successfully rearranged without a change of principle, so as to permit a raker to ride upon the McCormick reaper.

Because of the appearance of a number of business rivals after 1845, with machines which cut fairly well and permitted a rakeman to ride, Cyrus McCormick was justified in stating in 1848 that without these improvements he could not hope to sell his reapers. This does not constitute an admission that his original machine was worthless. He merely meant that a reaper which was salable in 1834 was by 1848 too far behind the times, without improvements, to be marketed. For this reason, when his implement began to bring him profits in 1845

[3] "Eureka," etc. (N. Y.), Dec., 1847, pp. 49, 50. "Journal of Franklin Institute," Jan., 1849, p. 26.

[4] The specification also included "the arrangement of the seat of the raker over the end of the finger-piece, which projects beyond the range of fingers and just back of the driving wheel . . . in combination with and placed at the end of the reel, whereby the raker can sit with his back toward the team, and thus have free access to the cut grain laid on the platform and back of the reel, and rake it from thence to the ground by a natural sweep of his body and lay it in a range at right angles with the swath," with the heads outward.

and in the years which followed, he could assert with much justice that his income was due to his new patents rather than to the elements described in the original one of 1834.

Consequently, when others saw the golden future for reaper-builders which Cyrus McCormick and Obed Hussey had prepared by their fifteen years of pioneering, it was not strange that they, lured by the same hopes, should make machines modeled upon one or the other of these implements or upon a selection of elements from each. McCormick could not sue a manufacturer who constructed a reaper with a reel, a divider, or a platform. He was not the inventor of any one of these by itself. But he could bring a manufacturer to court who marketed a machine which contained two or more of these elements in the combination covered by his patent, or who used any one of them in the distinctive form described in his 1834 grant—so long as that form was original. For these reasons the patent of 1834 was of great value to Cyrus McCormick even after he secured the two later ones in 1845 and 1847.

With a factory, sound credit, and considerable reputation among farmers in 1848, he could not be crushed by a refusal by the Government to extend his patent of 1834 for another seven years, but in such an event he would thenceforth be compelled to compete with his own ideas. It would be ironic if the very firms which had grown strong by constructing his reapers should use their power to his injury, and with no redress possible on his part. This was precisely the result to be anticipated, because Hussey's sub-manufacturers were unimportant, and the few reaper-makers of note outside of Baltimore were at Brockport, building McCormick machines. They—Seymour & Morgan, Backus, Fitch & Co., and J. Ganson & Co.—could be counted upon to work with might and main to defeat his efforts for a patent-extension. If they were successful, they would no longer need to pay the inventor a twenty-five- or thirty-dollar fee for each reaper they made. Very likely they would use the elements covered by his two later patents, but his fees could not be so large, and it might be possible for them to devise similar improvements of their own which would not invade his rights.

They could depend upon Hussey for aid in this struggle to defeat McCormick. His patent of 1833 expired about six months before his rival's, and he also was seeking an extension. Because he secured a patent on his famous open-back guard fingers in 1847, he was to contend less than a year later that his machine had reached perfection just at the time when his original monopoly lapsed. In other words, his case in this respect was very similar to McCormick's, but he needed to choose his arguments against his competitor's extension petition most carefully or they could be used with equal justice against his own. He could easily demonstrate that he had made less money than McCormick, and therefore was more deserving of a renewal in order that he might gain a fair recompense from his important invention. But could he explain his smaller financial return on other grounds than a poor machine or a lack of diligence on his part in its manufacture and sale?

Hussey's patent antedated McCormick's, but McCormick had often said that his reaper was first constructed and used in 1831, one year prior to his competitor's. Otherwise Hussey might work to defeat his rival by asserting that the latter had copied from him. However, this would be dangerous, because, if McCormick could prove that he had cut grain successfully with his machine in 1831, Hussey would have merely built up an argument against his own petition. In all likelihood the approximate coincidence in time of the two applications for patent-extension would mean that they would be yoked and would stand or fall together. If this were the case, it would be most unwise to work too strenuously against McCormick at the Patent Office.

On his part McCormick realized that Hussey would be his

main opponent, as always, in the effort to secure a patent-extension. For this reason, and judging that his foe would attack his claim to priority of invention, he began at least as early as the autumn of 1846 to lay his plans for the battle which would come in 1848. He wrote to his brother William in October, 1846, to keep John McCown, the sickle-maker, in good humor, because he could furnish convincing evidence that the reaper was first constructed in 1831.[5] There is reason to believe that his determination to have his own factory and to centralize production arose, at least in part, from a wish to be forearmed against a possible refusal of his application for extension. Such foresight was in accordance with McCormick's usual business acumen.[6]

Besides the opposition of Hussey, the Brockport firms, and of would-be reaper-makers everywhere, McCormick could expect resistance from the farmers, particularly if they were marshaled by business rivals whose ultimate purpose was quite at variance with the grain-growers' well-being. If his patent was not extended, competition among reaper-builders would increase and the stimulus of this rivalry pointed toward better machines at lower prices. Farmers were naturally attracted by this prospect at a time when an open field in business implied competition rather than combination. They can hardly be blamed for putting their own gain ahead of additional benefits for the one whose talents had helped them to grow more wheat. With a country predominantly rural, their will, if it could reach the Board of Extension of the Patent Office or Congress, would command respect from Whig and Democrat alike. A President was to be elected in 1848, and the Democrats were not sure enough of the Western rural vote to leave anything undone, no matter how trivial. Cyrus McCormick was not yet a power of political importance.

[5] C. H. to W. S. McCormick, Oct. 13, 1846.
[6] *Supra*, Chap. X, p. 248, ftn. 60.

He was not wise after the event, and naturally could not foresee the full force of the opposition which would meet his application for a patent-extension. He went ahead with assurance, happy in the realization that Hussey had failed to file his extension petition in time to satisfy the requirements of the law. Hussey consequently faced the necessity of pushing his claim through Congress, while McCormick, well versed in the regulations, forwarded the requisite papers to the Patent Office over six months before the date when his patent was to expire. So confident was he of success that he deemed it an extravagance to employ counsel, relying upon his experience in this field to carry through his case to success.[7] This proved to be a serious error. In the furnace-venture days he had been led into grave difficulties by his failure to secure legal advice. The lesson of 1848 was the last one on this subject which he would have to learn.

On December 10, 1847, McCormick first informally applied to the Patent Office for an extension of his 1834 patent, and paid the required forty dollars to the Treasury of the United States. The hearing before the Board of Patents—consisting of the Secretary of State, the Commissioner of Patents, and the Solicitor of the Treasury—was fixed for February 12, 1848.[8] On New Year's Day the inventor sent the commissioner, as required, a long report reviewing his reaper business under the patent. In summary he sought to demonstrate that he had diligently marketed his reaper; that it was a useful and valuable implement which had consistently defeated the Hussey machine, its only rival of importance in the field; that the monetary return had been slight and far less than was merited

[7] McCormick had just applied for an extension of the patent on his hillside plow. Pattison, II, i. McCormick to Commr. Burke, Mch. 27, 1848. "House Journal," 1st Sess., 30th Cong., 1847-48, pp. 277, 532.

[8] "Pattison," III, McCormick to Commr. Burke, Dec. 10, 1847. The formal application was made on Jan. 19, 1848. See, Senate, 1st Sess., 32d Cong., "Reports of Committees," No. 160, Mch. 30, 1852, pp. 1, 2.

by its great importance to the farmer; that the inventor's profits were derived from the patents of 1845 and 1847, rather than from the patent of 1834; that he had worked hard to improve it, and after years of effort a demand had finally been created, and the machine had proved its true worth, just as the patent was about to expire.

There is little doubt that McCormick minimized the profits he had received from the manufacture and sale of his invention. He estimated a gross income of about $23,000,[9] while his opponents—who, to be sure, could only guess—charged that the figure should be about $50,000. Certainly the major, if not the total, return had been since 1845, and no man could say how much of this was due to the elements patented in 1834 and how much to later improvements. McCormick at this time naturally tended to shift the credit to the latter, so completely, in fact, that unless the circumstances are borne in mind it will be concluded that he believed his machine was of no practical value before 1845. He had kept no account of his expenses and could only state that they had been "several thousand dollars." A large portion of his time for fourteen years had been devoted to the reaper, and even $50,000 was not a large gross return when the value of the invention is taken into account.

Perhaps it was unwise and unnecessary to champion the worth of his own implement by an invidious comparison with Hussey's. His competitor was aroused and soon explained his entrance into the battle solely on the grounds that McCormick was the aggressor and had unjustly attacked him.[10] There is some truth in this charge, but McCormick had never found Hussey a passive opponent in the past, and now that they were both once again in the same lists, each seeking the same objec-

[9] Pattison, II, q, patent fees of $20 each had yielded $15,560 and sales of county, etc., rights to manufacture, $7,083.

[10] Pattison, II, r, O. Hussey to Board of Patent Extensions, no date but between Mch. 18 and 27, 1848.

tive, he instinctively struck the first blow in an inevitable conflict. He would be content if both patents were extended, since
in his new field in the West he was almost unchallenged. But
it would give Hussey too great an advantage if he won and
McCormick failed.

In the account of his business, forwarded to the Commissioner of Patents, McCormick emphasized the failure of some
of his lessees to make salable reapers. This helped to explain
why his profits had not been larger, but it was irritating to the
parties thus indicted. An application for a renewal must be
received at least sixty days before the expiration of the patent,
in order that fair notice may be given in newspapers throughout the land. Consequently, any foe was afforded an opportunity to file reasons against the extension of the inventor's
monopoly. The Brockport firms were at once on the alert, and
soon the commissioner found on his desk a petition against
renewal, signed by over one hundred residents of Monroe
County, New York. Ansel Chappell's name headed the list.
He had purchased the first McCormick reaper sold in that
State and was a close ally, and at one time a partner, of Seymour & Morgan.

It is unnecessary to look further for the source of the opposition to McCormick's claim in the Genesee Valley. The Solicitor
of the Treasury, one of the three whose word was law in the
matter, was a resident of New York. James Buchanan, Secretary of State and another member of the board, had been long
schooled in practical politics, but very likely was too busy during these closing months of the Mexican War to give the matter much personal attention. Edmund Burke, the Commissioner
of Patents, and the last of the three upon whom McCormick
must rest his hopes in the first instance,[11] was friendly to the

[11] These three constituted the Board of Examiners for Patent Extensions.
The inventor who failed to secure a renewal from them had the privilege
of pressing his case before Congress or the Court of Claims.

inventor's petition. He was removed from office shortly after President Taylor, a Whig, succeeded President Polk in March, 1849, and is next heard from in the rôle of a McCormick lobbyist before Congress.

Cyrus McCormick had promised the Commissioner of Patents that he would forward all necessary evidence in support of his application by the fifteenth of January. His letter of January 1, 1848, partially fulfilled this guarantee and was soon supplemented by the statements of those who had witnessed either the building or the first field trial of the reaper in 1831. He evidently presumed that *ex-parte* statements were all that would be required, and, unadvised by counsel, he did not realize that his rivals could demand an opportunity to cross-examine these deponents. He probably prepared the depositions himself and secured the signatures of such persons as John McCown, who had made the sickle for the first machine, and of his mother, two brothers, John and Eliza Steele, and N. M. Hitt, who witnessed the first trial.

As a matter of routine, McCormick's application with its supporting evidence was turned over to Charles G. Page, the Chief Examiner of Patents, for report to the Board of Extensions. On January 22, 1848, this official recommended against renewal, on the grounds that the McCormick reaper embraced no new elements and that the conflicting Hussey patent antedated the one in question by almost six months.[12] The fact that Hussey's patent had been granted before McCormick's was *prima-facie* evidence that Hussey had anticipated McCormick in the invention of the parts common to both reapers. In other words, Page's opinion resolved itself into a statement that the patent should never have been granted to McCormick, since all of the principal features of his machine had been covered

[12] "Pattison," II, c, C. G. Page to the Commr. of Patents, Jan. 22, 1848. As late as 1856, Page reiterated his belief that his opinion of 1848 was sound. C. G. Page to P. H. Watson, May 12, 1856.

in prior grants. His two chief contentions on this point were that the McCormick reel was similar to Ten Eyck's, patented in 1825, and the knife, fingers, and the general arrangement of the cutter strongly resembled Hussey's. He apparently refused to accept the oft-repeated opinion of the federal courts that a new and effective combination of elements hitherto known is patentable.

The examiner's reference to the Ten Eyck reel was obviously absurd, as Cyrus McCormick made haste to point out.[13] Ten Eyck did employ a revolving knife-rack which suggested McCormick's reel in appearance, but it was devised to cut the grain as well as to bear it toward a separate knife. Page's emphasis upon the date of Hussey's patent would be unwarranted if McCormick could show that he had constructed and used a machine in 1831 which embraced all the essential parts of the one patented in 1834. By so doing he would establish a priority of two years over Hussey.

The Board of Extensions did not meet until one month after Page's report, but as early as the first of February, Cyrus McCormick had learned that his *ex-parte* evidence concerning the 1831 trials would not be accepted. To correct this oversight, he sought out Hussey at Baltimore, who admitted that his reaper did not antedate 1833, but declined to name a date when it would be convenient for him to cross-examine McCormick's witnesses.[14] Thereupon McCormick wrote twice to the Commissioner of Patents in early February, reporting this conversation and charging that all of Hussey's improvements since 1833, such as the large main wheel and the open-back guard

[13] Pattison, II, d, C. H. McCormick to Commr. Burke, Feb. 2, 1848.

[14] Stabler, *op. cit.* The author of this pamphlet, writing in 1854, asserts that McCormick asked Hussey to sign a paper agreeing to consider the *ex-parte* testimony as good evidence. Hussey declined, fearing to injure his own patent-extension hopes. Stabler states that Hussey did not know of McCormick's application until this interview. Save for this assertion, his narrative may well be accurate.

fingers, had been pirated from McCormick's own machine. He promised to furnish more formal evidence to demonstrate the value of his own reaper, if such was necessary, and urged Commissioner Burke on February 21 to appoint as early a date as possible for taking depositions to prove that he was entitled to priority of invention over Hussey.[15]

Obed Hussey was not idle. On this same day he wrote to Burke, objecting to a renewal of McCormick's patent on the ground that McCormick's reaper "has not proved a useful invention to the public," and that an extension would work injury to the one who had made "the best Reaping Machine which was ever offered to the world." McCormick had received sufficient financial reward before the poor quality of his machine was made evident and he had gained an unfair advantage in the Hutchinson trial of 1843.[16] It is hard to understand how Hussey could have written this. He must have known it was common knowledge that he was selling less than one hundred reapers each season, while McCormick and his licensees were marketing over ten times that number. It was hardly convincing to contend that so many farmers selected the poorer machine at a higher price.

Hussey also feared McCormick could prove at least one year's priority of invention. He therefore wrote a second letter two days later to the Board of Extension, in which he stated, "Our machines are different in principle, so far as regards these points, which either of us can justly claim to be the inventor of. I will admit that our machines in some respects are similar but these points of similarity are public property, and not the invention of either of us." [17] He thus prepared himself a place

[15] Pattison, II, d, j, and III, c, C. H. McCormick to Commr. Burke, Feb. 2, 12, and 21, 1848. McCormick hoped that Burke would designate Walnut Grove and Steele's Tavern, Va., as the places where this testimony should be taken.

[16] Pattison, II, i.

[17] *Ibid.*, II, k.

of refuge, in case McCormick could show that his reaper had operated successfully in 1831. Very likely this could be done, and unless Hussey persuaded the Patent Office and Congress that the two machines were essentially unlike (as they were), he stood small chance of securing an extension of his own patent. In other words, he foresaw that events were so shaping themselves that Page's report might have more justly referred to his own invention than to McCormick's. By the time of this letter he also sensed that his argument of February 21 could be easily answered by comparing the yearly sales of the two implements. Therefore he now shifted to higher ground: "One county is the extent of territory which I have sold. My desire has been to confine the manufacture as much as possible within my own control until I could give to the world a good reaping machine, which I have done just at the expiration of my Patent." This statement might serve to place his very small annual sales in a most commendable light and reconcile them with the excellent quality of the machines he had made.

On February 23, 1848, the Board of Extensions met with Page's adverse report, Hussey's objections, and McCormick's application for renewal and supporting evidence, before it. The Monroe County, New York, farmers' protest against the extension may also have been filed by the time of this first meeting. In any event, the three officials decided to postpone a decision until March 29, and in the meantime McCormick must furnish "satisfactory testimony that the invention of his machine was prior to the invention of a similar machine by Obed Hussey," and due notice must be given to the latter of the time when and the place where the testimony would be taken.[18]

The Commissioner of Patents was deputized to review this new evidence, together with all statements already filed, and recommend a decision for adoption by the board at its next meeting. In short, it is reasonable to suppose that neither the

[18] *Ibid.,* II, 1.

Secretary of State nor the Solicitor of the Treasury, with their manifold duties, at any time read and weighed the testimony. They would listen to Burke's recommendation, but, being a majority of the Board of Extension, they could decide differently if they so chose.

Accordingly McCormick informed Hussey on February 28, 1848, that depositions would be taken at Walnut Grove on March 10 (later changed to 17) and that he might attend if he thought proper.[19] On March 12, the inventor was ill with chills and fever at Charlottesville, Virginia, and wrote to his brother William that he doubted whether he could be at Walnut Grove by the 17.

> I don't think that Hussey will attend to it at all. I enclose copies of other depositions, which they can just repeat, leaving "stationary pieces" to support the grain, etc., out of Dr. Hitt's and putting in Steele's.[20] In your statement you had the double fingers or pieces "of iron or wood"—straight sickle, but not reversed teeth.[21] . . . You can say (as can also Mother and Leander) that you had written evidence in your possession of the year—dated 1831. It will *not be necessary* to show [it] as I think you can't either unless I was there. . . . Caroline can also say that she was at school in 1832, that I returned then from Ky. and she saw the reaper at work in a field near Cochran's,[22] and from the paper of father when I went to Ky. referring to the reaper, can also add that it was in operation in 1831.[23] Mrs. Steele will not be there, and it will be important to have the case as strong as can be, as that is probably the only question now. Mr. McCown stated that I called on him in 1831 to get a sickle made, which he did make . . . which he heard was put to such a machine that year but

[19] *Ibid.*, II, m, and III.

[20] Why this shift of phrase from one deposition to the other was felt to be necessary, is not clear.

[21] McCormick had lost the original statements of his two brothers and mother, and so he reminded them of their content. U. S. Patent Office Records, "McCormick Patent Extension Case, 1848," Photostat, Paper No. 13, C. H. McCormick to the Commr. of Patents, Feb. 21, 1848.

[22] For this incident, see Chap. IV, p. 86.

[23] For a discussion of the identity of this "paper," see *ibid.*

did not see.[24] . . . I wish you to go, or send, to see Sam Hite also. I think that he may recollect the year (1831) from changing places, and propose to pay him what he will charge if he will come. . . . McCown must be got. . . . See McCown as soon as possible and spare no pains to get all done right.

Notwithstanding McCormick's expectation that neither Hussey, Mrs. Steele, nor he would be present at Walnut Grove on March 17, all were there and his rival cross-examined the witnesses. Mrs. Steele saw the first public trial of the reaper on her husband's farm in 1831 and had described it in writing for Cyrus McCormick several months before. But in the meantime she had become mentally unbalanced and could remember nothing on the witness stand without the help of a paper which the inventor had prepared for her guidance. This naturally made her testimony worthless, but there were others who recalled the 1831 trial and Hussey was convinced that his rival's machine antedated his own. Cyrus McCormick's confidential letter to his brother, quoted in the preceding paragraph, indicates that he helped to shape the depositions of his witnesses, but it also reveals that he had no doubt in his own mind of the year in which his reaper was first used.

He thereupon forwarded this testimony to the Patent Office,[25] and Hussey wrote in protest that Mrs. Steele had been unable to testify "without her paper"; that Leander and William McCormick were too much interested in the manufacture of the reaper to be impartial witnesses, and that Cyrus had apparently shaped the depositions to fit his purpose. Despite these objections, he added that the testimony proved two things —that his rival had first tried his reaper in 1831, and that if

[24] For McCormick's part in the framing of these depositions, see his statements to the Committee on Patents and the Patent Office of the U. S. Senate, Apr. 3, 1853, in House of Reps., 1st Sess., 34th Cong., "Reports, Court of Claims," I, No. 11, May 16, 1856.

[25] Pattison, II, p, C. H. McCormick to E. Burke, Mch. 27, 1848.

McCormick ever employed the double finger, he had discontinued its use before Hussey's patent of 1847. While conceding McCormick priority of invention, Hussey underscored the word "trial" in order to emphasize his belief that his competitor's reaper had not cut successfully on the Steele farm in 1831; and he was careful to repeat that his machine did not conflict with the McCormick in any mechanical part actually invented by either himself or his rival. He admitted that his own machine entirely depended for its efficiency as a reaper upon its cutter, which he did not invent although he was the first to combine it with the double finger through which it vibrated.[26]

When the Extension Board reconvened on March 29, 1848, to make its final decision, it listened to a report in favor of McCormick by the Commissioner of Patents, Edmund Burke.[27] The major contention of Examiner Page that Hussey had anticipated McCormick in many elements common to both machines was shown, by the Walnut Grove depositions twelve days before, to be untrue. Burke argued that McCormick merited a decision in his favor[28] because of the "originality and priority" of his invention, the inadequate compensation he had received, the reaper's importance to agriculture, helping to begin a new era as had the jenny and power-loom, and because of the diligence and skill displayed by him in overcoming the difficulties attendant upon its improvement and introduction. Despite his recommendation, Buchanan, Secretary of State, and Gillett, Solicitor of the Treasury, decided against McCormick's application. Thus Burke was outvoted and, in accord-

[26] *Ibid.*, II, r, Hussey to the Board of Patent Extensions, undated but between Mch. 18 and 27, 1848.
[27] "McCormick Extension Case, Patent of 1845," p. 174, testimony of ex-Commr. Burke, in Dec., 1858. Burke stated that in 1848 ex-Governor Jas. McDowell of Virginia took much interest in McCormick's success and interviewed him in the inventor's behalf.
[28] Senate, 1st Sess., 32d Cong., "Reports of Committees," No. 160, Ex-Commr. Burke to Senators Douglas and Shields, Mch. 4, 1850.

ance with the custom, the report of the board was made unanimous.

The motives for Buchanan's and Gillett's opposition have not been certainly ascertained. Even if the Mexican War had not been coming to a victorious close, and the public had not been agog over the Wilmot Proviso, the Clayton Compromise, and the presidential election, it is doubtful whether the reaper battle of Hussey and McCormick before the Patent Board would have occasioned much stir. So far as is known, the Monroe County farmers alone, led by representatives of Brockport reaper-makers, were the only grain-growers whose opinion on the subject reached the table of the Board of Extensions. When the issue was carried to Congress and a ten-year fight was waged there by Hussey, McCormick, and others for patent-extension, public interest was actively aroused in behalf of or in opposition to one or the other of the principals concerned.

Burke wrote to Senators Douglas and Shields on March 4, 1850, that after the meeting of the board in February, 1848, when McCormick was ordered to take formal testimony, the inventor "subsequently made efforts to supply the defects but never did satisfactorily to the board and they declined to extend." That the renewal was refused for this reason was as pointedly denied by Gillett in 1856. "It was decided on its merits and not on technicalities. It was not because the testimony was informally taken because it was not." [29] Cyrus McCormick had yet another opinion as to the cause of his failure. He wrote to William McCormick from Washington, on April 4, 1848: "The Board of Commissioners decided against extending my patent . . . The profits was the strong cause of opposition, I believe, but the evidence was weakened, it was

[29] Pamphlet, "Documents in the Files of the Committee on Patents of the House of Representatives," in a bound volume of pamphlets entitled "U. S. Senate, Committee on Patents, Documents, Hussey, and Moore & Hascall Extension Cases, 1852-56" (Washington, 1857), R. H. Gillett to P. H. Watson, May 3, 1856.

said, by Mrs. Steele not answering 'for want of a paper' as
Hussey said." [30] McCormick always liked to regard the causes
of a checkmate as personal, since he then had something tangible to fight against. "Faulty testimony" or "the merits of the
case" offered no opportunities for a new contest. But if Hussey
was the chief reason, the foe could be met, and Hussey was a
rival whose tactics he understood. In all likelihood he should
have included Seymour & Morgan, who seem to have en-
gineered the petition of the Genesee farmers against his application, but that firm was needed for the moment, to build his
reapers.

Cyrus McCormick had the ability during a long lifetime of
business war to march ahead without vain regrets after a battle
was lost. His defeat before the Patent Extension Board must
have been a serious blow, but, judging from his correspondence, it was merely an incident of little consequence. On April
4 he wrote to his brother William: "I am now petitioning Congress for the extension which will be acted upon with Hussey's
case, and I have strong hopes will be extended, and also Hussey's which I should care not for. He would still be liable to
me . . . If I should fail of getting an extension, I calculate
I can hold my own without, but I think I shall succeed." Con-

[30] Pattison, II, s. The Monroe County, N. Y., petition had emphasized
McCormick's profits. It asserted that the inventor customarily charged manufacturers a $30 patent fee, and when he manufactured the reapers himself
he cleared $80 or $85 a machine. If an extension were to be granted, his
maximum patent fee should be reduced to $5 a machine, so as to do away
with "the odious feature of monopoly." The Senate Committee on Patents
and the Patent Office in 1854 reported a bill in favor of McCormick on
the premise that the decision in 1848 had been erroneous because the
Board of Patents had failed to recognize the essential differences between
the Hussey and McCormick reapers—Senate, 1st Sess., 33d Cong., "Reports
of Committees," No. 312, June 21, 1854. A bill was introduced in the House
on May 16, 1856, to extend McCormick's patent on the ground that the
adverse decision of the Board of Patent Extensions in 1848 had been due
to "an informality" in the evidence. See, House of Reps., 1st Sess., 34th
Cong., "Reports, Court of Claims, No. 11."

fidence of ultimate success after every defeat, and the will to fight on to the last ditch, are two reasons why McCormick outdistanced all his competitors.

In this case he planned and started a new campaign over a month before he heard the final decision of the extension board. The last Congress of Polk's Presidency was in session for its long term, and McCormick urged the Patent Office to appoint an early date for taking depositions at Walnut Grove, in order that he might present to Congress the evidence of his priority over Hussey before that body had acted upon his rival's petition for renewal. He might thus attain two objectives at a single stroke, since, if the Board of Extension decided against him, there was still time to win his suit before Congress and probably to defeat Hussey's hopes while doing so. As early as February 8, 1848, Senator Mason of Virginia presented to the Senate a petition of Cyrus McCormick for a renewal of his 1834 patent.[31] About the same time, his friend and former neighbor, Congressman James McDowell, ex-Governor of Virginia, acted in his behalf in the House of Representatives.

McCormick furnished Congress with copies of his statements to the Patent Office and of the depositions taken at Walnut Grove. In order to be prepared for any prejudice which might arise because Mrs. Steele had been unable to recall her *ex-parte* testimony, he secured a certificate from ex-Governor McDowell that she was mentally incompetent to testify.[32] For the first time he employed a lawyer to advise him in his course.[33]

---

[31] "Senate Journal," 1st Sess., 30th Cong., 1847-48, p. 157. "Congressional Globe," Apr. 11, 1848, p. 604. Many of the documents relating to the efforts of McCormick to win patent-extension from Congress have been printed in Pattison.

[32] Pattison, VII, b. C. H. McCormick to W. S. McCormick, Apr. 4, 1848.

[33] "McCormick Extension Case, Patent of 1845," pp. 171, 172, sworn testimony of Edmund Burke, Dec., 1858.

Between 1848 and 1858 effort was made in each session of Congress to secure an extension of his patent.[34]

Hussey was engaged in the same contest, on his own account, and soon Moore & Hascall of Michigan, who were seeking a similar favor, still further complicated the issue. The latter contended that McCormick was not the first to use the alternately reverse-angled sickle, since they had employed it in their harvester as early as 1838. Hussey continued to urge that he, and not McCormick, deserved the credit for, and the right of all financial return from, the sale or use of the double open-slotted fingers.

These are merely samples of the mechanical questions which bewildered the politicians and all others who tried to understand the merits of the case.[35] Congressional committee after committee reported in favor of the extension of McCormick's patent, and proclaimed that he had anticipated Hussey by two years in the invention and the successful use of a horse-power reaper.[36] Petitions of irate farmers and state legislatures year after year were sent to Congress in protest against the higher cost of agricultural machinery, which would result from patent renewals. A few memorials prayed that McCormick's, Hussey's, or Moore & Hascall's applications be granted, and, at least on

[34] Complete references in the Senate and House "Journals" to McCormick's ten-year struggle would demand too much space here. For samples see "Senate Journal," 1st Sess., 30th Cong., p. 157; *ibid.*, 1st Sess., 31st Cong., p. 175; *ibid.*, 1st Sess., 33d Cong., pp. 69, 449, 758; *ibid.*, 1st and 2d Sess., 34th Cong., pp. 169, 225, 253, 261, 318, 354, 355, 356, 440, 441; "House Journal," 1st Sess., 31st Cong., p. 899; *ibid.*, 1st Sess., 33d Cong., p. 110; *ibid.*, 2d Sess., 33d Cong., p. 445; *ibid.*, 1st and 2d Sess., 34th Cong., pt. 1, pp. 533, 538.

[35] Senator Fessenden of Maine could not understand why McCormick wanted an extension, since he admitted that his reaper was of little value prior to 1845. This may have been sarcasm, since the senator was a stanch Husseyite. Senator Seward also backed Hussey as "the pioneer of all." "Congressional Globe," July 14, 1856, p. 1601; July 19, 1856, p. 1660.

[36] Senate, 1st Sess., 32d Cong., "Reports of Committees," No. 160; *ibid.*, 1st Sess., 33d Cong., No. 312.

one occasion, McCormick paid his agents to get farmers to sign such a document.[37] Charge and countercharge about the paid lobbyists of McCormick and his rivals were heard in Congress. Edmund Burke, the former Commissioner of Patents, was employed for a season by McCormick "to get correct information before Congress." [38] The press and the agricultural magazines joined in the conflict, usually to speak for the farmers against such "monied monopolists" as McCormick.[39]

Generally speaking, Hussey and Moore & Hascall were supported by the senators and congressmen of the States in which their factories were located. Not so in the case of McCormick, for Senators Douglas and Shields of Illinois, with many other opponents of his patent-extension, were most complimentary to his genius as an inventor but, on constitutional grounds, hostile to his claim. After a patent has expired, said Douglas, there is no constitutional manner by which its privileges can be again vested by Congress in the inventor.[40] Others argued that Mc-

[37] MS. account of Wm. Marshall & Sons of Peoria, Ill., with C. H. McCormick, no date, but after Nov. 1850. For ten days' work at $1 a day, for obtaining signatures to a petition for extension of patent as per McCormick's letter of Nov. 15, 1850. "Senate Journal," 2d Sess., 31st Cong., p. 41. On Jan. 9, 1851, Douglas presented six memorials of Illinois citizens, praying an extension of McCormick's patent. "House Journal," 2d Sess., 31st Cong., pp. 222, 280.

[38] "McCormick Extension Case, Patent of 1845," pp. 162, 165, testimony in Dec., 1858, of E. Burke. "Congressional Globe," July 14 and 19, 1856, pp. 1601, 1660-1665. Senator Brown of Mississippi said that attorneys of parties with no inventive genius were blocking McCormick's bill. "I know, and state here, in the face of the American Senate and the world, that these men have beset me at every corner of the streets with their papers and their affidavits." Senator Pugh of Ohio denied this and said that the only lawyer who had come to him was one of McCormick's. McCormick wants a renewal "to protect his original failure from the improvements of anybody else and so to stop the whole inventive genius of the country for seven years."

[39] "Albany Cultivator," July, 1852, p. 259. "Prairie Farmer," Mch., 1852, p. 142. "Scientific American," Apr. 5, 1856, p. 237. Greeno, p. 27. *Post*, Chap. XIII, p. 324.

[40] "Congressional Globe," May 19 and June 16, 1854, pp. 1224, 1412; July 14, 1856, p. 1601.

Cormick's machine was not original with him. Some thought that if the grant were renewed it would be unfair to those who had begun to manufacture McCormick machines since the date of the expiration of his patent.

To the first charge, adequate answer had been made time and again. To the second, McCormick expressed his willingness, in case of a renewal, to guarantee to all independent manufacturers of his reaper since June 21, 1848, the property they had devoted to this purpose and the profits they had gained. If Congress would not grant an extension he would be content if his petition were merely referred back to the Extension Board for a rehearing.[41] An appeal from the decision of the Patent Office to the United States Court of Claims failed when the latter declined jurisdiction.[42] If congressmen and senators spoke in behalf of Hussey, others arose to champion McCormick. Senators Walker of Wisconsin and A. G. Brown of Mississippi were, with the two from Virginia, his main supporters in the upper house.[43] In the House of Representatives, Congressman McDowell, until his death in 1851, was ever loyal to his old neighbor. But the spokesmen of one inventor yearly managed to block the sponsors of the other. When, in 1855, McCormick and Hussey may have joined forces to get their respective patents renewed, the coalition likewise failed.[44]

Perhaps the contest was hopeless from the start. During the 1850's the number of reaper- and mower-manufacturers grew very rapidly. More and more capital was devoted to the

[41] Senate, 1st Sess., 35th Cong., "Miscellaneous Documents," No. 127, C. H. McCormick to the Senate and House of Reps., Dec. 18, 1853. Senate, 1st Sess., 33d Cong., "Reports of Committees," No. 312.

[42] "House Journal," 1st and 2d Sess., 34th Cong., pt. II, p. 991; *ibid.,* 3d Sess., 34th Cong., p. 206; *ibid.,* 1st Sess., 35th Cong., pp. 136, 137; *ibid.,* 2d Sess., 35th Cong., pp. 241, 242; House of Reps., 1st Sess., 34th Cong., "Reports, Court of Claims," No. 11.

[43] "Congressional Globe," June 16, 1854, p. 1412; *ibid.,* July 14, 1856, p. 1601.

[44] *Post,* Chap. XVIII, pp. 445-447.

business, and with few exceptions these rivals based their implements upon McCormick's principles of construction. No longer did McCormick and Hussey alone control the reaper market of the United States as they had done in the days before 1848 when the demand was small. McCormick, in spite of the failure to renew his original patent, was still the largest manufacturer of reapers in the country, while the Hussey factory at Baltimore did not grow, and was appraised at only $500 when the inventor was killed by a train in 1860.

By this date McCormick was one of the few millionaires in the United States, and as his profits multiplied each year during the preceding decade, it was not a very appealing argument in support of extension to point to his inadequate return before 1848 from his 1834 patent. Although he did not need a renewal, he characteristically kept on fighting for it because he believed that he deserved to win. And he did merit victory, from the standpoint of the value of his invention to the farmer. His profits after 1848 were due in large degree to his business boldness and skill, rather than to his genius as an inventor.[45] Before 1848 he had little more than paid his expenses, but after that year he became rich in spite of competitors who were using his own invention to lessen his profits. His brother wrote to him in 1859, at the close of the contest:

I enclose a slip from the Press (same in all the papers here). Well what of it? I suppose a man with ½ your present fortune is as well off in a *pecuniary* point of view *as he can be*. Suppose you had $500,000 *safely* invested in houses to rent or otherwise at ten per cent. . . . You would have an income of $50,000 a year in *interest*. I suppose you can safely count *double* that. I supposed it probable from your letters that in some way you *knew* the commissioner to be *in favor* with you and only upon that ground did I suppose it possible that you could reasonably hope for the extension. While I did my best here I have said in view of the

---

[45] Unsigned article, "Cyrus H. McCormick," in "Harper's Weekly," May 24, 1884, p. 338.

result that I did not expect it . . . and that I did not consider it material and that as I have often said your money has been made *not* out of your patents but by making and selling the machines. . . . I don't believe this decision will effect your business as compared with the past. Others *have* been making all they could *sell*. You will not be able to collect patent fees is I suppose about the only difference it will make.[46]

Cyrus McCormick never appears to better advantage than during the ten years after 1848. He doubled and quadrupled his sales, greatly enlarged his factory, dispensed with partners, fought his rivals in Congress and in the courts, abroad and at home, on countless harvest fields. He was admired and hated, fawned upon and eulogized. But he never aroused sympathy for himself and probably would have spurned the man who offered it. These are other reasons why he had little chance to win an extension of his patent from Congress.

Farmers became more and more vocal against patent-extensions on essential agricultural machinery as the years passed. No longer were the Genesee Valley wheat-growers unsupported in their efforts to prevent McCormick and other inventors from realizing their desires. Almost every State in the North and West was represented each year in the flood of remonstrances which came to Congress, and local legislatures instructed their senators and requested their representatives "to vote right" on patent-extension bills.[47] It is difficult, if not impossible, to prove that political pressure from the rural constituencies of many members of Congress led to a policy in regard to McCormick

[46] W. S. to C. H. McCormick, Feb. 1, 1859, L.P.C.B., No. 18, pp. 92, 93, 98. W. S. McCormick has in mind the refusal to extend the 1845 patent as well as the one issued in 1834.

[47] Between 1848 and 1853, there were 103 petitions of citizens and resolutions of legislatures or rival manufacturers of various States against the extension of McCormick's patent—and sometimes Hussey and Moore & Hascall are coupled with him. These were sent to either house of Congress and probably some were duplicates.

of compliment, and refusal to support.[48] But certainly this is
the most obvious and likely explanation of his failure to win his
long fight. The loss of this battle was a challenge rather than a
discouragement. After 1848 he changed his business tactics
and proved himself as skilful an industrialist as he was an
inventor.

[48] See, Senate, 1st Sess., 32d Cong., "Reports of Committees," No. 160:
"It is one of those great and valuable inventions which commence a new era
in the progress of improvement, and whose beneficial influence is felt in all
coming time. . . ." Equally eulogistic statements about Hussey's reaper may
be found, *ibid.*, 1st Sess., 30th Cong., No. 154, and *ibid.*, 1st Sess., 33d
Cong., No. 207.

CHAPTER XIII

MANUFACTURING THE McCORMICK REAPER AND MOWER

THE blacksmith shop at Walnut Grove was large enough for the manufacture of the reapers as long as the demand for them was local. Robert and Leander McCormick, with the help of the slaves and an occasional hired man, formed the factory personnel. The nature of the arrangements made by Cyrus McCormick with his father and brother is not clear. No record remains of wages given, and it is likely that Robert, who owned the plant, did not until 1844 begin to pay Cyrus a fifteen- or twenty-dollar patent fee on the reapers made and sold. Prior to that year all of the male members of the family were so closely associated with the enterprise that it is impossible to trace the allocation of the profits. Reaper-building was doubtless a mutual family concern in which all coöperated with the hope of discharging the iron-furnace debts as quickly as possible. Between 1844 and his father's death in 1846, Cyrus McCormick apparently contributed nothing toward the expense of manufacturing. William McCormick, who devoted most of his attention to the management of his father's farms, kept an account of the business transacted by Robert and Cyrus, but furnace business, reaper sales, farm expenses, transportation charges, and advertisement costs are so inextricably mingled that very little certain information can be gained from its study. Initials and abbreviations are customarily used for persons and things, familiar to William but mysteries to the student to-day.[1]

---

[1] *McCormick vs. Manny*, II, pp. 234, 235; 275-287. W. S. McCormick testified that Cyrus paid him nothing prior to 1850.

The business year at Walnut Grove was divided into three parts. In the winter and spring chief attention was given to manufacturing and soliciting sales. When production increased to almost fifty reapers, as it did in 1845, the winters at Walnut Grove must have been very busy ones. Fortunately, iron and wood, the two chief materials used, were convenient and cheap. Ash, hickory, and maple were principally employed, and Robert McCormick had his own timber, sawmills, and carpenter shops, as well as his smithy.[2] The steel sickles demanded fine workmanship, and in 1842, when John McCown, whose tilt-hammer shop had produced the knife for the first McCormick machine in 1831, was found unreliable because of his fondness for liquor, Cyrus was compelled to make the cutters at Walnut Grove.[3] This proved impracticable after trial, and for the next year his knives were fashioned by Selah Holbrook at Port Republic, twenty miles away, and Cyrus brought them home on horseback.

Because the farmers hesitated to order until they were reasonably sure that their crops would be abundant and the market price of grain fair, the advance sales and the ultimate demand were rarely identical. The impossibility of prognosticating the weather or the size of the harvest, and the fact that all alterations of construction were of doubtful value until they could be tested in the harvest field, rendered even the little business at Walnut Grove a highly speculative one. With meager capital and many iron-furnace debts still to pay, the McCormicks in these early years generally confined their annual production of reapers to the number of orders received. Because the experience in each harvest at this time proved the

[2] Lumber was sometimes purchased. See C. H. McCormick to Wm. Massie, Dec. 24, 1842, where the inventor seeks "some heavy seasoned stuff." "There is some 3 in. plank (or over) which I think would suit us well to put into our machines. We would not want much of it at this time I suppose, and might be glad to get a little that is not so thick."

[3] C. H. McCormick to J. Newton, May 16, 1842.

desirability of mechanical alterations, surplus reapers represented a loss too heavy to be borne.

Paint, polish, and "furbelows" were largely omitted from the first McCormick reapers and the machines consequently failed to win a reputation for beauty. The emphasis was for long upon durability and performance rather than upon appearance. The flapping canvas and the huge six-foot reel must have appeared to the sensitive eye and ear an awkward substitute for the swinging cradle and the song of the reaper.[4] Those who rejoiced in any advancement of the cause of temperance were rendered happy by a machine which made fewer harvest hands necessary, and easier work under a summer's sun. The reaper helped to reduce the consumption of liquor in harvest-time and consequently had an ethical as well as an economic reason for being.[5]

During the month or six weeks of the Virginia harvest, the McCormicks faced the problems of transportation and delivery. The completed reapers were freighted by canal, river, or road to a spot most accessible to the purchaser. One of the family often accompanied the machine to its destination and spent several days or a week putting it in working order and testing it in the grain-field. Speedy alterations had to be made when field tests proved their advisability; experiments were conducted in order to discover improvements which might be added before the next harvest, and Cyrus McCormick was on the alert to meet Obed Hussey's challenge whenever and wherever given. This close personal attention bestowed upon each purchaser could continue only as long as the yearly sales were few and grouped within a circle whose circumference was not far distant from the Walnut Grove center. In the autumn, bills were collected, manufacturing materials assembled, and

---

[4] *Hussey vs. McCormick,* p. 139. It was not until 1859 or 1860 that considerable attention was given to the "finish" of the machines.

[5] Parsons, Miller, and Steward, pp. 10-18. *Supra,* Chap. III, p. 71.

plans laid for the coming season. During the years from 1839 to 1845 the liquidation of the iron business and the farming of a large estate necessarily required a portion of the time of the father and his sons.

The $15 or $20 per reaper which Robert McCormick paid as a patent fee to his eldest son was something less than one half of the net profit resulting from each sale. In 1839 manufacturing was begun with the intention of selling each machine for $50 cash. The inventor discovered that the production cost was about this amount, and Abraham Smith, the first purchaser, was the only one who was favored with a reaper at this price. Richard Sampson, the other buyer of 1840, paid $90, and reapers were soon selling for $100 cash.[6] A variation from the usual arrangement with his father occurred in 1844, when Cyrus McCormick bought from him eight or nine machines he intended to introduce in the West. Thus in the business relations within the family were first used two of the standard principles that guided the inventor in making his contracts with other manufacturers between 1843 and 1850. Either the privilege of construction and sale in exchange for a patent fee, or the production of machines at an agreed price for the inventor's own use, remained the customary terms upon which manufacturing rights were leased. Many of the contracts were made to expire in 1848, when the 1834 patent lapsed, while the balance were restricted to a single harvest.

As early as 1843, Cyrus McCormick closed several contracts for the harvest of the next year that much curtailed the area in which Walnut Grove machines might be sold.[7] In the agreement with his father in 1846 the fee paid by the latter was reduced by five dollars, and this was possibly a result of the

[6] The cash requirement was frequently waived. A deposit on delivery and the balance in four months were the usual terms for many years. Occasionally, relatives or distinguished farmers were given special rates.

[7] "Richmond Semi-Weekly Whig," Oct. 27, 1843.

diminution of sales territory open to the output of the Walnut Grove shop as a result of the leases to other reaper-builders. The arrangements of 1843 with Jabez Parker of Richmond, James M. Hite of Clarke County, and Martin Tutwiler of Fluvanna County need not be detailed here, but in each case a definite territory was assigned for a five-year period upon payment of a price fixed in the written contract.[8] The price per county varied with the patronage the lessee might expect to enjoy in each. Jabez Parker was granted a five-year monopoly right to manufacture and sell in five counties around Richmond for $500,[9] while at the same time J. M. Hite contracted to pay $1,333 for the same privileges in eight counties in his vicinity.[10] In that year McCormick found two men who were willing to pay him $200 apiece for a county in Michigan and one in Maryland.[11]

On the other hand, for 1845, besides a number of sales of county rights for a cash price similar to the above,[12] he also agreed that Henry Bear of Cooper County, Missouri, might manufacture at will and pay him a twenty-dollar patent fee for each machine sold.[13] For the same season similar arrangements were made with Backus, Fitch & Co. of Brockport, New York, and with A. C. Brown of Cincinnati, Ohio. The Genesee Valley firm received the right to make forty reapers, for sale in four designated counties, while Brown could build two hundred if

[8] "Southern Planter," Jan., 1846, pp. 5-8. "Richmond Enquirer," May 16, 1845, and Jan. 16, 1846. *Supra,* Chap. VIII, pp. 194-195.
[9] "Lynchburg Virginian," May 8, 15, 19, 29, 1845.
[10] Pattison, II, a, C. H. McCormick to E. Burke, Jan. 1, 1848. *Ibid.,* IX, J. M. Hite to C. H. McCormick, Mch. 16, 1848.
[11] "Richmond Enquirer," Nov. 19, 1844.
[12] C. H. to W. S. McCormick, Apr. 2, 1845. "Genesee Farmer," Apr., 1846, p. 100. Backus, Fitch & Co. of Brockport, N. Y., were sold the right to make reapers for Monroe and Orleans counties at $100 each. Mr. McCoy of Southport (Kenosha), Wis., was leased four counties until 1848, for $1,000.
[13] C. H. McCormick to E. Burke, Jan. 1, 1848.

sufficient orders were secured. Brown employed agents to canvass the West, and Cyrus not only traveled as a salesman in his behalf but exercised some supervision over the construction work at Cincinnati. For each purchaser whom he found, he received a commission of five dollars in addition to the patent fee.[14] These contracts resemble the agreement with Robert McCormick at Walnut Grove.

In the case of both the Cincinnati and the Brockport lessees, the firms employed sub-manufacturers to assist them. Cyrus McCormick apparently had no authority to prevent this delegation of work, but it contributed to the poor quality of the output.[15] On the other hand, in the case of the cutter-blades the services of a skilled craftsman were necessary. Jabez Parker at Richmond had his sickles fashioned by an edged-tool maker; Robert McCormick relied upon John McCown's blacksmith shop or Selah Holbrook's tilt-hammer foundry for this same careful work, and Henry Bear sent from Missouri to the Brown factory for his knives.[16] It was customary for Cyrus McCormick to forward a model machine or patterns for the guidance of these manufacturers, but he was never sure that they would be faithfully copied.

The arrangements for the harvests of 1846 and 1847 furnish further illustrations of the manner in which the inventor accumulated capital so that he could strike out for himself in 1848. Additional county rights to manufacture were sold in 1846, and A. C. Brown paid about $1,900 for the right to supply sixteen Ohio counties for four years from August 1,

---

[14] *McCormick vs. Manny,* I, pp. 206-209. "McCormick Extension Case, Patent of 1845," adverse testimony, testimony of Jos. Ganson.

[15] "McCormick Extension Case, Patent of 1847," pp. 93-96, 113-117.

[16] C. H. to W. S. McCormick, May 15, 1845, and Oct. 13, 1846. "Richmond Enquirer," May 16, 1845. C. H. to R. McCormick, May 3, 1845: Cyrus wrote that he was supervising the making of blades at Cincinnati. "Genesee Farmer," Nov., 1847, adv. section, p. 5. D. J. Townsend, a sub-manufacturer of Illinois, secured his castings in Brockport.

1845.[17] Backus, Fitch & Co. agreed to make one hundred for western New York, and Seymour, Chappell & Co., of the same town, one hundred for the Western harvest of 1846.[18] Cyrus McCormick wrote to his brother William on August 6, 1845:

> I have after much chaffering with B. F. and Co. contracted with them to build 100 machines for next harvest (improved) charging me with a fifth part of the cost @ $40, but for which they are to be allowed $50, and then they and I divide the profits equally as each is sold. That is, they charge $50, and say $10 for all expenses of selling and collecting makes $60, leaving $50 to be divided @ $110 which it is proposed to sell at. I (or Leander) to give 1 month's assistance without charge (boarded) and if wanted longer to get $2 a day. . . . I have also contracted with Seymour, Chappell and Co. of the same place . . . to build any number to 100 that may be ordered, say 25 by 1st Nov'r; 25 by 1st Jan'y, and all by 1st Ap'l, at $25 each, and probably more if wanted.[19]

For 1847 two contracts were made in Illinois,[20] and for a time Cyrus McCormick contemplated establishing a factory of his own to supply the Southern demand.[21] However, after learning that his two brothers did not care to manufacture for

[17] *Supra*, p. 232, ftn. 7. C. H. to W. S. McCormick, Apr. 2 and May 15, 1845; to R. McCormick, May 3, 1845.

[18] Pattison, II, a, C. H. McCormick to E. Burke, Jan. 1, 1848.

[19] "New Genesee Farmer," Sept., 1844, pp. 76, 77. "McCormick Extension Case, Patent of 1845," adverse testimony, pp. 14-16, 35-37. *McCormick vs. Manny,* II, pp. 409-411. *Seymour & Morgan vs. McCormick,* pp. 36-40. Pattison, II, a, C. H. McCormick to E. Burke, Jan. 1, 1848: "For 75 of the 100 made by Seymour, Chappell & Co., I paid about $58 each, and sold them in the West; and for 20 of the remaining 25 they paid me $20 each as a patent fee, and I may yet pay the same for 2 or 3 others but not certain."

[20] These were with Gray & Warner of Chicago, whose contract lasted for one year, and D. J. Townsend of Au Sable Grove, Ill., who made reapers in 1847, 1848, and 1849. "Chicago Daily Journal," July 28 and 30, 1846. "Chicago Daily Democrat," Oct. 19, 1848. "Richmond Enquirer," Mch. 18, 1847. "Genesee Farmer," Nov., 1847, adv. dept., p. 5. "Ohio Cultivator," Jan. 15, 1850, p. 31.

[21] C. H. to W. S. McCormick, Oct. 13 and Dec. 11, 1846.

the West, at Walnut Grove, he eventually made new agreements with Brown at Cincinnati and with the Brockport firms. Under the former, in which Leander joined as a one-third partner of Cyrus, the McCormicks agreed to pay Brown $60 for each machine constructed, but he promised to hire Leander to supervise the building at $15 per week. For the same season, Seymour & Morgan of Brockport paid Cyrus a thirty-five dollar patent fee for each of about two hundred reapers which they made and sold, as well as a commission for each order that he secured for them.[22] C. M. Gray and Seth P. Warner, of Chicago, contracted to make one hundred reapers for three or more Illinois counties and to pay the inventor a royalty of $30 a machine as well as a commission of $5 on orders which he might send in.[23] The partnership agreements of the years 1848 to 1850 have been discussed in the preceding chapter.

This annual extension of manufacturing was due not only to the growing popularity and use of the reaper but also to the inventor's realization that the homestead in Virginia was not properly situated and equipped to supply a wide market. The period of decentralized production ends with the removal to Chicago in 1848, and thenceforward Cyrus McCormick was

[22] C. H. to L. J. McCormick, Jan. 8, 1847. C. H. McCormick to Seymour & Morgan, Mch. 19, 1847, in the "Farm Implement News," XXIII (1902), pt. 1. "McCormick Extension Case, Patent of 1845," adverse testimony, pp. 17, 35-37. "Chicago Weekly Journal," Sept. 6, 1847. "Genesee Farmer," June, 1847, p. 140; Nov., 1847, adv. dept., p. 5; July, 1850, p. 173. Fitch, Barry & Co. of Brockport also made about 50 McCormick reapers in 1847, and paid the inventor a $25 patent fee. H. E. Smith, of Fowlersville, N. Y., also had a contract to manufacture, but his output has not been ascertained.

[23] McCormick vs. Gray and Ogden, p. 17. The contract was made on July 31, 1846. Gray & Warner were to supply DuPage, McHenry, and Boone counties, Ill. If one hundred orders could not be secured there, Lake, Cook, and Will counties might be added. If these were not enough, then Iroquois, Grundy, and Putnam counties might be included. "Chicago Daily Democrat," June 30, 1847.

content to enlarge his plant in that city as the national and
international demand for his reaper increased. By 1856 the Mc-
Cormick factory completed forty machines a day in the rush
season, and made over four thousand each year.[24] No description of the buildings during this harvest has been found, but
three years later five brick-and-wood structures of from two to
five stories each, furnished a total floor space of 110,000 square
feet.

Leander McCormick was in immediate charge of all construction work and was assisted by the foremen of the wood,
iron, casting, and repair departments.[25] At seven o'clock each
morning, except Sunday and the few holidays, 120 carpenters,
115 iron-finishers, 40 blacksmiths, and 25 laborers reported
for a ten-hour working day. "In the screw cutting room, a
bevy of boys picked up from our streets, under the supervision of a capable mechanic, tended each his own machine,
with a solemn air of responsibility, novel to some of them at
least." [26] The laborers were non-unionized and the wages seem
pitiable to-day, until it is remembered that room and board
could be procured in the city for $3 a week. Smiths received
$1.25 a day; foremen, bricklayers, and carpenters, $2.50;
teamsters, "who could sleep at the office," $1.00; watchmen,
$1.50 a night for thirteen hours of service, "not hard on the

[24] J. L. Wilson, for C. H. McCormick, to A. Johnson, May 2, 1856,
L.P.C.B. No. 1, p. 259.

[25] "Lexington Gazette," Apr. 28, 1859, copying from the "Chicago Tribune." Each department sent in weekly reports of materials made and
used. The reporter noted with admiration that in the repair room there.
were duplicates of every model of machine which had been sold. "Here
. . . is the whole story told in the identical reapers, one of each kind ever
sold, and a farmer of Illinois or Missouri, who in an earlier year bought
a Machine, has only to mention the part he wishes duplicated with the
year of his purchase, and from the 'Repair Room' the pattern maker or
the foundryman takes his pattern and fills the order promptly."

[26] Ibid., the "Tribune" called this an "excellent and benevolent policy."
See also W. S. McCormick to W. T. Rush, Steele's Tavern, Va., Jan. 29,
1858, L.P.C.B. No. 10, p. 491.

The McCormick Works at Chicago about 1860

clothes," seven nights in a week.[27] As William McCormick wrote in 1857, "A man of some sprightliness and business tact along with his trade could probably soon work his way up to fifty dollars per month of 26 days, ten hours work. This might take a year or more to acquire. Chicago is getting to be a great City and in it good men can always find employment at fair wages." [28] And yet it was worth much, during the hard times from 1856 to 1859, to work for an employer who never failed to pay on Saturday nights, and who was enlarging his plant and installing new machinery while many of his competitors were closing their factories and dismissing their help.

· Although the output of grain-harvesters steadily increased, many farmers needed mowers as much, or more, than reapers. The Southerner grew little hay on his plantation, but in the Northern seaboard States where grain-growers could no longer compete with Western wheat, more and more stock was grazed and larger and larger acreage was devoted to grass.[29] Nearly fourteen million tons of hay were cut in 1850 and it was estimated that this was harvested by hand at a cost of one dollar a ton. A good mowing machine would do the same work more easily and speedily and for one quarter of that cost.[30] Granting that every farmer would use an efficient horse-power machine, if available, the annual saving in money alone would be considerable.

The problem of cutting grass is quite different from that

[27] Letters of W. S. McCormick to D. Zimmerman, Youngstown, Pa., Sept. 6, 1856, L.P.C.B. No. 3, p. 374; to Jas. Campbell of Westons, N. J., *ibid.*, No. 3, p. 551; No. 4, p. 85; to Mr. McNair, Decatur, Wis., Aug. 28, 1857; *ibid.*, No. 8, p. 609½.
[28] W. S. McCormick to J. M. Lilley, Greenville, Va., Feb. 25, 1857; *ibid.*, No. 5, p. 322.
[29] *Supra*, Chap. IX, pp. 204. See also T. J. Paterson, from Rochester, N. Y., Feb. 28 and July 6, 1854; D. Zimmerman, from Connellsville, Pa., Apr. 5, 1855.
[30] "Michigan Farmer," Nov., 1852, pp. 348, 349. "Indiana Farmer" (Indianapolis), June, 1858, pp. 82-84.

of harvesting grain. A ripe grain stalk is usually brittle and stands apart from its fellows near the ground. Grass ready for harvest is matted and tangled from root to tip. It is often tough and wiry, full of moisture, and usually so low that it cannot be bent toward the sickle with a reel. The mowing knife must be adapted for use in grass of all kinds, ranging from heavy clover and timothy to the native prairie varieties. It is economical to cut as close to the ground as possible, and consequently the mowing arm must skim the surface, where stones and other obstructions are likely to break off sickle-sections and guard fingers. A wooden finger-beam, such as was customarily used in the reaper, would soon wear out if retained in a mower. Few fields are level, and thrifty farmers naturally demanded a machine whose cutter-bar would automatically accommodate itself to the undulations of the ground. This mattered little in grain, where the valuable seed is wholly at the tip of the stalk and a few inches more or less of stubble was of no great consequence. On the other hand, the delivery problem in mowing is simpler than that in reaping. The cut grass needs only to be spread so that it can dry as quickly as possible in the sun and wind.

For these reasons, a more stoutly built machine was required for cutting grass. It was soon discovered that a framework which was durable in a reaper was racked to pieces quickly in a field of heavy tangled clover. But, while this was true, the blunt broad guard fingers and the heavy divider of the reaper would not penetrate the maze of grass stems and effect the separation which was necessary in order to cut effectively. Yet, if the fingers and the divider were made longer, narrower, and more pointed, they would easily break when driven against a stone or a root. Some material less brittle than cast-iron and more durable than wood was necessary. Tough grass clogged the knife and stopped the forward motion of the machine.

Most farmers grew both grass and grain, but few could

afford to purchase both a reaper and a mower. The owner of an eighty-acre farm secured from the Government for a hundred dollars would hardly consider spending three times that amount for two machines with an average life of nine or ten years. To secure large sales the manufacturer must devise one implement which could be converted quickly from a mower to a reaper and back again, at the will of the owner. A stout framework, a reel, a removable platform, and two knife-bars—one for reaping and the other for mowing—would be the essential parts of such a combined machine.

By 1849, when McCormick had so improved his reaper that it gave almost complete satisfaction, there were already several mowers in the market which worked well. The Ketchum machine, made at Buffalo, was the most popular of these, and was to remain so for some years to come. This implement, designed only for mowing, gained a reputation among farmers which it was difficult for McCormick to supplant when his mower was finally perfected about 1855. Hussey, and soon J. H. Manny, Burrall, Rugg, Danford, and others, had mowers for sale which added to the competition.

Aside from the rivalry of Hussey and inadequate transportation, McCormick's marketing problem in the early years of the reaper consisted largely of teaching farmers to use machinery. Because he was not the first in the field with a mower, the implements of other manufacturers were a challenge from the outset. The largest field for the sale of reapers was in the West, where the McCormick factory was situated. On the other hand, Eastern farmers in the 1850's were the best customers for mowers and looked with distrust upon a machine that was made so far from their own neighborhood. Cyrus McCormick had difficulty in selling his reapers on the seaboard after his removal to Chicago, although his only competitor there was Hussey. It was to be even harder to build up a mower market in a territory already supplied with a number

of machines which cut grass as well, or better, than the Mc-
Cormick. Until the harvest of 1854, Cyrus McCormick was
annually disappointed with the operation of his mower.

In the summer of 1849, McCormick tried his mower for the
first time in a field of prairie grass a short distance from
Chicago. The machine was very like his reaper, save that the
platform was removed, the sickle shortened, and a device called
a scraper-board added, which was designed to supplement the
divider in its work of separating from the standing grass the
swath to be cut. Even the reel was retained with the hope that
it would assist in bending the grass toward the knife. Only one
machine was made for trial purposes and more than likely the
optimistic public statement of the inventor concerning its operation should be somewhat discounted.[31] Nevertheless, when
Cyrus McCormick concluded the partnership agreement with
Orloff M. Dorman on September 22, 1849, it was stipulated
that one hundred separate mowers or reaper-mowers should be
made for the harvest of 1850, the inventor receiving a patent
fee of $20 from each.[32] In the same month he advertised that
he would sell mowers in 1850 for $100 and reaper-mowers
for about $175. The mowers would be warranted to operate
well on smooth land.[33]

Despite these pre-season hopes, he manufactured only mowing attachments for the harvest of 1850, consisting of a knife-

[31] For the McCormick mower in 1849, see the "Chicago Daily Journal,"
Sept. 8, 1849; "Prairie Farmer," Oct., 1849, p. 320; "Ohio Cultivator,"
Jan. 15, 1850, p. 31; "Chicago Commercial Advertiser," Apr. 3, 1850; U. S.
Patent Office Records, "C. H. McCormick-W. F. Ketchum Interference,
1852" (typed copy), pp. 28-34, 40, 130-137. The first trial of the mower
was held on the farm of W. E. Carrington of Flag Creek, Ill. Carrington
stated that he cut his hay crop of 100 tons with it.
[32] MS. agreement between C. H. McCormick and O. M. Dorman, Sept.
22, 1849.
[33] "Chicago Daily Journal," Sept. 8, 1849. "Ohio Cultivator," Jan. 15,
1850, p. 34. McCormick believed that his mower would cut 12 to 15 acres
a day.

bar and scraper-board which could be quickly attached to his reaper. Several of these so-called "combined" machines were sold that year, and McCormick was enough encouraged by their performance to announce in the autumn that he would make "a considerable number" for 1851.[34]

All of his reapers in 1851 were made so that a mowing attachment could be added whenever desired, and in that season the mowing-bars were not manufactured in sufficient quantity to meet the demand.[35] Nevertheless, William S. McCormick testified at this time that his brother's mowers were still experimental and had not yet been introduced successfully.[36] During the summer of 1851 further trials led to the adoption of a new type of guard finger and an iron beam.[37] A contest in the autumn, staged by the Mechanics' Institute of Chicago, resulted in a victory for the McCormick mower over Rugg's and Danford's.[38] Thereupon Ketchum contended that McCormick's scraper-board had been anticipated in his machine, and Rugg protested that the curved guard finger, in combination with the rivet heads on the cutter-blades, was an infringement upon his own.[39] McCormick's competitor won in each instance before the courts, and the inventor was compelled to alter these parts of his implement in order to escape the payment of royalties. Notwithstanding the award of the Me-

[34] "Albany Evening Journal," Oct. 17, 1850. "Prairie Farmer," Jan., 1851, pp. 44, 45. "Albany Cultivator," July, 1851, p. 253.

[35] "Albany Cultivator," July, 1851, p. 253. "Ohio Cultivator," June 1, 1851, p. 176: Here is shown a cut of the McCormick reaper-mower, and the inventor writes, "After many experiments and comparisons, I have now adopted the best possible arrangement and combination for cutting grain and grass, and yet the simplest and most durable."

[36] "C. H. McCormick-W. F. Ketchum Interference, 1852," p. 40.

[37] Photostat of order blank, 1852. *Hussey vs. McCormick,* p. 169.

[38] "Prairie Farmer," Apr., 1852, p. 194. "Albany Cultivator," June, 1852, p. 228.

[39] "McCormick-Ketchum Interference, 1852." "Prairie Farmer," Apr., 1852, p. 194; June, 1852, pp. 295, 296. U. S. Patent Office Records, "G. H. Rugg-C. H. McCormick Interference, 1852."

chanics' Institute of 1851, there is no doubt that the mowing
attachment failed to work well during that harvest.[40] In the
following year McCormick assured all purchasers of 1851, that
he would send them the new improvements without charge.[41]

In 1852 mowing attachments were priced at $25 and several
hundred were sold.[42] But the reports from agents and farmers
were not favorable. There was something wrong with the
knife and guard fingers. They were too similar to those used
for reaping to be effective, while a self-adjustment device for
raising and lowering the sickle, which was added that season,
was merely an improvement in detail and not a remedy for
the basic defects.[43] In the mower trials of the New York Agricultural Society at Geneva in the autumn, stones snapped off
the fingers and sickle-sections of the McCormick mower, and
the knife clogged. McCormick admitted that he must place the
guard teeth closer together in order better to protect the
sickle.[44] Since the successful mowers were generally employing
a smooth-edged cutter, many agricultural editors doubted that

[40] "McCormick-Ketchum Interference, 1852," p. 40. W. S. to J. B. Mc-
Cormick, Apr. 21, 1859, L.P.C.B. No. 19, p. 550: "I spent *months* that
summer [1851] and for the *first* time got *fingers, sickle, divider* and scraper
so we could mow."
[41] In an order blank for 1852 the guard finger of 1851 was blamed.
[42] "Ohio Cultivator," Apr. 15, 1852, p. 128. McCormick advertises that
his mower and mowing attachment are now warranted to cut wider and
cleaner, all kinds of grass, standing or lodged, tangled or clean, wet or
dry, with less power and nearer perfection than any ever offered before.
[43] C. H. McCormick to W. T. Rush, Feb. 20, 1852. "Albany Cultivator,"
Dec., 1852, pp. 412, 413.
[44] "Albany Cultivator," Sept., 1852, pp. 312-313; Oct., 1852, p. 355; Feb.,
1853, p. 69. "Michigan Farmer," Nov., 1852, pp. 348, 349. It was the
general opinion that mechanical mowing was shown to be practical by the
Geneva trials, although all machines had to be driven at a horse-killing
pace in order to secure sufficient velocity in the vibrating knife. The
McCormick machine also failed to find favor with the judges at the trials
of the Clark and Madison Counties Agricultural Society in Ohio. It was
said that one or two men had to stand on its frame to make it leave as
short a stubble as was desired. "American Farmer," Sept., 1852, pp. 100, 101.

the McCormick sickle-edged knife could ever be adapted for cutting grass.[45]

The machines of the next year were as unsuccessful. Not only did they fail to cut fine grass but, because of unwise changes in the gearing, they operated less satisfactorily than in the preceding harvest.[46] Of course this gearing trouble affected the reapers also, and the season of 1853 closed with much prejudice among farmers against the McCormick machines. Therefore the inventor continued his experiments, lessened the length of the mowing knife, made it of still finer cut, and advertised a mower for $100, altogether separate from the reaper. He would sell at Buffalo for this price without any charge for freight from Chicago.[47] Thus he invaded Ketchum's territory, resolved to undersell him in the State which at this time needed more mowers than any other.

It is difficult to be certain of the degree of success attained by the McCormick mower in the harvest of 1854. At least, for the first time, a strong note of commendation from some agents and purchasers was heard amid the complaints which were sent in by others.[48] Those who were not pleased, usually wrote that Ketchum's was better, that the divider was too big, that the knife clogged, that the fingers were too large, and that the

[45] "Albany Cultivator," Sept., 1852, pp. 312, 313. "Michigan Farmer," Nov., 1852, pp. 348-349.

[46] T. J. Paterson from Rochester, N. Y., July 12, 1853; Jan. 3 and Mch. 21, 1854. E. P. Tayloe from Powhatan Hill, Va., Feb. 3, 1854. W. S. to J. B. McCormick, Apr. 21, 1859, L.P.C.B. No. 19, p. 550: "In 1853 the *second time* I had a 1000 disaffected *farmers* and a 100 *disappointed* Agents and again I spent *all* the harvest in the field and worked the *parts* that led to the improvements of 1854."

[47] MS. order blank for 1853. "Albany Cultivator," Dec., 1852, pp. 412, 413. "American Farmer," May, 1853, p. 375. Cyrus McCormick experimented with his mower in 1854 in Virginia, on the farm of W. B. Randolph. A. H. Drewry, from Chesterfield County, Va., to C. H. McCormick, Apr. 28, 1855.

[48] H. M. Smith, from Richmond, Va., June 4 and 10, 1854; W. B. Silver, from Sugar Valley, O., July 30, 1854.

framework was not sufficiently strong to stand the strain of cutting heavy clover.[49] McCormick sent machines to several of his principal agents in the East for experimental purposes, and by the close of the season he was ready to introduce those alterations which were to make the chorus of praise in 1855 drown out the lesser undertone of discontent. By 1865 experts agreed that efficient reaping and mowing could not be done by a single implement.

Wrought-iron and malleable iron were substituted for cast-iron in the mowing beam and guard fingers. Fingers and divider were made narrower and more pointed. The framework was reinforced and the knife shortened. The reel was still retained, since it permitted the horses to go more slowly and allowed the machine to cut long grass when the wind was blowing away from the knife.[50] The panic of 1857 soon came to eliminate some of his rivals who had hitherto offered so much opposition, and further experiments led to improvements which by the end of the decade made the McCormick machine the equal of any in the field. Despite the growing popularity of his machine as a mower, the inventor was still chiefly known as the man who was setting the standard for most of the reaper-makers of the world.

Although Cyrus McCormick's business grew so rapidly between 1848 and 1856, it was some years before all parts of his reaper and mower were made at the factory. At the beginning of this period the sickles were manufactured at Fitchburg, Massachusetts, by Aldrich & White for from $1.10 to $1.30 each. Guard fingers were made at Elizabethport, New Jersey, and elsewhere, and iron castings were furnished by Elihu Granger

[49] A. R. Metcalf, from Constantine, Mich., Sept. 27, 1854; T. J. Paterson, from Rochester, N. Y., Mch. 21, 1854; H. D. May, from Belvidere, Ill., Sept. 18, 1854.

[50] J. Campbell, from Westons, N. J., June 27, 1855. McCormick handbill for Pennsylvania, 1855. *Hussey vs. McCormick*, pp. 228-232. "American Farmer," May, 1855, p. 382.

and Thomas Sherry of Chicago for from $48 to $50 per ton.[51] Each reaper was given one coat of paint, and this work was done separately, at least in 1851, by Chicago painters for fourteen cents a machine.[52] Whitewood, pine, and ash were purchased from Indiana and Michigan sawmill-owners for about $15 per thousand feet; coal, boated from Cleveland or Buffalo to Chicago, cost from $6.25 to $9.50 a ton, and iron was usually secured in the East for from $24 to $30 a ton.[53] These materials began to arrive at the McCormick dock as soon as it was cleared of reapers, in early August of each year.

The total cost of building a reaper in 1849, including factory depreciation, rent, materials, interest, commissions to agents, and allowance for bad debts, was estimated to be $64.29.[54] In that year farmers paid $115 cash or $120 on time for a machine.[55] In other words, the implements were sold at an advance of almost a hundred per cent over cost. This, together with the annual increase of sales, helps to explain McCormick's rapid march toward great wealth. The business was shared with William B. Ogden and William E. Jones in 1849, and, since McCormick received a patent fee of $28 or $30 on each reaper, besides his four ninths of the manufacturers' profits, he pocketed a net return of about $44 on each of the 1,450 reapers

[51] Agreement of C. H. McCormick with Aldrich & White, July 23, 1849. Agreements of C. H. McCormick with Thomas Sherry, Sept. 20, 1849, and Sept. 16, 1850. "Gem of the Prairie," Apr. 24, 1849.

[52] Contract of Jan. 20, 1851, with Magnus Norboe and Tobias Jackson.

[53] Contract of Feb. 3, 1855, with Nelson, Ferris & Co. of Mishawaka, Ind. C. W. Bevins, from Goshen, Ill., Aug. 26, 1855; G. R. Wilson & Co., from Buffalo, N. Y., Aug. 10 and Sept. 14, 1854; Crawford & Price, from Cleveland, O., Jan. 29 and Sept. 28, 1855; Curtis & Boyce, from Erie, Pa., Sept. 28, 1855.

[54] "McCormick Extension Case, Patent of 1845," adverse testimony, pp. 37-40, 42. O. M. Dorman, on Sept. 26, 1850, stated that machines were made for "not much over" $37, and that the net profit averaged about $60 per machine. Profit-and-loss statement for 1849, in C. H. McCormick's handwriting. This estimates the cost of manufacturing at about $55 per machine.

[55] Poster of McCormick, Ogden & Co., 1849.

sold.[56] After he had dispensed with all partners by 1851, and the price of the reaper had been raised, his income was even larger, although, of course, his patent fee ceased.[57]

The reaper, reaper-mower, and mower were the only machines manufactured by McCormick between 1848 and 1856. On several occasions prior to 1852 the inventor announced that he would broaden the variety of his output, but these expectations were not realized. In December, 1848, he published his intention to improve and manufacture a traveling thresher.[58] Early in 1851, he advertised that:

We have a new and complete Thresher and Separator invented by my brother, Leander J. McCormick, combining some important advantages over the others in use. While I am in the East this winter I intend to examine agricultural implements generally to find those suited to the wants of western farmers, with a view to making them.[59]

Horse-powers and seed-drills were also in prospect. The fire at the factory in March of that year prevented the completion of this program.[60]

All McCormick reapers legally made in the United States after 1851 were produced at the Chicago factory. The last

[56] Profit-and-loss sheet, 1849. Here McCormick totals his profits and patent fees from the Chicago factory at $64,142.86. This does not include his patent fees of that season from D. J. Townsend, of Au Sable Grove, Ill., or from J. Ganson & Co., of Brockport, N. Y.

[57] *Seymour & Morgan vs. McCormick,* p. 189, testimony of W. S. McCormick, Oct. 18, 1851.

[58] "Chicago Daily Journal," Dec. 15, 1848. In the letter files of the McCormick Hist. Asso. Library there is an undated contract of C. H. McCormick to make Jacques & Love threshers for States west of Ohio, and to pay Jacques $5 for each one made.

[59] "Albany Evening Journal," Oct. 17, 1850. "Wisconsin and Iowa Farmer and Northwestern Cultivator" (Racine, Wis.), Jan., 1851, pp. 23, 24. "Chicago Daily Journal," Mch. 22, 1851.

[60] W. S. McCormick to D. R. Burt, July 28, 1857, L.P.C.B. No. 8, p. 222.

outside contract of the period following 1844 expired in that year,[61] and henceforward reaper-building was kept closely under the supervision of the inventor. Despite this fact, McCormick was tempted on several occasions to make arrangements with firms in Ohio and New York to produce his machines.[62] He was handicapped in his efforts to win the patronage of the seaboard by his distance from these markets, and by the high freight rates. The taunts of Hussey, who advertised that he had driven McCormick across the mountains, were particularly irritating. In late 1851 and in 1852, when his rival was ridiculing his success in England and was apparently planning to open a Chicago factory, McCormick retorted that he would sell his reapers in New York City at Chicago prices and would begin production in Baltimore.[63] The latter threat was never made good, although his principal Eastern agents, such as Campbell of New Jersey, continued to urge him to open a seaboard branch.[64]

Transportation from factory to farmer was expensive. A reaper-mower weighed about twelve hundred pounds in 1854, and as a rule most of the freight and storage charges were paid by the purchaser.[65] A chief reliance was placed upon

[61] "Ohio Cultivator," Jan. 15, 1850. "Genesee Farmer," May, 1850, p. 126; June, 1850, p. 149.

[62] C. H. to W. S. McCormick, Mch. 7, 1854: Chappell, Whiteside & Burnett of Brockport, N. Y., wished to build 25 or 30 McCormick reapers and were told by the inventor that they might do so if they would pay him a $20 patent fee. They apparently declined. "I don't like to have anything to do *with Brockport*, but might it not be well to let them there build that many. . . ." T. J. Paterson, from Rochester, N. Y., May 3, 1854; W. A. Gill, from Columbus, O., May 29, 1855; A. D. Hager, from Springfield, O., Dec. 31, 1854. "McCormick Extension Case, Patent of 1845," pp. 243 ff., testimony of Israel S. Love.

[63] "Chicago Daily Democrat," Dec. 23, 1851. Pamphlet of C. H. McCormick, "The McCormick Patent Reaping and Mowing Machine in America," Mch. 15, 1852.

[64] James Campbell, from Westons, N. J., July 15 and Aug. 14, 1854.

[65] "Chicago Daily Journal," Sept. 8, 1849. "Ohio Cultivator," Jan. 15, 1850.

canal and steamboat in the Middle West, and rough handling
by stevedores and careless delivery by indifferent captains
brought many complaints from agents and consignees.[66] When
a district was assigned to a salesman, effort was made to have
it front upon a navigable river or lake, so that machines might
be delivered with comparative ease.[67] Because farmers would
not grow a surplus unless there was an accessible market, and
as the bottom-lands were often the most fertile, grain-production tended to concentrate at this time in counties accessible
to deep water. Although reapers and mowers were sometimes
sold to farmers who lived at a distance from the main highways of commerce, the letters of the period show that railroad
penetration meant prosperity for the maker of agricultural machinery, as well as better days for the grain-grower.[68] If the
transition from a frontier civilization is largely conditioned by
the ability of the settler to produce an agricultural surplus, then
the reaper and the railroad were two agents of prime importance in the forward march of the West. The farmer invested in railroad stock, often to his regret, and occasionally
an agent complained that no reaper sales were possible because
all of the cash in his district was tied up in such transportation
ventures.[69]

[66] Chester Weed, from Muscatine, Ia., July 18, 1849. W. J. Hanna to
D. Williams, Indianapolis, Ind., Apr. 6, 1857, L.P.C.B. No. 6, p. 93:
"I find it almost impossible to get a Canal Boat to leave 3 machines at
one place, 5 at another, and so on, without making grievous mistakes."
He voiced the same complaint about railways.

[67] "Chicago Commercial Advertiser," June 13, 1849: McCormick states
that sample machines may be seen at most of the towns and steamboat
landings along the Illinois and upper Mississippi rivers, and at several of
the ports of Lake Michigan.

[68] J. L. Wilson, from Burlington, Ia., Feb. 6, 1852; from Indianapolis,
Ind., Apr. 3, 1854, and from Cordova, Ill., Dec. 17, 1854: An agent is
needed in Champaign and Vermilion counties, Ill., since the railroad will
open this year.

[69] John Ott, of Parke County, Ia., wrote in 1854: "There are 3 distinct
Rail Roads building through this county and most farmers have pledged

Notwithstanding this exceptional situation, it is generally true that the railroad meant more sales for the agricultural-machinery manufacturer, and the use of these implements by the farmer brought more freight to the transportation company. Each being of service to the other, it might be expected that a railroad company would carry reapers at a very low charge. The company office wrote to the freight agent of the Pittsburgh and Fort Wayne Railroad, on February 2, 1859:

It *strikes* me forcibly that RR. corporations should treat agricultural implements as a favored exception in common freight from the fact that the *sales* and use of them tend to develop the *resources* of the country on which the road depends for its traffic and support; besides the manufacture of machines at a distance from the places where sold, and used, affords directly so much additional business to a road. I have often discussed the question of establishing a factory in Baltimore in view of avoiding the cost of freight on Eastern Sales, while if I can get freights put down to a low figure, the question would be one of only nominal importance. As you are probably aware my Patents are one by one rapidly drawing to a close, and competition consequently increasing, which impells me to seek cheap facilities for transportation in order to compete with Eastern *manufacturers.*[70]

Nevertheless transportation was too vital to the welfare of the reaper business to necessitate large favors to the manufacturer from the railroad companies, unless there were several lines serving the same territory. A reaper could be moved by boat to Cleveland, and thence by rail to Philadelphia, for a total cost of fifteen or twenty dollars. This included drayage and commission charges at such transfer points as Cleveland and Pittsburgh.[71] Eastern farmers naturally hesitated to pay

stock in some one of these roads and think they can't spare more money this year."

[70] L.P.C.B. No. 18, pp. 161, 162.

[71] "Gem of the Prairie," May 24, 1851. "Ohio Cultivator," July 15, 1850, p. 217. E. S. Troxel, from Waynesboro, Pa., Sept. 29, 1854; J. M. Ransom, from Lexington, Va., June 21, 1855.

fifteen per cent of the Chicago price of a reaper in freight, and agents on the seaboard urged McCormick to erect a factory in their neighborhood. Freight rates were not proportioned to distance, and Peoria, Illinois, farmers complained that they must pay eleven dollars to get their reapers by canal and steamboat from Chicago.[72]

By 1854 the company was making yearly agreements with such railroad companies as the Galena and Chicago Union, the Cleveland and Pittsburgh, and the Pennsylvania.[73] For example, the Cleveland and Pittsburgh line contracted to carry reapers between those two cities for thirty cents per one hundred pounds, provided that McCormick gave it all of his business in their territory.[74] The Pennsylvania Central consented to put machines in the same class of freight as coal, stone, and lumber, and McCormick's Philadelphia agent wrote that the line had "done as much as can be expected." [75] At the close of the 1854 harvest McCormick was informed that 247 of his machines had been carried from Chicago to Philadelphia at an average cost of $12.61, or about $4 from Chicago to Cleveland, $3.60 from Cleveland to Pittsburgh, and $4.80 from Pittsburgh to Philadelphia.[76] Canal-boat companies attempted to compete with railroads for reaper-carriage between Chicago and Pittsburgh, promising to transport machines the entire distance in about five days at a cost of thirty-seven and a half cents per

[72] J. L. Wilson, from Pleasant Valley, Ia., Jan. 31, 1852: He complained that local agents were imposing upon the farmers by charging too much freight. He suggested that the company should inform each purchaser of the exact freight and warehouse charges. W. O. Leyburn, from Stoughton, Wis., May 26, 1855; J. Preston, from Peoria, Ill., Mch. 29, 1855.

[73] D. R. Burt, from Waterloo, Ia., Apr. 2, 1854. The Galena & Chicago Union R. R. would not lease a car for transporting anything save coal and cattle. They charged 1½ times the usual rate for agricultural machinery.

[74] Agt. of Cleveland and Pittsburgh R. R. Co., from Pittsburgh, Jan. 2 and May 10, 1854; A. D. Hager, from Pittsburgh, May 3, 1854.

[75] R. T. Elkinton, from Philadelphia, Sept. 24, 1854.

[76] *Idem,* Sept. 6 and 13, 1854.

one hundred pounds. This was only slightly more than the railroad charge from Cleveland to Pittsburgh, but the firm continued to rely largely upon the latter for eastward hauls.[77] Reaper depots or distribution centers were established in the East in such cities as Baltimore, Philadelphia, and Rochester.[78]

The price of the McCormick reaper advanced from $115 cash and the freight charges in 1849, to $130 with a maximum of $5 for freight in 1854.[79] But in the latter year most of the machines which were sold were combined reapers and mowers, and they were priced at $155 in addition to the cost of transportation. The rising cost of materials and labor was said to justify the increased price. It is a somewhat striking fact that in the face of growing competition and the appearance of the self-rake machine, Cyrus McCormick could charge more for his hand-rake reaper than any rival, and could not only hold his ground but lead the market and increase his output annually.[80] He charged "all that the traffic would bear," and farmers were favored with bargain prices when they lived in areas hitherto unsupplied with reapers or in localities where the competition was keen. In the partnership contract with O. M. Dorman for the harvest of 1850, it was agreed to sell for $120 in Ohio and Missouri, for $105 along the Erie Canal, and for $115 in Illinois. In other words, the company paid the

[77] J. D. Shepard, from Hutsonville, Ill., Feb. 25, 1855; G. M. Gault, from Annapolis, O., Aug. 18, 1855; Hussey & Sinclair, from Cleveland, Ohio, Apr. 14, 1855.
[78] "Albany Cultivator," July, 1851, p. 253. "McCormick Patent Reaping and Mowing Machine in America," Mch. 15, 1852.
[79] "Chicago Daily Democrat," Oct. 19, 1848. Agreement of C. H. McCormick and O. M. Dorman, Dec. 28, 1849. "Ohio Cultivator," Jan. 15, 1850, p. 34. "Genesee Farmer," July, 1850, p. 173. "Albany Cultivator," Jan., 1851, pp. 40, 41; June, 1852, p. 228. Printed McCormick sales form for 1854.
[80] "Prairie Farmer," Mch., 1854, p. 128. McCormick writes, "I have witnessed the operations of all the so-called self-rakers, and other new fangled experiments, and have been solicited by the inventors to manufacture them, but . . ."

freight of $4 or $5 by boat to Buffalo, and charged the New York farmer $10 less than the Chicago price.[81] Reapers were also sold in New York and Philadelphia on Chicago terms as late as 1855.[82]

These concessions to the seaboard reflect the efforts of the inventor to find favor in an area which looked with suspicion upon a reaper from the West.[83] They were also merely another phase of the long battle between Hussey and McCormick. In 1855, James Campbell, the principal agent in New Jersey, wrote William S. McCormick of the "rascally combination that exists against C. H. at the East." Because of the inventor's proneness to seek redress in the courts against infringers—

they raise this cry among farmers that McCormick is rich and is making hundreds of thousands a year out of the farmers in the country and is bringing all under tribute to him; that he is a great monopolist, etc., and that the money paid for one of his machines here goes immediately out of the country into the West. . . . I find they have carried prejudice to the Agricultural Implement dealers as I find they are all down on McCormick.[84]

One reason for the advance in the price of the McCormick reaper was due to changes in construction and the gradual replacement of wood by iron. A complete story of the mechanical evolution of the reaper between 1848 and 1855 would involve technicalities beyond the purpose of this narrative, but several changes of considerable importance were introduced

[81] "McCormick Extension Case, Patent of 1845," adverse testimony, pp. 37-40. "Genesee Farmer," July, 1850, p. 173; June, 1853, p. 195. "Albany Cultivator," June, 1852, p. 228.
[82] McCormick handbill for Pennsylvania, 1855.
[83] The West, in like manner, looked with disfavor upon Eastern reapers. "Gem of the Prairie," May 24, 1851: "We would prefer seeing our western farmers patronizing western manufacturers." Jas. Campbell, from Westons, N. J., July 15, 1854.
[84] J. Campbell, from Westons, N. J., June 27, 1855; T. J. Paterson, from Rochester, N. Y., Feb. 10, 1854; J. Andrews, from Richland, Ind., Mch. 31, 1855.

which require mention.[85] Scarcely a single element was left untouched. The main wheel was enlarged, the gearing was altered almost every year, the platform shortened and covered with zinc, the reel improved in detail, and a seat added for driver as well as raker.[86] The two most significant innovations, besides the mowing attachment already discussed, were the substitution of a scalloped for a smooth-edged sickle for reaping, and the abandonment of the knife-bearer after a new guard finger was adopted.[87] Although no basic changes were made, the alterations made annually are evidence of the never-ending experimental work in progress and of the pressure of competition. Because the reaper had not been standardized, spare parts to fit the models of each year had to be kept on hand at the factory and with the agents.[88] These frequent improvements made it necessary to sell the surplus machines of one harvest in the following season at reduced prices, unless they could be marketed in Canada, California, or some other territory where rivalry was not keen and where reaper literature rarely circulated.[89]

[85] Poster of McCormick, Ogden & Co., 1849. "Chicago Daily Democrat," Oct. 19, 1848. "Gem of the Prairie," Apr. 24, 1849. "Chicago Daily Journal," Sept. 8, 1849. "New York Tribune," Oct. 5, 1849. "Ohio Cultivator," Jan. 15, 1850, pp. 31, 34. "American Farmer," July, 1850, Pictorial Supplement. For an able discussion of McCormick reaper mechanics, see R. B. Swift, "Who Invented the Reaper," in the "Implement Age," Apr. 15, 1897.

[86] Zinc was used on the platform in 1849, but sheet-iron was substituted in 1851. This caused complaint because it rusted. See J. L. Wilson, from Pleasant Valley, Ia., Jan. 31, 1852; C. H. to W. S. McCormick, Mch. 7, 1854; J. L. Wilson, from Albany, N. Y., Oct. 25, 1854; "American Farmer," May, 1855, p. 382.

[87] Photostat of a McCormick Poster, 1850. "Scientific American," Feb. 8, 1851, p. 164. "Albany Cultivator," July, 1851, p. 253. *Hussey vs. McCormick*, pp. 172 ff. "The Plough, The Loom, and the Anvil" (Phila.), June, 1851, pp. 785, 786. *McCormick vs. Manny*, II, pp. 231, 232, testimony of W. S. McCormick.

[88] *Supra*, p. 308, ftn. 25.

[89] T. J. Paterson, from Rochester, N. Y., Nov. 10, 1851; C. H. to W. S. McCormick, Mch. 7, 1854; Henry Jackey, from Grayson County, Tex.,

From the beginning of reaper-building in 1839, through 1856, Cyrus McCormick placed nearly sixteen thousand reapers, reaper-mowers, and mowers upon the farms of America. If it is borne in mind that the number of his sales increased from 2 in 1840 to 4,095 in 1856, the rapid expansion of his business can be visualized. From 1851 to 1853 there was a slump when only about 1,000 were sold in each harvest.[90] His rivals were busy, particularly after 1848, but McCormick's total output probably equaled over one third of all the others combined.[91] The expansion of his market depended in part upon a shrewd advertising policy and an adequate force of capable agents. While he increased his capacity for production, he simultaneously evolved a system for reaching the farmer with the news of his reaper which was unique in his own day for its scope and its effectiveness.

no date; Father J. B. Duerinck, from St. Mary's Pottawatomie Mission, Kan., Oct. 10, 1854, Jan. 3 and July 28, 1855. He thought he was the first to use the reaper-mower in Kansas.

[90] *Hussey vs. McCormick,* pp. 228-232.

[91] The "Albany Cultivator," of Aug., 1849, p. 257, quotes from the "Prairie Farmer" that McCormick had sold 2,800 machines in three years, and other firms about 100, not including 180 harvesters. But this was before most of the rivals appeared. "Scientific American," Oct. 19, 1850, p. 34. The editor judges that 1,800 machines were sold during the harvest. McCormick made 1,597 and sold about 1,550. "Prairie Farmer," July, 1852, p. 341. Here it is stated that no less than 3,500 new reapers would be used in the Northwest in that harvest. *Ibid.,* Aug., 1854, p. 321. McCormick built 1,550 reapers, Manny, 1,100, Wright-Atkins, 300; Danford built 500 mowers. "Albany Cultivator," Apr., 1857, p. 127. In Chicago alone 3,286 reapers and mowers were built in 1855 and 5,860 in 1856.

CHAPTER XIV

ADVERTISING THE McCORMICK REAPER AND MOWER

THE marketing problem which Cyrus McCormick faced about 1840, when he first decided to devote his entire attention to the sale of his reaper, was most baffling. His experience in the iron business was of value in acquainting him with the routine of a factory and with certain financial practices to be avoided, but the metal was largely sold to a few dealers at Richmond and Lynchburg who made it their business to locate the ultimate consumer. The sale of reapers required quite different tactics. The demand for the machine was highly seasonal and potential purchasers were as widely scattered as the grain-fields of the world.

Furthermore, American farmers knew nothing about mechanical grain-cutting; McCormick had first to demonstrate the utility of his reaper—and to men who were accustomed to view innovations with skepticism. The prospective buyer naturally wished to see the machine before he placed his order. This was a demand which it was difficult to satisfy. The reaper was large and heavy, while roads were of indifferent quality and railroads were few. In view of his slight acquaintance with the world outside of his own State, his small experience in salesmanship, and his meager capital, it is remarkable that Cyrus McCormick so soon worked out by trial and error a business practice which served him so well. His methods of publicity were so forward-looking that they are in use to-day without essential change.

The years from 1831 to 1843 may be appropriately called

the Virginia phase of the McCormick reaper. Slight effort, if any, was made to sell the machine before 1840 and it is not at all clear that the implement itself claimed much of the inventor's attention between 1835 and 1839. The causes for this interlude have already been mentioned.[1] In a history of the reaper, this period is mainly significant as a time when Cyrus was experimenting at home while his future rival, Obed Hussey, never dreaming that he would hear again from the McCormick reaper, was drawing considerable attention to his own invention in the neighboring State of Maryland.

With the harvest of 1839, McCormick resumed the policy of publicity which had been suspended during the preceding five years. As the reaper was a new and useful invention, the newspapers and agricultural magazines gave it more and more free advertising. Because it was ingenious and promised to revolutionize grain-culture, local and state pride in Virginia was at least temporarily enlisted in its support. When the inventor began to neglect the home market for the larger opportunities of the North and West, after 1844, Virginia editors tended to bestow their favor upon Hussey, whose factory was at Baltimore and who always emphasized Eastern sales. But, at the same time, McCormick was spreading the reaper gospel among the leading grain-growers of the United States with long advertisements in such prominent publications as the "Prairie Farmer" of Chicago, the "Ohio Cultivator" of Columbus, the "Michigan Farmer" of Detroit, the "Genesee Farmer" and the "Cultivator" of Rochester and Albany respectively. Chicago and Albany newspapers also were regularly used.

The columns of these periodicals were opened to him for a price, but the editors often discussed the reaper gratuitously, both while it was a curiosity and after it had proved its worth. Naturally they could not do otherwise if they were to serve the best interests of the farmer and promote every device and

---

[1] *Supra,* pp. 97, 98.

method which made for better agriculture.[2] An outstanding performance, such as the award of the Council Medal of the London exposition of 1851, was widely heralded in the papers of the United States, and P. T. Barnum in 1851 advanced the same end when he charged twenty-five cents to view the Grand Moving Picture of the Crystal Palace—a "brilliant chronicle of our success on the great battlefield of rural industry."[3] No proof has been found that McCormick ever directly subsidized any editor to champion his reaper rather than a rival's, but in 1851 he threatened to establish his own paper when the publisher of the influential "Prairie Farmer" formed a momentary partnership with Hussey and shortly afterward began to manufacture the Atkins self-raking reaper.[4]

Although an editor could not afford to lend his support to a machine which worked poorly, he naturally gave his powerful endorsement to the manufacturer who advertised most liberally in his paper. With so many disputes arising about the best type of knife, guard finger, or delivery, it was easy for a publisher to profess neutrality and at the same time to influence his subscribers to favor principles of construction and operation which were peculiar to a particular, but unnamed, machine. The manufacturer was especially fortunate if he could persuade an editor to be an agent for his reaper. Charles T. Botts of the Richmond "Southern Planter" served McCormick between 1843 and 1847 in this capacity, but he so shifted in his affections as reaper opinion veered in Virginia that the inventor was never quite sure of his whole-hearted support, and by 1853 Botts was

[2] "Western Farmer and Gardener," Oct., 1844, p. 57. The editor, E. J. Hooper, wrote, "We cannot but consider that this Reaper [the McCormick] is by far the best of the horse-power kind, that has ever been invented in America." "Chicago Daily Journal," July 21, 1848. T. J. Paterson, Feb. 19, 1855, recommended that an advertisement should be given to the "Rural New Yorker," a weekly, with the largest circulation in the State.

[3] "The Plow" (N. Y.), Mch., 1852, p. 103.

[4] *Post*, Chap. XVII, pp. 413, 416.

openly hostile to his former employer.[5] M. B. Bateham, editor
of the "Ohio Cultivator," was a salesman for McCormick in
1850 and 1851. These men were not expected to travel through
the rural districts canvassing for orders, but were to receive
and forward all requests for reapers which should come to
them, and to display sample machines where they could be
examined by all who were interested.[6] Both publishers announced their agencies through the columns of their magazines
and thus gave their public endorsement to the McCormick
grain-cutter.[7]

Judging from the advertisements then in vogue, the best
way to catch the eye of the buying public was to display a cut
showing a reaper pulled at an easy trot by two fine horses, one
of which was ridden by a smiling boy contentedly cracking
a formidable whip. Beside the machine strode a rake-wielding
farmer whose neat attire and serene countenance were designed
to inform the reader that "raking off" was not half so hard a
task as swinging a cradle. Numbers were attached to the most
important parts of the machine, and beneath the picture was a
long, technical, and, to the modern reader, wearisome explanation of the construction, operation, and function of each of
these designated elements. This was one method by which
McCormick educated the farmer in the use of horse-drawn

[5] "Southern Planter," Jan., 1846, pp. 5, 6; July, 1846; Mch., 1847, p. 95.
Supra, pp. 198, 233. "Richmond Whig," Apr. 25, 1853. "American Farmer,"
June, 1853, pp. 401, 404, 405; July, 1853, p. 20.
[6] "Ohio Cultivator," July 15, 1849, p. 214; Apr. 15, 1850, p. 120.
[7] Edmund Ruffin, editor of the "Farmers' Register," who refused all
advertising, wrote in Aug., 1839 (pp. 455, 456) of "the great injury inflicted
on deserving inventors themselves, as well as on the gulled public, by the
puffing system, which is in such universal use in this country. Every new
invention, or scheme, or publication, whatever may be its degree of merit
or demerit, is ushered forth with puffs upon puffs. Dupes are made, and
the knaves who puff, and sell, profit at the expense of the fools who believe
and buy. And the more discreet or cautious, who know the working of
the puffing system, stand aloof, and trust as little to true statements as
to false."

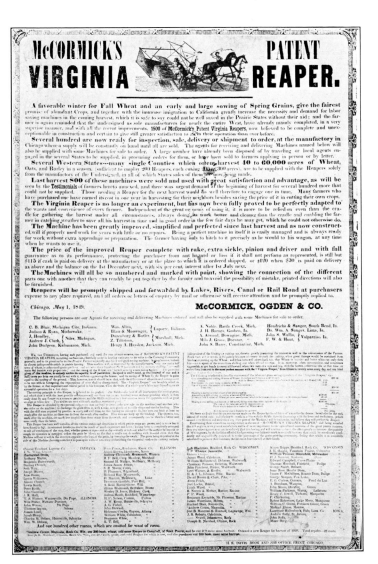

McCormick, Ogden & Co. Poster

machinery. Finally, a letter of the inventor assured the public that the reaper was now even more satisfactory in its operation than last year [8]; that its field of usefulness was wide, the terms of sale easy, early orders imperative; and that the failure of rival machines in the harvest field had been complete.

All of this information was given in the characteristically pompous language of the day, unrelieved by conscious humor, and set forth with a sincerity which carried conviction. McCormick's early letters of advertisement reveal a shrewd appreciation of sales psychology. Much emphasis was placed upon the care exercised to withhold the reaper from sale for several years until it had been thoroughly tested.[9] This was a stroke at Hussey, who had allowed the farmer to suffer with him during his first decade of experiment. The success of the reaper was both boldly asserted by McCormick, and also subtly conveyed to the reader by incidental mention of the yearly increase in the number of sales. If any machines had not been disposed of in the preceding harvest, poor transportation facilities, faulty distribution, wheat blight or bad weather were often

[8] "Richmond Enquirer," Feb. 15, 1842. It is interesting to note how many times between 1845 and 1852 Cyrus McCormick announced that his reaper was perfected. *Ibid.*, Feb. 26, 1845: The addition of the raker's seat and other improvements are believed to "perfect the reaper." "Prairie Farmer," Dec., 1846, p. 372: McCormick describes the improvements in the 1847 machine and trusts that now a "perfect article may be expected." "Chicago Daily Democrat," Oct. 19, 1848: Great improvements for the next harvest, and now "a perfect reaper." Poster of McCormick, Ogden & Co. for 1849: "The Virginia Reaper . . . has now been fully proved to be perfectly adapted to the wants . . . of every farmer. It has been much improved since last harvest." "Ohio Cultivator," Jan. 15, 1850, p. 34: "The improvements made during the past year in the estimation of many increase the value of the Reaper 100%." *Ibid.*, Apr. 15, 1852, p. 128: "A more perfect Reaping and Mowing Machine than any ever before offered to the public." Hussey did likewise. See "Southern Planter," Mch., 1845, pp. 54-57: "My machines are now as near perfection, I apprehend, as such an implement can be expected to be." Two years later he patented new improvements.

[9] "Albany Cultivator," May, 1846, p. 165. "Richmond Enquirer," Aug. 17, 24 and Sept. 30, 1842.

blamed for the surplus.[10] More frequently, and with truth, the inventor informed the public that the demand exceeded the supply and that only the early orders could be filled.[11] No assurance could be given that the next year's price would not be higher, and it would be good economy to buy at once.

McCormick was alert to the advantage gained by stressing the number of "pirates" who were infringing his patents and by advising users of machines sold by these unlicensed factories that they were as liable to prosecution as the builders themselves.[12] This implied that his reaper was so well made that others desiring to manufacture were unable to discover different principles of construction which would function with equal efficiency.[13] Such suits were never brought, and very likely never contemplated, but the inclusion of these warnings in his advertisements may have made many a farmer hesitate to purchase a rival machine of which he might be dispossessed after an expensive court action.[14] By 1842, McCormick had named his invention the "Virginia Reaper" and thus associated it with a State name which perhaps of all others carried the most sentimental appeal.[15] Occasionally he published figures to prove that his machine would pay for itself in one harvest on a farm of

[10] "Chicago Daily Journal," Sept. 8, 1849.

[11] "Chicago Commercial Advertiser," June 13, 1849. "Chicago Daily Democrat," Oct. 19, 1848.

[12] "Albany Evening Journal," Oct. 17, 1850. "Ohio Cultivator," Jan. 15, 1850, p. 31; Feb. 15, 1850, p. 63. "Prairie Farmer," Dec., 1849. "Chicago Commercial Advertiser," Apr. 3, 1850.

[13] In the "Genesee Farmer," of June, 1853, p. 195, McCormick states that the number of those pirating his machine is the best evidence of its superiority.

[14] T. J. Paterson of Rochester, N. Y., to C. H. McCormick, Feb. 28, 1854: He complains that farmers scorn the warning not to buy infringing machines. "The same warning has been given year after year at considerable expense but I have not learned that it has prevented a single sale."

[15] "Richmond Enquirer," Sept. 30, 1842.

moderate size.[16] In short, the reaper was an economy and a profitable investment—not a luxury—and its use saved money as well as time, labor, and grain.

To reëmphasize the truths contained in such a letter of advertisement, testimonials of prominent purchasers were added. These men frequently assured the reader that So and So's machine had been abandoned as useless in their neighborhood. Letters of endorsement were necessarily written by well-known Virginian planters up to 1844, but after that year they were furnished by farmers from almost every State of the West and North, excluding New England. It was good policy to prove that the article for sale was universally used, and this could be best shown by publishing certificates from a wide geographic range. Testimonials were customarily solicited, and their similarity of expression suggests that they were often written by the manufacturer. If they voiced the sincere opinion of the signers, this made little difference, but the extravagant praise which was so often given would inspire slight confidence to-day.

Indeed, the farmers of that time were not long deluded about their value. Manufacturers began to view with scorn the commendations procured by their competitors, and editors of agricultural magazines warned their readers not to place faith in them.[17] The grain-grower soon looked with suspicion upon all such "point with pride" paragraphs and demanded an opportunity either to see the reaper in operation or to test it for himself.

As the testimonial declined in value as an advertising medium, although never wholly outworn, the long-established

[16] *Supra*, Chap. III, p. 73, ftn. 50. As early as 1842 ["Richmond Enquirer," Aug. 24 and Sept. 30, 1842] a reaper and seven attendants did the daily work of 5 cradlers and 10 helpers. "Albany Cultivator," May, 1846, p. 105.

[17] "Prairie Farmer," Jan., 1850, p. 30.

firms announced that their machines were too well known to
require the published endorsements of satisfied purchasers.
Because these certificates often filled half the space taken by the
entire advertisement in a journal, considerable money was saved
by discontinuing their use. As early as 1845, Cyrus McCormick
told the readers of the "Richmond Enquirer" that he deemed
it unnecessary to publish more testimonials for that harvest
than had already appeared in his earlier advertisements of the
same season. The names of those who owned reapers in the
neighborhood and copies of their written statements would be
mailed upon request or would be filed for interested persons
to read at the office of the editor. By 1849 he stated that long
advertisements were unnecessary,[18] and the previous year he
had deemed it superfluous to print any testimonials in support
of his machine.[19] In their place were substituted lists of agents
or of satisfied farmers with whom prospective purchasers might
correspond. Nevertheless, he did not altogether abandon the
testimonial, and when his mower was introduced in 1849 he
temporarily returned to an extensive publication of letters from
farmers endorsing its use.[20]

As most farmers were unaccustomed to complicated machinery, the inventor had the problem not only of selling but
also of teaching his purchasers how to use the reaper. Otherwise, because of the ease with which advantage could be taken
of the guarantee, McCormick might expect many farmers to
give his machine a half-hearted trial and then demand that
their money be returned. The horses and mules, as well as the
negroes, needed to share in this training, and the reaction of

[18] *Ibid.*, Jan., 1850, p. 34, letter of C. H. McCormick, Dec. 4, 1849.
"Chicago Daily Journal," Sept. 8, 1849. "Chicago Commercial Advertiser,"
Apr. 3, 1850. "Albany Evening Journal," Oct. 17, 1850. "Genesee Farmer,"
June, 1851, p. 148.
[19] "Chicago Daily Democrat," Oct. 19, 1848.
[20] "Chicago Daily Journal," Sept. 8, 1849. "Ohio Cultivator," Jan. 15,
1850, p. 31. "Chicago Commercial Advertiser," Apr. 3, 1850.

animals to the noise of the first automobiles illustrates the attitude of a team pulling a rattling reaper which it could neither see nor escape.

Occasionally there were grounds for the suspicion that the workmen who operated the machine, and followed it to bind the sheaves, endeavored to make it do poor work, because they were unwilling to contribute to their own future unemployment.[21] The knife required sharpening after cutting about fifty acres of grain, and this had to be done skilfully. The reel and the knife could be raised and lowered if the operator understood the method, and there was a "knack" in raking from the platform which could be gained only by instruction and from experience. The owner must learn that the moving parts of the reaper required frequent oiling and that the knife would not permit careless driving against stumps and stones.

Modern common sense in the use of machinery was uncommon then, and explanations which would now be resented as insulting to the intelligence of the purchaser were necessary during these years, as the farmer slowly learned to rely upon horse-power. For these reasons Cyrus McCormick soon found it advisable to send printed directions to the purchaser, explaining how to use and care for the machine.[22]

So many reapers had seemed perfect on paper and had proved to be worthless in practice, that a farmer could not be expected to purchase unless the machine were accompanied by a guarantee which permitted its return in case it would not operate. Prior to 1842, Cyrus McCormick did not warrant the performance of his reaper, although he was willing to repair one which broke because of its poor construction, or to replace a

---

[21] *Supra,* Chap. VII, p. 171, ftn. 70.

[22] "Richmond Enquirer," Aug. 24 and Sept. 30, 1842, advertisement of C. H. McCormick. "The undersigned expects soon to have *cuts* and printed *descriptions* in detail of the reaper, which he can forward by mail to persons desiring to know more of it, and which will enable anyone to understand its construction perfectly."

faulty sickle with a better one.[23] However, after the satisfactory season of 1841 he advertised that henceforward purchasers would run no risk, for, if the reapers for 1842 were not strong and durable, and would not cut fifteen acres a day and save one bushel of wheat per acre, ordinarily lost by shelling when the cradle was used, they could be returned.[24] The inventor of course expected that he would be given an opportunity to replace or to repair a broken reaper and to instruct a farmer in its use. If it continued to function poorly, the farmer might have it for a reduced price or return it to Walnut Grove.[25]

In 1844, Hussey warranted his reaper to cut twenty acres a day,[26] but as late as 1846, after a raker's seat was added, McCormick advanced his speed guarantee only from fifteen to "fifteen or twenty" acres a day.[27] The 1833 machine had cut ten acres a day, and therefore an increase of almost one hundred per cent in harvesting efficiency had been attained by his experiments of the first twelve years. Before 1855 this guarantee was changed to one and a half acres an hour, and occasionally as much as two acres an hour were promised.[28] The inventor announced in 1852: "I warrant them superior to Hussey's and to all others. I have a reputation to maintain. Let a farmer take both and keep the one which he likes best."

[23] Corbin Braxton to C. H. McCormick, Mch. 10, 1845.

[24] *Hussey vs. McCormick,* p. 147. "Albany Cultivator," Feb., 1845, p. 58. Agents sometimes complained that the right of the farmer to return a machine, if not satisfactory, injured sales. H. M. Smith of Richmond, Va., wrote on Aug. 18, 1854: "To work under a guarantee is a sure mode to kill the reputation of any machine. For if the smallest failure occurs to prevent making themselves liable for the purchase money they will not persevere in the use of it." T. J. Paterson, from Rochester, N. Y., May 6, 1854.

[25] C. H. McCormick to E. Burke, Jan. 1, 1848, Pattison, II, a.

[26] "Albany Cultivator," May, 1844, p. 168.

[27] "Southern Planter," Jan., 1846, pp. 5, 6.

[28] "Ohio Cultivator," May 15, 1852. Order blank for 1852, Missouri, Ohio, and Wabash Delivery. Handbill for Pennsylvania, 1855.

Until the close of the 1842 harvest, cash was expected upon delivery, although there were exceptions made to this rule. The price varied, but by 1842, $100 at Walnut Grove and $105 at Richmond tended to be the usual charge. In the harvests of 1843 and 1844 McCormick extended four months' credit, and in 1844, and thereafter, he provided each machine with an extra sickle.[29] In 1846 he offered to sell his reaper "on time for good paper drawing interest," and to send it "to any responsible farmer who may desire to try it on the same terms with any other, to be purchased or refused as decided on making such trial." [30] The next year the price was advanced to $115 cash or $120 on time, but from that season on, for several years, there was little change.[31] Soon an extra pinion and driver were given with each reaper, as well as a spare sickle and guard fingers.[32]

These long reaper advertisements, consisting of a cut and description of the machine, an announcement by the manufacturer often in the form of a letter, testimonials, and the terms of sale, generally first appeared in the December issues of the leading agricultural journals. Herein they were repeated month by month, almost unchanged in content, until the harvest. No mercy was shown to competitors, nor was any effort made to camouflage an attack under the language of insinuation. McCormick frankly struck at Hussey by name, and "turn about was fair play," with charge and countercharge supported by the testimony of purchasers whose pride arose in defense of an

[29] "Richmond Semi-Weekly Whig," Oct. 27, 1843. "Southern Planter," Dec., 1844, pp. 271, 272. "Richmond Enquirer," Nov. 19, 1844.
[30] "Southern Planter," Jan., 1846, pp. 5-8. "Albany Cultivator," May, 1846, p. 165. "Richmond Enquirer," Dec. 19, 1845. "Prairie Farmer," Nov., 1845, p. 275. "New Genesee Farmer," Apr., 1846, p. 100, June, 1853, p. 195.
[31] Poster of McCormick, Ogden & Co., 1849: $115 cash, or $120 when $30 is paid on delivery and balance on Dec. 1, 6% interest from July 1.
[32] "McCormick Patent Reaping and Mowing Machine in America," Mch. 15, 1852, p. 10.

implement for which they had spent money. The farmer was not enticed by the subtle devices of to-day. The cuts were crude, the language technical, and the disquisition upon the machine so long that the present-day newspaper-racer would rarely read beyond the title. The modern employment of feminine grace to add attractiveness to the commodity was unknown, and the prevailing point of view would have precluded its use even if it had been thought of. The assurance of a quality of performance far beyond the actual capacity of the product was as commonplace then as now, but this was usually accompanied by a guarantee to take back the reaper if it did not cut as well or as fast as the warrant promised.

The manufacturer always tried to make his machine have news value. Free advertisement could best be procured by appealing to the sport-loving disposition of rural communities suffering from a lack of the unusual and the exciting. The reaper permitted such a use during the harvest-time if a rival could be found who was willing to enter his implement in a grain-cutting contest. As interruptions in the monotony of country life and as entertainment at county and state fairs, these reaper races were a decided success. Heralded long in advance by newspapers and agricultural journals, they were often held under the ægis of a state or county agricultural society which made the necessary arrangements and provided a board of judges. Occasionally the spectators determined the award by the relative volume of the cheers which greeted the name of each machine at the close of the race. Shrewd exhibitors provided adequate meat and drink to sustain the onlookers as they followed the reapers under a scorching sun. Each contestant was accompanied by a band, to awaken enthusiasm and sway the opinion of the crowd in his favor. In most instances, the trial was of short duration, and accidental occurrences such as the breaking of a part, or the selection by lot of a section of the field where the grain was down, might determine the result.

Not infrequently a highly polished reaper, made with particular care, was employed for exhibition purposes, and the farmer was never quite certain that the victor's ordinary implement would be of equal quality. Specially trained drivers and "rakers-off" were used, as well as horses long accustomed to move more swiftly when they heard the noise of the reaper behind them. The work was done with a rush and an éclat which the average farmer could not duplicate with ordinary laborers and an ordinary machine in his own grain. The horse or the team was driven as fast as possible, in order to cut a maximum in the allotted time and also to impress the crowd with the lightness of draft of the machine. The prize was usually money, a ribbon, or a medal, and the winner made capital from his victory by incorporating in his advertisements and posters for the next harvest an account of the remarkable performance of his reaper and the ludicrous failure of his competitors.

As a fair test of the merits of two or more reapers these exhibitions were a failure. At first the farmers, and the manufacturers also, laid great emphasis upon them. By the time of the Civil War the established reaper-makers hesitated to risk the reputation of their implements on a "flirt," as a short contest was sometimes called, and the farmer had learned to select his reaper after seeing it perform in a harvest field under the usual conditions.

In 1854 it was surmised by a McCormick agent who witnessed a five days' trial at Belvidere, Illinois, between the Manny and Atkins machines, that the competitors gave brandy to their horses in order to prevent them from collapsing because of the great speed at which they were driven in the hot

July sun.[33] This Manny-Atkins contest illustrates a method of advertisement wherein an agricultural organization or a county fair had no share. It was fought for a prize of $1,500, and, like other similar contests, was born of a challenge by one of the rivals in the local press. Neither won, because the jury failed to agree, and suspicion is warranted that it was arranged solely for publicity and was not intended by either manufacturer to be conclusive.

The contests were too short, juries were prejudiced, unforeseen accidents often spoiled the performance of the best machine, and the points upon which the superiority of any reaper should be judged were so many that the decisions were usually satisfactory only to the manufacturer who gained the palm. The defeated and their champions immediately pointed out factors of superiority overlooked by the trial board, but which in their opinion were far more important than those that had determined the award.

The inconclusive nature of field trials was due not alone to accidents arising during the course of the contest but also to the equivocal and sometimes unfair decisions rendered by the judges. It was perhaps natural that any locality should favor a machine made on the spot, selling for a lower price than a "foreign" implement, and with spare parts always on hand. The patentee was well known to his patrons and in his factory gave employment, during the winter, to his neighbors. But it could hardly be expected that reapers of long-established reputation would be entered in a local trial arranged to boost an untried machine offered to the farmers for the first time. To be sure, in the vicinity of the plant manufacturing a new reaper, a long-tested machine suffered at least a temporary setback. If a challenge to a field trial was not accepted, the local press

[33] "Michigan Farmer," Aug., 1854, p. 263. A. D. Hager, from Belvidere, Ill., to C. H. McCormick, July 26, 28, and 30, 1854. The loser was to pay the $1,500 to the state agricultural society.

told its subscribers that the "valued implement of our respected townsman, Mr. X., has scared away that formerly redoubtable reaper of Mr. Y., who has hitherto taken so much money from the pockets of our friends."

Very often the judges owned reapers of their own and personal pride prevented them from showing favor to a machine they had "almost bought." It was more satisfying to possess an implement that had swept the field at the local county fair. Sometimes circumstances seem to indicate that manufacturers tampered with the probity of the judges, either by bribes or by offers of their reapers at reduced prices. Often the press accounts of the trial make it clear to the reader that one particular machine far outdistanced its rivals in the contest and yet the judges expressed the utmost hesitation to award the prize, because of the excellent performance of every entry. For example, accounts of the Hussey-McCormick contest at the Hutchinson farm, in 1843, agree that the McCormick machine won without effort. The fact that Hussey did not have his best reaper in the race was beside the point. Nevertheless, the judges announced:

"We are unanimously of the opinion, that both of them are valuable inventions, and richly merit the encouragement of the farming community. They both performed most admirably. The committee feel great reluctance in deciding between them, but upon the whole, prefer McCormick's." [34] Reading this by itself, one would naturally believe that the competitors had been most evenly matched.

Because of the unfairness of the brief field contest, prominent reaper-makers were wont to suggest that a season-long trial should be made. Beginning in Virginia or Kentucky, rival machines should cut day by day, under all conditions of weather and grain, following the harvest north until the last Wisconsin

[34] "Richmond Enquirer," July 4, 1843. "Southern Planter," Aug., 1843, pp. 183, 184. *Supra,* Chap. VIII, pp. 190 ff.

or New York oats were in the barn.[35] The machine which did the best after such arduous usage, where the factor of chance was reduced to a minimum, would have a feat to its credit that would really prove something. So far as is known, no reaper marathon of this nature was ever staged, but the periodic challenge issued by this or that manufacturer was an advertising device calculated to attract a farmer who was considering the purchase of a machine.[36]

The longest reaper and mower contest in the United States prior to 1854 extended for six days at Geneva, New York, in 1852. It was held under the auspices of the New York State Agricultural Society, and nine reapers and seven mowers competed for the prizes. A dynamometer was attached to each machine to determine the draft required to move it forward at the speed necessary for effective cutting.[37] Attempts were made to gage the power used per inch of cutting blade, and also the amount of side draft—that bane of all machines which were pulled rather than pushed through the grain. Which cut the cleanest, which was most efficient at lowest speed, which was least wasteful of grain, which performed best on uneven ground, which was cheapest, which was lightest and most

---

[35] "Michigan Farmer," Jan., 1855, pp. 23, 25. Proposition of Aaron Palmer, reaper-manufacturer of Brockport, N. Y., Dec. 12, 1854. He stated that the two weeks' trial in wheat in 1854 of the Illinois State Agricultural Society at Bloomington was the only adequate test of reapers yet held in the United States. His machine won first prize and this fact doubtless affected his viewpoint. *Ibid.*, Mch., 1854, p. 83. "American Farmer," Mch., 1854, pp. 289-290. Proposition of J. S. Wright.

[36] In the "Pennsylvania Farm Journal," Aug., 1855, pp. 235-237, is an elaborate scale of points by which, it is contended, reapers and mowers may be fairly judged. This is an earnest effort to standardize implement competition and make the trials equitable, wherever held. There are eleven qualifications given for both the mower and the reaper. Each of the eleven is assigned a relative point value. The perfect mower score is 212, and the reaper, 300. This illustrates the intricacy of this solution, as well as its impracticability. *Ibid.*, Oct., 1855, pp. 301, 302.

[37] "Albany Cultivator," Feb., 1853, p. 69.

durable? From which machine could the gavels be discharged most neatly and most easily, and on which reaper did the raker-off have the least arm-breaking task?

In such a manner were the reapers judged, and, although it could hardly be expected that any one implement would best meet all of these tests, the jury decided that the Burrall machine, manufactured at Geneva, made the highest score, with Manny's second and Seymour & Morgan's third.[38] So also, after similar examination, Manny's mower was given the first prize and Ketchum's the second. McCormick did not place with either his reaper or his mower, nor had he done so earlier in the same season at the trials at Springfield, Ohio, under the patronage of the agricultural society of that State. Here the first reaper award was bestowed upon the Densmore Self-Rake, manufactured by a Mr. Warder, on whose farm the contest had been staged.[39] Ketchum won the mower championship, with a Hussey machine second both as a reaper and as a mower.

The customary battle with the pen ensued. While editors declared that such trials were excellent methods of detecting "humbugs," [40] Cyrus McCormick endeavored to demonstrate that the decisions of the judges had been unfair in each instance. He did not "mean to impugn the motives" of the jury. He had not been present at either trial, although his brother Leander had represented him at Springfield. He considered that the Geneva award "was calculated to do the grossest injustice to myself, and to the public." The machine he had carefully groomed for this trial had arrived too late and his

[38] Ibid., Sept., 1852, pp. 312, 313. "Genesee Farmer," Aug., 1852, p. 257; Nov., 1852, p. 353.
[39] "Albany Cultivator," Dec., 1852, pp. 412, 413. "American Farmer," Aug., 1852, p. 75; Sept., 1852, p. 99. "Michigan Farmer," Aug., 1852, pp. 248, 249.
[40] "Albany Cultivator," Sept., 1852, pp. 312-314. "Michigan Farmer," Nov., 1852, pp. 348, 349.

ordinary reaper had been used. Stones raked off the teeth of the sickle and he admitted that the guard fingers would have to be placed closer together in order to afford more protection to the mower knife. By statistics he showed that his reaper required less power than Manny's or Burrall's, and that it cut a wider swath and delivered the grain in better form for binding. Because spectators agreed that his machine reaped better than the two Geneva prize-winners, the award of the judges was contrary to the expert opinion of practical farmers.

Thus did McCormick protest in a public letter, reinforcing his complaint by the assertion that the Manny and Seymour & Morgan machines were close copies of his own.[41] After the Springfield trial, his brother had purchased the victorious Densmore machine and a subsequent test against his own proved its worthlessness.

As it now is, we shall be thrown over to another reaping season for further *reaper trials,* when I design to have my machine in the field at the earliest day possible, say on the James River, Virginia, that its superiority may again, as heretofore, be contested in *any thorough manner,* and *that* in time to govern sales further north.

Then Manny replied that "the flutterings of a wounded bird are so mingled with expressions of pain, that it is perfectly natural that sympathy should be excited," and much more in the same tenor.[42] Another war of letters thus ran its course to a harmless close—the inevitable aftermath of field trials, so interesting to watch, so effective for advertising, so replete with rivalry, but so indeterminate in result.

The advertising value arising from the use of a McCormick reaper by an agricultural society or a prominent farmer was early recognized. If the local celebrity did not feel that his patronage justified irritating procrastination in paying for his

[41] "Albany Cultivator," Oct., 1852, p. 355; Dec., 1852, pp. 412, 413.
[42] *Ibid.,* Feb., 1853, p. 69.

machine, the advantage of his support was worth having.[43] Agricultural clubs and distinguished farmers were occasionally sold reapers at reduced prices, and extra effort was made at the factory to send them excellent ones.[44] The value of the resulting publicity is realized to-day, and the prospective buyer, then as now, was prone to conclude that if a nationally known figure, even though he had never owned a field of grain, endorsed a particular make of reaper, he could safely buy one also. An Iowa agent wrote to McCormick in 1854 that he sold a reaper for a reduced price to Judge Lovell, the president of the Dubuque County Agricultural Society. "He [Lovell] is not known as an Agent but recommends out of interest felt for the society and out of interest which I feel for his prosperity. I shall give him five dollars for each Reaper which he may assist me in selling." To account still further for his secret salesman, the same agent added a week later: "I found it necessary to continue the successful fight with Manny and others to have a man *out* as well as *in the Ring.*" [45]

Manufacturers also exhibited their reapers at early autumn county and state fairs and at "institutes" held in New York, Philadelphia, and Chicago. Prizes were occasionally awarded to implements which had not been tested in the field, and premiums were given on the strength of testimonials written by farmers

[43] T. J. Paterson, from Rochester, N. Y., to C. H. McCormick, Dec. 1, 1854. T. J. Walker & Co., Belleville, Ill., account for 1856. Opposite their record of a sale to Frederick Hecker of Lebanon, is noted: "This is the 'big gun' of the Republican Party. His time has been so much taken up with politics, we suppose he has entirely forgotten to pay. Will probably hear from him after the election. His certificate will take well with the Germans throughout the West."

[44] E. S. Troxel, from Waynesboro, Pa., May 17, 1854, to C. H. Mc-Cormick. He had procured three orders in Washington County, Md., through the aid of a member of an agricultural society there, "and agreed on 5% off on all sold within bounds of that society in order to get its backing and have thus won out over Seymour and Morgan's agent."

[45] D. R. Burt to C. H. McCormick, from Waterloo, Ia., Apr. 30 and May 7, 1854.

many miles away. In fact, it was not unknown for the board of
judges to consist of men who had never seen any machine cut
grain in the field, but who, on appearance alone, felt competent
to rank rival exhibits according to their respective merits. An
award similar to this, shortly after McCormick had moved to
Chicago, started a newspaper controversy almost as prolonged
and bitter as the dispute with Hussey in Virginia between 1843
and 1846.[46]

When the Virginia Reaper was introduced to the grain-fields
of Illinois and Wisconsin, in and after the harvest of 1844,
the competition Hussey had offered in the East was left behind.
In his stead appeared George Esterly, of Heart Prairie, Wisconsin, who built at his home and elsewhere a large and costly
header suitable for use by prairie farmers who devoted a broad
acreage to wheat. Esterly planned to establish a branch factory
in Chicago at about the time when Cyrus McCormick began his
residence in that city. In the autumn of 1848 the Chicago Mechanics' Institute held its second Annual Fair at the Market
House, and both McCormick and Esterly decided that a display
of their machines at this exhibition would be a worth-while
method of advertisement.[47] A gold medal awaited the inventor
whose implement should be adjudged best by the Committee
of Award, consisting of Mayor Woodworth, Alderman Foss,
and John S. Wright, editor of the "Prairie Farmer" and
Esterly's agent.

[46] "Western Farmer and Gardener," Nov., 1844, p. 82. "Transactions of
the New York State Agricultural Society," V (1845), p. 107. At the
Utica Fair of this society, O. Hussey received a $15 premium for his
reaper. His brother, T. R. Hussey, was one of the three judges. The next
year (ibid., VI, p. 97), the society at its Auburn Fair gave McCormick
a $5 premium, although Hussey also exhibited. The jury admitted that
they had been unable to test either machine and based their award upon
testimonials. Supra, Chap. IX, p. 211. C. H. to W. S. McCormick, Oct. 13,
1846.
[47] "Chicago Daily Journal," Nov. 16, 1848. "Prairie Farmer," Feb., 1847,
p. 71.

The judges had no opportunity to see the reapers in action and were compelled to rest their decision upon testimonials of "reliable farmers" and editorial "puffs" which each competitor furnished for their information. The medal was bestowed upon Esterly, but the explanation published by the judges in defense of their choice afforded the nettled McCormick an opportunity to reply with some very effective ridicule. It was not a prudent policy, almost at the outset of his Western venture, to offend the editor of the most powerful agricultural paper of the Middle West, not to mention the mayor of the city and a politician of consequence. But McCormick rarely, if ever, hesitated to vent his anger when he felt that he had a righteous grievance.

Despite the immediate and lasting enmity of the "Prairie Farmer," he probably never regretted his outburst on this occasion, for it was not his nature to do so. The judges confessed that they experienced difficulty in reaching a decision, since they "knew the award of the Institute would have a strong effect upon the public mind. . . . No one of the Committee having seen any one of the machines . . . in actual operation in the field, our decision is not entitled to the credit of a thorough examination." They admitted that the McCormick reaper was "more in demand on the prairies than all others united," but if Esterly's would operate in accordance with its inventor's guarantee and the testimonials which he presented, "we consider [it] to be a more important labor-saving improvement, and that it is entitled to the premium offered by the Institute, of a gold medal for the 'best harvesting machine.' " [48]

Immediately the editor of the "Chicago Daily Journal" rushed to the defense of McCormick. The judges' decision was against their own premises,—rejecting positive evidence in one case, in favor of *ex parte* statements and certificates in the other.

[48] "Chicago Daily Journal," Nov. 24, 1848.

. . . It is believed such an award cannot weigh a feather against the onward progress of Mr. McCormick's Reaper. . . . On the whole, it seems that what the Committee had at heart was the *encouragement* of Esterly without the injury of McCormick or the public.[49]

Encouraged by this support and irritated because Esterly boasted of his success in his advertisements, McCormick wrote to the friendly editor a public letter which appeared in the "Journal" on December 15, 1848. The inventor stressed the obvious inconsistency of an award, admittedly based upon purchasers' testimonials, which gave the medal to the competitor whose machine was less favored by farmers, as evidenced by the relative volume of sales and as stated by the jury itself.[50] The balance of the controversy need not be detailed; its inclusion here is merely intended to illustrate the use of exhibitions to promote sales, and the doubtful value of the judgments rendered by committees of award.

Because of such decisions, McCormick naturally tended more and more to shun fairs unless the occasion was unusual and the prospect of advantage most favorable. In this instance the subsequent debate between Esterly and McCormick in the press was of undoubted value to both contestants. Editors would print the letters of the rivals so long as their subscribers showed an interest in the subject at issue. It is not difficult to believe, after following the course of the argument in this and other similar controversies, that the competitors raged at each other in terrifying phrase not so much because they were really angry as because they knew that if they could amuse the public

[49] *Ibid.,* Nov. 25, 1848. "Chicago Daily Democrat," Nov. 27, 1848. "Gem of the Prairie," Dec. 9, 1848.

[50] "Chicago Daily Journal," Dec. 15 and 16, 1848. In the latter issue the editor compliments McCormick upon his letter: "We have seldom seen an article of the kind more clearly and forcibly written." The fact that McCormick, Ogden & Co. . . . "can't supply the demand . . . is worth more than all the 'reports' and 'certificates' in Christendom."

they would arouse a deal of interest in their implements and would secure a valuable bit of free advertisement.

"What is all this frothy and long-winded fuss about," queried Esterly, sarcastically, and "why does Mr. McCormick expend several hundred dollars in publishing circulars . . . to injure the character of the Mechanics' Institute, the report of the Committee and other men's machines?"

As to his treatment of the Committee during the time they were making up the award, and for some days previous his advances intended to influence their decision,—that is their matter, and not mine. . . . I will sell a machine for what it will clear in twenty days over his Virginia Reaper. . . . McCormick warrants his machine to cut 1½ acres of wheat in one hour. Will it? Yes! How? Have everything in the best of order, and then drive on as hard as you can for one hour. The next hour must take care of itself. . . . I find many of my best customers among those who own McCormick's. . . . I . . . tender him my thanks for the pains he has taken to advertise my machine. . . . I wonder whether I could sell Mr. McCormick a few Virginia Reapers as I am frequently offered them at half price in exchange for my Harvester.[51]

With such taunts and Yankee humor the battle of the reapers was fought in many a column of the press of the land during these years. The complete frankness, the brag and swagger, the bludgeon-like charges and retorts, delighted a people who talked very much that way themselves in the blustering fifties. Boasting and bold speech were the fashion of America, and reaper advertisements reflect in miniature the spread-eagle style which brought upon the diplomatic correspondence of the Secretaries of State of this time the ridicule and contempt of Old World statesmen.

[51] "Chicago Daily Democrat," Jan. 11, 1849, letter of George Esterly from City Hotel, Chicago, Jan. 9, 1849.

CHAPTER XV

SELLING THE McCORMICK REAPER AND MOWER

PRIOR to 1843 the members of the McCormick family were the sole agents for the sale of the reaper. Following the successful harvest of that year, Cyrus granted manufacturing rights for particular localities and the lessees occasionally performed services for him akin to those later expected of regular salesmen. Jabez Parker (later Parker & Smith) of Richmond received orders for reapers from men living outside his territory and forwarded them to Walnut Grove. He also kept a supply of spare parts and his shop was equipped to repair broken machines. Probably J. M. Hite and Martin Tutwiler played similar rôles, although the sources are silent concerning them. Corbin Braxton, a planter of influence on the lower James River, concerned himself with Cyrus McCormick's interests and kept him informed of reaper opinion and potential purchasers in his neighborhood.[1] W. H. H. Taylor and L. Tucker, of Cincinnati residence and Virginian antecedents, and Colonel Joshua Brown of St. Louis, similarly assisted McCormick in 1845.[2] The first two advertised in the press that orders for machines might be mailed either to A. C. Brown, the Cincinnati manufacturer, or to themselves. Whether or not William and Leander McCormick received commissions for the orders they procured is not known.

Cyrus McCormick was his own chief agent during these

[1] Corbin Braxton to C. H. McCormick, Mch. 10, 1845.
[2] "Ohio Cultivator," Mch. 15, 1845, p. 47. *McCormick vs. Manny,* I, defendant's testimony, pp. 209 ff.

early years. In and after 1844 he traveled widely through New York and the West, his pockets filled with order blanks, urging farmers to buy his reapers. The first regularly employed agents appeared in 1845. During this harvest his cousin, J. B. McCormick of Woodford County, Kentucky, began a reaper service of over twenty years. At this time he rode through the Ohio Valley drumming orders for the A. C. Brown plant at Cincinnati.[3] He was one of the two most picturesque agents in the early years of McCormick reaper history. Caustic and facile of pen, apt in criticism, proud, and confident of his own inventive and business ability, prone to prophesy disaster, sounding every depth and height of pessimism and joy in two succeeding letters to his employer, he alternately pleased and irritated his kinsmen with his long and rambling communications.

This agent made the lower Ohio Valley, Tennessee, and Missouri his stamping-ground, and was indulged with his enormous sales territory long after the scope of the business and his own health counseled him to accept a smaller one. Because of his tirelessness, his mechanical skill, and his keen appreciation of farmer psychology, he was an excellent salesman during the early years of his career. He wrote with complete frankness to his relatives and they often discovered many grains of wisdom amid the chaff of his discontent. Incidentally he was an ardent Clay Whig and delighted to rally his cousins upon their stanch adherence to the opposing party.[4]

For the same harvest of 1845, one R. Mitchell of Clarksville, Tenn., and J. M. Hite, Jr., of Virginia, also traveled through the West, searching for McCormick customers.[5] In the Gene-

[3] C. H. to W. S. McCormick, Aug. 6, 1845, and Dec. 11, 1846.

[4] J. B. McCormick supported the Whig party in 1848, but he was a Jacksonite in early life. He had been Atty. Genl. of Tennessee. He died in Dayton, O., in 1873. See the "Quincy Whig" (Quincy, Ill.), quoted in the "Chicago Daily Journal," Oct. 31, 1848.

[5] C. H. to W. S. McCormick, May 15 and Aug. 6, 1845, and Oct 13, 1846.

see Valley, Ansel Chappell of Brockport, the first New York purchaser of a McCormick reaper and later a bitter foe, acted as an agent.[6] The agency of Botts of the "Southern Planter," as early as 1843, has been mentioned in another connection.[7] In 1846 a representative of the reaper appeared in Laporte, Indiana, and for the same harvest Chappell was expected to canvass the West. Cyrus hoped that his youngest brother, John McCormick, would "ride" with their cousin in 1847, in order to gain experience in salesmanship, but this wish was probably not gratified.[8]

Following 1846, and particularly after McCormick's removal to Chicago in 1848, the appointment of new agents and the development of an effective sales system went on apace. Before 1855 the network of agencies covered most of the States of the Union and Canada.[9] The New England States and the lower South were naturally the two regions in which slight effort was made, during these years, to sell reapers. The number of salesmen along the middle seaboard and in Virginia also was relatively few, and McCormick had great difficulty in building a profitable market in the Genesee Valley. The evolution of a successful mower increased the attention given by the company to the Eastern farmer, and about 1850, McCormick entered upon a definite program to reinvade the coastal area and the South. Thereafter more salesmen appear each year in the East, but as late as 1855 three fourths of all the reapers annually produced by McCormick at his Chicago factory were sold in Illinois, Wisconsin, Iowa, and Missouri.

[6] "Genesee Farmer," Jan., 1850, p. 31, testimonial of Ansel Chappell.
[7] "Southern Planter," Jan., 1843.
[8] C. H. to W. S. McCormick, Dec. 11, 1846.
[9] Poster of McCormick, Ogden & Co., for 1849. "Ohio Cultivator," June 1, 1851, p. 176; Apr. 15, 1852, p. 128. "Albany Cultivator," July, 1851, p. 253. "American Farmer," July, 1850, Pictorial Supplement, and Dec., 1850, p. 210. Memo. of David Zimmerman, Genl. Agt., 1855.

In these States the agency system was, consequently, most highly developed.[10]

When McCormick left Walnut Grove for Chicago, the roving commissions under which his few agents had hitherto operated in the West came to an end. J. B. McCormick was finally persuaded to limit his field to Kentucky, Tennessee, and Missouri.[11] Ansel Chappell and the other representatives already named disappeared from the pay-roll. Cyrus McCormick and his two brothers no longer could afford the time to solicit sales by long winter and spring trips among the farmers. Their presence was required at the factory, but frequently one or all of them traveled during the harvest season through the wheat country, talking with grain-growers and agents, watching their machines in operation, and gathering from observation valuable suggestions for the improvement of the reaper and for more effective salesmanship. This was an excellent way to note the progress of competitors, detect infringements of patents, and, withal, to gain a needed change from the drudgery of close confinement to desk or shop in Chicago.[12] As the McCormick reaper gained fame through the country-side, it was gratifying to the farmer to find one of the brothers stopping at his house, inquiring about his reaper, or perhaps even mounting the machine and driving it through the wheat for his instruction. This was particularly true after the great World's Fair in London in 1851, where the McCor-

[10] "McCormick Extension Case, Patent of 1845," adverse testimony, pp. 37-40. "Ohio Cultivator," Jan. 15, 1850, p. 31; Aug. 1, 1850, p. 226. "Albany Evening Journal," Oct. 17, 1850. "Prairie Farmer," Jan., 1851, pp. 44, 45. "Albany Cultivator," July, 1851, p. 253.

[11] He was indulged with this large territory, which he could not adequately cover, for a decade. In 1859, much against his will, he was restricted to Missouri. By that time he was associated with one Baker at St. Louis and forwarded, for a fee, many McCormick reapers bound down the river. *Hussey vs. McCormick,* pp. 235-239.

[12] T. J. Paterson, from Rochester, N. Y., to C. H. McCormick & Co., Nov. 10, 1851.

mick reaper won the highest award and the name of its inventor became a household word in rural America.

After 1848 the employees of the company who most closely resembled the early salesmen, journeying almost at will over the land, were the traveling agents. By 1856 these men usually had a definite territory, comprising several States, under their supervision. Trusted helpers in Chicago, such as H. G. Hubbard, A. D. Hager, and J. L. Wilson, were often despatched on long business trips to introduce the reaper to a new grain region; to overcome the prejudice of a particular locality; [13] to the trial of rival machines where a secret observer might discover much for the advantage of the company, or to Providence or Boston to look for a new boiler or steam-engine for the factory.[14]

Thus A. D. Hager, in 1854, watched incognito the Manny-Atkins contest at Belvidere, Illinois,[15] and attempted to overcome the dislike for his employer's machine in the Roanoke and Yadkin valleys of North Carolina.[16] Such men were usually sent out in winter to talk with agents and farmers, collect money, appoint new salesmen, and discharge inefficient and dishonest ones. In this manner the office personnel at Chicago kept in intimate touch with the real problems of the field force. It led to sympathetic understanding when matters went awry, and it also prevented the local agent from hiding his inefficiency be-

[13] MS. instructions to Henry G. Hubbard, Oct. 18, 1849. "Prairie Farmer," Jan., 1851, pp. 44, 45. D. R. Burt from Waterloo, N. Y., Mch. 13, 1853. Burt, a traveling salesman, was endeavoring to secure agents to promote the reaper in Canada by writing to applicants and forwarding handbills.

[14] Horace White from Indianapolis, July 11, 1854. White was engaged in locating and returning to the factory all returned and unsold machines. He found 40 or more of 1848 and 1849 vintage at Vincennes, rusting and accumulating storage charges at excessive rates. A. D. Hager from N. Y. City, Aug. 21, Oct. 23, 27, 1854; from Lowell, Mass., Aug. 30, 1854; from Boston, Aug. 31, 1854; from Springfield, Mass., Sept. 1, 1854.

[15] A. D. Hager, from Belvidere, Ill., July 26, 28, and 30, 1854.

[16] *Post,* pp. 370 ff.

hind a story of unsurmountable obstacles in his sales territory. These confidential assistants were paid from $600 to $1,000 a year and traveling expenses.[17]

Similar in purpose but somewhat different in kind were the State-wide agents like T. J. Paterson of Rochester, James Campbell of Westons, New Jersey, and R. T. Elkinton of Philadelphia.[18] Usually their sphere of work was confined to their own States, but they might be asked to purchase iron or coal for the factory, to bargain with railways for transportation, to try out new devices and report, or to gather evidence for use in a lawsuit.[19] Nevertheless their normal duties were the appointment of agents and the supervision of sales, deliveries, and collections within their own particular district. Although they were state agents, Paterson was expected to push the sale of the reaper in Canada, and Campbell was for a time the representative for Delaware and Maryland, as well as for New Jersey.[20] Several of these men were conspicuous for their unswerving loyalty to their employer during long years of hard service, and Campbell, who resigned to be a state senator in 1857, found an ethical sanction for his devotion to his task. "The only object I had in view at first," he wrote to Leander McCormick in 1854, "was to aid agriculture and place the farmer beyond the power of a set

[17] In 1855, A. D. Hager was paid $600 and expenses. J. L. Wilson to David Zimmerman of Youngstown, Pa., Aug. 20, 1856, L.P.C.B. No. 3, p. 267. W. S. McCormick to W. A. Lewis, Kanawha Court House, Va., Nov. 16, 1857, L.P.C.B. No. 9, p. 538.

[18] "Fourth Annual Rept. of the Ohio State Board of Agriculture," 1849, pp. 88, 90, 106, 130, 207; "3d Annual Report," 1848, p. 181. "Ohio Cultivator," Jan. 15, 1850. "Genesee Farmer," July, 1850, p. 173. McCormick states that T. J. Paterson of Rochester is his general agent for western New York. Paterson had undergone a period of training in the West. "Albany Cultivator," July, 1851, p. 253. J. B. McCormick from St. Louis, Mch. 14, 1855.

[19] Jas. Campbell, from Westons, N. J., May 19, 1855.

[20] Idem to L. J. McCormick, May 15, 1854. T. J. Paterson from Rochester, N. Y., Nov. 10, 1851. MS. agreement of Apr. 1, 1852, with Paterson.

of drinking Harvest Hands with which we have been greatly annoyed." [21]

There were similar agents in other States, and each usually worked on a commission basis rather than for a fixed annual salary. The amount of their commissions varied, generally corresponding to the degree of sales resistance in the districts under their supervision. This resistance, of course, was relative to the activity of competitors, the quantity of grain grown, and the newness of the territory under their charge. Thus Eastern state representatives received a higher percentage on sales and collections than those of the West. The commissions varied from five per cent to fifteen per cent of the price of the reaper, but from this they must pay the smaller fees to the subagents who actually made contact with the individual farmer.

By 1848, if not earlier, yearly agreements in writing were made by McCormick with his principal agents. The 1849 contract with Messrs. Phelps & Bourland of Peoria, Illinois, will serve as an example of many others. They promised to "travel thoroughly over and through the wheat growing portions of" the eight counties named, during the winter and spring until the next harvest. "Responsible and trustworthy farmers only" would be solicited to buy, and "efficient assistant agents" would be hired. They agreed to superintend the delivery of machines at convenient points, and to "devote themselves actively to putting up, starting and setting to work the said Reapers, to receiving the cash payments, and to taking promptly the notes therefore, in, during and after the harvest." They engaged to pay their own traveling expenses and to report semi-monthly by mail to the company.

The company, on its part, guaranteed to give them $6 for each machine which they sold. One half of this might be re-

[21] Jas. Campbell from Westons, N. J., to L. J. McCormick, Feb. 6, 1854, and to C. H. McCormick, Nov. 4, 1857.

tained by the agent from the first payment made on each reaper, and the balance at the time of final settlement by the purchaser. If no more than $55 were collected on a machine, the agent would receive nothing for that sale; if from $55 to $85 were paid in, only $3 would be due to the salesman. If the company should inform Phelps & Bourland that it could no longer supply orders, the agent must stop canvassing, but the firm would pay $3 for all orders already engaged which could not be filled. The company promised to pay all court costs and attorney fees when a suit was necessary in order to collect from the farmer.[22]

Thus in Illinois and in a few other midwestern States where sales were many, there was no one principal agent, but several counties were assigned to an individual or to a firm in the same manner that New York and New Jersey were allotted to Paterson and Campbell. The presence of a general representative did not prevent direct contact between the factory and the lowliest assistant agent. Not infrequently the local salesman was appointed by the home office of the company, and in any case he was expected to send in monthly reports in the slack season and weekly or bi-weekly ones during the late spring and harvest-time. In fact, reapers were sold by the Chicago factory without the assistance of any agent, because some farmers were of the opinion that they could get better service and easier terms if they wrote directly to the place of production. Then too, as late as 1855, many localities had no salesmen.

The promotion of sales rested in the first instance upon the home office of the company. Much space has already been devoted to the methods by which C. H. McCormick advertised his reaper. The agent was naturally one of the manufacturer's principal publicity mediums, and he was assisted in his work by the posters and handbills his employer sent to him each year.

[22] MS. contract with Phelps & Bourland, Dec. 28, 1849. Feb. 24, 1851, they were assigned 12 counties and promised $10 for each machine sold. "McCormick Extension Case, Patent of 1845," pp. 51-53.

Salesmen sometimes informed the company that farmers overlooked reaper advertisements in the papers and magazines,
and that circulars and broadsides widely distributed about the
country-side were a far more profitable means of carrying the
news to the grain-grower.[23] Posters were attached to a snake
fence, a village tie-rail, or were used as wrappers for wares
sold at a country store. Circulars were often distributed from
farm to farm in winter by the agent astride his horse, or, if
he was particularly businesslike, he had a mailing-list and
sent one with a personal letter to each farmer in his district.

McCormick occasionally prepared a descriptive pamphlet,
but this was for instruction as well as for advertisement. Besides the terms of sale, testimonials, and a colorful exposition
of the merits of the reaper, this booklet furnished minute instructions to guide the farmer in "setting up," using, and
repairing the machine, and cautioned him to house it properly
during the winter. One cut or more aided the manufacturer to
make his lesson clear. Sometimes the directions were printed
on a separate circular, with another one devoted wholly to
advertising matter.[24] As early as 1842, McCormick used
printed directions to aid the purchaser in operating his reaper.[25]
Whatever the form this literature assumed from season to season, such material was mailed to any prospective buyer upon
request and was forwarded to each agent for distribution wherever it would do the most good. In addition to advertising
and educational aids of this nature, there were printed order-
blanks and reaper notes. These need mention here only to
illustrate the extent of the system which McCormick evolved

[23] A. D. Hager, from Greencastle, Ind., Dec. 13, 1854; Jas. Shields, from
Montevideo, Pa., Feb. 15, 1855; Thos. Dunsmore, from Bellevue, Ky.,
Apr. 25, 1855.
[24] "Richmond Semi-Weekly Whig," Oct. 27, 1843. "Ohio Cultivator,"
Mch. 15, 1845, p. 47. "Albany Cultivator," May, 1846, p. 165. "Ohio
Cultivator," Apr. 15, 1847, p. 64.
[25] "Richmond Enquirer," Aug. 24 and Sept. 30, 1842.

Directions for Assembling and Operating a McCormick
Reaper-Mower, 1857

to help the agent, attract the farmer, and bind the purchaser. It was a long cry, by 1850, from the slipshod business methods of the iron-furnace venture of a decade before.

Occasionally an energetic and bold agent complained that the McCormick "sales talk" did not make the proper appeal in his territory and forwarded material of local interest for inclusion in the handbills sent for his use.[26] Posters were sometimes printed in German, for in sections of Illinois, Wisconsin, and Missouri many of the farmers were German and were accounted thrifty and "sure-pay." [27] The company even issued "styratyped" forms which suggested arguments to render a salesman's eloquence particularly persuasive in regions where competition was keen.[28] Notwithstanding this close control exercised from the center, and although the advertising material, then as now, was superlative in its optimism, no instance has been discovered where the company suggested questionable methods to procure sales.[29]

Despite this valuable assistance given to agents to aid them in selling reapers, the success of the individual canvasser mainly depended upon his own initiative and energy. His efficiency was gaged by the number of orders sent in and by the

[26] J. B. McCormick, from Versailles, Ky., Feb. 18 and Mch. 14, 1854.
[27] T. J. Walker & Co., from Belleville, Ill., Jan. 20 and Apr. 10, 1854; Mch. 8, 1856. Wm. Marshall, from Adeline, Ill., Apr. 22, 1854. Nevertheless, W. J. Hanna wrote from the company office to F. W. Smith of Woodstock, Ill., June 8, 1859: "In these northern counties [of Ill.] the risk is fifty per cent greater in selling any machinery to the general run of customers than it is in the south half of the state, and the greatest risk is in McHenry Co. . . . There are so many men in that county hailing from over the water (none the worse for that of course) but of very limited means, and many of them only renters that more than ordinary caution is absolutely necessary." L.P.C.B. No. 22, p. 439.
[28] D. R. Burt, from Waterloo, N. Y., Mch. 13, 1853.
[29] J. L. Wilson, from Genoa, Ill., Jan. 2, 1852. Wilson persuaded a Seymour & Morgan Co. salesman to work secretly for the McCormick interests, but this does not appear to have been done with the sanction of the Chicago office.

promptness with which he collected and forwarded all money due. The amount of penetration by competitors within his district was another test of his ability. The local salesman was most effective when he was favorably known to the farmers of his territory and had sufficient mechanical skill to set up and repair the reapers. He need not be a scholar, but he must know how to keep accounts carefully and honestly. Since frequent reports were required, he must write legibly, and while perfect spelling was not expected, the company was undoubtedly justified in refusing the applicant for work who wrote: "I can Bee of Goodel of Surases in asisting the Sail of your Mashines for Wich I will Spair noe Pains." [30]

By 1850 the McCormick reaper had a reputation and was no longer experimental. This was, of course, a self-selling feature which aided the agents and worked to the advantage of the company, since the latter did not find it necessary to pay as large commissions as its rivals. McCormick's salesmen often complained that Manny's or Seymour & Morgan's employees received as high as twenty-five per cent on sales, while they had to be content with five or ten dollars per machine. [31] However, very few resignations have been found, and the volume of sales usually made up for the smallness of their fees. As in the case of the general agents, there was no fixed rule which determined the compensation of all salesmen, and the pay was scaled to the difficulty and value of the service. [32]

[30] J. Burk, from Wright's Corner, Ind., Aug. 4, 1854.

[31] For a typical agent's contract see the agreement with Andrew Claycomb, of Warren County, Ill., for 1849. Contract with Abner Thompson, Mifflin County, Pa., Feb. 16, 1852. He was to receive $2 a day and expenses, for each day that he was employed as an agent. In the supplementary agreement with O. M. Dorman, Jan. 16, 1850, the partners stipulated that no commission of over $10 should be paid.

[32] "McCormick Extension Case, Patent of 1845," adverse testimony, pp. 37-40, deposition of O. M. Dorman, Sept. 26, 1850: "We paid agents $5 to $6 per machine for selling and collecting. In two instances, $7 to $8 per machine, and in Wisconsin, where Seymour & Morgan machines offer keen

Although these local agents did not write to one another, their sales methods were very similar whether they were working in Iowa or in New Jersey. The company forwarded a sample machine as early each year as possible, and the agent exhibited it in his barn or store, or pulled it along the roads of his district, to show it to the farmers. Court days or Saturdays were the best times to display it in the court-house square or in front of the general store at the county-seat. Very often rival reapers also were on hand, and the crowd delighted to listen to the cut and thrust of the competitors. The following extract from the letter of an Iowa agent to his employer is a fair sample of the eloquence used to gain the favor of the farmer:

I found in the neighborhood supplied from Cassville quite early in the season one of Manny's agents with a fancyfully painted machine cutting the old prairie grass to the no small delight of the witnesses, making sweeping and bold declarations about what his machine could do and how it could beat yours, etc., etc. Well, he had the start of me, I must head him some how. I began by breaking down on his fancy machine pointed out every objection that I could see and all that I had learned last year . . . gave the statements of those that had seen the one work in my grass . . . all of which I could prove. And then stated to all my opinion of what would be the result should they purchase from Manny. You pay one half money and give your note for the balance, are prosecuted for the last note and the cheapest way to get out of the scrape is to pay the note, keep the poor machine and in a short time purchase one from McCormick. . . . Now gentlemen I am an old settler, have shared all the hardships of this new country with you, have taken it Rough and Smooth . . . have often been imposed on in the way I allmost know you would be by purchasing the machine offered you to day. I would say to all, try your machine before you [pay] one half or any except the freight. I can offer you one on such terms, warrant it against this machine

rivalry, we paid one agent $9 per machine. In Ohio and Missouri, where we were anxious to make an entry, we paid more than in Illinois. We gave agents 10% along the Erie Canal."

or any other you can produce, and if after a fair trial . . . any other prooves superior and you prefer it to mine, keep [it]. I will take mine back, say not a word, refund the freight, all is right again. No Gentlemen this man dare not do this. The Result you have seen. He sold not one. I sold 20. About the same circumstances occured in Lafayette Cy.[33]

Although Cyrus McCormick did not exhibit his machine so often at county and state fairs after 1850 as in the early years, the agent might do so, and if he fortunately won the premium, he thereby boosted the reputation of the implement in his own district.[34] Very rarely an agent was also selling for some other company, but unless circumstances were exceptional McCormick preferred a man of undivided allegiance.[35] The farmer who bought the first Virginia Reaper in his neighborhood was sometimes permitted to pay for it by inducing his acquaintances to purchase also.[36]

When the agent sold a reaper he was expected to secure the signature of the farmer on a printed sales form stipulating that he would make a first payment when he received the machine, and remit the balance on December 1, with interest at six per cent from July 1. Salesmen wrote to the company, complaining that rivals did not require so much formality and that many farmers were loath to bind themselves in this way.[37] In fact, the regulation seems to have been honored as much in

[33] D. R. Burt, from Waterloo, Ia., June 26, 1854. There is no punctuation in this letter, as written, and a minimum has been inserted to make its meaning clear.

[34] John Erb, from Durlach, Pa., Dec. 26, 1854; E. S. Troxel, from Hagerstown, Md., Sept. 9, 1854, and from Waynesboro, Pa., Sept. 29 and Dec. 13, 1854.

[35] H. M. Smith, from Richmond, Va., June 10, 1854. Smith was also an agent for Hussey and Burrall.

[36] I. I. Hite, from White Post, Va., June 16, 1855; L. P. Armstrong, from Shipman, Ill., Mch. 20, 1855.

[37] D. R. Burt, from Potosi, Wis., June 12, 1854.

the breach as in its observance,[38] for the correspondence reveals that frequently no cash was paid when the reaper was
delivered and only after the harvest had begun did the agent
go from purchaser to purchaser to secure their signatures to
reaper notes.[39]

Prior to 1848, Cyrus McCormick did not sue a farmer for
the price of his reaper, and court actions for this purpose were
infrequent before 1855, although each agency contract included
a clause to the effect that the salesman should begin suit when
directed by the company. McCormick bore the expense, but
unless the situation became desperate it was impolitic to hale
a delinquent purchaser before a court. The sympathy of the
country-side was usually with the debtor and prejudice against
the "hard-hearted" manufacturer meant a serious loss of business. On the other hand, everything possible was done to
satisfy the farmer and make him willing to pay without pressure. Though December was the date for final settlement, it
was usual for additional time to be given upon request.

The agent was supplied with spare parts for the reaper and
mower, and either replaced those in the machine which broke
despite the care of the owner, or sold them at a nominal price.[40]
This was a real service. In harvest-time speed was necessary
and a farmer who found his reaper useless because of the
breaking of some small element was faced with a serious loss
of time and money if he had to send to Chicago or rely upon
the slow skill of the cross-roads blacksmith. Because spare
parts accompanied every machine that left the factory, the
buyer under ordinary circumstances could get through the
harvest without leaving his farm on account of the reaper. In

[38] J. L. Wilson, from Cordova, Ia., Nov. 25, 1854; J. B. Fairbanks, from
Concord, Ill., Mch. 31, 1855.

[39] H. D. and O. N. May from Belvidere, Ill., Aug. 2, 1849. This letter
is printed in the "Chicago Daily Journal" of Sept. 8, 1849.

[40] B. M. Rhodes, from Baltimore, May 26, 1855. "American Farmer,"
May, 1855, p. 382.

1853 the McCormick machine worked poorly, because of faulty gearing. The following winter each purchaser was sent replacements free of charge, in order to make their implements give satisfaction.[41]

If an agent had too much repair work to do, or if he lacked the ability, the Chicago factory despatched a mechanic in the winter, to go through the country putting the reapers in good condition for the next season.[42] This, of course, was not altruism, but it helps to explain why McCormick's sales grew from year to year. Farmers who owed money to the factory were given as much, if not more, attention of this kind, and debts often were paid as a result. The basic reasons for the rapidly increasing business were the value of the implement and the extension of markets, means of transportation, and the grain area, but this careful effort to please the farmer in little matters and this highly organized agency system, unexampled in its day, also contributed to McCormick's success. At a time when nation-wide industries were few, and modern advertising methods and salesmanship were in their infancy, McCormick, with no precedents in his own field of manufacturing to serve as a model, worked out a method of operation which was generally pleasing to the farmer and profitable to himself.

The agent's task was often difficult. The output and the variety of reapers and mowers grew by leaps and bounds after 1850, and farmers became more and more critical.[43] In some

[41] T. J. Paterson, from Rochester, N. Y., Jan. 3, 1854; C. F. Keener, from Naples, Ill., Apr. 17, 1854; Edmund Ruffin, from Old Church Point, Va., Feb. 2, 1855.

[42] Hiram Austin, a Chicago mechanic, from Peoria, Ill., Feb. 22, 1854.

[43] Amos Bailey, from Walworth, Wis., Feb. 3, 1854. Some agents in the Middle West already complained that their districts were over-supplied with machines. J. L. Wilson, from Burlington, Ia., Feb. 6, 1852: Farmers are turning from wheat- to corn-production and have enough reapers. J. L. Wilson, from Genoa, Ill., Jan. 2, 1852: There are enough reapers in this section to last five years. G. M. Gault, from Annapolis, O., Apr. 14, 1855: Farmers are planting corn instead of wheat and are importing

sections of the country they were besieged by salesmen, and, as a result, they constantly demanded better reapers and easier terms of payment. According to some McCormick agents, many farmers felt so independent of any one make of reaper that they were wont to return machines upon the slightest evidence of failure to meet the warranty.[44] Furthermore, they were so confident of the solicitation of the salesman that unless need dictated they refused to do the most trivial repair-work themselves, relying upon the company's repair-man or the agent to visit them and do it free of charge. The farmer in the 1850's was not often "machine-minded," and, regardless of the cost of the reaper, was likely to leave it in the field where he last had used it, exposed to rain, snow, and sun until the next harvest. The wood warped, the paint disappeared, and the iron rusted.[45] The owner was surprised and disappointed to find that his implement would not operate when next year's wheat was ready to cut. Progressive farmers were building larger barns to protect implements, as well as crops, from the weather, and a few equipped themselves with the facilities to do their own repair work.

The usual grievances of the reaper salesman were underselling by competitors and larger commissions paid to rival agents,[46] bad weather, poor crops, late delivery of reapers,

wheat from Illinois. For the same thought see J. L. Wilson, from Havana, Ill., Mch. 15, 1854; D. R. Burt, from Waterloo, Ia., Apr. 30, 1854.

[44] T. J. Paterson, from Rochester, N. Y., May 6, 1854; H. M. Smith, from Richmond, Va., June 15, 1854; Edmund Ruffin, from Old Church Point, Va., Dec. 16, 1854. *Supra,* Chap. XIV, p. 336, ftn. 24.

[45] Hiram Austin, from Peoria, Ill., Jan. 22, 1854. He had been sent out from the factory to repair reapers. "I am sory I enlisted but ther is no use I shall go through with the Job if I live . . . the machiens are in the worst plight imaginable. I have found them out doors and frozen down Just where they used them last." "Pennsylvania Farm Journal," Sept., 1855, pp. 270, 271.

[46] J. L. Wilson, from Genoa, Ill., Jan. 2, 1852; T. J. Walker & Co., from Belleville, Ill., Jan. 20, 1854; T. J. Paterson, from Rochester, N. Y., Mch. 21, 1854; R. T. Elkinton, from Philadelphia, Mch. 29, 1855.

faulty construction, and depreciated currency.[47] The number of sales depended upon the weather more than in other businesses, and a late spring, excessive rain or drought, or any other of the abnormal and uncontrollable circumstances to which the farmer was subjected, spelled a bad season for agent and manufacturer alike.[48] Most grain-growers had no surplus in the bank and could not buy machinery unless there were prospects of a good crop and a fair market price for grain. Nor would a salesman wish to press a machine upon a farmer who did not seem able to pay. A crop outlook that was discouraging late in April frequently became favorable within a month, and under such circumstances more orders for reapers would be rushed to the factory than could be filled. Late shipments on slow canal-boats often arrived at their destination too late and Eastern agents in particular complained of tardy deliveries.[49] Because the regional demand could never be accurately forecast, a few reapers were left over even after the best of seasons.

If choice had to be made, McCormick apparently gave preference to the Western market, in his shipments, notwithstanding

[47] Farmers who preferred the cradle to the reaper are occasionally found. See the letter of E. Brown, from Leesburg, O., in the "Ohio Cultivator," of Aug. 15, 1850, p. 245. "Albany Cultivator," Sept., 1852, p. 314. "Prairie Farmer," Sept., 1850, pp. 266-269.

[48] "Ohio Cultivator," July 15, 1850, p. 217. H. B. Shepard, from West Union, Ind., Nov. 12, 1854; Isaac Hite, from White Post, Va., Apr. 27, 1855. A complaint of a different nature came from L. P. Armstrong, of Shipman, Ill., Mch. 20, 1855: "Your agent called here last year on Sunday and as we profess to be a God-serving community we of course did not trade with him."

[49] "Chicago Commercial Advertiser," June 13, 1849. "Chicago Daily Journal," Sept. 8, 1849. Last-minute orders were particularly embarrassing in 1856. The office wrote to J. B. McCormick, at St. Louis, June 15, 1856, L.P.C.B. No. 2, p. 226½: "All creation is howling for machines all at once. . . . Will ship your last carload tomorrow. Had to *steal* them for you. . . . You raised h—ll in shipping too many machines up the Mo. river. Can't you get them back? The Kansas fellows will indict you for high treason."

the fact that he emphasized his intention in and after 1850 of
placing great stress upon Eastern and Southern sales.[50] Hessian fly, weevil, army-worm, wheat blight, and chinch-bug were
other "dispensations of Providence" which quickly turned rural
joy into gloom and seriously affected the annual profits of the
reaper-maker.[51]

Many agents seemed to enjoy grumbling, and the company
files are filled with letters written during these years, lamenting
faulty woodwork, breaking sickle-sections and fingers, heavy
side draft, parts missing upon delivery, and bad weather.[52]
The salesmen often were mechanics and Cyrus McCormick
must have been wearied by the constant suggestions sent to
him for the improvement of this or that part of the reaper, for
the defeat of rivals, and for more extensive publicity.[53] In some
cases the agents were merely passing along what they had been
told by farmers, and there is little evidence to show that the
company altered the construction of the reaper or mower to
conform to recommendations of local agents. The factory experimented with its machines and seems to have relied almost
solely upon these trials to prove the desirability of change.

The work of collecting from purchasers involved many
problems. Grain-growing was so speculative because of the
weather, blight, and uncertain markets, that the manufacturer
of agricultural machinery must be willing to make adjustments

[50] "Ohio Cultivator," Jan. 15, 1850, p. 31; Feb. 15, 1850, p. 63. "Genesee
Farmer," July, 1850, p. 173. "Albany Evening Journal," Oct. 17, 1850.
"Chicago Daily Journal," Dec. 13, 1851. "McCormick Patent Reaping and
Mowing Machine in America," Mch. 15, 1852.

[51] Richard Morrow, from Piqua, O., June 28, 1854; H. G. Emery, from
Indianapolis, May 31, 1854; Isaac Goon, from Marshallville, O., May 14,
1855; Sam'l Park, from Hutsonville, Ill., May 14, 1855.

[52] Phelps & Bourland, from Peoria, Ill., July 24, 1849; T. J. Paterson,
from Rochester, N. Y., Nov. 10, 1851; J. L. Wilson, from Pleasant Valley,
Ia., Jan. 31, 1852.

[53] W. B. Silver, from Hamilton, O., Jan. 7, 1855, J. Andrews, from
Richland, Ind., Nov. 9, 1855; W. O. Leyburn, from Waterford, Wis.,
May 12, 1855.

in terms of payment in order to retain the friendship and patronage of the farmer.[54] This was particularly true in 1854 and 1855, when crop failures were numerous and good money was scarce. There were many depreciated "free-stock" bills in circulation in the Middle West, and frequently farmers had neither sound state bank-notes nor specie with which to pay.[55] They rarely consulted the bank-note detectors and were often angered to find that agents would not receive their money in payment for machines. In some cases, where other funds were impossible to procure, any paper bills that were available were taken at a discount, and were then rushed to their source of issue or to a bank, to be exchanged for money current at its face-value in Chicago.[56]

In the Middle West agents discovered that a vital connection existed between prompt payments and a good corn crop and pork market. Grain-growers often relied upon the sale of corn and pork to raise the funds necessary to meet their reaper notes on December 1, and if money was scarce and the produce agents could pay for these commodities only in manufactured goods, both the reaper-owner and the agent were in a dilemma.[57] There was always the last resort of receiving farm

[54] D. Zimmerman, from Lewistown, Pa., Nov. 27, 1854; Jas. Burk, from Wright's Corner, Ind., Aug. 4, 1854.

[55] D. Williams, from Indianapolis, Oct. 25 and 30, 1854; A. D. Hager, from Indianapolis, Ind., Nov. 17, 1854, and from Greencastle, Ind., Dec. 13, 1854; M. Nowlan, from LaFayette, Ill., Nov., 1854; E. S. Troxel, from Waynesboro, Pa., Dec. 18, 1854; A. P. Dickey, from Racine, Wis., Jan. 4 and Feb. 13, 1855; Harrison & Son, from Newark, Del., Mch. 27, 1855; D. Zimmerman, from Venango, Pa., May 6, 1855.

[56] S. D. Gartrell, from Terre Haute, Ind., Dec. 11, 1854. He was compelled to take state stock money at 12% discount on Eastern exchange. He wrote that he could possibly exchange it for Illinois bank notes, but "I hear that most of them [Illinois banks] are broke."

[57] T. J. Walker & Co., from Belleville, Ill., Sept. 19, 1854; J. L. Wilson, from Keokuk, Ia., Dec. 3, 1854, and from Cordova, Ia., Dec. 17, 1854: There are no cash buyers of pork along the Mississippi. The river is closing. Farmers are packing their pork and letting their grain remain in

products in discharge of the debt, but this was firmly dis-
countenanced by McCormick, prior to the panic of 1857, although exceptions can be found.[58] The inadvisability of lawsuits has already been mentioned. Not only would legal
proceedings cause hostility to the firm, but even if a court order
to distrain were granted, the company would be saddled with
farm property, real or personal, difficult to convert into cash.[59]

Arrears in payments totaling thousands of dollars followed
each harvest and only the very large profits made on each sale
allowed the business to go on. Cyrus McCormick was often
forced to borrow funds in Chicago or New York to operate
the factory, although many times the amount of his loan was
due from those who had purchased his reapers.[60] Farmers paid
him six-per-cent interest upon their debt, but he could have
derived much more than this return from the money if it had
been available for his own use. Investments in Chicago real

the stack until spring. You must have money, but should you sue? Bank
failures and suspensions also make collections hard.

[58] C. Weed, from Muscatine, Ia., Sept. 3, 1849. This agent reports that
two farmers have paid their reaper notes in wheat and that he will sell it.

[59] J. L. Wilson, from Cordova, Ia., Nov. 25, 1854: "I have *positively instructed* the Messrs. M. to sue all paper that falls due and is unpaid." This
was unusual at the time, but suits were frequent during the panic, 1857-59.

[60] "McCormick Extension Case, Patent of 1845," pro testimony, p. 197.
L.P.C.B. No. 16, p. 537, No. 17, p. 48, financial statements of Nov. 6,
1858, and Dec. 20, 1858.

Year	Number of machines made	Cost including materials and labor	Number on hand	Number to be acc't'd for by agents	Notes on hand unpaid	Amount of sales
1849	1,490	$72,149.82	0	0	$2,589.77	$172,504.73
1850	1,603	?	5	0	2,976.37	89,016.89
1851	1,004	36,290.26	5	0	5,113.87	105,000.04
1852	1,011	38,701.79	17	0	3,753.16	112,530.70
1853	1,108	62,572.83	22	0	5,840.84	124,973.59
1854	1,558	86,736.51	9	0	12,855.02	209,373.94
1855	2,534	138,344.40	10	0	34,557.80	363,483.72
1856	4,095	194,397.52	56	100	125,414.81	574,011.32
1857	4,091	199,892.00	154	39	315,690.67	541,346.06
1858	4,561	194,586.43	644	403	393,587.14	466,659.44

estate were yielding large profits, but the inventor was unable
to participate to any great extent prior to 1855.

The thousands of letters which poured in to the central office of the firm during these years, from agents in almost
every State of the Union, are still in existence. Nevertheless
these salesmen usually reported because they were required to,
and viewed their task without imagination. Save for J. B.
McCormick, already mentioned, only one man in the period
before 1855 so wrote that his letters furnish enjoyable as well
as instructive reading. In 1854, Cyrus McCormick sent A. D.
Hager, a Vermont Yankee, to reintroduce the reaper in North
Carolina, and to overcome the prejudice in the Halifax neighborhood which had resulted from its initial failure about ten
years before. T. Pollock Burgwyn, with his brother and father,
grew 1,700 acres of wheat in 1854 and had favored Hussey's
machine since 1845.[61] He was a vice-president of the United
States Agricultural Society, a man of great influence in his
own State, and, what was still worse for McCormick, one who
felt that it was his duty to write about his reaper problems, to
prominent agricultural papers. Hussey of course used these
letters to advance his own fortunes and McCormick selected
Hager to win Burgwyn to his own standard. To expect a New
Englander to ingratiate himself with a proud planter was somewhat fantastic, but Hager at least brought to his task a saving
sense of humor and a determination not to be discouraged.
His letters of 1854, although not typical, may appropriately be
quoted to illustrate the work and the problems of a reaper agent
during this period.

Hager's first problem was to freight the reapers to the Burgwyn estate. "I find 'our' Canal from Raleigh west is only a
paper one, and the only way I am to get those machines east is

<hr>

[61] For a description of the Burgwyn estate, see the "American Agriculturist," of Jan., 1850, p. 27. "American Farmer," Mch., 1851, p. 307. "Albany
Cultivator," Aug., 1852, p. 284.

to get them *waggoned* to Fayetteville on plank road (most of the way) and from thence by Steam Boat to Wilmington." This was on May 12, when Hager was at Raleigh. Three days later he had reached Jamestown, North Carolina:

> I arrived here yesterday after a tedious stage ride from Raleigh. Upset once on the road with a stage load of 14 passengers, but not severely hurt. . . . Wheat fields here are small, hence the prospect is not the best for selling. I go to night to Greensboro to attend *court* and a public examination of the Students of the Female Seminary. . . . I hope to meet the wealthy patrons of that institute and find some *customers*. I made a *rap* with Burgwyn and a *public trial* of Burralls, Husseys, and McCormicks Reapers comes off after we have set up and *got the hang* of McCormicks. He and his "Brother Tom" have plantations adjoining and have quit cotton raising and gone to raising corn and *wheat*. They raise 1700 (!) acres of wheat this year. . . . My fare for 98 ms. was $6.75 and 50 cents for every poor meal of victuals I had on the road. It costs like sixty to travel here and rather "poor doins" at that. . . . Burgwyns will have 14 machines to work in their fields this season. . . .

A week later in the same town he still viewed his task with a light heart:

> I have strove in vain, to get a horse to use a week, but now have concluded to take Stage and then foot it. This is decidedly a one horse country all but the *horse*. The land is good, but as long as they have a negro to plow it, with one mule and an antediluvian plow with *shafts* to draw by, they will have little use for reapers. I hope I am Yankee enough to sell what we have on hand here, and am inclined to think I shall, when the rubs of harvest come.

Two weeks elapsed and then Hager found time at Halifax to write:

> I should have written more had I any thing worth writing but to tell you of the "Old Fogies" and those opposed to Reaping machines on the grounds that "if we use these labor saving

machines we shan't have anything for our *niggers* to do." I thought such news would not pay. . . . I go to Burgwyns tomorrow morn. I "sort of *dread*" the result, but I don't show it. I recollect your instructions to carry the impression that they had *almost* seen Mr. McCormick when they had seen me.

After he had reached Burgwyn's plantation he was unable to conceal the humor of the situation:

Wednesday and Thursday are the days for *Napoleon* to either win or lose the battle of Roanoke Valley. I will have the *darkeys* on my side as all want to rake on the machine that the man owns that "give Bob de half dollar to carry him to de ferry."

Burgwyn bought five Hussey reapers and a mechanic from the Baltimore factory had been at this plantation for a month "rigging them up." Hager forwarded a preliminary report on June 13:

Hussey's, Burrall's and your machine . . . worked till noon today. All cut well. The raking on yours was the poorest done of any. Hussey's and B's both delivered in the rear and the hands understood. . . . If Burgwyn's negroes and I am not too stupid to learn to rake tomorrow, I think we will show the World's Wonder off to advantage. I would give ten Dollars out of my own pocket to know how to rake off *well* myself. . . . I have promised the Raker a Premium provided he rakes so well as to bring out my machine ahead. . . . But I say and think now of North Carolina as I did before I came. It never will be an extra place for selling machines. New England will be worth a dozen of it provided it will continue to *mow* as it *mowed* here Saturday. . . . As for *mowing* here it is all out of the question. They raise no grass for hay. What I mowed at this place was on a lawn in front of his residence, kept as a sort of curiosity,—turkey's retreat, etc. He don't know now what to do with the hay, but talked yesterday of having it "toted" to the pasture ground for his cattle and mules to pick over. . . . Mocking Birds can be bought from one to Five Dollars each. I have offered the darkeys $2 for an old one. If they get one I will present it to Mrs. [W. S.] McCormick.

The next day he was still happy:

> The day is past. All machs. worked well. . . . . Yours cut equal to any of them but the delivery is not as good as the others. They [negroes] are too slow motioned, and lack gumption [for raking]. Burgwyn *threatens* them and I *hire* them. Between us they do the best they can. . . . I will just remark that I am treated, with the best his house affords (and he lives in tall style), have twice during a time of leizure been invited to take a ride with him, once with his family, am furnished with the latest papers, etc.—but Hussey's Agent eats not at Burgwyn's table but with his *overseer* and never to my knowledge has been invited into the house. Today I was furnished with a horse saddled but Hussey's Agt. walked it.

Notwithstanding this entertainment, Hager left Halifax on June 16 uncertain of the result. Burrall's had failed, but Burgwyn reserved his decision between the McCormick and Hussey reapers until he found time to write about the trials to the "American Farmer" of Baltimore. This was ominous, since the editor of this paper always favored the Hussey machine, manufactured in his own city. Probably Hager did not leave the plantation in the best of spirits and the events of the next few days further irritated him. He wrote from Greensboro on June 20:

> I am this far on my road to Yadkin Valley. Yesterday and today I have been made a tool of by some of the chivalry (?) of the South. I worked the refused '52 machine and ground it and fixed it so that it worked first rate and to the satisfaction of all—still the d——d villains won't agree to take it. I hold still, but I *think* swear—and nothing would suit me better than to give them a high fall. One thing I must say for the honorable (?) southerners that I have become acquainted with here—that is, they are the smallest specimens of real men that I ever saw—their word, or a sense of what we Yankees call honor they don't regard half as much as the lowest Dutchman I ever dealt with. I've got the *Blues* but it is the *mad,* and not the desponding kind—and the way I do, is to fight the Devil on his own grounds. I'm for *selling* the *machines* and if anybody does it, I'll do it. You may see some

flaming a/c's of McCormick's Reaper in N. C. I have forty plans
for attack and thirty nine for retreat and when the battle is over
I will tell you who is *winner*. I am bound for the Yadkin Valley
and the probability is that I shall not write while I am there as
P. Offices are things they have "up North." . . . Health good
. . . weather hot and no rain for one week. Everybody but myself
has bowel complaint. If they would take less liquor and keep more
honor about them, think might enjoy better health.

Records largely fail from this point on. Hager seems to
have sold several machines and to have left the balance of the
eleven or twelve, which he took to North Carolina, on trial
with planters about Halifax and in the Yadkin Valley. As
late as 1857, he was writing to the company, trying to untangle
the North Carolina business of 1854. But by that time he had
left reaper employ and was still buoyant as Assistant Naturalist
of Vermont, arranging that State's collection of minerals and
fossils. He was an outstanding agent, not because of his efficiency, for he apparently was not a good salesman, but because he brought joy and enthusiasm to his task.

Not only had the wheat sections of the United States been
covered with a network of McCormick agencies by 1856, but
by that time the directing force at the factory had been carefully systematized. During the first years of manufacturing at
Chicago the major emphasis at the plant had naturally been
placed upon the production department. It was 1859 before
Wm. S. McCormick felt that the office staff under his management was adequately housed in rooms equipped with pine tables
and illuminated by gas.[62] On the walls were maps of the chief
grain areas of the United States, divided into districts, each
bearing the name of the local agent and showing the sale of
reapers there in successive years. For the inspiration of the
clerks and the edification of visitors who came to admire
Chicago's largest factory, the medals, diplomas, and certificates

---

[62] W. S. to C. H. McCormick, Feb. 15, 1859, L.P.C.B. No. 18, p. 456.

of merit won by the McCormick reaper during the past fifteen years were conspicuously displayed.[63] To insure expert attention to the varied problems of each day's business, one man in the office supervised the agents; another, collections; a third, purchasing; a fourth, the shipment and allocation of machines; a fifth, repairs and spare parts; while in the background hovered the bookkeeper, who was ready to give financial information pertinent to the work in each field.

The correspondence for any one year shows a natural seasonal variation of subject-matter. In the spring most of the letters were to agents, urging many and early orders, and to transportation companies seeking favorable freight rates for car-load shipments of machines. During the rush season from May 1 to August 10 the focus of the factory's attention gradually moved northward with the harvest, from the belt of the border States to the Canadian grain-fields. The shipment and reshipment of reapers and mowers, and the forwarding of spare parts were the topics of the hour. As the local agents were urged in the spring to sell, so in the autumn they were pressed for their collections, their account-sheets, reaper notes, and for certificates from satisfied purchasers to use in advertising pamphlets and posters. Iron- and lumber-men were given the word that the McCormick dock was cleared and ready to receive pigs and castings, sickles and lumber for the next season's machines.[64]

Traveling agents, and even members of the office personnel, then about the country checking up salesmen and appointing new ones, required a deal of information and advice, which kept the office force busy in Chicago. In December of each

[63] "Lexington Gazette," Apr. 28, 1859, copying from the "Chicago Tribune."
[64] W. J. Hanna, for C. H. McCormick, to the American Transportation Co., Buffalo, N. Y., Nov. 10, 1857, L.P.C.B. No. 9, p. 445: "My dock is on the pier and is well known as the most commodious and roomy Dock in the City, with plenty of Water always for the largest boats." It was 300 feet in length. The annual factory inventory was taken in late August.

year the letter-books, despite the Christmas season, are filled with admonitions to dilatory agents and farmers, threatening suit and demanding adequate security for the settlement of the debts which were still outstanding.

Outgoing letters were tediously written in longhand, and copies were kept in huge tissue-paper letter-books of about nine hundred pages each. Cyrus McCormick was rarely in the office, and William wrote fewer and fewer business letters as the years passed, save to some favored agents or old friends, or upon an important question which needed the emphasis of his penmanship, so difficult to decipher. The blotter-board, water-brush, and letter-press—the chief tools with which retained copies were made—were in the charge of a copyist clerk, whose day began at half-past six each morning, when he started the fire in the office stove and wielded broom and dust-pan before his superiors arrived at seven.[65] Beginning in 1856, these letter-books—now dog-eared, their script faded and often illegible—record a part of the story of the rise of one of the major industries of the United States. When supplemented by the hundreds of impersonal reports sent it annually by agents all over the land, describing conditions in their particular localities, these files transcend the reaper business in their importance and constitute a storehouse from which much valuable data for an agricultural history of the United States may be drawn.

[65] W. S. McCormick to M. Rountree, Dec. 4, 1858, L.P.C.B. No. 15, p. 233.

CHAPTER XVI

THE INVASION OF ENGLAND, 1851-55

BY 1850 the experimental period of mechanical grain-reaping in the United States was over. Cyrus McCormick, securely established at Chicago, marketed each season about fifteen hundred machines to farmers as widely separated as New York and California, Texas and New Jersey. The reaper of Obed Hussey also had proved its worth, if a small but very vocal clientele on the Eastern seaboard may be believed. The total output of reapers since the beginning of manufacturing, about a decade before, was relatively small, and the presence of the seven or eight thousand machines by 1850, in the grain-fields of America, does not demand much emphasis in any explanation of the mounting production and export of wheat to Europe during these years. Railroad penetration of the North and West, better agriculture, more farmers on more land, a general prosperity heightened by a war demand, crop-failures in Europe, and the repeal of the English corn laws, are reasons which better explain why the United States grew forty-eight per cent more wheat and fifty per cent more corn in 1850 than in 1840.[1]

If the importation of wheat was necessary in 1838, to tide America over a period of panic, ten years later the serious

[1] "Landwirthschaftliche Zeitung für Nord und Mittel Deutschland," May 22, 1857, p. 168. "Gardeners' Chronicle," Feb. 11, 1854, p. 90; Sept. 1, 1855, p. 589. The price of wheat per bushel in England dropped steadily from 8s. 8½d. in 1847 to 4s. 9¾d. in 1851, but then rose to 5s. 1d. in 1852, and 6s. 8d. in 1853. The English bushel weighs 60 pounds and the American, 40 pounds.

problem of an increasing grain surplus found a partial and seemingly providential solution in a starving Ireland. As so often in the history of the United States, the distress of Europe was the gain of America, while the agricultural press demonstrated to the Western farmer that wheat produced at a cost of forty-two cents a bushel could still undersell foreign grain at Liverpool.[2]

English writers, unable to deny that grain was needed from abroad, urged the landlord and the tenant farmer to devote more land to cereal-culture and to bend every effort to increase the yield per acre. Already the English farmer could reap thirty-five or more bushels an acre, while his American cousin was very well satisfied with twenty-five.[3] But Great Britain needed eighteen million quarters of wheat a year. Scotland produced about one thirtieth of that amount, Ireland about one fifteenth, and England approximately three fifths. Four or five million quarters annually had to be brought from Russia, Prussia, the Scandinavian countries, and the United States.[4]

[2] "American Agriculturist," Aug., 1848, pp. 241-244. "Prairie Farmer," May, 1849, p. 159. Wheat could be grown in Michigan, Indiana, and Ohio at an estimated average cost of 42 cents a bushel. Five bushels of wheat equaled 1 barrel of flour; five times 42 cents is $2.10, plus 31 cents for the barrel; 25 cents for cartage to the Lakes or a canal; 25 cents freight to Buffalo; 85 cents freight from Buffalo to New York; 40 cents from New York to Liverpool; 25 cents insurance and wharfage—totals $4.41 in Liverpool. It was said to cost about $6.87 to produce a barrel of European flour and transport it to England. The lesson was obvious.

[3] "Gardeners' Chronicle," Feb. 21, 1852, p. 140; Apr. 17, 1852, p. 251; July 24, 1852, p. 473; Aug. 21, 1852, p. 541; Sept. 25, 1852, p. 620; Mch. 3, 1855, pp. 138, 139; Nov. 3, 1855, p. 731. "London Times," Aug. 16, 1851.

[4] "Gardeners' Chronicle," Mch. 8, 1856, p. 162. English wheat importation mounted from an average of a million quarters between 1830 and 1840, to nearly two million between 1840 and 1846. Between 1846 and 1856, under unrestricted trade, the average increased to nearly five million. Up to 1840, England needed to import each year a quantity sufficient to feed its population for three weeks. Between 1840 and 1856 this rose to about eleven weeks. Consequently, the editor believed that these statistics furnished "a very lively challenge to the improvement of wheat soils."

Even if self-sufficiency were too chimerical a goal, there seemed to be no justifiable reason why less land should be under cultivation in the United Kingdom in 1851 than twenty years before.[5]

Harvest labor could be procured much more cheaply in Great Britain than in the United States, but by 1850 the supply was threatened with serious curtailment. England relied for her harvest hands, in large part, upon a seasonal migration from Ireland. Entire families came, working from sunrise to sunset with sickle and hook in the harvest, eating the cheese, bread, and beer rationed out by their employers, and often spending the night in the open fields.[6] The wage was pitiable. One shilling sixpence in addition to a meager dole of food was the average compensation paid to an able-bodied man for a full day's labor during the harvest season.[7] While a skilled workman in America with a cradle-scythe could reap as much as two acres in a day, the Irish harvester, acquainted only with the sickle and hook, found less than an acre of heavy English wheat enough of a task to keep him busy until night came.[8] Hard times in Ireland after 1846, the consequent loss of man-power due to starvation and immigration, and the opening of the California and Australian gold-fields, combined to decrease the numbers of workers ready each summer to move north through England, following the ripening grain. Better wages paid in other trades also served to lure the laborer from the drudgery

---

[5] *Ibid.*, Apr. 14, 1855, p. 247.

[6] "Michigan Farmer," Nov., 1851, pp. 326, 388, letters of Warren Isham, the editor, from Stockton-on-Tees and Perth, Scotland, Aug. 18 and 29, 1851.

[7] "Gardeners' Chronicle," Sept. 1, 1855, p. 589; June 5 and 19, 1852, pp. 363, 397; Oct. 21 and Nov. 11, 1854, pp. 683, 730, 731; Mch. 17 and Nov. 10, 1855, pp. 181, 746. The average daily farm laborer's wage decreased from 2s. 2d. in 1847 to 1s. 2½d. in 1851. It rose a penny a day by 1852, and averaged 1s. 8d. in 1853. By 1854 a man's weekly wage had risen to 10s. or 15s. a week; women, 10d. a day, and boys, 7d. a day.

[8] *Ibid.*, Nov. 8, 1856, p. 745.

of the farm.[9] By 1850, England required a substitute for hand harvesting but an appreciation of the need for a reaper did not mean that conservative squires would quickly adopt one upon its first appearance.

Clever men in Scotland and England tried for over sixty years prior to 1850 to invent a practical horse-power reaper. The Ogle machine of 1822, which so much resembled the McCormick of a decade later, did not outlast a single harvest. The creation of the Rev. Patrick Bell, promising when first invented in 1826, had long since been relegated to the obscurity of a farm in Scotland and was forgotten. During the twenty years after 1830 several patents had been issued on machines which usually incorporated some modification of the revolving scythe device of a generation before, but in 1848 there was probably not one reaper at work in all England.

After McCormick and Hussey arrived with their machines and the initial wave of exultation had subsided, the reapers of Bell and Ogle were to be remembered in England as the originals from which the American machines had been derived. This afterthought, so stanchly upheld until the present day, has already been shown to have no basis of fact.[10] The patriotic explained to the world that, because England was not ready for a reaper before 1850, the Bell machine had been invented before its time. The resurrection of this reaper after the arrival of machines from the United States, and its failure until its manufacturers had adopted the McCormick knife, justify the belief that it would have been neither remembered nor successful without this assistance from the outside. Without question, the competition of foreign wheat and the labor situation in England, about 1850, made the moment especially

[9] *Ibid.*, Aug. 30, 1851, p. 553; Aug. 14, 1852, p. 523; Jan. 15, 1853, p. 44. "Farmer's Magazine" (London), Sept., 1852, pp. 227, 243. W. S. King (ed.), "Journal of Agriculture" (Boston), Aug. 20, 1851, pp. 90, 91.
[10] *Supra,* 64 ff.; 181, ftn. 10.

auspicious for the advent of the McCormick and Hussey machines.

With McCormick and Hussey in America ready for new fields to conquer and with England ripe for their harvest, the preparations in London for an Exhibition of the Industries of All Nations merely furnished an opportune and spectacular occasion for the first appearance of reapers from the United States in the grain-fields of Great Britain. A great Crystal Palace was in process of erection. America had reserved eighty-five thousand square feet of floor space, which her citizens might or might not be able to fill with their exhibits, and Congress was ready to furnish ships to carry without cost the many examples of New World genius which were expected to astonish Europe. In the language of the commissioners of the exhibition, this was to be "the first occasion on which the productions of the different nations of the globe have ever been brought together for the purpose of comparing their several merits." [11]

The people of the United States were at the peak of their ante-bellum pride. They had just fought a most successful war; the specter of slavery had again been laid, and it was good politics, as well as most satisfying to the general feeling of national well-being, to display some evidence of American greatness to a mother country whose people had always been skeptical. Charles Dickens and others had recently found little to praise in the United States; England had clashed with her interests in Oregon and Texas; everything, in fact, conspired in 1850 to make Americans confident of their glory and eager to prove that the strictures of English travelers were most undeserved.

Two years prior to the opening of the great exposition,

[11] "First Report of the Commissioners for the Exhibition of 1851 to the Right Hon. Spencer H. Walpole" (London, 1852), Appendix XIX, pp. 101-103.

Cyrus McCormick was already planning an invasion of England. In the summer of 1849 the Chicago papers told of a marvelous reaper at the factory of McCormick, Ogden & Company, built of highly varnished Michigan ash, its ironwork transformed into straw-colored bronze, and its canvas screen emblazoned with an American eagle, "talons, bolts, and all." "The gilding may perhaps wear off, and the mountain bird's proud plumage be a little ruffled by the trial upon English acres," confessed the editor of the "Chicago Daily Journal," "but the machine will be there still, another creditable exponent of the ingenuity and enterprise of the Universal Yankee Nation." [12] McCormick intended to present this reaper to the Royal Agricultural Society of England through its president, Prince Albert, and thus gracefully and effectively introduce his invention to the British grain-grower. The method was characteristic. The favor of an agricultural society had often been the first step in the march of the machine across unexploited wheat lands in America.

In 1851, after the success of the first McCormick reaper in England was heralded as an event of great significance, W. C. Rives of Virginia, United States Minister to France, announced that he had been the one to suggest the enterprise to McCormick. He asserted that after noting the need for a reaper in England, upon a visit to that country in 1850, he told the inventor through a friend that his fortune would be made if he exhibited it at the great exposition of the next year.[13] This boast is untenable. There is nothing to show that Cyrus McCormick had the exhibition in mind when the English machine was constructed; and, above all, this reaper was finished over a year before Rives visited England. William B. Ogden, Mc-

[12] "Chicago Daily Journal," June 16, 21, 1849. "Gem of the Prairie," June 16, 1849.
[13] "Chicago Daily Democrat," Dec. 1, 1851, letter of W. C. Rives, Sept. 30, 1851. "The Plough, the Loom and the Anvil," Jan., 1852, pp. 428, 429.

Cormick's partner, also has been designated as the one who first visualized the wealth which awaited the reaper overseas.[14] The correspondence of the period gives no hint of the inception of the idea, and while Ogden's adventuresome spirit would have found the undertaking a congenial one, the character and career of McCormick equally well support the belief that the enterprise was of his own planning. To enter a virgin field, with or without a hope of pecuniary gain, was ever near to his heart. The Ogden-McCormick partnership dissolved in August, 1849, and the former's share, if any, in the project ended.

For some unknown reason this specially built reaper did not leave the United States until the early spring of 1851.[15] Perhaps Cyrus McCormick heard of the great exhibition, which was to open on May 1 of that year, and decided to take advantage of the publicity which would surely come from an introduction of his machine at that time. With visitors in London from all parts of the world, news of his implement would be carried to every grain area of the globe. To enter England through the Crystal Palace was an opportunity beyond McCormick's fondest hopes. He had been accustomed in America to take his reaper to the farmer, using such slow and expensive methods of travel as were available. By displaying his machine at the exhibition, he could make the best farmers of England, and the only ones who would at once be interested, come to him. It was a situation perfectly adapted to his original purpose and permitted him to broadcast the news of his invention far and wide at small expense.

Under such circumstances Cyrus McCormick used the interval between the harvest of 1849 and the spring of 1851 to

[14] "The Chicago Magazine, The West as It Is," Mch., 1857, p. 33.
[15] "The Prairie Farmer," Aug., 1849, p. 264. The McCormick reaper, finished in superior fashion and intended as a gift to Prince Albert, "has been sent." Probably it was freighted to New York at this time and was held there until further orders.

secure an English patent,[16] and to win for his machine the gold medal and the diploma of the American Institute of New York at its annual fairs in 1849 and 1850.[17] When an Englishman wrote to the editor of the "Albany Cultivator" in the autumn of 1850, inquiring about American reaping machines, McCormick replied at length, assuring the writer that he was coming to his country with an implement which would greatly increase the speed and much reduce the cost of harvesting grain.[18]

Nor had Hussey been idle. Either by independent decision or because of the published intention of his rival he also prepared a reaper for the London exposition.[19] He had already sold a machine to a resident of Liverpool, who, for a fee, permitted the firm of Garrett & Sons of Leiston to make drawings of its mechanism. This company, unknown to the inventor, planned to have an "improved" Hussey in the field by 1851, ready to furnish competition when the Americans arrived.[20]

[16] "Copies of Specifications of English Patents," 1850, No. 13398. Patented, Dec. 7, 1850, for "a certain foreigner, residing abroad," by Richard A. Brooman of the firm of J. C. Robertson, Patent Agents of London.

[17] "Eighth Annual Report of the American Institute of New York, 1849," p. 37. *Ibid.*, "Ninth Annual Report, 1850," p. 31. "Scientific American," Oct. 19, 1850, p. 34. It is once again noted that McCormick intends to give the machine to Prince Albert, but after the exhibition. "Wisconsin Farmer and Northwestern Cultivator," Feb., 1850, p. 42.

[18] "Albany Evening Journal," Oct. 17, 1850. "Albany Cultivator," Nov., 1850, p. 379, letter of Wm. Dennison of Manor Farms, Blackheath, London, dated Sept. 15, 1850. *Ibid.*, see McCormick's reply, Jan., 1851, pp. 41, 42.

[19] "Albany Cultivator," Apr., 1851, p. 149. As early as June, 1848, in the "American Agriculturist," p. 195, it was stated that Hussey had been granted a request to exhibit his reaper in England before the Royal Agricultural Society. *Supra, 171,* ftn. 72.

[20] The usual story concerning this machine is as follows: Hon. Thos. Tollemache, M. P., visited America in 1849. He was so pleased with the Hussey reaper that he induced a friend, Mr. John Ellis of Liverpool, to purchase one. This reaper was shipped from Rochester, N. Y., in June, 1850 ("Genesee Farmer," July, 1850, p. 154). R. Garrett & Son of Leiston, hearing of the machine, paid Ellis £10 for the privilege of copying it. This firm had constructed two by 1851, calling their machine the Tollemache Reaper. One was exhibited at the Crystal Palace. Hussey protested against

Once again Cyrus McCormick outgeneraled Obed Hussey. Neither inventor found it expedient to sail for England until the harvest season of 1851 in the United States was well advanced. Both men necessarily consigned their machines to the care of agents in London who were unacquainted with their operation. But McCormick, unlike his rival, was careful to send along an expert mechanic and raker-off, D. C. McKenzie, "a brown, rough, homespun Yankee" of Livingston County, New York.[21]

When Hussey and McCormick arrived in London in the late summer, the exhibition at the Crystal Palace had been in progress for three months. The English press ridiculed the American exhibit during these first weeks. Over-confidence had led the commissioners of the United States to reserve far more floor space than could be filled. With extremely bad taste a great gilded spread eagle was used to make up in quantity what was lacking in quality. This "prairie ground," as the scoffers called it, seemed the more barren and ridiculous because it was flanked with magnificent displays of Russian, Austrian, and French art.[22]

the piracy, but not until after an agreement with Dray & Co. in 1851 to manufacture his machines for the English market. By this time Garrett had applied for patents for improvements on the Tollemache, including a modification of the well-known Hussey knife. For a somewhat different story see the "Farmer's Magazine" (London), of Sept., 1851, pp. 271, 272 and Jan., 1852, p. 14; Geo. Dodd, "The Curiosities of Industry" (London, 1852), pp. 10-12.

[21] "McCormick Patent Reaping and Mowing Machine in America," Mch. 15, 1852. McCormick states that he first met McKenzie in the Crystal Palace and that the man was not skilled with the reaper. All other evidence confutes his last assertion. Since McKenzie was of New York, probably T. J. Paterson secured his services for McCormick.

[22] "Report of Benj. P. Johnson, Agent of New York, Appointed to Attend the Exhibition of the Industry of All Nations" (Albany, 1852), pp. 14, 15. Geo. Vail, "Report of the New Jersey Commissioners to the World's Fair" (Trenton, 1852), pp. 17-20. "Art Journal" (London), III (1851), pp. 208-210. "Michigan Farmer," Nov., 1851, p. 321, letter of the editor from England, July 23, 1851.

To compete with the silks, statuary, and jewelry of Europe, Americans could only point to Hiram Powers's Greek Slave and his Fisher Boy, a plaster cast of Daniel Webster, and embroidery by "a lady of Boston," portraying the "raising of Jairus's daughter." Nicholas Longworth of Ohio exhibited some of his famous Catawba wine; Wade Hampton of South Carolina, cotton; John Ericsson of New York, nautical instruments; Charles Goodyear of Connecticut, india-rubber shoes and life-boats; Samuel Colt of the same State, a six-shooter; and Carter Braxton of Virginia, a sample of green sand marl. There were gold-filled teeth, air-exhausted coffins, fireproofed paint and safes, sewing-machines, ice-making machines, silk stockings, cotton cloth, buggies, velocipedes, artificial eyes and legs, maple sugar, slate pencils, cod-liver oil, corn-husk mattresses, magic-lantern slides, railroad switches, and telegraph instruments. A "stuffed buck-eyed squirrel" from Ohio, gold ore from Virginia, zinc from New Jersey, flour from the Genesee Valley, Hebrew dictionaries from New York City, and autumn leaves and clipper-ship models from New England also were on display. In short, the exhibitors presented a cross-section of American life, emphasizing the useful rather than the beautiful, and unaware or unconcerned that they would appear strange in the eyes of Europe.[23]

Among this curious assortment of wares from America, Cyrus McCormick's Virginia Reaper had a conspicuous place. "A cross between a flying machine, a wheelbarrow and an Astley chariot," said the "London Times." "An extravagant Yankee contrivance," . . . "huge, unwieldy, unsightly and incomprehensible," concluded others. "Other nations rely upon their proficiency in the arts, or in manufactures, or in machin-

[23] "Official Descriptive and Illustrated Catalogue of the Great Exposition . . . 1851" (3 vols., London, 1851), III, pp. 1437-1439. The Americans also displayed books for the blind, daguerreotypes, telescopic rifles, shoes, and extract of sarsaparilla.

ery, for producing effect. Not so with America. She is proud of
her agricultural implements which Garrett, or Ransome and
May, would reject as worthless; she is proud of her machinery,
which would hardly fill one corner of our Exhibition." [24] The
scorn of England was difficult to face, but an atmosphere was
created which made the subsequent success of the United States
at the fair peculiarly gratifying. After the yacht *America* had
outsailed all competitors, after the Colt revolver had found no
equal, when the significance of india-rubber was made clear,
when Day & Newell's Parautoptic Permutating Lock had successfully defied all English locksmiths, and Gail Borden's meat
biscuit was shown to contain a maximum of nourishment in a
minimum of space, the tone of the English press completely
changed.[25]

If these wonders were not sufficient, the victorious march of
the Virginia Reaper across England was a fitting climax. By
August the scornful "London Times" admitted that the Mc-
Cormick reaper alone was doubtless worth more to England
than the cost of the entire exhibition.[26] There were four hundred and ninety-nine exhibits from the United States. To these
were awarded five Council Medals, one hundred and two prize
medals, and fifty-three Honorable Mentions. In proportion to
the number of entries, Americans won more prizes than did
the exhibitors of England.[27] The Council Medal "was almost

[24] "London Times," May 1, 1851.
[25] "Michigan Farmer," Nov., 1851, letter of the editor from England.
[26] "London Times," Aug. 12 and Sept. 27, 1851. "Economist" (London),
Aug. 16, 1851, p. 899. "Gardeners' Chronicle," Aug. 23, 1851, p. 538: "May
we not congratulate the inhabitants of the New World who, by their genius,
have conferred so great a benefit upon the Old World." *Ibid.,* Sept. 2, 1851:
"It is beyond all denial that every practical success of the season belongs
to the Americans."
[27] "Ohio Cultivator," Nov. 15, 1851, p. 341. Charles B. Norton, "World's
Fairs, from London, 1851, to Chicago, 1893" (Chicago, 1890, 1893), pp. 14,
20. 171 Council Medals, 2,954 Prize Medals, and 2,123 Honorable Mentions
were awarded in all. There were only 5,048 visitors from the United States

exclusively reserved as a reward for remarkable inventions, and was considered not to be applicable in cases where excellence of execution, however great, was the only merit." [28] The Virginia Reaper was one of the five American products to win this highest honor.[29]

The award to McCormick by the Jury on Agricultural Implements, consisting of fifteen men representing six countries, was not bestowed simply because his machine appeared to surpass Hussey's and all other reapers displayed on the floor of the Crystal Palace. B. P. Johnson of New York, the American member of the jury, suggested that the Hussey, McCormick, and Tollemache machines should be given a practical test in wheat.[30] It was the month of July, and although the grain was still green, J. J. Mechi, a rich manufacturer of cutlery in London, with a model farm at Tiptree Heath about forty-five miles away, invited the commissioners to stage their test in his grain. For several years Mechi had held "annual gatherings" on his estate in order to display to neighboring landlords and friends the yearly advances he had made toward better agriculture. It seemed to him a most fortunate coincidence that the reapers sought an arena at the very time when he had planned to hold his yearly meeting.[31]

to the fair. About 17,000 exhibitors displayed 1,000,000 articles. "Report by the Juries of the Great Exhibition of the Works of Industry of All Nations, 1851," pp. lxxxiii, civ, cxiii, cxv, cxcii.

[28] "First Report of Commissioners for Exhibition of 1851," pp. xl-xli; 101-103; Appendix, xix.

[29] "Scientific American," Nov. 8, 1851, p. 58. The other Americans to whom Council Medals were given were: D. Dick, for engineers' tools and presses; Gail Borden for his meat biscuit; Wm. Bond & Son for astronomical instruments, and C. Goodyear for india-rubber. Three Council Medals were granted to Englishmen for displays of agricultural implements.

[30] For a description of the English and French reapers exhibited at the fair see "Farmer's Magazine" (London), Nov., 1851, p. 440; "Report by the Juries," p. 481.

[31] "Michigan Farmer," Oct., 1851, p. 297. The editor describes the Mechi Farm. "No. British Agriculturist," July 19, 1893, p. 478. A brief sketch of

The trial at Tiptree Heath on July 24, 1851, was the first appearance of the McCormick reaper in English grain. Neither Hussey nor McCormick was present, but nearly two hundred spectators braved the "sour, dark, drenching day," as Horace Greeley described it, to witness the contest in the dripping green wheat.[32] Three members of the Committee on Agricultural Implements of the Exhibition constituted the jury. The Virginia Reaper was operated by McKenzie, while an English mechanic, who had been in charge of Hussey's machine for three months but had never seen it work, sought to win laurels for his employer.[33] The knife clogged, and, due to a maladjustment of the platform, raking-off was impossible. If Hussey had been present his reaper might have performed more creditably. The Tollemache machine could not start and joyful skeptics saw their prophecies fulfilled.

Then McKenzie moved ahead through the wheat with the McCormick reaper, cutting well in spite of the rain and soggy stalks, with a speed which the jury estimated to be equal to twenty acres a day.[34] The crowd gave four cheers for McCormick, but, on the suggestion of Baron Martens, the Belgian member of the jury, the final decision was reserved until an-

the life of J. J. Mechi is given. He had made farming his hobby after accumulating a considerable fortune from the sale of the "Magic Razor Strop" and cutlery. He was a member of Parliament, Sheriff of London in 1856, alderman in 1857, and with high chances to be Lord Mayor in 1864, when a bank failure cost him £30,000. He died a bankrupt in 1880. "Genesee Farmer," Nov., 1863, p. 340.

[32] "Gem of the Prairie," Aug. 30, 1851; "New York Tribune," July 26, 1851.

[33] The jury consisted of B. P. Johnson, Secretary of the New York State Agricultural Society, Colonel Challoner of England, and Baron Martens of Belgium. "Albany Cultivator," Oct., 1851, p. 327. Parsons, Miller, and Steward, op. cit., pp. 48, 49, letter of O. Hussey, Jan. 1, 1852. Hussey complained that his reaper was in charge of "ignorant mechanics." When it was sent from America it was fixed to cut too high, and English workmen, endeavoring to lower the knife, put the machine out of proper adjustment.

[34] "Gardeners' Chronicle," Aug. 2, 1851, p. 493. "London Times," July 25 and Aug. 23, 1851. "Hull Advertiser," Sept. 5, 1851.

other trial under more favorable circumstances should give the McCormick reaper an opportunity to demonstrate that it was also a fair-weather machine. In such an event the award of a Council Medal would be recommended, but if Hussey's proved to be of equal merit under ordinary harvesting conditions in dry, ripe grain, both reapers would receive this highest prize of the exhibition.[35]

After Squire Mechi had furnished a bountiful dinner for his mud-spattered guests and the McCormick machine had been further extolled over the wine by the host, Lord Ebrington, and Prince Frederick of Holstein, the "annual gathering" ended and McKenzie transferred his now famous charge back to the Crystal Palace. "You can't imagine how the tone is altered," wrote B. P. Johnson to the "Albany Cultivator" five days later. " 'The Prairie Ground' of America is now thronged. McCormick's machine is put back in its place and I believe yesterday more visited it than the Kohinoor diamond itself." [36] No more convincing evidence of popularity could have been cited.

The English press carried long accounts of the Tiptree trial and probably McCormick and his reaper were momentarily the most talked-about topics associated with the exhibition. It was high time for the inventor to arrive in London and catch his popularity at its peak. McKenzie was nervous by July 29: "Mr. McCormick has not yet arrived," he wrote, "and I look for him with great anxiety, as it is highly necessary he should be here. . . . When putting the reaper up in the Exhibition

[35] Article by P. Pusey in the "Journal of Royal Agrl. Soc., 1851," XII, pt. II, No. 28, pp. 611-616. "Report by Juries of Great Exhibition . . . 1851," p. 497. "Albany Cultivator," Oct., 1851, p. 327, letter of B. P. Johnson, from London, July 29, 1851.
[36] Ibid., "Report of B. P. Johnson, Agt. N. Y. State," pp. 93-100. "Michigan Farmer," Nov., 1851, p. 321, letter of the editor, dated England, July 23, 1851: The English people "begin to find that there is something besides the baubles of royalty worth looking at." "Gem of the Prairie," Aug. 23, 1851, quoting from the "London Times" of July 25, 1851.

Cyrus Hall McCormick about 1860

after the trial, Mr. Greeley came by and congratulated me for having taken the wind out of John Bull's sails." [37]

At exactly the proper moment McCormick's ship reached port and the inventor, happy at the completion of his first sea voyage without illness, appeared in London on August 4.[38] If the coincidence of events had been carefully planned in advance his arrival could not have been better timed. Hussey, who had reached England before his rival, was now absent in France on a profitless excursion and the deciding trial was set for August 6, on the farm of Philip Pusey, the Chairman of the Committee on Agricultural Implements. In this contest, at which Cyrus McCormick was present, both machines were thoroughly tested,[39] and the Hussey reaper again failed to work well. McCormick's operated admirably.

The jury was now fully satisfied and recommended that a Grand Council Medal be awarded to the Virginia Reaper.[40] The "London Times" was convinced that "the reaping machine from the United States is the most valuable contribution from abroad, to the stock of our previous knowledge, that we have yet discovered." [41] It was January, 1853, before Peter Force, Chairman of the American Executive Committee, was able to deliver the medal to McCormick, "in consideration of the superior excellence and originality of the American Reaper," [42]

[37] "Gem of the Prairie," Aug. 30, 1851, letter of D. C. McKenzie to T. J. Paterson, of Rochester, N. Y., July 29, 1851.

[38] W. S. McCormick to J. D. Davidson, Aug. 23, 1851.

[39] "Report by the Juries," op. cit., p. 497. McCormick pamphlet, "The McCormick Patent Reaping and Mowing Machine in America," 1852. "Michigan Farmer," Nov., 1851, p. 340, letter of Warren Isham, the editor, describing the Pusey farm.

[40] For the ceremony attending the award of the Council Medals at the exposition see the "London Times," of Oct. 16, 1851.

[41] "London Times," Sept. 27, 1851: "The reaper will amply remunerate England for all her outlay connected with the Great Exhibition." Ibid., Oct. 16, 1851.

[42] "Richmond [Va.] Whig and Public Advertiser," Feb. 12, 1853, letter of President Fillmore to C. H. McCormick, Jan. 25, 1853.

but from the moment of the inventor's arrival in England he found himself favored with more fame and attention than he had ever received in his own country.

After the Pusey trial McCormick's implement was not returned to the Crystal Palace but was first taken to Tiptree Heath to harvest Mechi's wheat [43] for the instruction of all who wished to come and watch. On August 11 the inventor began a triumphal tour of three weeks' duration through the English country-side, displaying his machine in operation at Farningham, Leiston, Guildford, Lincoln, Hitchin, and the Royal Agricultural College at Cirencester.[44] In each instance it performed well, and McCormick sailed for home on the S.S. *Pacific* in early September assured that the prospect for many English sales in 1852 was most promising. Before his departure he arranged with Burgess & Key of London to be his representatives and warned them not to meet Hussey's machine in a field test unless the Virginia Reaper were in charge of an experienced operator.[45] Upon his arrival in New York on September 14, the "Scientific American" announced that "the proprietor will be ready to bear witness that he found no impediments from British jealousy, and that his success was hailed with as much enthusiasm as the damp weather would

[43] "Illustrated London News," Aug. 16, 1851, letter of J. J. Mechi.
[44] "London Times," Aug. 16, 1851. "Farmer's Magazine," Sept., 1851. "Mechanics' Magazine" (London), LV, p. 148. "London Spectator," Sept. 13, 1851, p. 874. "Magazine of Science, and Artists', Architects', and Miners' Journal" (London), XIV, p. 360. "Gardeners' Chronicle," Aug. 30, 1851, p. 554.
[45] *Ibid.*, Sept. 20, 1851, p. 606. Burgess & Key, in turn, engaged Mr. Samuelson of Banbury to manufacture the McCormick reaper. "Catalogue of the Bath and West of England Agricultural Society Exhibition, 1853" (Plymouth, 1853), p. 40. "The Plough, the Loom, and the Anvil," Dec., 1851, p. 384. Here it is stated that McCormick had arranged to have five hundred reapers made in England for 1852. By 1855, Garrett & Son of Saxmundham, and Ransome & Sims of Ipswich were manufacturing for Burgess & Key. "Gardeners' Chronicle," Sept. 1, 1855, p. 589. "Scientific American," Nov. 15, 1851, p. 69.

allow." [46] A lawsuit with Seymour & Morgan necessitated his return, but it would have been well if he could have remained in England for a few weeks longer.

Even before the inventor sailed for America, Hussey hastened across the Channel from France and publicly protested that the verdicts of the Mechi and Pusey trials were unjust. At the same time he began a progress of his own through England with his reaper.[47] Under his personal supervision his machine performed efficiently, and after satisfactory exhibitions at Lewisham, Hull, Driffield, Blenheim, Carlisle, and other places, before agricultural societies and such noble gentlemen as the Duke of Marlborough and Earl Lonsdale, his reputation revived.[48] A third meeting with the Virginia Reaper was avoided while McCormick was in England, but on September 18, Burgess & Key challenged Hussey to a trial before the Cleveland Agricultural Society at their annual show at Stockton-on-Tees on September 25.[49] William Dray & Co., manufacturers for Hussey, accepted.

The day of the contest was rainy and the wind blew with gale force. Although weather conditions were so severe that no farmer would ordinarily harvest grain, the Hussey reaper managed to cut a few swaths, while the McCormick was unable to start. The judges decided to repeat the trial on September 27, and again, on that day, the Virginia Reaper failed to measure up to the performance of its rival.[50] As a result of Burgess &

[46] "Scientific American," Sept. 27, 1851, p. 11.

[47] "London Times," Sept. 17, 1851, letter of Obed Hussey.

[48] For the Hussey tour with his reaper see "Hull Advertiser," Sept. 5 and 12, 1851; "Maidstone and Southeastern Gazette," Oct. 21, 1851; "Kentish Gazette" (Canterbury), Nov. 11, 1851; "Gardeners' Chronicle," Nov. 1, 1851; "Prairie Farmer," May, 1852, pp. 258-274.

[49] "London Times," Sept. 18 and 23, 1851: Garrett & Sons of Leiston, manufacturers of the modified Hussey machine, explain their inability to accept the challenge.

[50] Parsons, Miller, and Steward, op. cit., pp. 51-59. "Albany Cultivator," Jan., 1852, pp. 46, 47. "Farmer's Magazine," Nov., 1851, p. 432. "Gardeners'

Key's ill-advised challenge, Hussey gained considerable prestige, and some doubted whether the award of the exhibition had been merited. In a public letter Pusey stated his belief that Hussey's reaper also deserved a Council Medal, and Mechi ordered one of the implements for his own farm.[51] Both machines continued to cut grain and grass in England and Scotland as long as the harvest lasted, and while each did well, Hussey had the unique privilege of exhibiting before Prince Albert, who thereupon ordered two machines for the royal estates of Windsor and Osborne.[52]

As the year 1852 opened, agricultural opinion in England was divided in its favor toward the two reapers, and the coming harvest was expected to reveal their relative worth more accurately. Many believed that skilful English mechanics would find ways to improve each, while those with long memories were satisfied that the Bell machine was the prototype of both.[53] When news of the American reapers reached the Carse of Gowrie in Scotland, the reaper of Patrick Bell was again brought forward and plans were made to manufacture a few machines of this model for use in the summer's grain.

The belief of English machinists that they could improve the McCormick and Hussey reapers was not wholly based upon

Chronicle," Nov. 8, 1851, p. 717. In "The McCormick Patent Reaping and Mowing Machine in America," 1852, McCormick argues that Hussey bribed the binders, and that he pleaded ill health when he was asked to cut grain bending away from the knife.

[51] "Report by the Juries," op. cit., p. 497. P. Pusey in "Journal of Royal Agrl. Soc.," 1851, XII, pt. II, No. 28, pp. 611-616. Parsons, Miller, and Steward, op. cit., pp. 59-64. "London Times," Oct. 7, 1851.

[52] Parsons, Miller, and Steward, pp. 64-66. "Farmer's Magazine," Oct., 1851, p. 351. "Gardeners' Chronicle," Nov. 22, 1851, p. 747; Dec. 6, 1851, p. 781. "McCormick Patent Reaping and Mowing Machine in America," 1852.

[53] "Farmer's Magazine," Dec., 1851, pp. 528, 529. McCormick was characterized as a Scotch emigrant, for some years settled in Chicago. "Gardeners' Chronicle," Nov. 22, 1851, p. 747.

scorn of American ingenuity. As McCormick had found it necessary to readjust his reaper to meet prairie conditions when he first crossed the Appalachians in 1844, so English harvest problems differed from those in the United States. A weight of custom held the English farmer to time-honored methods of harvesting.[54] Because the moist climate and more intensive cultivation of the soil produced very heavy wheat, there were problems of cutting and delivery rarely present in America.[55] If raking off by hand was a difficult task in the United States, it required a superman in Great Britain, and a self-rake was almost a necessity. The pliable stalks of English grain were harder to cut than the light, brittle straw of America. Clogging of the knife was more likely to occur, and a more precise adjustment of the blade and the guard fingers was essential. Unless the ridges and furrows of many English fields were leveled off, mechanical harvesting was hardly possible. Hedges, rather than snake fences, were common, and these could not be temporarily broken down to permit the passage of a machine. English fields were usually smaller than those in the United States, and a reaper did its best work in a large expanse of grain where it was unnecessary to turn corners so frequently.[56]

Hired men were paid a much lower wage in England than in America, and therefore the price of the Hussey and McCormick machines seemed exorbitant. Unless cheaper reapers were made, hand labor appeared to be the more economical

---

[54] *Ibid.*, Aug. 30, 1851, p. 553; Sept. 13, 1851, p. 585; Sept. 2, 1854, pp. 570, 571; Sept. 23, 1854, p. 617.

[55] Pusey's article in the "Journal of Royal Agrl. Soc.," 1851, XII, pt. II, No. 28, pp. 611-616. "Prairie Farmer," Mch., 1854, p. 106. The editor includes an article in this issue by Jas. Sleght, Curator of the Museum of the Highland Agricultural Society of Scotland. "Gardeners' Chronicle," Aug. 30, 1851, p. 554; Sept. 2, 1854, pp. 557-571; Dec. 23, 1854, p. 124; Sept. 1, 1855, p. 589.

[56] *Ibid.*, Sept. 18, 1852, p. 601.

method of harvesting.[57] The English preferred side delivery in swath, but the McCormick machine delivered at the side in gavels with a raker's help, and on the Hussey the bundles of grain were usually pushed off at the rear. Both reapers cut too high to suit the average English farmer.[58]

Despite these differences editors of English agricultural magazines, without exception, urged their readers to reap with machinery.[59] Of course our skilful manufacturers will soon perfect these American harvesters, wrote they; and to be sure, the Bell machine furnished the inspiration for the Yankees, but if England is to compete with foreign grain and if our laborers are to be kept at home, our farmers must adopt this time-, work-, and money-saving device. We must cut wide gates through our hedge-rows; enlarge our fields, drain our land, and smooth off our ridges. Our farm laborers have an ingrained prejudice against the use of machinery. This short-sightedness has stifled English mechanical genius and has diverted it to inventions in the field of manufacturing.

Why, nine-tenths of the mechanics in this country are as mentally superior to the smaller farmers as the improved Berkshire pig is physically to its long-eared, long-legged ancestor. When our glory and greatness are boasted of, it is with shame and sorrow that the condition of the agricultural population forces itself on my mind.[60]

[57] *Ibid.*, Aug. 14, 1852. It is noted that wages are rising in England despite the 1,500 reapers at work. The number of machines is not keeping pace with the emigration. "Farmer's Magazine," Dec., 1851, pp. 528, 529. The McCormick reaper was then advertised to sell for £28. "Albany Cultivator," Mch., 1853, p. 79.

[58] "Gardeners' Chronicle," Sept. 13, 1851, p. 585; Oct. 16, 1852, p. 668; Sept. 1, 1855, p. 589.

[59] "Report by the Juries," *op. cit.*, pp. 495, 496. Pusey believed that the use of the reaper would save the farmer 5s. 10d. per acre, calculating that hand harvesting cost 9s. an acre. "Gardeners' Chronicle," Sept. 16, 1854, p. 601. It was estimated that the McCormick reaper, with one man, one boy, and one horse, cost between 7s. 7d. and 9s. per acre to use.

[60] "Gardeners' Chronicle," Mch. 18, 1854, p. 171.

The adoption of reaping machines will mean that more grain will be grown and consequently there will be more work for more men. The farm-hand will need to learn how to operate machinery, and the attainment of this skill, together with the increase of wheat-production, will lead inevitably to higher wages.[61] The emigration from Ireland overseas should be turned to Canada rather than to the United States,[62] but, in any event, it is almost providential that when England for the first time in many years suffers from a lack of harvest labor, a machine should appear to fill the gap.[63] The social and economic condition of the impoverished Irish peasantry, who cross the Irish Sea each summer to work in our harvest fields, is deplorable, and a blot upon our country-side. The reaper will raise the standard of living in the rural districts and will effect a revolution there comparable to that caused by the concentration of manufacturing in our cities.

Thus, in summary, did the agricultural press call upon the English landlords to be up and doing, for patriotic, economic, and social reasons.

"Punch" published a poem, in 1853, purporting to show that the Irish laborer was most willing to yield his backbreaking harvest job to the tireless reaper [64]:

PAT'S WELCOME TO THE REAPING-MACHINE

I'm sick of the sickle, Molly dear, and stooping so long and so low;
And it's little grief it gives me, to give the ould bother the go!
And when another harvest comes, by the Saints! I'd like to see
The money or anything else that 'ud make a Raping-Machine
    of me!

[61] *Ibid.*, Aug. 30 and Sept. 13, 1851.
[62] *Ibid.*, Feb. 21, 1852, p. 140; Apr. 17, 1852; Apr. 24, 1852, p. 267; Dec. 16, 1854, p. 811.
[63] "Farmer's Magazine," Sept., 1852, pp. 227, 243.
[64] "Punch, or the London Charivari" (London), XXV (1853), p. 127; by permission.

I've raped in Scotland and England, and I've raped in the Lothians
 three,
And I dar' say its twenty year since first I crossed the Irish Sea;
I've raped yer wheat, and yer barley, and oats and beans, sez Pat;
But as for Profit—its sorrow the raping that ever I raped of that!

So, good luck to you, Misther MacCormack, and Yer Reverence,
 Misther Bell,
And good luck to yer, Misther Hussey—I wish yer Honours well;
The shearer's footing on the fields ye've fairly cut away;
But it's not been worth the standing on, bedad, this many a day.

But we'll throw the sickle aside, Molly, and go and try our luck
On the banks of the far Australian strames, where the otter is
 billed like a duck;
For there's mate, and drink, and clothes, Molly, and riches and
 rank to be won,
At the Anti—what d'ye call the place, on t'other side of the sun?

The experience of the harvest of 1851 led those interested
in mechanical reaping to the opinion that the McCormick machine had a more practical delivery than Hussey's and excelled
in damp grain, but that the Hussey performed better in grass,
and in grain bending away from the knife. Some also believed that Hussey's reaper surpassed McCormick's in deep-
furrowed fields, and the lower price of the machine was
always a factor of influence.[65] In short, when the harvest of
1852 opened, neither reaper held undisputed first place and
English agricultural societies were ready to sponsor a continuance of the rivalry that had opened in the preceding year.
Men in Scotland, ever nationally minded, prepared to demonstrate that the title to preëminence rightfully belonged to Bell's
machine. Garrett, also, with his modified Hussey implement,
eagerly sought the favor of the public.

[65] "Report by the Juries," *op. cit.,* p. 497. Pusey thought McCormick's
reaper was best in barley and oats, and Hussey's in laid grain and on steep
ridges. "Illustrated London News," Aug. 16, 1851, letter of J. J. Mechi.

In August, 1852, the editor of the "Gardeners' Chronicle and Agricultural Gazette" surmised that fifteen hundred reapers were at work in England.[66] Probably one half of this figure would be more accurate, but, without question, the reaper-makers of the kingdom were not to experience the same discouragements that had met McCormick and Hussey when they started production in America a decade before. The farmers of the United States had taught the English the significance and the necessity of mechanical reaping. In the 1852 harvest there were McCormick reapers made by Burgess & Key and by Samuelson; Hussey's made by Garrett, William Dray, and William Crosskill, and Bell machines manufactured by Crosskill also.[67] North in Scotland, Lord Kinnaird sought to construct a modified McCormick; in fact, all British manufacturers were experimenting with the reapers in their charge.

William McCormick, with McKenzie, the expert mechanic, was in England to push the fortunes of the Virginia Reaper, and Obed Hussey once again crossed the ocean to promote his own interests.[68] Many contests were held from July to October, and at the end of the harvest it was still possible to champion

[66] "Gardeners' Chronicle," Aug. 14, 1852. "Abridgement of Specifications Relating to Agriculture, Div. I, Field Implements, A. D. 1618-1866," pp. 206, 220, 222, 231, Patent to W. Dray for O. Hussey, Jan. 27, 1852. *McCormick vs. Manny,* I, p. 316; II, p. 683; Obed Hussey testified on Aug. 28, 1855, that "according to the common report of manufacturers," 1,400 of his reapers were made in England in 1852.

[67] "Farmer's Magazine," Jan., 1852, p. 14. "Gardeners' Chronicle," Dec. 23, 1854, p. 124. There were thirty-two patents on reapers issued in England in 1849-54. This was over half the number granted between 1786 and 1849. This large increase was credited to the Great Exhibition.

[68] O. Hussey to E. Stabler, from Manchester, Eng., Sept. 10, 1852. W. S. McCormick sailed for England on July 24, 1852, in order to attend his brother's reaper for two or three months. *McCormick vs. Manny,* II, p. 205. He took a machine with him, but part of it was lost in transit from the steamer to London. "London Times," Aug. 30, 1852. *McCormick vs. Manny,* II, p. 700, Hussey states that he went to England late in the 1852 harvest and, so far as he remembers, the only trial he attended was before the Cleveland Agricultural Society of Yorkshire.

either machine.[69] Hussey's outstanding triumphs occurred early in the season on the Mechi farm at Tiptree Heath and before the Royal Agricultural Society at Lewes. He was then so indiscreet as to take his reaper into Scotland, where Caledonian juries repeatedly awarded the palm to Bell.[70]

In England the tide turned in favor of McCormick as the summer grew older. The most severe reaper trial ever held up to that time was a nine-day contest in August at the Cirencester Agricultural College, which had purchased several Hussey machines for its own use. Here the prize was won by McCormick, and his reaper also was judged by the Yorkshire Agricultural Society, the Driffield Farmers' Club, and the Durham County Agricultural Society to be best.[71] In early September, fortified by these victories, William McCormick moved to the Scottish border and challenged any reaper to meet his machine in the vicinity of Sunderland.

The gantlet was thus thrown down with the hope that the Bell reaper would emerge from its highland glens and meet its rival on more or less neutral ground. The gage was not accepted and McCormick was too wise to imitate Hussey and carry the conflict into the enemy's own territory before hostile judges.[72] An exhibition at the Smithfield Cattle Show at London in December completed the season.[73] In the autumn the Manny reaper and the Atkins-Wright Self-Raker appeared

[69] O. Hussey to E. Stabler, from Manchester, Eng., Sept. 10, 1852, and Oct. 22, 1852. "Farmer's Magazine," Oct., 1852, pp. 363, 364.

[70] "N. Y. Farmer and Mechanic," Sept. 4, 1852, p. 447. "Gardeners' Chronicle," July 17, 1852, p. 459; July 24, 1852, p. 477; July 31, 1852, p. 489; Aug. 28, 1852, p. 553; Sept. 18, 1852, p. 602; Sept. 25, 1852, p. 621.

[71] *Ibid.*, Aug. 21, 1852, p. 537; Sept. 25, 1852, p. 617. "London Times," Aug. 25, 28, 30, Sept. 9, 1852, and Feb. 5, 1853. "Farmer's Magazine," Sept., 1852, pp. 227-229. "Catalogue of Bath and West of England Agrl. Soc. Exhibition, 1852," p. 40; "Albany Cultivator," Dec., 1852, p. 407.

[72] "Albany Cultivator," Dec., 1852, p. 408, copying an article from the "Sunderland Times," Sept. 18, 1852.

[73] "Gardeners' Chronicle," Dec. 25, 1852, p. 826.

in England, and thus two more of McCormick's keenest competitors crossed the ocean to fight him anew on foreign soil.[74]

During the next three harvests the battle for popular favor continued, with the trend of opinion gradually turning toward the McCormick machine manufactured by Burgess & Key.[75] The makers of the Bell reaper, notwithstanding their surprising success in the summer of 1853, virtually admitted its inferiority to the Virginia Reaper, that autumn, by seeking the privilege of using the McCormick knife.[76] Lord Kinnaird, McCormick's spokesman in Scotland, wrote to the inventor on December 19:

I saw Mr. Bell on Saturday, and he says Mr. Crosskill [maker of Bell's machines] will give you three pounds *royalty* for your Cutter. . . . If . . . you give me authority, I will settle with him for you. You should do this without loss of *time* as it would put a stop to attempts to evade your patent, and with three pounds for Bell's, and five pounds for your own improved machines, as I proposed, you would secure all the machines in the country.[77]

The financial arrangements which were eventually concluded are unknown, but presumably some such bargain was closed, for the Bell reaper appeared in the harvest of 1854 equipped with McCormick's sickle.[78] It cut well, but its weight and cost

[74] "Ohio Cultivator," July 1, 1853, p. 215; Sept. 15, 1853, p. 278. "Illustrated London News," Sept. 10, 1853, p. 133.

[75] "Farmer's Magazine," July, 1853, p. 67; Sept., 1853, pp. 241, 263, 245, 246; Oct., 1853, pp. 330, 331. "Gardeners' Chronicle," July 16, 1853, pp. 459, 460; July 30, 1853, p. 490; Aug. 27, 1853, p. 554; Sept. 10, 1853, p. 587; Sept. 17, 1853, p. 601; Oct. 15, 1853, pp. 666, 667. "American Farmer," Aug., 1853, pp. 54, 55; Apr., 1854, p. 330. Both McCormick and Hussey visited England in 1853. See *McCormick vs. Manny*, II, p. 699. In the "American Farmer" of Jan., 1854, p. 216, it is stated that Hussey has just returned from over a year's absence in Europe.

[76] Letter of Lord Kinnaird, in the "Mechanics' Magazine" (London), Dec., 1853.

[77] "Lord Kinnaird, from Rossie Priory, Luchture, N. B., to C. H. McCormick, Dec. 19, 1853, in the "American Farmer," Mch., 1854, p. 301.

[78] "Gardeners' Chronicle," Apr. 8, 1854, pp. 226, 227; Oct. 21, 1854, p. 682.

still handicapped it in its rivalry with the McCormick. In like manner Dray and Crosskill, the two manufacturers of the Hussey reaper, as well as Garrett, remodeled their original machines so that they resembled the Virgina Reaper in principle.[79] The knife was modified with a hole cut in each sickle-section to prevent clogging, and a side delivery was added,[80] but probably McCormick received no patent fees because of these alterations. The lightness and comparatively low price of the Hussey reaper insured it a continued sale. Hussey spent many months in England in 1853 and when he returned to the United States early the next year apparently was well content with his success abroad.[81]

In England the chief objections to the McCormick reaper had always been its cost and hand delivery. Lord Kinnaird, in Scotland, sought to solve this last problem by adding an endless web designed to lay the cut grain in swath without the assistance of a raker.[82] This was a failure, and no remedy was found until Burgess & Key, in August, 1854, patented an Archimedian screw device which pleased the grain-growers.[83] The delicate and complex arrangement of the Atkins Self-Raker proved to be impracticable in the heavy English grain,[84] but the lifting screw appliance of Burgess & Key was durable and effective, as well as a relatively simple means of discharging the grain in the orderly swath so much preferred, by the British farmer, to gavel delivery.

[79] "N. Y. Farmer and Mechanic," Sept. 4, 1852, p. 447. "Gardeners' Chronicle," Oct. 15, 1853, pp. 666, 667; Apr. 8, 1854, pp. 226, 227.
[80] "Specifications of English Patents, 1852," No. 697, Nov. 9, 1852, to Wm. Dray. "Mechanics' Magazine" (London), LVII, p. 113.
[81] "American Farmer," Jan., 1854, p. 216.
[82] "Gardeners' Chronicle," Oct. 21, 1854, p. 682; July 28, 1855, p. 507. "Farmer's Magazine," Sept., 1855, p. 239.
[83] "Abridgement of Specifications Relating to Agriculture, Division I, Field Implements, A. D. 1618-1866," p. 299, patent to Wm. Burgess, Aug. 16, 1854. "Mechanics' Magazine" (London), Mch. 17, 1855, pp. 241, 242.
[84] "Gardeners' Chronicle," Oct. 15, 1853, pp. 666, 667.

This improvement was first given wide advertisement in the harvest of 1855, and its success in large measure marks the end of the first battle of the reapers in England. By it the problem of adapting the McCormick machine to English harvest conditions was solved. The price of the reaper was still a deterrent to wide sales, and the apathy of the farmer was ever a subject of remark by agricultural magazine editors.[85] But the Crimean War, with the temporary stoppage of grain-importation from Russia, boosted the price of cereals and gave a fresh impetus to wheat-culture and to the use of horse-power reapers in England.

While McCormick, Hussey, and Bell contended for the patronage of English landlords, a less intense rivalry was in progress across the Channel in France. In the years preceding 1850, French inventors had made a few efforts to harvest grain by machinery,[86] but they had not advanced much farther toward success than the crude header of their Gallic ancestors. Although a French reaper was exhibited at the Crystal Palace in 1851, it was not tried in grain, and received no recognition either from practical farmers or from the agricultural juries of the exhibition.[87] During the same year the American

[85] "Farmer's Magazine," July 19, 1856, p. 490: "Why these reaping machines are not more generally adopted we must confess surprises us." "Gardeners' Chronicle," Nov. 8, 1856, p. 745.

[86] "Descriptions des Machines et Procédés Consignés dans les Brevets d'Invention." Tables des Quarante Premiers Tomes (Paris, 1843), p. 28; ibid., Table Générale des Vingt Premiers Tomes (Paris, 1856), pp. 7-11, 13. These list six French reapers in the period 1834-50. See Jules Burat, "Exposition de l'Industrie Française" (Paris, 1844), 2d part, pp. 52, 53, for four others.

[87] "Farmer's Magazine," Nov., 1851, p. 440. "Albany Cultivator," Jan., 1847, pp. 12, 13, article signed "Caius": Our instruments of agriculture are nearly twenty years in advance of those shown at the Paris Conservatoire. "What would New York farmers think of seeing a pitch fork with wooden tines, ticketed among the resources of modern agricultural art? And a hay rake, such as a 'cute' country boy could make on a rainy day, with his jackknife and knee for a lathe, and his thumb and fore finger for compass, displayed in the great Conservatoire of Paris!"

machines were described in French magazines, and the Imperial Conservatory of Arts and Trades declared its intention of securing one of the McCormicks for exhibition at Paris.[88]

Nevertheless it was 1855 before French farmers accorded much attention to mechanical harvesting. The International Exposition in Paris at that time and the Agricultural Congress in the same city in 1856 furnished the occasions upon which the McCormick, Hussey, Wright, and Manny reapers were introduced to the wheat-fields of France. Hussey was sent to the exposition of 1855 as the commissioner for the State of Maryland,[89] while McCormick was most effectively represented by McKenzie, who had rendered such noteworthy service to his chief in England.[90]

Two preliminary trials of mowers and reapers near Paris that summer were climaxed with a great contest at la Trappe in Normandy on the farm of M. Dailly, the Postmaster-General of France. Seven reapers were entered and the trial was witnessed by Prince Jerome, nine Arab sheiks, General Toombs, Mr. Corcoran the banker, and, according to the "Genesee Farmer," "in this group the fine form of Mr. Fillmore, who had climbed on to a shock of fallen wheat, was conspicuous." [91] The McCormick reaper won and the exposi-

[88] "Journal de l'Agriculture Pratique et de Jardinage" (Paris), 3d ser., III (1851), p. 124. This magazine notes the two American reapers at the London exhibition, but adds, "It is evident that they are not in a state to enter into practical use." "Exhibition Universelle de 1851, Travaux de la Commission Française sur l'Industrie des Nations" (Paris), I, pp. 62-65.

[89] "American Farmer," Dec., 1854, p. 190. "Gardeners' Chronicle," June 24, 1854, p. 412.

[90] "Pennsylvania Farm Journal," Oct., 1855, pp. 291, 592.

[91] "Genesee Farmer," Oct., 1855, pp. 308-511. "Albany Cultivator," Oct., 1855, p. 315. Harper's Encyclopædia of United States History, VI, pp. 68-70. For the two preliminary trials, one private and the other at the Imperial College of Agriculture at Grignon, see "Journal de l'Agriculture Pratique," IV (4th ser.), July-Dec., 1855, pp. 155-165; 261-265, 437-440. "American Agriculturist," Aug. 30, 1855, p. 387.

tion awarded it the Grand Gold Medal of Honor.[92] Once again, as in England, the inventor had gained the most coveted prize.

The la Trappe trial was heralded in Belgium as "one of the most happy and grandest events of our century in the annals of agriculture," [93] and Horace Greeley informed the readers of the "New York Tribune" that it was "more beneficent and creditable for the United States than if fifty thousand of her troops had defeated one hundred thousand choice European soldiers." [94] The Emperor of France purchased a McCormick reaper and the inventor sold rights to manufacture for the French harvest of 1856.[95] Manny and Wright, who had received first- and second-class silver medals, respectively, at the exposition of 1855, also made arrangements to supply the French market, and Manny, then being sued in America by McCormick, added to the heat of the conflict by advertising at home that he had defeated his rival in France.[96]

[92] McCormick handbill of 1856. "Rapports du Jury International, Grandes Médailles d'Honneur et Médailles d'Honneur" (Paris, n.d.) III Classe, p. 8.

[93] "Journal de l'Agriculture Pratique" (Brussells, 1856), pp. 200-203, 210-212.

[94] "New Jersey Farmer" (Freehold, N. J.), Sept., 1855, pp. 11, 12, copying from the "New York Tribune." Report of Hon. Wm. Elliott, Commr. of South Carolina, quoted in H. Howe, "Adventures and Achievements of Americans," pp. 153-157.

[95] McCormick handbill of 1856. C. H. to W. S. McCormick, Mch. 20, 1856: "Fleischmann has contracted for fifty machines in France (added to the ten before), paying me £5 each, and therefore we will only send the first lot which I directed to be shipped through to him. If more are now under way, it may be well to send them to England or Belgium,—think a few should be so sent."

[96] "Michigan Farmer," Oct., 1855, pp. 296, 297. "Albany Cultivator," Nov., 1855, p. 356. C. H. McCormick to J. L. Wilson, Aug. 28, 1855. Wm. D. Hudson, Sand Hill, Mo., to C. H. McCormick, Apr. 6, 1856: "I thought the Devil was at work when I saw last winter that spurious report of the French trial of your reaper. I grated my teeth and called them Know Nothings, but I noticed a short time since in my 'Tribune' that all is right. . . ." To correct the error, McCormick secured certificates from the U. S. consul in Paris and from the editor of the Paris "Constitutionnel."

English machines now sought favor in Europe and added spice to the rivalry arising from the Agricultural Congress at Paris in 1856. On July 3, at Courcelles, Belgium, each of seven reapers attempted to cut an allotted twenty acres of wheat in the best fashion. A Dray-Hussey and two McCormick reapers made in France were the only ones which finished. No first prize was awarded, but a silver medal and four hundred francs were given to each of the McCormicks, and a bronze medal and three hundred francs to the Dray machine.[97] By 1856 the McCormick reaper was in use in Algeria, although one of Bell's preceded it there by about a year.[98]

Even before the London exposition of 1851, Cyrus McCormick, under date of November 5, 1850, announced that his reaper had reached Austria.[99] In fact, there is some evidence to show that, as early as 1845, Prince Lichnowski introduced this implement to his native land, and that by 1850, Anton Burg, the imperial court machinist of Vienna, had copied it and sold almost two hundred machines.[100] However this may be, in 1850, an influential agricultural paper of Prague, while admitting that the Burg machines were not wholly successful, because of the difficulty of raking off, optimistically prophesied

[97] "American Farmer," Dec., 1856, p. 175. The two McCormick machines had been manufactured by M. Bella of Grignon and by M. Laurent of Paris. "Journal de l'Agriculture Pratique," VI (4th ser.), p. 125.
[98] "Journal de l'Agriculture Pratique," VI (4th ser.), p. 228.
[99] "Prairie Farmer," Jan., 1851, pp. 44, 45. In this advertisement, McCormick also mentions South America as a region which will soon know his reaper. "Albany Evening Journal," Oct. 17, 1850.
[100] Louis Moll, "Exposition Universelle de 1851, Travaux de la Commission Française sur l'Industrie des Nations" (Paris), III, pt. 2, pp. 62-67. C. L. Fleischmann, "Der Nordamerikanische Landwirth, ein Handbuch für Ansiedler in den Vereinigten Staaten" (Frankfurt, 1848), pp. 154-156. "Journal de l'Agriculture Pratique," III (6th ser.), pp. 285, 286. "Centralblatt der Land und Forstwirthschaft in Böhmen" (Prague), June 18, 1850, p. 88. Gustav Ritter von Suttner gave Burg the McCormick reaper he brought back from the United States in 1849. Burg's price in 1850 was 400 florins, but he would sell for 350 if he received ten orders.

that the American reaper would solve the labor scarcity in Austria and check the spread of communism among the peasants.[101] In 1851 a Hussey reaper, made in England, reached Austria, and Baron Ward, an Englishman living near Vienna, attempted to perfect it.[102]

From Austria the news of the American machines traveled to Prussia and Poland and in 1856 the editors of the "Landwirthschaftliche Zeitung für Nord und Mittel Deutschland" of Berlin imported a Burgess & Key McCormick with the purpose of introducing it to the junkers.[103] In the same year a Virginia Reaper left America, consigned to Jacob Beylen of Cologne.[104] Evans & Lilpop, manufacturers of Warsaw, are said to have marketed about thirty McCormick reapers in 1856.[105] Two years later Butenose Brothers of Moscow wrote to Cyrus McCormick that they had received his reaper in excellent condition and were confident of large sales in Russia if it proved satisfactory.[106]

In such fashion did the news of the McCormick reaper spread from Algeria to Moscow and from London to Vienna. Many sales, particularly on the Continent, could not be expected

---

[101] *Ibid.*, Sept. 17, 1850, pp. 171, 185-187; *ibid.*, Aug. 20, 1850, p. 153; Oct. 10, 1851, pp. 349-351, and Nov. 21, 1851, p. 394.

[102] "Landwirthschaftliche Zeitung für Nord and Mittel Deutschland," Oct. 31, 1856, pp. 349-351; Nov. 7, 1856, pp. 354, 355. The Hussey reaper, brought from London in 1851, was tried at Wieselburg in 1852 in wet grain and it clogged. By 1856 it was in the collection of the K. K. Higher Agricultural Institute of Hungary. *Ibid.*, Aug. 7, 1857, pp. 254, 255. "Gardeners' Chronicle," Oct. 18, 1856, pp. 699, 700. By 1856 several McCormicks made in England were working in Prussia and in Austria-Hungary.

[103] "Landwirthschaftliche Zeitung," Aug. 15, 1856, pp. 257, 258.

[104] P. B. Truax, from Toledo, O., Apr. 26, 1856. W. Hanna to the Freight Agent, Cleveland and Toledo R.R., Apr. 17, 1856, L.P.C.B., No. 1.

[105] "Landwirthschaftliche Zeitung," Sept. 8, 15, 1859, pp. 282-285, 293-296.

[106] Butenose Bros., Moscow, July 20, 1858, to C. H. McCormick. John A. Pitts, from Buffalo, N. Y., Sept. 2, 1857. He wished a reaper to ship to Chile. H. Van Houten, from Pella, Iowa, Mch. 30, 1857. He ordered a machine to send to Holland.

at once, and the American farmer, early persuaded of the advantage of mechanical harvesting, was soon to pour such a flood of grain into Europe that many peasants, unable to compete with hook and sickle, sought the New World to ward off starvation. This was still in the future in 1855, but even at that time far-sighted agriculturists of Europe foresaw the social and economic consequences of reaping by horse-power. The American Civil War would shortly add the impressive lesson that when choice must be made between cotton for cloth and grain for food, friendship must be maintained with the people who produce the wheat.

CHAPTER XVII

THE SECOND REAPER WAR, 1848-55

THE successful introduction of McCormick and Hussey reapers to England and Europe quickened the interest of American farmers in these implements.[1] Both inventors used their triumphs abroad to advertise their machines at home, and the overseas battles were refought in their pamphlets, order blanks, and posters during the decade.[2] Several prominent agricultural editors visited the great exposition at London, and their papers, and others as well, detailed for the entertainment of their subscribers the progress of the European reaper rivalry.[3]

In fact, it has been said that the recognition accorded to McCormick and Hussey abroad gave the greatest impetus, thus far, to the manufacture and use of reapers in the United States.[4] Whether this was the chief cause for the appearance

---

[1] McCormick was honored by agricultural societies because of his victories abroad. See, "Transactions of the New York State Agricultural Society" (1851-52), pp. 154, 155. "Journal of the National Agricultural Society, 4th Annual Meeting" (Boston, 1856), p. 37. "Transactions of American Institute," X (1851-52), pp. 223, 224.

[2] Photostat of a McCormick order blank for 1852. Advertisements, and the McCormick-Hussey controversy in the "American Farmer," Apr., 1852, pp. 361, 368; May, 1852, pp. 398, 411; June, 1853, pp. 404, 405. "Prairie Farmer," Dec., 1851, p. 592. "Genesee Farmer," June, 1853, p. 195. "Albany Cultivator," Dec., 1851, p. 407. "Chicago Weekly Democrat," Jan. 24, 1852. "Chicago Daily Journal," Dec. 19, 23, 24, 27, 1851.

[3] "Gem of the Prairie," Aug. 30, 1851. "Richmond Republican and General Advertiser," Sept. 2, 1851. "Spirit of the Times" (N. Y.), XXI (1851), pp. 328, 329. "Farmer and Planter" (Pendleton, S. C.), Feb., 1852, p. 31. "The Plow," Feb., 1852, pp. 56, 57.

[4] "Michigan Farmer," Oct., 1853, p. 296. "The Plough, the Loom and the Anvil," Feb., 1852, pp. 56, 57.

of so many new firms in America, with the phenomenal increase of sales, may well be questioned.[5] For over a decade
McCormick and Hussey had been preparing the way for the
prosperity of the reaper-makers of the 1850's. They had, after
a long period of trial and error, evolved good machines; their
original patents had expired, more grain areas and wider markets were ever opening to the farmer, and the Crimean War
soon came to increase the foreign demand for wheat. In August, 1854, the editor of the "Pennsylvania Farm Journal"
announced somewhat optimistically:

The age of scythes and cradles may now be said to have passed
very much away, and to be among the things that were. The history of 1854, when written, will record their exit. Reaping and
mowing machines are hereafter to be a fixed fact, and specimens
of the others may now be secured and hung up in the different
county museums, to illustrate to a future age what barbarous and
labor killing instruments were wielded in the harvest field. Who
knows but that some future Barnum may make them prominent
in his cabinet of curiosities, and have to explain their uses to
incredulous spectators.

Extraordinary strides in railway-construction were made between 1848 and 1857, and the farmer, hitherto isolated, could
now grow surplus grain with the assurance of adequate transportation to profitable markets. If Hussey's and McCormick's
original patents had been in force under these conditions,
scarcely a reaper or a mower could have been made without the
payment of a heavy patent fee to one or both of them. McCormick, at least, with his unusual business skill, would probably

    [5] J. L. Bishop, "A History of American Manufactures from 1608 to
1860" (3d ed., London and Phila., no date), II, p. 483. By 1857, 176 grain-
and grass-harvesters and 62 mowing machines had been patented in the
United States. The trials of the United States Agricultural Society in that
year brought 40 different machines into the lists. C. H. McCormick received
the first reaper prize. "Valley Star," Sept. 10, 1857.

have soon become one of the richest, as well as one of the most hated, men in America.[6]

During these years the rivalry between McCormick and Hussey in the United States continued with unabated intensity. The year 1848 has been considered a dividing line in the contest, because the expiration of their original patents carried the competition before the Patent Office and Congress; the move of McCormick to Chicago widened the arena, and the London exhibition came shortly to add still another battle-front. By 1850, in a measure owing to the failure of these inventors to win an extension of their patents, there were new rivals in the field, several of whom were far more formidable antagonists of the Virginia Reaper than the Baltimore Quaker had ever been. Thus the original duel, confined to the Eastern seaboard, grew into an economic war of more than continental proportions in which many manufacturers were engaged.

By 1848 the supremacy of Cyrus McCormick west of the Alleghenies was a perpetual challenge to Obed Hussey to invade that country in force. The latter still contended that he had driven his rival from the seaboard, although McCormick's annual reaper output, twenty times larger than Hussey's, made this assertion an extravagant boast.[7] McCormick countered that he had won the undivided affection of one of the world's greatest grain-growing areas, while the yearly increase of his sales left no doubt of the victor in the contest. A few Hussey reapers were made by sub-manufacturers in Ohio, Pennsylvania, Illinois, and Wisconsin, as well as at Baltimore and by the inventor's brother at Auburn, New York.[8]

Thus, when Cyrus McCormick made Chicago the sole home

[6] "Congressional Globe," 34th Cong., 1st Sess., July 14, 1856, p. 1601, speech of Senator Jones of Tennessee.
[7] "Albany Cultivator," Apr., 1851, p. 149.
[8] "Ohio Cultivator," Apr. 15, 1848, pp. 60, 64; Oct. 1, 1848, p. 145; July 15, 1849, p. 214. "Genesee Farmer," July and Aug., 1848, advertising sec-

of his reaper, Hussey decentralized production. His Baltimore factory rarely turned out over five hundred machines a year, while the McCormick plant annually completed several thousand. Perhaps many unauthorized builders in the West were making a few Hussey reapers each harvest, regardless of the inventor's threats to sue them for an infringement of his 1847 patent.[9] The powerful McCormick made good his warnings by action in the courts, but Hussey, hampered by lack of capital, was usually forced to content himself with futile admonitions. He did sue the manufacturers of the Ketchum Mower and won his case, and shortly before his death in 1860 compelled McCormick to pay him a royalty and heavy damages for use of the open-back guard, although McCormick brought forward much evidence to prove that he had employed it long before his rival's patent of 1847. Not manufacturer's profits, but the sale of patent rights, explains Hussey's modest fortune by 1860.

In January, 1849, John S. Wright, the editor of the "Prairie Farmer" of Chicago, contended that the reapers which were made in Illinois were so superior to Hussey's that within three years his machine would be as obsolete as "the old wrought iron, three pound pitchfork was when the neat, light, steel fork came into use. . . . Our eastern friends had better be rubbing their eyes or they will be caught in the fix of Rip Van Winkle." [10] Notwithstanding this scorn, a few Husseys were sold as far west as Iowa during this harvest, and the "Ohio Cultivator" was certain that they gave much better service in

tions; May, 1849, p. 125. Patent Office Records, "Hussey Extension Case, Patent of 1847," p. 127. "Prairie Farmer," May, 1850, p. 146.

[9] "American Farmer," Mch., 1848, p. 292; Feb., 1849, p. 264. "Ohio Cultivator," Dec. 15, 1848, p. 186. "Albany Cultivator," Mch., 1849, p. 93; Mch., 1851, p. 186; Apr., 1851, p. 149; May, 1851, p. 192. "Genesee Farmer," July, 1848, p. 176; June, 1851, p. 148.

[10] "Prairie Farmer," Jan., 1849, p. 39; Aug., 1849, pp. 246, 247. "Ohio Cultivator," Oct. 1, 1849, p. 298.

Ohio than did McCormick's.[11] By the autumn Wright, who had been so scathing as the year opened, noted that Hussey was in Chicago looking for some one to build his machines, and within two years he joined forces with the inventor in a short-lived partnership.[12] After the harvest of 1849, McCormick won a premium over his rival at the Syracuse Fair of the New York State Agricultural Society,[13] while Hussey, unopposed, gained the award at a similar exhibition in his home State of Maryland.[14]

In 1850, Hussey made arrangements in Illinois for the manufacture of his reapers, and exhibited a model at the Mechanics' Institute in Chicago.[15] In a letter published in the "Prairie Farmer" he compared his machine with McCormick's, to the great disadvantage of the latter. He declared that he had driven his rival from Virginia, Maryland, North Carolina, Kentucky, New York, and Ohio. "Whether this is to be the destiny of the two machines in the other states remains to be developed." [16] McCormick thereupon concentrated more attention upon those States where his competitor said that he was "extinct," and in the autumn exhibited his reaper at the fair of the Maryland Agricultural Society.[17]

During the next harvest, Cyrus McCormick printed sales' statistics to show that he had sold a larger number of reapers each year on the seaboard than had Hussey, and accompanied this evidence with the appointment of more agents in the East

[11] *Ibid.,* July 15, 1849, pp. 214, 216; Aug. 1, 1850, p. 226. "Genesee Farmer," July, 1850, p. 173. Chester Weed, of Muscatine, Ia., to McCormick, Ogden & Co., July 18, 1849.

[12] "Prairie Farmer," Oct., 1849, p. 322; Sept., 1850, pp. 266-269.

[13] "Genesee Farmer," July, 1850, p. 173.

[14] "American Farmer," Nov., 1849, p. 147.

[15] "Prairie Farmer," Jan., 1850, p. 30; May, 1850, p. 146; June, 1850, p. 185.

[16] *Ibid.,* Mch., 1850, pp. 75, 76. "Albany Cultivator," Apr., 1851, p. 149.

[17] "American Farmer," Dec., 1850, p. 210; July, 1850, Pictorial Supplement.

than ever before. "Hussey can have 'his only genuine article,' "
wrote McCormick, "as long as he lets me continue to supply
the demand of the country." [18] This marks his first serious
attempt since 1845 to recapture the Eastern market. The results justified the effort. Nevertheless, high transportation
charges, the comparatively heavy draft of his reaper, and its
failure to mow successfully prior to 1854, handicapped him in
this region. He later threatened to build an Eastern branch
factory if the railroads would not give him lower rates on
through car-load shipments to the coast.

McCormick's Eastern sales in 1851 were double those of the
preceding year, and he won the first reaper premium at the
Pennsylvania State Fair. In the West he received other prizes
at state fairs in Michigan and Wisconsin, and at the Mechanics'
Institute of Chicago.[19] The Maryland State Agricultural Society again honored Obed Hussey, but the judges at the state
fair held in Rochester, New York, were unable to decide which
of the two machines was the better.[20] By the close of the year
Hussey faced a competitor who had just won the Grand Council Medal at the World's Fair in London and w: stronger than
ever. He thereupon formed a partnership w i the editor of
the "Prairie Farmer" whereby five hundr⟋ of his machines
were to be made in Chicago for the coming harvest.[21]

[18] "Albany Cultivator," July, 1851, p. 253: McCormick sold 100 in the
East in 1850 and Hussey made a total of 114 reape⟋s in Baltimore for his
entire market. In 1851 the figures were 200 and . ⟋8, respectively.

[19] "Prairie Farmer," Dec., 1851, p. 592. It is ⟋erhaps significant that for
the first time in several years the Husseyite editor of the "American
Farmer" of Baltimore allowed a letter to be printed which favored Mc-
Cormick. See the issue for May, 1851, pp. 412, 413.

[20] Ibid., Nov., 1851, p. 176. "Albany Cultivator," Nov., 1851, pp. 369-371.
"Ohio Cultivator," Oct. 15, 1851, p. 313.

[21] "Prairie Farmer," Dec., 1851, p. 592. "Chicago Daily Journal," Dec.
23, 1851: McCormick suggests to Wright and Hussey that they "observe
the good old doctrine,—prove your faith by your works." This was prob-

Once again it is apparent that the oft-emphasized lack of aggressiveness on the part of Obed Hussey is disproved by almost every move of his career.

In the McCormick-Hussey polemics of 1851 and of the years immediately following, the rivalry in England and the justice of the honors there received hold the most prominent place. This endless debate furnished excellent advertisement, but it naturally did not lead either inventor to accept the viewpoint of the other. The mutual contest for extension of patents also was echoed in the press, but the chief dispute dealing with the American harvest fields turned about McCormick's efforts between 1851 and 1855 to supplant his rival among the farmers of the Southern seaboard.

The outstanding Hussey champions were Samuel Sands, the editor of the Baltimore "American Farmer," Edward Stabler, a Maryland Quaker and a personal friend of the inventor, Robert B. Bolling, a proud Virginian planter, and T. P. and H. K. Burgwyn who boasted of broad acres devoted to wheat-culture in North Carolina.[22] Solon Robinson, the itinerant apostle of better agriculture, now and again used his pen in defense of Hussey, while Edmund Ruffin of Virginia, stanch Southern patriot and a distinguished proponent of better methods of farming, led the old "stalwarts" who saw little good in any reaper. In the West, McCormick contended against the outspoken antagonism of John S. Wright, the editor of the widely circulated "Prairie Farmer" of Chicago.[23]

ably an answer to Wright and Hussey's letter in the same paper for December 19, in which they sarcastically beg McCormick to allow them to sell the 500 reapers which they intend to make in Chicago.

[22] "The Plow," edited by A. B. Allen of New York, was also favorable to Hussey. See the issues of Feb., 1852, pp. 56, 57; Mch., 1852, pp. 92, 93. A. B. Allen & Co., were Hussey's agents.

[23] For the press battle between McCormick and Wright-Hussey, see the "Chicago Weekly Democrat," Jan. 24, 1852; the "Chicago Daily Journal," Dec. 1, 19, 23, 24, 27, 1851. Much of this debate turned about the relative value of the McCormick and Hussey cutters. "Chicago Daily Journal,"

In early 1852 Hussey and Wright dissolved their partnership and Wright delegated his editorial duties to his brother, so that he might be free to manufacture the Atkins Self-Raker, an ingenious mechanical delivery device attached to a Hussey machine.[24] In the face of this formidable opposition, Cyrus McCormick fought almost alone. He was too strong and forthright to elicit sympathy and support.

Early in 1852, Obed Hussey published a pamphlet which reviewed the rivalry with McCormick in England and the relative merits of the cutting principles of the two reapers. A newspaper war upon the same subjects had been in progress for several months.[25] In mid-March Cyrus McCormick answered this pamphlet with an attack in kind, explaining that his action was due to a wish to counteract any harmful results Hussey's strictures might have had upon the Eastern grain-grower. In this manner he announced his intention to come East again with even more force than he had used in the preceding harvest.[26] He purposed "to pay his respects" to Hussey in the South also, but he would especially welcome a contest in a prairie wheat-field against his competitor's reel-less reaper and smooth-edged cutter.[27]

Mch. 22 and Dec. 27, 1851. McCormick spent part of Christmas Day, 1851, writing a reply to Hussey.

[24] "Prairie Farmer," May, 1852, pp. 258, 274: J. S. Wright states that he has arranged to make 150 or 200 Hussey reapers for the Western market. In "McCormick Patent Reaping and Mowing Machine in America," Mch. 15, 1852, the author says that the Wright-Hussey partnership first came to his attention in Nov., 1851, and that it was dissolved in Jan., 1852.

[25] O. Hussey, "Hussey's Reaping and Mowing Machine in England" (Baltimore, 1852). Letter of W. S. McCormick in the "Chicago Weekly Journal" of Jan. 24, 1852. "Genesee Farmer," June, 1853, p. 195. "Chicago Weekly Democrat," Jan. 24, 1852, letter of O. Hussey.

[26] The appearance of the McCormick pamphlet was merely an incident, not the end, of the contest in the press. "American Farmer," Apr., 1852, p. 368; May, 1852, pp. 398, 411; June, 1852, p. 439.

[27] "Chicago Daily Democrat," Dec. 23, 1851: McCormick writes of opening a factory in Baltimore.

The friends of Hussey were only too eager to afford Mc-Cormick an opportunity to meet his rival in the East. Samuel Sands announced that a field contest would be held in Maryland during the coming harvest, and that the state agricultural society would award a premium of one hundred dollars to the best machine. Thereupon, T. P. Burgwyn, who harvested fourteen thousand bushels of wheat with Hussey reapers in 1851, declared that he would add another one hundred dollars to the prize offered.[28] The trial was finally arranged for July 7, 1852, at Edward Lloyd's farm near Easton, Maryland. Although steamboats from Baltimore offered to transport reapers to the field without charge, Hussey appeared as the only noteworthy contestant for the award.[29]

The pages of the "American Farmer" smoke with its editor's ire. McCormick had protested the slate of judges on the score that they were all friends of Hussey, and his Baltimore agent was then permitted to name five more. "After this courtesy to him, why he refused to be present, or to permit his agent to represent his interests, he can best explain." [30] No good reason for McCormick's absence has been found. After his frequently expressed intention to press his campaign in the East, his failure to respond to this opportunity to gain favor in hostile territory could only be interpreted to his disadvantage. Perhaps he was convinced that he would not receive justice, even from the reconstituted board of judges, and certainly he never wittingly played into the hands of his enemies.

Nor was his Maryland fiasco the only checkmate he suffered

[28] "American Farmer," Apr., 1852, p. 341. His brother, H. K. Burgwyn, was then a vice-president of the United States Agricultural Society. "Albany Cultivator," Aug., 1852, p. 284.

[29] "American Farmer," July, 1852, p. 16; Dec., 1852, pp. 194, 195.

[30] Ibid., Aug., 1852, pp. 59, 60. Here is also given an article from a Maryland paper, "The Eastern Star." "Of course Hussey reaped the honor of having backed out the gentleman who took the 'great medal' at the World's Fair."

in his competition with Hussey during this harvest. In an Ohio
contest Hussey's machine received prizes both as a mower
and a reaper, while McCormick's did not place.[31] McCormick
was unable to defeat his rival in the widely heralded Geneva,
New York, trials, staged by the state agricultural society.[32] In
England, as we have seen, Hussey temporarily halted the tide
of opinion rising in favor of his opponent. As the season closed,
the latter announced that he would be along the James River, in
Virginia, early in the next harvest, prepared to meet all
comers.[33]

McCormick's troubles in Virginia, Maryland, and North
Carolina increased with the harvests of 1853 and 1854. As if in
answer to his James River challenge, Edwin G. Booth, an
officer of the Virginia State Agricultural Society, wrote to
the "American Farmer" in March, 1853, that the McCormick machine "was the most magnificent and costly humbug in its line." He referred to its lack of success upon the
large plantations of William Allen, Corbin Warwick, and
Robert Bolling, and went so far in his criticism as to assert:
"Not one of McCormick's Reapers has ever operated any
profitable length of time in this region." [34] Even the hostile
editor felt that Booth had been "hard on McCormick." But
the inventor's reply in the June number of this magazine was

[31] "American Farmer," Sept., 1852, pp. 99, 100, 101. This was the trial
at Springfield, O., of the Clark and Madison Counties Agricultural Society. "Annual Report of the Ohio State Board of Agriculture, 1852." "The
Plough, the Loom, and the Anvil," V (1852), pt. 1, pp. 165, 166. "Albany
Cultivator," Dec., 1852, pp. 412, 413; supra, p. 343.
[32] "Albany Cultivator," Sept., 1852, pp. 312-314; Oct., 1852, pp. 338, 355;
Dec., 1852, pp. 412, 413.
[33] Ibid., Dec., 1852, pp. 412, 413.
[34] "American Farmer," Mch., 1853, pp. 298-300. "Southern Planter," Dec.,
1852. This was not Booth's first attack on McCormick; see the "American
Farmer," Mch., 1851, p. 303; the "N. Y. Farmer and Mechanic," Sept. 16,
1847, p. 447; the "Monthly Journal of Agriculture," Mch., 1848, p. 461.

more of an attack upon Hussey than a defense of his own machine.[35]

In the meantime the Virginia Agricultural Society had proposed a reaper contest on Booth's farm in Nottoway County for a fifty-dollar premium, but at McCormick's request it was shifted to William Allen's "Maiden Hall" estate on the James River. After the battle here on June 21 and 22, the judges failed to agree: two were for Hussey, two for Burrall, and one for McCormick.[36] Once again McCormick had lost in the East, nor could his success against Hussey that year in England serve to counteract the prejudice of the seaboard farmer.[37]

McCormick had now failed to defeat Hussey both in Maryland and in Virginia, and in midsummer, 1853, H. K. Burgwyn, after discoursing upon the great harm done to those farmers who innocently purchased worthless reapers, classified McCormick's among "the miserable failures" he had in mind. The Burgwyns had long used the Hussey machines with satisfaction, but they probably revealed the chief cause for their animus when they wrote some months later that Southerners were growing suspicious of all "Yankee wares," particularly those marked "built for the southern market." [38] Since the Hussey reaper was made at Baltimore, it did not bear this Northern stigma.

Nevertheless, McCormick decided to carry the conflict to

[35] "American Farmer," June, 1853, pp. 401, 404, 405. Apr., 1853, p. 343; May, 1853, pp. 368, 375, 378. "Richmond Whig," Apr. 25, 1853.

[36] "American Farmer," July, 1853, p. 20. "Richmond [Va.] Daily Despatch," June 23, 1853. "Richmond Enquirer," July 19, 1853.

[37] "Albany Cultivator," Aug., 1853, p. 257. "Pennsylvania Farm Journal," Sept., 1853, p. 189: Hussey made 306 machines in Baltimore in 1853.

[38] "American Farmer," June, 1853, pp. 402, 403. For earlier articles of like tenor from North Carolina see an account signed "Davie," *ibid.*, March, 1851, p. 307; Jan., 1849, p. 207; July, 1849, pp. 22, 24; Dec., 1850, p. 364. "American Agriculturist," Jan., 1850, p. 27. "North Carolina Planter" (Raleigh, N. C.), July, 1849, p. 33.

Burgwyn's own plantation in 1854. The contest had rolled southward—1852 in Maryland, 1853 in Virginia, and now in North Carolina. The somewhat humorous story of the vain attempt of McCormick's Yankee agent, A. D. Hager, to supplant Hussey on the Yadkin River, has already been told.[39] During the same season Edmund Ruffin of Virginia found his previous opinion confirmed, that all reapers, including McCormick's, were of very little practical value unless there were "a Blacksmith shop at each corner of the field." [40] Edward Stabler of Maryland published a lengthy pamphlet in defense of his friend Hussey,[41] who was boldly contending that he was the originator of the "first successful reaping and mowing machine," [42] and McCormick's principal agent in New York wrote to his chief that his competitor was doing him much harm in that State and in Canada.[43]

After 1848, McCormick sold each year as many or more reapers in the East than did Hussey, whose Baltimore factory reached its maximum annual output in 1855 with 521 ma-

[39] *Supra*, pp. 370 ff.
[40] H. M. Smith, of Richmond, Va., May 6, 1854, to C. H. McCormick; Edmund Ruffin, of Old Church Point, Va., to C. H. McCormick, Dec. 16, 1854.
[41] E. Stabler in "A Brief Narrative," etc., emphasized that McCormick had admitted his reaper was of little practical value before 1845. He failed to mention Hussey's statement that his was not of real service until his improvements of 1847. Stabler's account was based on information furnished by Hussey, who paid the printer's bill. See Stabler, in the "Prairie Farmer" of Feb., 1854, p. 71. *McCormick vs. Manny*, II, 696-698.
[42] "Scientific American," Dec. 23, 1854, p. 120. "American Agriculturist," Feb. 21, 1855, p. 371. "American Farmer," Jan., 1854, p. 216; Aug., 1854, p. 52; June, 1855, p. 383; May, 1855, p. 382.
[43] T. J. Paterson to C. H. McCormick, Mch. 21 and July 14, 1854. Hussey manufactured 385 machines in 1854. He and McCormick each received a bronze medal at the New York Crystal Palace, and Hussey won a premium of $10 and McCormick a diploma at the annual fair of the Pennsylvania Agricultural Society. "American Farmer," Feb., 1854, p. 253. "Pennsylvania Farm Journal," Nov., 1854, p. 346.

chines.[44] For the next harvest he manufactured less than one third of that number, and by 1859 only ten reapers were completed at his plant.[45] By this time Cyrus McCormick, who was marketing over four thousand annually, was hardly aware of Hussey's competition west of Ohio.[46] In other words, the rivalry of these veterans was keen chiefly because questions of patents were at stake and because McCormick carried the war vigorously into the enemy's territory. The simultaneous contest for the English trade added much fuel to the fire. In 1858, Hussey closed the twenty years of conflict by suing McCormick for an infringement of his 1847 patent. A summary of the questions at issue in this case will be given in the next chapter of this narrative.

The number of reaper and mower manufacturers increased very rapidly after 1848.[47] While Obed Hussey continued to be Cyrus McCormick's chief competitor abroad until 1855, the latter by that date faced far more powerful antagonists at

[44] Patent Office Records, "Hussey Extension Case, Patent of 1847" (Washington, 1861), p. 5. Hussey made 163 reapers in 1856; 95 in 1857; 19 in 1858; 10 in 1859, and 24 in 1860. He manufactured a total of 2,216 between 1848 and 1860, and sold 1,845. In the same period, McCormick manufactured 31,252. Ardrey, "The Harvesting Machine Industry," in the "Scientific American," Supplement, Dec. 20, 1902, p. 22545. He writes that Hussey made no money until 1859, when a "syndicate of patent lawyers" bought his patents for $200,000.

[45] Hussey was bitter by 1857. He wrote in the "American Farmer," Mch., 1857, p. 6 (adv. supplement): "While I have not drawn money from the pockets of farmers to enrich myself, other manufacturers have become rich through my invention, and honourable gentlemen, misled by the clamor of such manufacturers have withheld from me what equity and justice would give me [the extension of my patent]. . . . These manufacturers are the identical persons . . . who took up my invention to make money by it, after I had endured the toil, expense, and vexation to produce a valuable implement for the farmer through fourteen long years without profit."

[46] B. M. Rhodes, from Baltimore, to C. H. McCormick, Jan. 20, May 26, 28 and June 30, 1855.

[47] An excellent survey of the history of mechanical reaping in the United States and in England, up to 1854, will be found in the "American Agriculturist," Sept. 27, 1854, p. 35, and Oct. 25, 1854, p. 99.

home. Seymour & Morgan at Brockport, New York, Howard & Co., of Buffalo, John S. Wright of Chicago, and, above all, John H. Manny of Waddam's Grove, Illinois, each made annually more reapers and mowers than Hussey had sold since 1833. A score and more of smaller producers reared their heads to disappear after a season, causing Cyrus McCormick momentary embarrassment in the locality of their factories.

During the decade of the fifties, self-raking reapers, which mechanically delivered the cut grain at the side of the machine, either in gavels or in swath, were gaining popularity. They mark the transition between the hand-rake reaper and the binder, but neither McCormick nor Hussey adopted the appliance at this time. Many of these improvements were more clever than practical, and William McCormick wrote on one occasion that his brother had had an opportunity to buy almost every such device of note which had been invented, including the Atkins Automaton, but he had decided after an examination of each that the advantages from its use were much too uncertain to be relied upon.[48] Since he more than held his own against all rivals who manufactured self-rake reapers, his judgment was doubtless a wise one.

Perhaps the most ingenious and popular of the mechanical rakes was constructed by a bedridden Chicago mechanic, Jearum Atkins, who skilfully arranged a pair of mechanical arms that as nearly as possible approximated the motion of human hands in raking gavels of grain from the platform. From 1852 to 1858 this invention was one of the curiosities of the agricultural world. Large numbers were sold in all sections of the North and West, and the powerful "Prairie Farmer" was its most effective sponsor. McCormick was aware

[48] W. S. McCormick to T. J. Walker & Co. of Belleville, Ill., Apr. 30, 1857, L.P.C.B. No. 6, p. 504. Adv. of C. H. McCormick in the "American Farmer," June, 1854, p. 392. "Prairie Farmer," Mch., 1854, p. 128.

of its competition and doubtless felt relieved in 1858 when its meteoric career closed, partly owing to the financial panic and partly because all of the machines for that harvest were built of green, unseasoned wood.[49]

Cyrus McCormick followed several lines of policy in opposing these rivals. He fought to the finish for an extension of his 1834 patent. He expanded his Chicago factory as rapidly as possible and concentrated all manufacturing under his own able supervision. He closely scanned the machines of his competitors and brought suit when they appeared to infringe his 1845 and 1847 patents. This seemed especially advisable. He could not prevent the use of the combination of mechanical principles employed in his original reaper, but a manufacturer could not hope to sell many reapers unequipped with a raker's seat, a reverse-angled sickle, and the other improvements covered by McCormick's later patents. These would expire in 1859 and 1861, respectively, but until that time they were effective weapons.

Seymour & Morgan were the first to feel the weight of McCormick's displeasure. This firm had, with several others of the town of Brockport, New York, manufactured under license seven or eight hundred of his reapers in the period from 1845 to 1849.[50] Their influence had been exerted to prevent an extension of the 1834 patent. Following the 1849 harvest, Seymour & Morgan decided to manufacture reapers independently, constructing a machine very similar to McCormick's, although they claimed that their patented, hollow, guard finger

[49] J. L. Walker to J. B. Fairbanks, Concord, Ill., Feb. 8, 1858, L.P.C.B. No. 10, p. 633: "Wright & Co. have failed and will not pay 10¢ upon the dollar."

[50] McCormick's warnings to all infringers may be found in the "Prairie Farmer," Dec., 1849; the "Ohio Cultivator," Jan. 15, 1850, p. 31; Feb. 15, 1850, p. 63; the "Chicago Daily Journal," Sept. 8, 1849.

was original.[51] McCormick warned the firm orally and through the press to desist unless they chose to defend themselves in the courts for infringement of his 1845 and 1847 patents, and he included all purchasers of this reaper in his admonition.[52] The Brockport partners, disregarding McCormick's threat, made about three hundred reapers for the next harvest, and guaranteed their patrons from liability to the inventor.[53]

Thereupon McCormick asked the United States Circuit Court at Albany in the summer of 1850 to issue an injunction restraining Seymour & Morgan from further manufacture, on the grounds that their divider and reel-post infringed his 1845 patent, and that their raker's seat invaded his monopoly of 1847.[54] Judge Nelson refused to grant the petition, but ordered the firm to "keep and render under oath" a true account of all machines made and sold. Because of McCormick's failure to win an injunction, Seymour & Morgan were able to market almost all of the machines they had made for that season. McCormick now sued for $15,000 damages, and, pending the trial, was granted an injunction in the autumn of 1850, restraining his rivals from making any more reapers of the model sold in the late harvest.[55]

[51] A cut of Seymour & Morgan's reaper is in the "Genesee Farmer," Jan., 1850, p. 31.

[52] *Seymour & Morgan vs. McCormick,* pp. 5 ff., 84, 89, 93, 94. "Genesee Farmer," June, 1850, p. 149; July, 1850, p. 173.

[53] *Seymour & Morgan vs. McCormick,* pp. 75, 95. "Albany Evening Journal," Oct. 17, 1850, letter of C. H. McCormick. "Chicago Daily Journal," Oct. 25, 1850, letter of C. H. McCormick. "Chicago Weekly Journal," Nov. 4, 1850.

[54] *McCormick vs. Manny,* II, 4-9, 369 ff., 391 ff.

[55] "Prairie Farmer," Jan., 1851, pp. 44, 45. The injunction was issued on Oct. 15, 1850, restraining Seymour & Morgan, under a penalty of $20,000, from making or selling any more reapers known as "Seymour & Morgan's Reaping Machines," incorporating the improvements of McCormick's patent of Oct. 23, 1847. The injunction may be found in the "Albany Evening Journal," Oct. 17, 1850; the "Scientific American," Oct. 26, 1850, p. 42; the "Wisconsin and Iowa Farmer and Northwestern Cultivator," Jan., 1851.

This did not end the contest. The firm merely moved the offending raker's seat to a new position, changed the trade name of the machine to the "New York Reaper," and went ahead with a large building program for 1851. In the winter of 1850-51, McCormick called the attention of the public to this defiance of the injunction and ridiculed the quality of Seymour & Morgan's output. "They are the first pirates ever prosecuted by me for infringement. . . . Everyone who uses one is liable to suit by me and they will be. So Seymour & Morgan had better make a lot of money to compensate their purchasers." [56] The partners were not driven from business by these threats but even more widely advertised their 1851 reaper and taunted their competitor in language as scornful as he had used when referring to them. "C. H. McCormick can no longer monopolize the Reaper business to the great damage of all save himself. . . . Buyers of our machine need not fear. If McCormick wins, we can pay." [57] They sold some of their machines in 1851 in the vicinity of Chicago, and others as far west as Iowa.[58]

The course of the suits against Seymour & Morgan between 1851 and 1855 is most devious, and a complete presentation of the story would require more space than its importance warrants. They were able to postpone the trial by pleading that their depositions and models were not completed, and, by the

[56] "Chicago Daily Journal," Mch. 22, 1851, letter of C. H. McCormick.
[57] "Chicago Weekly Democrat," Mch. 29, Apr. 2 and Apr. 19, 1851. "Genesee Farmer," Feb., 1851, p. 54; June, 1851, p. 148; July, 1850, pp. 173, 175. Seymour & Morgan state that their machine defeated McCormick's whenever they were tried together, "and the gentleman having *learned from experience* that he cannot compete with us in a fair business-like manner in selling, has tried to frighten us from making our machine. . . . We shall show Mr. McCormick, should he ever give us occasion, that *our only infringement is on his business, and not on his patent.*"
[58] "Gem of the Prairie," May 24, 1851. J. L. Wilson to C. H. McCormick, from Genoa, Ill., Jan. 2, 1852; Phelps & Bourland, of Peoria, Ill., to C. H. McCormick, June 9, 1851.

autumn of 1851, McCormick was so exasperated by their dilatory action that he consented to rest his case solely upon an alleged infringement of his patent of 1847—the defendants admitting their readiness to stand trial on this issue.[59]

Although constructed differently, the raker's seat on the Seymour & Morgan machine was identical in position and purpose with McCormick's, but they argued that this device had been used long before their rival's 1847 patent, and hence it was not his exclusive property. Nevertheless, Justice Nelson held that the patent was not for a seat but for that arrangement and combination of the parts of the reaper which allowed a place for the rakeman to ride where he could work effectively without disturbing the equilibrium of the reaper. Accepting this interpretation of the patent, infringement by Seymour & Morgan was unquestionable, and the jury brought in a verdict of $17,306.66 damages.[60] This award was supposed to equal the entire profits which the offending firm had gained from the sale of about two hundred and eighty machines. In other words, the court held that if Seymour & Morgan had not made these reapers unlawfully, McCormick would have sold two hundred and eighty more in the harvest of 1850.[61] This would have been difficult to prove.

The defendants immediately appealed to the United States Supreme Court, and this tribunal, in May, 1854, upheld the validity of McCormick's patent of 1847 and decided that his Bill of Complaint was just. However, the case was sent back to the lower court for retrial on the grounds that Seymour & Morgan were bound to McCormick only for their profits from

[59] *McCormick vs. Manny*, II, pp. 403-419.

[60] "Chicago Daily Journal," Nov. 3, 1851.

[61] *McCormick vs. Manny*, II, pp. 299-309, Justice Nelson's charge to the jury at Canandaigua, New York, July 2, 1851, and at Albany, Oct., 1851. The jury agreed that McCormick's estimate of the net profits from the manufacture and sale of a reaper was correct. He had claimed $60, while Seymour & Morgan, quite naturally, had said $30.

his raker's seat, and not for those gained by using the mechanical principles of his 1834 patent, now expired. In other words, the penalty was too severe.[62]

In the meantime Cyrus McCormick secured a reissue of his 1847 patent, on the plea that the original specification was defective. He was surprised to learn that by this action he waived any rights that he had possessed under it before its emendation. For this reason, when the case was returned for a rehearing before Justice Nelson and a jury in 1854, McCormick necessarily shifted the grounds for his attack to the patent of 1845.[63] This involved a discussion of dividers and reel-bearers rather than of rakers' seats. William H. Seward was the leading counsel for McCormick.[64] The exact points at issue were most technical and involved an understanding of reaper mechanics which cannot be presumed here. Seymour & Morgan were at a disadvantage, since they had been licensees of McCormick for several years under his patents and had thereby tacitly admitted that he was the inventor of the elements described in them.[65] The jury awarded damages of $7,750 to the inventor, and this sum was increased to over $10,000 by the addition of the costs and charges of the trials.[66] On appeal, the United States

[62] "McCormick Reaping Machine; Charge of His Honor Mr. Justice Nelson to the Jury in the Circuit Court of the United States for the Northern District of New York at Albany, October 24, 1854, in the Case of Cyrus H. McCormick vs. William H. Seymour and Dayton S. Morgan" (N. Y., 1854), p. 14. The court reached its decision by a four to three vote.

[63] T. J. Paterson to W. S. McCormick, Oct. 21, 1854: "C. H. in obtaining the renewal of his patent thought he had achieved a great triumph over Seymour and Morgan, but as it turns out if he is defeated that will be the sole cause."

[64] Chas. M. Keller and Sam'l Blatchford also were counsel for McCormick.

[65] "The Reaper; Argument of William H. Seward in the Circuit Court of the United States, October 24, 1854" (Auburn, N. Y., 1854), pp. 10, 11, 23, 24. Here will be found an excellent summary of the mechanical questions at issue. This pamphlet will be hereafter cited as "Seward."

[66] *Seymour & Morgan vs. McCormick,* pp. 28, 29. *McCormick vs. Seymour & Morgan,* 3 Blatchford 216. *McCormick vs. Manny,* II, 390, 391.

Supreme Court sustained this decision in 1857.[67] An associate wrote from Albany to William McCormick when the award of the Circuit Court was made known:

Judge Nelson's charge . . . was strong in favor of C. H.— but very muddy and thick—so everybody says. How the jury ever agreed was a mystery. C. H. is not exactly *satisfied,* but law is uncertain and he had better let *well enough alone,* as the verdict is substantially as great a triumph as if the damages had been greater and the principle just as well settled as to his Patent upon divider and reel post (the former trial settling the Rakers Seat question).[68]

Thus ended one phase of the court battle with Seymour & Morgan.

While this case was slowly making its way through the federal courts, the company continued to be a serious competitor, particularly in New York and Canada. In the field trials of the New York State Agricultural Society at Geneva in the summer of 1852, their reaper placed third, although it failed to win any prize in a similar contest conducted by the Ohio State Agricultural Society at Springfield.[69] "If Seymour and Morgan are out of the way," wrote McCormick's chief New York agent in November, 1851, "a much more extensive and profitable business may be done, it is hoped, in this State." [70] Cyrus McCormick widely published the first verdict of the federal circuit court as a warning to other infringers,

[67] The decision of the Supreme Court was on Jan. 7, 1857. Since one claim in the patent of 1845 was for a feature non-patentable, the taxation of costs was stricken out of the circuit court's decision. McCormick received $9,354.05 by May 30, 1857. See C. H. to W. S. McCormick, Jan. 6, 13, 17, Apr. 9 and May 30, 1857.
[68] J. L. Wilson, from Albany, N. Y., Oct. 25, 1854.
[69] "Albany Cultivator," Sept., 1852, pp. 312-314; Dec., 1852, pp. 412, 413. "American Farmer," Sept., 1852, p. 99.
[70] T. J. Paterson to C. H. McCormick, Nov. 10, 1851, and June 12, 1853.

and he charged that the machines made by Seymour & Morgan since 1850 were also infringements of his 1845 patent.[71]

After the injunction of 1850 was issued, Seymour & Morgan moved their raker's seat from McCormick's position, on the extension of the finger-bar, to the rear of their reaper platform, thus hoping to avoid an infringement of his patent. For this reason, and probably also with his eye on John H. Manny & Co., Cyrus McCormick secured a reissue of his 1847 patent on May 24, 1853, with a revised specification intended to cover the seat wherever it was placed on the reaper. In his own words—

it was uncertain whether the language of the specification annexed to the said original letters patent did not limit your orator [McCormick] to one particular place on the platform of the machine for locating the raker; and that, therefore, your orator surrendered his said letters patent, in order to remedy the insufficiency of the said specification, and to define in more certain and exact terms the extent and limit of his invention.[72]

Believing that he now had the means to crush Seymour & Morgan, and knowing that they were building about four hundred machines for 1853, equipped with a raker's seat on the platform,[73] he petitioned the United States Circuit Court on June 1 of that year for an injunction to restrain the firm from selling these reapers. His request was immediately granted by

[71] "Prairie Farmer," Dec., 1851, p. 592. "Genesee Farmer," May, 1852, p. 165; June, 1852, p. 196. "American Farmer," May, 1852, p. 411. "Albany Cultivator," June, 1852, p. 228.

[72] Certified copy of "Patent Office Records, Reissue, May 24, 1853," No. 239. Another reissue of this same patent was granted on Dec. 21, 1858. *McCormick vs. Manny,* II, p. 327, C. H. McCormick's Bill of Complaint vs. Seymour and Morgan, June 1, 1853. For a further discussion of this reissue, from the standpoint of the Manny case, see the next chapter.

[73] For this season, Warder & Brokaw of Springfield, O., also manufactured the New York Reaper, and won first prize with it at the contest held by the state agricultural society on Sept. 1. "Ohio Cultivator," Apr. 15, 1853, pp. 119, 126, 159; Sept. 1, 1853, p. 260.

Justice Nelson and a permanent injunction was issued by the same court on September 18, 1854.[74] Apparently McCormick's plea for damages in this instance was denied, but Seymour & Morgan were driven to market the infringing reapers of 1853 in Canada, and to busy themselves thereafter with the manufacture of Palmer & Williams Self-Rakers, and Ketchum Mowers.[75]

Although the contests with Hussey and Seymour & Morgan dragged along for many years and eventually reached the highest court of the land, a still more important and bitterly fought campaign in this war of the reapers has yet to be described. Cyrus McCormick was fighting on three important, and on many minor, fronts simultaneously. Generally speaking, by 1853 all of the reaper-makers in the United States were leagued against him and among these foes none was more formidable than John H. Manny, whose machines were made in large numbers in a dozen places in the North and West. The next chapter will present his conspicuous part in this combined effort to compass McCormick's downfall, and also the final attempt of Obed Hussey to injure his ancient rival.

In the harvest field the weapon was the reaper; in Congress, lobbyists, farmers' petitions, and pressure of all kinds; while in the courts "injunctions" and "infringements" were the two words most frequently heard. It was an age of business war, rather than of manufacturers' trusts, although the following pages will show that the contestants talked of consolidation even while they fought each other in Congress and in the courts.

[74] *McCormick vs. Manny*, II., pp. 6-9, 342.
[75] T. J. Paterson, from Albany, N. Y., Jan. 7 and Feb. 10, 1854. "Michigan Farmer," Aug., 1854, p. 251. "Prairie Farmer," Mch., 1854, p. 128. "Ohio Cultivator," May 1, 1854, p. 143. "Genesee Farmer," May, 1854, p. 166. "American Farmer," June, 1854, p. 392.

CHAPTER XVIII

THE COURT CLIMAX

JOHN H. MANNY of Waddam's Grove, Stephenson County, Illinois, sold almost one thousand reapers in 1854, and more than double that number in the next harvest.[1] Here was a most dangerous opponent, with a rapidly growing business in McCormick's own State, and in the very heart of the wheat region he had hitherto considered peculiarly his own.

Pells Manny and his son John gained their first interest in mechanical reaping in the late forties, when they purchased an Esterly header. They presently advertised a similar implement of their own manufacture,[2] but the market for headers was limited, and by 1850 they turned their attention to a combined reaper-mower which soon won the approbation of many prairie farmers. A casual observer would have believed that it was merely the McCormick reaper under a new name, but closer inspection revealed that the cutting angle of its knife-sections was more acute, the fingers were sharp-edged; the platform was different in shape; the forker's stand was on the rear of the platform instead of the extended finger-bar, and there was also an appliance by which the cutter-bar could be automatically raised or lowered at the will of the operator.[3] Without doubt,

[1] *McCormick vs. Manny*, II, p. 70.
[2] "Prairie Farmer," Oct., 1847, p. 324; Oct., 1848, p. 316; Nov., 1849, p. 347; Jan., 1850, p. 30; Sept., 1850, pp. 266-269; Jan., 1851, p. 51. "Gem of the Prairie," July 22, 1848.
[3] "Before the Hon. Thomas C. Theaker, Commissioner of Patents. In the Matter of the Application of Mary Manny, Executrix, et als. for the Extension of Letters Patent dated Sept. 23d, 1851, granted to John H. Manny" (Washington, 1865), pp. 72, 73. Hereafter cited as "The Manny

the two machines were very similar in principle, and McCormick was convinced that Manny infringed his patents of 1845 and 1847.

The first serious clash between these two manufacturers occurred at the trials of the New York State Agricultural Society at Geneva in the summer of 1852. Here Manny received first prize for his mower and second for his reaper, while the McCormick machines did not place in either class. The editor of the "Albany Cultivator" ventured the opinion that Manny had the best combined machine on the market.[4] As soon as the awards were made known in the autumn, McCormick published a long analysis of the trials to show that he, rather than Manny, should have received the prizes. He declared that his competitor's implement was substantially his own, save for the cutter-gage, "which materially deteriorates the machine in other respects." Manny answered with similar strictures, and there the contest rested until the next harvest.[5]

In the season of 1853, at a trial held at Mount Holly, New Jersey, McCormick's machine was declared to be a better reaper-mower than Manny's, although the latter was acclaimed the best reaper.[6] By this time McCormick advertised that Manny was making the McCormick machine, "altered much to its prejudice," with the hope of thus avoiding the responsibility for violating his patents. "They [Seymour & Morgan and Manny] will be held responsible and arrested in their

Extension Case." "Albany Cultivator," Sept., 1852, pp. 312, 313. The editor shows cuts of the McCormick and Manny knives and compares them, to the disadvantage of the former.

[4] *Ibid.*, Oct., 1852, p. 338. "Michigan Farmer," Nov., 1852, pp. 348, 349. "Genesee Farmer," Aug., 1852, p. 257; Nov., 1852, p. 353. "Chicago Weekly Democrat," Dec. 4, 1852. At the annual fair of the Mechanics' Institute of Chicago, McCormick received a silver medal for the second best reaper-mower, and Manny a gold medal for the best. *Supra,* Chap. XIV, pp. 342 ff.

[5] "Albany Cultivator," Dec., 1852, pp. 412, 413; Feb., 1853, p. 69.

[6] *Ibid.*, Aug., 1853, p. 257. "Pennsylvania Farm Journal," Aug., 1854, pp. 252, 253.

course as soon as the law which is sure can reach them." [7]
Disregarding this warning, J. H. Manny organized a company
at Rockford, Illinois, while his father continued to produce a
few machines at the home factory at Waddam's Grove. Others
were made at Hoosick Falls, New York, by Walter A. Wood
and by Ball & Parsons.[8] In 1854, J. H. Manny announced that
his sickle, guard fingers, platform, forker's stand, and other
elements were protected by patents, and warned all manufacturers not to infringe.[9] His triumphs were repeated in this
harvest and the increasing volume of his sales indicated the
measure of his growing popularity.[10]

On November 22, 1854, James Campbell, an agent of Mc-
Cormick, journeyed to Rockford and purchased a Manny
reaper from the factory.[11] This was immediately sent to Chicago for study, and less than a week later Cyrus McCormick
filed a Bill of Complaint against his competitor in the United
States Circuit Court, charging that the implement infringed
both his 1845 and 1847 patents.[12] Calling attention to the large
business done by his rival, McCormick alleged that he had

[7] "Genesee Farmer," June, 1853, p. 195.

[8] "Prairie Farmer," Feb., 1854, p. 91 a. Here will be found a complete
description of the Manny machine. Walter A. Wood was persuaded that
the Manny machines of his manufacture infringed the McCormick patents.
He therefore came to terms with McCormick in 1855, 1856, and 1857, agreeing to pay a patent fee. Agreements with Wood, Apr. 25, 1856, Apr. 22
and 29, 1857. "Ohio Cultivator," May 15, 1855. A list of Manny's sub-
manufacturers, 1851-60, showing the license fees paid by each, is in "Manny
Extension Case, 1865," pp. 12-14.

[9] "Prairie Farmer," Feb., 1854, p. 91 a. "Michigan Farmer," June, 1854,
p. 192.

[10] E. Wagoner, from Westminster, Md., Dec. 19, 1853; Wm. Marshall,
from Ogle County, Ill., Apr. 22, 1854; D. R. Burt, from Waterloo, Ia.,
Apr. 30, 1854; J. B. McCormick, from Versailles, Ky., Feb. 18 and Mch. 7,
1854; A. D. Hager, from Belvidere, Ill., July 26, 28, 30, 1854.

[11] McCormick vs. Manny, I, complainant's testimony, pp. 4, 5.

[12] Ibid., II, 2 ff., McCormick gave his residence as Rockbridge County,
Va., although he had not lived there for over six years.

already been deprived of at least $30,000 in profits and petitioned the court both for an injunction to restrain Manny from further manufacture and for an order to compel him to publish his accounts.[13] Justice McLean granted McCormick's request, and, early in 1855, Manny and his associates posted a bond for $10,000, payable to Cyrus McCormick, as security that they would keep an accurate record of their business and would satisfy the judgment of the court, whatever it might be.[14]

Both McCormick and Manny made elaborate and expensive preparations during the eleven months which intervened before the case came up for trial. The former secured Edward N. Dickerson of New York, one of the ablest of patent lawyers, and Reverdy Johnson, a leader of the American bar, to plead his cause. Many depositions concerning the construction of old and new McCormick and Manny reapers were secured for presentation to the court and model machines of various inventors were made ready by both parties to the case.[15] Financial outlay seemed to be a minor consideration. In September, 1855, an employee of McCormick wrote from the scene of the trial:

I should not be willing to pay the costs in this case for one of the best patents in the country. The marshall's bill for moving

[13] *Ibid.*, II, pp. 12, 13.
[14] *Ibid.*, II, pp. 28, 64. C. H. to W. S. McCormick, from Washington, Mch. 7, 1854, and from New York, Oct. 4, 1854.
[15] T. J. Paterson, a trusted employee, to W. S. McCormick, May 4, 1855: "I did not write C. H. knowing he was on the jump having trouble from mistakes of lawyers—rather nervous and in a fever generally. . . . His letters recently have been short and written in such haste and with such a twitch that it would puzzell *Old Nick* to read them. By the way the Brockport folks [Seymour & Morgan] think he is a *brother* to Old Nick, indeed some of them claim him to be Belzebub himself. . . . C. H. and Dickerson start tonight from N. York for Cincinnati where they are to be on Monday. They go out to cut up *dog* I suppose and raise the *Deivle* generally." *Idem* to *idem,* June 25, 1855. C. H. McCormick to J. L. Wilson, Aug. 11, 16, 21, 1855.

Mack's machine from the sidewalk to the Exhibition room over the Court Room was $56—which includes nothing for putting up. This is but a slender idea of the expense of a suit in the United States Court. The Maryland, New York, and Virginia aristocracy, Johnson, Dickerson, and C. H. are swelling considerably here. Champain is an every day affair.[16]

Similar efforts were exerted by the defense. Much hinged upon the decision, since if McCormick won he could place most of the reaper-makers of the land under tribute to him. For this reason funds poured in from all parts of the North and West to aid Manny in the suit and his lawyers were among the ablest in the country. George Harding of Philadelphia, an equal of Dickerson in the field of patent law, was assisted by the astute and redoubtable Peter H. Watson of Washington. Edwin M. Stanton, however, was Harding's chief associate; while in the background, carefully prepared but not permitted by his colleagues to speak, was Abraham Lincoln. When the trial was scheduled to be held in Springfield, Illinois, Manny's counsel shrewdly decided that a popular local lawyer would help their cause, and since Lincoln was known to be a friend of Judge Drummond, in whose court the case would be heard, he was retained. Later, by the consent of both parties, the suit was transferred to Cincinnati before Justice McLean [17] and Judge Drummond, and Lincoln, happy because of his first great case, came to that city in September, 1855, bringing with him a brief which he had written after long study in the unfamiliar fields of reaper mechanics and patent law.

The late A. J. Beveridge, in his "Abraham Lincoln," [18]

[16] T. J. Paterson to W. S. McCormick, Sept. 24, 1855. *McCormick vs. Manny*, II, pp. 67, 68. On May 2, 1855, Watson testified that "draughtsmen, model-makers, copies from the Patent Office, exclusive of counsel fees," had totaled to date nearly $5,000.

[17] Justice McLean was the father-in-law of George Harding.

[18] Albert J. Beveridge, "Abraham Lincoln, 1809-1858" (2 vols., Boston, 1928), I, 575-583.

tells the story of the cool reception given the Springfield lawyer by Harding and Stanton, and of the unceremonious and insulting way in which they maneuvered him into the obscure rôle of a silent watcher in the court-room. According to this distinguished author, the Manny trial was a milestone of importance in Lincoln's life. Lincoln admired the brilliance and polish of his associates, stored their names deep in his memory, and returned to Springfield with his fee of $1,000, determined to be the equal of college-bred lawyers before they should become numerous in Illinois. Others have pointed out that the large check he received in this case, combined with his compensation for representing the Illinois Central Railroad in a suit at about the same time, made it possible for him to finance his campaign against Douglas in 1858.[19] If Edwin M. Stanton, Secretary of War in Lincoln's cabinet, and the momentous Lincoln-Douglas debates are so closely related to this battle of the reapers, the case of *McCormick vs. Manny* has a national significance far broader than the immediate issues involved.

The defendants fortunately retained Peter H. Watson [20] as counsel with Harding, Stanton and Lincoln. Any inventor seeking favors from the Patent Office was glad to have Watson on his side, as he had a seemingly magic method of carrying such business through to success. As an advocate his shrewdness was scarcely less amazing than his profound knowledge of harvesting machinery and patent law.

The originality of Manny's divider and forker's stand was the issue chiefly at stake. William P. Wood, a model-maker of Washington, was commissioned to go to McCormick's natal

---

[19] "Chicago Record-Herald," Feb. 14, 1909. "Harvester World," Dec., 1909, p. 2. In "Manny Extension Case, 1865," pp. 35 ff., is a statement of the receipts and expenditures of Manny and his heirs during this period. On p. 40 it is noted that A. Lincoln was paid a retainer fee of $400 on Oct. 15, 1855. His name is otherwise unmentioned.

[20] He was later Assistant Secretary of War, and president of the Erie Ry.

Valley of Virginia.[21] Here Wood found Isaac Hite, whose father had purchased the right to manufacture McCormick reapers in 1844. In that year Isaac constructed a raker's platform to attach behind the McCormick reaper so that the rakeman might ride as he worked, but he was refused a patent by the Government.[22] Hearing of this invention, Manny persuaded Hite to assign his right therein, and, through Watson, it was patented in 1855, in the name of a third person acting as a blind. The Commissioner of Patents at that time held that a raker's seat was a raker's seat in principle, no matter how constructed, and therefore Manny now owned a device which was unquestionably in use for a year before the seat described in the McCormick patent of 1847.[23]

Having thus disposed of the plaintiff's claim to the first use of a riding raker with his machine, the defendants had now to find support for Manny's divider. McCormick's case on this point would be greatly weakened if it could be shown that his divider, patented in 1845, consisting of a dividing bow and a dividing iron, had been used by other inventors prior to that date. An obsolete reaper, built by Ferdinand Woodward of Monmouth County, New Jersey, in 1844, was disinterred and its divider was skillfully transformed under expert direction so as to resemble McCormick's. Witnesses were procured who were ready to inform the court that Woodward had used his

---

[21] Wood was active in the U. S. Secret Service during the Civil War. See his affidavits of Dec. 16, 1897, and Mch. 12, 1903, filed in the McCormick Historical Association Library in Chicago.

[22] *McCormick vs. Manny,* II, 810 ff. *Supra*, p. 216.

[23] *Ibid.,* I, defendant's testimony, pp. 482 ff., 496, 498, 505, 508, 509-531. U. S. Patent Office Records, "McCormick-Hite Interference," 1855. The assignment by Hite to one Washington Pagett was on Apr. 21, 1855. When the interference issue between Hite and McCormick was heard by the Commr. of Patents in June, 1855, McCormick's lawyer vainly pointed out the underlying cause for the revival of this old invention. "The purpose is obvious. To facilitate the defense in some of the suits instituted by McCormick against infringers, and now pending."

machine as early as 1842 or 1843. This, if true, would demonstrate that McCormick's invention of the compound divider had been anticipated, and that his patent of 1845 should
never have been issued, so far as it related to this element.
But the defendant's witnesses broke down under cross-examination, and Dickerson, McCormick's counsel, pointed out to
the court that the Woodward machine was worthless as evidence.[24]

There was yet another expedient which, if successful, would
help immeasurably. If McCormick neglected to patent his peculiar divider for five or six years after its invention, his right
to its exclusive use might well be questioned.[25] An old McCormick reaper of 1845 was found on the plantation of Richard
Sampson in Goochland County, Virginia. Sampson, now eighty-
two years old and nearly blind, also had purchased a machine
from Cyrus in 1840. He was led to depose that the implement
had not been altered since its purchase by him, fifteen years before.[26] In other words, his senility was found to be an asset, and
Sampson confused the 1845 reaper with the one he had bought
five years prior to that harvest. This old machine was then
carried to the court-room at Cincinnati as conclusive evidence
that McCormick had employed his peculiar divider, patented
in 1845, as early as 1840. Because of this it was argued that,
in accordance with the law of 1839, the device "had passed into
public use" and was not patentable in 1845. For all their
shrewdness, the defense overlooked several important facts.
This reaper had an iron divider, and there were three holes in

[24] *McCormick vs. Manny*, II, p. 1228.

[25] *Ibid.*, II, p. 295. Justice Nelson stated, "Since the Act of Mch. 3d, 1839,
a patentee may make and vend or use his improvement or invention within
two whole years of the time when he makes his application for a patent,
without forfeiting or necessarily abandoning his right to a patent."

[26] *Ibid.*, I, defendant's testimony, p. 532; II, 851-855. "Southern Planter,"
Oct., 1844, pp. 237-239: Hussey stated that he saw the 1840 McCormick
reaper lying "in ruins" in Sampson's *field*.

its 'framework which had been bored for the purpose of attaching a raker's seat. William McCormick, testifying at the trial, quickly pointed out that this could not be the reaper of 1840, since a raker's seat was not added until 1845, and that a wooden, rather than an iron, divider had been employed in 1840.[27]

Besides employing able counsel and ordering depositions and elaborate model machines to be prepared, Cyrus McCormick took steps before the opening of the trial to strengthen his patent of 1847 in such a way that his success seemed doubly assured. The wording of the specification accompanying his patent could be interpreted to mean that it embraced a raker's seat only, without any reference to the combination of that improvement with the other elements of his reaper.[28] In the suit against Seymour & Morgan the defendants' counsel argued that as this patent was simply for placing a seat upon the machine, it was void, because other inventors had used a seat prior to McCormick.[29] Unconvinced by this contention,

[27] *Ibid.*, I, defendant's testimony, pp. 534-537; II, 181 ff., 194. Affidavits of Wm. P. Wood, Dec. 16, 1897, and Mch. 12, 1903, and of A. E. H. Johnson on Mch. 12, 1903. Johnson was Watson's assistant in 1855. These depositions were secured by Frank A. Flower, a biographer of E. M. Stanton. In the McCormick Historical Association Library there are numerous letters between 1897 and 1903 from Flower dealing with this matter. Wood and Johnson, in their affidavits, tell a quite different story from that given in the text. They seem to have confused the Woodward and Sampson incidents. They state that they found the 1840 machine on the Sampson plantation. By careful welding they altered its divider to suit the purposes of the defendants. The significance of their chicanery, as told by them forty-five years later, is not clear, and the present account is based upon the testimony given in the case. These affidavits, made in the case of Wood when he was on his death-bed, doubtless reveal the devious course pursued in the case, but the records do not support their contention that their cleverness had much influence upon the court. Frank A. Flower, "Edwin McMasters Stanton" (Akron, O., 1905), pp. 62-65.

[28] "Eureka," etc., Dec., 1847, pp. 49, 50, for the original specification.

[29] For the importance of this action in the Seymour & Morgan case, see the preceding chapter.

Justice Nelson held that the patent covered a combination and arrangement of parts whereby the patentee had made room for his particular type of seat upon his reaper.

This explanation answered Seymour & Morgan's charges of lack of novelty and patentability, but it greatly limited the rights which McCormick hoped the grant guaranteed exclusively to him. Consequently, because of Nelson's decision, the ambiguity of his own original specification, and the contemplated Manny suit, in 1853 McCormick petitioned the Patent Office for a reissue of his patent. He explained that it was "inoperative by reason of the defective specification, which defect has arisen from inadvertence and mistake." [30] Accompanying McCormick's petition was a revised specification which significantly differed from the one it was hoped to replace.[31] Much care was exercised to make clear that the raker's seat applied only to machines utilizing a reel and side delivery (i.e., like Manny's), but this was wholly omitted from the original specification of 1847.

Furthermore, McCormick now placed a stronger emphasis upon the fact that he claimed every combination of a raker's seat and a reel on side-delivery reapers. The import of this will be lost if it is not remembered that his patent of 1834, incorporating a reel as an essential element of his reaper, had failed of renewal. So it seems that McCormick was prompted, at least in part, by a desire to accomplish by indirection what had been directly denied to him by the Patent Office and Congress. If he could, by a rewording of his 1847 specification, gain exclusive control of all reapers using a raker's seat in combination with a reel, he would have in his power all machines using a reel, since implements without a raker's seat, or a self-rake, were

[30] *McCormick vs. Manny, I*, defendant's testimony, pp. 100 ff., letter of C. H. McCormick to the Actg. Commr. of Patents, Apr. 14, 1852: "The very critical condition of my rights requires that the question of the reissue should be decided at the earliest possible moment."

[31] For a comparison of the two specifications see *ibid.*, II, 21-24, 25-28.

obsolete by 1853. The Commissioner of Patents realized the implication of McCormick's action, and refused to reissue the patent with its new specification until the inventor had explicitly affirmed in writing that "the claim was not broadly to a combination of the reel with the seat, but to their combination *as arranged.*" [32] That is, the patent should only cover his seat, combined with the reel and the rearrangement of parts necessary to make it serviceable on *his* reaper.

With such qualifications, the patent of 1847 was reissued on May 24, 1853,[33] but two years later, when the suit against Manny was in progress, McCormick contended that he had an "exclusive right to every arrangement of the seat in combination with the reel." [34] Manny used a forker instead of a raker, and his stand was placed upon the rear of the platform rather than on the extended finger-bar, as in the case of McCormick's. Manny's answer to the plaintiff's Bill of Complaint charged that the reissue was secured not because the original specification was "defective or insufficient" but in order that his rival might include in his monopoly "new and additional matters—more . . . than were first and originally invented by the said McCormick.[35] With still more bluntness, McCormick's 1853 specification was said to be "artfully and fraudulently drawn . . . for the purpose of inducing the Commissioner of Patents to secure to the said McCormick exclusive rights greater than by law the Commissioner was authorized to grant." [36]

[32] The italics above are the author's. *McCormick vs. Manny*, **II,** pp. 1139-1143.

[33] *Ibid.*, I, defendant's testimony, p. 112.

[34] *Ibid.*, II, pp. 1139-1143.

[35] *Ibid.*, II, p. 46.

[36] *Ibid.*, I, defendant's points, p. 9: "The claims for the seat, the reel post, and the divider, are efforts to acquire a monopoly of the reaping machine, by enlarging, modifying, and changing the description and specification of particular improvements, and expanding them so as to cover principles, methods, and results, in violation of the principles and avowed

Besides the question of Manny's forker's stand, McCormick based his case upon two other principal grounds. He claimed that his angled divider (consisting of a dividing iron and iron bow) in combination with his reel, covered by his 1845 patent, was infringed by Manny's oblique wooden divider and reel. In like manner he asserted that the defendant's reel-bearer had been anticipated in the same patent, which conferred a monopoly upon this device in the form of a post fixed upon the platform of the reaper. In his Bill of Complaint McCormick naturally laid great stress upon his recent victory over Seymour & Morgan on issues which, at least when superficially considered, were identical with those involved in the present case.[37]

The trial began on September 20, 1855, at Cincinnati, before Justice McLean and Judge Drummond, and the counsel argued for ten days. At its start Cyrus McCormick, as always, was confident of success. Two weeks before the opening of the trial, William McCormick, after talking with his elder brother, reported his impressions to a friend: "We *expect* to use up Manny and Co. so far as *making* Reapers go and make them *pay well* for the past. We shall see ere long at all events. . . . I believe there is *scarcely a doubt* but we can stop *all* who use the Reel (Self Raker or not) upon the *necessary combination,* though the old patent is out. If we do we can choose our makers of machines."[38] This assurance yielded to uncertainty after George Harding, in a masterly argument, had answered Edward Dickerson, McCormick's counsel, on every point. "The

policy of the patent laws. And the result aimed at by the complainant would withdraw, from the public, the contribution of many minds, and subject an instrument of great public utility to a private monopoly, without even a decent color of right."

[37] *Ibid.,* II, pp. 2-11.

[38] W. S. McCormick, from Kerr's Creek, Va., to W. J. Hanna, Sept. 5, 1855. C. H. McCormick, from Washington, to J. L. Wilson, Sept. 4, 1855, and to H. Blakesley, from New York, Sept. 11, 1855.

case looks now rather dubious," confided T. J. Paterson to William McCormick on September 28. "Johnson [who was to close for McCormick] may bring all up right, if not, look out for Squalls and Breakers ahead."

Johnson was unable to convince the bench, and when the verdict was announced on January 16, 1856, it supported Manny in every particular.[39] The bitterness of complete defeat, including the payment of the heavy costs of the suit, could not have been much relieved by the compliment which Justice McLean paid to McCormick in his decision. "He [McCormick] is left in full possession of his invention, which has so justly secured to him, at home and in foreign countries, a renown honorable to him and to his country, a renown which can never fade from the memory, so long as the harvest home shall be gathered. The bill is dismissed at the cost of the complainant."

Justice McLean held that Manny's use of a reel in combination with a divider, which was different from the plaintiff's, was not an infringement of the latter's patent of 1845. "A patent, which claims mechanical powers or things in combination, is not infringed by using a part of the combination." [40] In like manner, Manny's counsel had shown without difficulty that McCormick had abandoned the reel-post, covered by this patent, and had substituted a reel-bearer, which had been used by many inventors before his adoption of it. The court sustained this view and ruled that Manny had not infringed.[41]

On the third charge the opinion of Justice McLean can best be quoted: "It must be admitted that the combination of the raker's seat with the reel, as claimed by the plaintiff, was new. And a very important question arises, how far this claim extends." The judge then pointed out the difference in position

[39] *McCormick vs. Manny*, I, opinion of Justice McLean, p. 19. "American Agriculturist," Feb., 1856, p. 98.
[40] *McCormick vs. Manny*, I, opinion of Justice McLean, pp. 10, 11.
[41] *Ibid.*, p. 12.

and in construction of the two seats at issue. "To seat the raker on Manny's machine does not require the same elements of combination that were essential in McCormick's invention. . . . It [Manny's] is consequently substantially different from his [McCormick's]. The seat was not the thing invented (in either case), but the change of the machinery, to make a place for it. And where the seat may be placed on the platform, or on any part of the machine, which does not require substantially the same invention and improvement as McCormick's, there can be no infringement of his right." [42]

Cyrus McCormick immediately took steps to appeal the case to the United States Supreme Court.[43] John H. Manny died of consumption at Rockford on January 30, 1856, shortly after the news of his victory reached him, and his former associates and heirs now became the defendants in the case.[44] McCormick announced that a higher tribunal had yet to speak, and that because in all probability the decision would be reversed, all makers and users of Manny machines would be held responsible.[45] Of course this was merely a gesture of defiance which neither restrained the Manny company from manufacturing nor checked the widespread sale of its reapers.[46]

Nevertheless the letters of McCormick during the two years which elapsed while the case awaited its turn on the docket of the Supreme Court, make clear that the Manny heirs were

[42] Ibid., pp. 14, 18-19.
[43] Ibid., II, p. 1026. He appealed on Mch. 22, 1856.
[44] "Ohio Cultivator," Mch. 1, 1856, p. 73. "Michigan Farmer," Mch., 1856, p. 87.
[45] Notice of C. H. McCormick, dated Feb. 26, 1856, in the "Valley Star" of Apr. 10, 1856.
[46] During the years 1856-58, McCormick, through his agents, kept a careful account of the Manny sales and of those of other competitors whose machines were believed to infringe upon his patents. See the form letter, signed by C. H. McCormick and sent to all agents, in L.P.C.B. No. 8, p. 411. C. H. to W. S. McCormick, from Baltimore, Sept. 29, Oct. 1, 23, 1856. W. S. McCormick to J. L. Wilson, June 25, 1856.

not so certain of success as their published boasts would lead one to believe. The course of this lawsuit from 1856 to 1858 was tangled with the efforts of Cyrus McCormick and others to gain from Congress renewals of their patents. Early in 1857 steps were taken to form the first great reaper combine in history. Peter Watson approached McCormick with the authorization of the Manny interests, Seymour & Morgan, Atkins-Wright, Wood & Co., Palmer & Williams, and Howard & Co. (Ketchum Mower).

These were the largest agricultural implement concerns in the United States and they had been most active for some years in thwarting McCormick's efforts to extend his 1834 patent, and to defeat him in his suit against Manny. They now appeared ready to withdraw their opposition and henceforward to pay McCormick a fee of $30 a machine, if his patent were extended and if all would agree to fix the price of each reaper at $160, and to stabilize all agents' commissions on sales.

Cyrus McCormick was naturally most favorably inclined toward this plan when it was under discussion early in 1857. Such an arrangement would give him almost complete control of the reaper output of the country, since he would have at least a thirty-dollar advantage per machine over every other builder.[47] Why these negotiations were dropped about one year after they were begun, is not clear. McCormick's letters suggest that Congress was too busy with corruption investigation committees, Kansas, slavery, and the Dred Scott decision to bother with his patent-extension. Reverdy Johnson ap-

---

[47] The details of the scheme varied. On Jan. 23, 1857, Cyrus wrote to W. S. from Washington: "The parties above [named in text], if [patent is] extended, to be licensed and to pay [me] $30 fee, and then a *separate* arrangement with Manny and Co. to unite with me in getting patent of '45 extended, they then to pay $10 under *it,* and *others, all others,* to pay what I choose to charge. While Watson has the power at the Patent Office, and has no doubt that we *can extend it.* . . . Price of machines to be $160, and Manny's to be the same, and same *commissions.*"

parently convinced him that the Supreme Court would decide favorably in the Manny suit, and that he could make better terms with his rivals after he was armed with that verdict.[48]

At the same time his competitors had in mind another scheme which was quite different in purport from the one just mentioned. They urged Howard & Co. to bring suit, for patent-infringement, against McCormick in Chicago, and thus to embarrass him in his efforts at Washington before Congress and the Supreme Court.[49] On April 17, 1857, McCormick wrote a letter to his brother which sheds much light upon the nature of the business war that was being waged:

I write you a line to say that I *now* think there is no danger of a suit by Howard and Co. (Ketchum machine). I agreed to pay Keller [a prominent patent lawyer] $1500 if no suit, or he not in the case for them,—had been with them—and after seeing them he accepted, though I told him would just as soon he would go with them. I had talked with him about case, and felt due to make the offer. I then explained my case to him, and he was to, and did see Howard, and is to see him again, and I think the case is so plain that there can not be much danger of an effort by them, while I doubt not they had contemplated a move at Chicago.

Possibly the panic of 1857, crippling or eliminating McCormick's competitors, played its part in rendering these plans abortive.

Certainly Cyrus McCormick was most hopeful of victory at the close of 1857. His marriage was planned for early in 1858 and it would be gratifying to have that auspicious event accompanied by success in the courts and by the large increase in

[48] C. H. to W. S. McCormick, from Washington, Jan. 23, Feb. 7 and 20, 1857, and from New York, Apr. 3 and May 21, 1857.

[49] *Idem* to *idem,* from Baltimore, Oct. 23, 1856: "I have strong doubt whether I should go to Chicago this fall, as it may be the intention of the combined Reaper enemies to sue me there . . . for the purpose of troubling me when I must be in Washington. . . . My last effort probably to get my extension."

business that would surely result. He wrote of buying land in Chicago to provide for the anticipated growth of his factory, and suggested that the new prosperity would warrant the inclusion of other members of his family in the business. Even if he failed to win his decade-long fight for the extension of his 1834 patent, a victory over Manny would bring him almost equivalent advantages. In this mood he wrote to his brother on Christmas Day, 1857:

I have in fact the strongest confidence in carrying the Manny case, and if I do, I believe it will result in everything *I have hoped for from patent extension.* The opposing parties are very uneasy, have been sounding me. . . . If I permit [?] them, they are all anxious to unite with me in getting my 2nd and 3rd patents extended at P. Office, they (some select firms) paying me a fee under them, and there is, I think *strong* ground to calculate upon this. So that, in fact, I think there is just now the strongest prospect that I have had, and I don't badly err in these things generally. It is a *favorable time* too just now (in view of my expected change [marriage]) for such a turn, if so. If I can bring all this out successfully it may make such an *increase of business* as to engage all in it better than not.[50]

He had not been pleased with the way Edward Dickerson had handled his case and had released him as counsel. Justice Curtis, pleading an inadequate salary, resigned from the Supreme Court in 1857, and McCormick wished to secure his services. Reverdy Johnson advised strongly against this, and succeeded in persuading him to reëngage Dickerson. Johnson felt that Curtis's dissenting opinion in the Dred Scott case, delivered in March, 1857, with other matters connected with that famous decision, was the real cause for his resignation, and that he would be almost the last person to choose to appear in McCormick's behalf before his recent associates.[51]

[50] C. H. to W. S. McCormick, Dec. 25, 1857, and Dec. 21 and Dec. 29, 1857.
[51] Jas. Campbell to C. H. McCormick, Oct. 22, 23, 29, 1857.

Notwithstanding the care with which his lawyers were selected, and despite his expectations of victory, the United States Supreme Court, in May, 1858, upheld the decision of the Circuit Court, and the Manny case was over. On May 1, 1858, the "Ohio Cultivator" announced with pleasure:

The Supreme Court this morning, decided the suit between . . . McCormick and Manny, in favor of Manny on every point. The case involved several important principles, and a large amount of money. It was elaborately argued during five days, with an unprecedented array of working models and illustrations, showing the operation of various reaping machines in the grain field.

The decision affects all the manufacturers and users of reaping machines throughout the country. Mr. Justice Grier delivered the opinion of the Supreme Court, affirming the former decision and dismissing McCormick's bill with costs.[52]

Cyrus McCormick was still the largest producer of reapers in the world.[53] Two of his patents were in force, although neither of them was sufficiently inclusive to cause his rivals much embarrassment. One of them covered his raker's seat, in combination with the other parts of his reaper, and would

[52] "Ohio Cultivator," May 1, 1858, p. 133. McCormick circular, of May, 1858: "I am in the same position as before the suit, and although others may, as heretofore, study to imitate my machines according to my original patent, and as nearly copy my patented improvements as possible, yet after all they cannot build and sell my identical machine. They are still obliged to *haul the raker on the platform,* where he must submit to having the dust thrown in his eyes by the operation of the reel, and to be jolted over the clods by the little platform wheel, necessarily *racking their machines to pieces.* This accounts for the great durability of my machine as compared with others."

[53] This statement needs a slight qualification. In 1855, Manny manufactured 2,893 machines, and McCormick 2,534. In 1857 the Manny firm, to its sorrow, made 4,565, and the latter 4,091. *Hussey vs. McCormick,* pp. 75, 232. The next year the Manny output dropped to 2,500. "McCormick's Extension Case, Patent of 1845," pp. 109, 235 ff. Manny was said to have sold in the Middle West, from 1848 to 1858, about 15,000 machines. This total does not include the output of other manufacturers making his machine.

protect him in this regard for three more years. The other, due to expire in 1859, embraced a reel-post which the inventor had long since abandoned, a divider—still most effective—and a reverse-angled sickle which McCormick had greatly modified in 1850. The temper of Congress was hostile to any patent-extensions on implements essential to the farmer, and unless their mood changed, McCormick would be stripped of all his monopolies by 1861.

Herein lies the great significance of the Manny case for the grain farmer and the reaper-manufacturer. If McCormick had, like Hussey, lacked business ability, the decision would have foreshadowed the end of his career. On the other hand, if he had not been aggressive, the suit would never have been brought. The vigor with which he was opposed symbolizes the power that he wielded in the reaper and farmer world, and the value of the principles he had invented, to every manufacturer who wished to produce a successful reaper. By the extent of the opposition aroused against his claims, his rivals had paid him a great tribute. He was to prove during the next twenty-five years that he could lead in reaper-manufacturing without the assistance of his three first patents.

By 1857, Cyrus McCormick, defeated by Manny, refused an extension of his patent of 1834, and threatened by the manufacturers of the Ketchum Mower, seemed a legitimate prey for all comers. Hussey, no longer a serious competitor in the harvest field, joined the hue and cry and struck at his rival through the courts. He forearmed himself for the battle by securing a reissue of his 1847 patent, on the grounds that his original specification was void because of a "defective and insufficient description" of his improvement. This was a common strategy of inventors, and McCormick had practised it four years before, when engaged in his contest with Seymour & Morgan. In his amended specification Hussey restated with added emphasis the fact that his patent of 1847 covered the use of an open-back guard finger in combination with a vibrating scallop-edged cutter.[54]

Exactly one month later Hussey, through his counsel, Peter Watson, filed his Bill of Complaint against McCormick in the United States Circuit Court for the northern district of Illinois. He asked for damages for past infringements and an injunction to restrain McCormick from selling the three thousand or more 1857 machines in course of construction, which incorporated elements covered by his reissued patent of 1847. More particularly, he charged that his competitor had pirated his—

combination of a vibrating scalloped cutter, the indentations of whose edge act as a series of moving shear-blades, with slotted guard fingers, the sides of which act as a corresponding series of fixed shear-blades, the parts of such fingers forming the slot being connected at the front ends only, leaving the rear of the slot open and free for the escape of material that would otherwise clog the cutter.[55]

McCormick, assisted by Edward N. Dickerson and Charles M. Keller,[56] in his answer to this Bill of Complaint and by the testimony of many witnesses at the ensuing trial in 1858,[57] attempted to show that there were but three new things in Hussey's 1847 patent—the slots in the top of his guard fingers, the use of a smooth-edged, scalloped cutter in combination with these fingers, and the close contact which the under side of this blade made with these fingers; that the patent should be strictly construed to embrace only these three improvements; that, in

[54] The reissue was dated Apr. 14, 1857. For a comparison of the specification accompanying this reissue, with the one of 1847, see *Hussey vs. McCormick*, pp. 7-9, 261-263; "Emery's Journal of Agriculture and Prairie Farmer" (Chicago), July 22, 1858, p. 55.

[55] *Hussey vs. McCormick*, Hussey's Bill of Complaint, May 14, 1857, pp. 1-6, 20.

[56] *Ibid.*, p. 24.

[57] *Ibid.*, pp. 10-19. L.P.C.B. No. 12, pp. 42, 236, 307-310, 393-395, 445, 446.

such case, there had been no infringement; that, if it were broadly interpreted, McCormick's use of a humpbacked guard finger cut away on its under side, prior to 1844, had anticipated Hussey's improvements; that McCormick's cutter did not operate with a shear-action and therefore did not infringe, and that Hussey's amended specification was, by design, made more inclusive than the original of 1847.[58]

These contentions did not convince the court, and on September 19, 1859,[59] Justice McLean upheld Hussey's claims. An injunction was issued restraining McCormick from a further use, without license, of the elements in question. A Master was appointed to adjudicate the damages,[60] and an assessment of over $80,000 was eventually made.[61] In the decision of the court Hussey was declared to be the first inventor of the combination of the open-slotted guard finger and scalloped cutter, and his patent of 1847 was held to cover any such combination, no matter whether the blade was smooth or sickle-edged. McCormick's patent of 1834 did not embrace this appliance, and he had abandoned and never patented the combination of the straight-edged sickle blade and slotted wooden fingers, which he had used for several years after 1840.[62] This open-back guard finger, that McCormick, and perhaps others, seem to have used before Hussey, was the only noteworthy element patented by Hussey which survives in the

[58] Ibid., p. 269.
[59] Ibid., pp. 303, 304.
[60] Ibid., pp. 311, 312.
[61] Patent Office Records, "Hussey Extension Case, Patent of 1847" (Washington, 1861), pp. 13-22. The case against McCormick, and his efforts to win an extension of his 1833 patent, had cost him over $44,000. He received $80,618.73 from McCormick, and Watson took 10% of this as his fee. Ibid., p. 31, McCormick seems to have paid him $18,595 as a license fee in 1858.
[62] Hussey vs. McCormick, pp. 303-308. "Ohio Cultivator," Jan. 15, 1860, p. 25. "Rural Register," July 1, 1859, p. 8; Oct. 1, 1859, p. 106. "Michigan Farmer," Jan. 28, 1860, p. 28.

452 CYRUS HALL McCORMICK

modern reaper. Hussey was killed in 1860, in a railroad accident, and his heirs secured a reissue of his 1847 patent in 1861.[63]

The second chapter in the history of reaper rivalry naturally closes on the eve of the Civil War, with Cyrus McCormick much stronger at the end than he had been at the outset of the decade. He was helping the farmers and they were aiding him by growing more grain and pushing ever farther toward the West. Unquestionably his wealth would have been much greater if he had won the Manny case and if he had been able to renew his 1834 patent, but by 1858 he was ready to distribute as well as to make money, and the Presbyterian Church was characteristically the first object of his philanthropy.[64]

[63] "Hussey Extension Case, Patent of 1847," pp. 5, 11, 12, 23, 28. When Hussey died, the value of his estate, excepting his patent, was $84,158.27. The appraised value of his Baltimore shop was $500, the same figure as in 1848. The expense of his business for the twelve years was over $195,000, and the proceeds, including over $37,000 in outstanding and doubtful debts, were over $277,000. "Rural Register," Aug. 15, 1860, p. 58; Jan. 1, 1861, p. 201.

[64] W. S. to C. H. McCormick, Mch. 14, 1857, L.P.C.B. No. 5, p. 561, "Last year's business was in all quarters highly successful and I think will show a profit of some $300,000, though yet impossible to make a statement." "McCormick Extension Case, Patent of 1845," pp. 11-15, McCormick's own statement of profits up to Dec. 7, 1858.

CHAPTER XIX

CYRUS McCORMICK AND HIS REAPER IN RETROSPECT

BETWEEN 1850 and 1860, Cyrus McCormick spent many days in the court-room and even more in searching for witnesses, securing depositions, supervising the building of models, and consulting with his counsel. If to these engagements are added his decade-long patent-extension battle in Congress, his many controversies in the press, his several trips abroad, his attendance in the harvest field and at agricultural fairs, and the manifold duties and responsibilities connected with the manufacture and sale of reapers at his growing factory in Chicago, the complexity of his existence becomes apparent. Concern for his church and his relatives, trips to the springs of New York, and, in 1857 and 1858, his courtship and marriage, filled the interstices of his life—or, rather, overlapped with the other important subjects which commanded his attention. Fortunately he was blessed with a powerful physique and good health. From dawn until late at night he concerned himself with his task. Working almost two ordinary business days in every one, he had a decided advantage over competitors whose health and temperament demanded a more moderate schedule.

Although the McCormick reaper was of such great importance to the farmer, and although its inventor was surprisingly indulgent with his debtors, it is not strange that the graingrowers tended to picture him as one who was amassing an enormous fortune at their expense. His enterprise grew from a country blacksmith shop to almost world-wide proportions within fifteen years, and he changed perforce during the same period from a farmer of the Valley of Virginia to one of the outstanding figures in the big-business group of that time. Notwithstanding the half-million dollars owed to him by farmers in 1858, of which he estimated that perhaps forty per cent might eventually be collected, he was very wealthy, as wealthy men were reckoned then.[1] He was one of the great of the land, and took pride in the friendship of distinguished men. Justifiably enough, his fame rested upon his genius as an inventor, although his money had accumulated after his original patent lapsed. In 1858 he still led the field, and was to continue in the forefront until his death, over twenty-five years later. His talent for invention had not waned, and his letters of the late 1850's are often filled with suggestions for the improvement of his reaper and mower.[2]

In the press of business and litigation he came to be regarded as a hard man, respected by all but loved by few. He had reason to be proud, and his status in life permitted him to leave the petty details of his business to his subordinates. He held himself somewhat aloof, traveling from city to city accompanied by his secretaries and lawyers, writing lengthy letters to his brothers in Chicago upon matters of broad policy, and tiring the half-dozen helpers around him who sought to keep step with his ceaseless energy.[3] In the autumn of 1854 when the suit against Seymour & Morgan reached a crisis, one of his assistants wrote to William McCormick from Albany:

C. H. is in good health but has been bothered to death. I wonder how he can have a distinct idea on any subject. It was my intention

[1] *Supra*, p. 369, ftn. His net assets on Feb. 28, 1858, were estimated to be $1,132,095.88. See L.P.C.B. No. 11, pp. 217-223. "McCormick Extension Case, Patent of 1845," pro testimony, p. 197.
[2] E.g., C. H. to W. S. McCormick, Aug. 11, 13, Oct. 14, Dec. 20, 1856.
[3] C. H. McCormick, Jr., "In the Days of the Elder McCormick," in the "Harvester World," Mch., 1925, p. 2.

to have got off this morning but C. H. wished to see me in his room yesterday and on going up with him he soon became so absorbed in matters pertaining to the case that my presence was unknown to him, and I will wait till I can learn his wishes.[4]

In the early days of his enterprise he rode a horse as the only means to get quickly from place to place. An occasional early morning or evening canter remained his sole method of physical exercise, after prosperity came. Brief visits to the springs of New York State, more for reasons of health than for recreation, were his only vacations during these years. He had implicit faith in the efficacy of Congress Water, and other similar mineral beverages, to ward off most ills. So he wrote late in 1856, "Say to L[eander] and H[enrietta] I think they had better buy either *Congress* water from *Saratoga Springs* and at all *Hotels,* or Avon Springs water, write *proprietor.* I have used a bottle Congress water a day for at least six weeks, and have *much improved flesh and digestion.*" [5]

A brief paragraph written by him in 1860 describes his appearance and in it he also unconsciously reveals his conception of the art of portrait-painting:

It may be proper for the artist to know should I not reach Philadelphia in time for the finish of my portrait, that my hair is a very dark brown,—eyes dark, though not black, complexion fresh and health good, 5 ft. 11½ inc. high, weighing 200 lbs. I prefer my portrait taken with more of a front face, if consistent with the position assigned me in the painting and would send you a likeness if wanted.[6]

[4] J. L. Wilson to W. S. McCormick, Oct. 25, 1854.

[5] On Oct. 8, 1857, he wrote to William McCormick from Avon Springs, "I suppose it [Congress Water] would not cost more than 12 cents a bottle (I paid 25 cts at Hotels) which would be for 5 weeks say $5 each, which would be comparatively nothing . . . should *think* it would be useful for Caroline and Mr. S[hields] too,—may not be for C[aroline]." At a time when he was dealing in very large sums of money, it is curious and significant to find him so meticulous about the price of bottled spring water.

[6] C. H. McCormick to John Skirving, Apr. 25, 1860. This was a large canvas, portraying the leading inventors of the United States.

He wished to look squarely at the world, whether peering at it from a canvas or facing it in real life.

He appreciated the need for relaxation and exercise but rarely found the time to follow his own better judgment. He expected hard work from his associates, although he came to realize that his own strength and capacity for sustained effort were unique, and that it was unfair to use himself as a gage with which to measure the efficiency of his employees. He wrote his brother in 1857:

It will be necessary for you and L. J. to *take care* to *avoid interruptions* from attention of body and mind to business, as much as possible. . . . The business is entirely too large and the responsibilities *now* too immense to admit of a departure from *regular business system* and *hours* (of course some *exceptions*). This success in business is the foundation of *everything*. . . . I don't want to be severe but you will know the importance of all I say, and *you* could *not fail* to feel it in my position. Think of the *times,* and now there is near $50,000 drawn out and applied to investments (I think) etc. etc.[7]

And yet William McCormick, to whom this letter was directed, disliked the routine and confinement of office life, suffered from dyspepsia, longed for the apple-butter and home-cured Virginia hams of his boyhood days, and frequently made a summer pilgrimage to his beloved Valley of Virginia to breathe the pure mountain air and talk once again to his old neighbors.[8]

[7] Letter of Sept. 12, 1857; again on Dec. 16, 1857, he wrote even more sharply to William: "Do you and L. get to the factory at 7 *regularly*— and keep things up there regularly in proportion to the responsibility and magnitude of that concern? I know the liability to get *worse* and *worse* in regard to *promptness,* and if it is *anything like* it was in summer, it is bad enough. . . . Retire at 9 if need be, and get up . . . at 5. . . ."

[8] Letters of W. S. McCormick in L.P.C.B. No. 3, p. 444; No. 9, pp. 107, 152, 283, 430, 452, 486, 498, 750; No. 14, p. 337. He was also seeking a milch cow at this time to bring to Chicago for the use of his family. He wrote concerning apple-butter: "My old Mother used to always make it and I do not like to do without it."

Nor was Cyrus McCormick always so stern with his younger brothers. Less than four months after the letter from which a quotation has just been made, he wrote on the same subject, but in a very different spirit:

And then, of course, first of all things, as I have always said, your place is to arrange to take as much time and exercise for yourself as your health requires to recruit it properly. This I have *always* urged upon you, and you can only judge of. While, as I said, I write and talk entirely about business, as necessary for so large a concern, I am sure I do feel constantly for the interests of you all, as a father does, being the oldest, and from the circumstances of my position in business, at the head, in a business point of view.[9]

Society and the lighter side of life had slight attraction for McCormick prior to 1858. Those who knew him well and accompanied him on his never-ending trips about the country, occasionally wrote of him to his brothers in a tone of raillery which would hardly have pleased the serious-minded inventor if he had known. Thomas J. Paterson informed William McCormick in February, 1855, that "the last time I saw him [C. H.] at Washington the Women were in full cry after him. He thought the *Dear Angels* wanted his money and ran the other way as fast as they pursued. If justice had been done him they would have caught him, put him in leading strings, hung him before this time. He would not want the peril of this escape brought to public notice, would he?" [10] Over two years later, in August, 1857, he was writing in the same vein of the "glorious nibbles" which Cyrus might have from ladies *"wealthier, fairer and lovelier by odds* than they were last

[9] C. H. to W. S. McCormick, Dec. 25, 1857.
[10] T. J. Paterson to W. S. McCormick, Feb. 18, 1855. See also *idem* to *idem*, Sept. 23, 1854. C. H. McCormick, Jr., was told by his father many years later that the latter was greatly attracted by a daughter of Reverdy Johnson, his counsel, for some months during the mid 1850's.

year," if he would only consent to come and stay a month at the springs of Avon, New York.[11]

But at this time Cyrus was spending over six weeks in Chicago, the longest stay he had made in that city for more than two years.[12] On the very day that Paterson mailed his letter William and Leander McCormick wrote to their sister Mary Caroline Shields that they "wouldn't be surprised if C. H. picked up a wife." [13] The young and charming Nancy Fowler, of Clayton, Jefferson County, New York, was visiting Mr. and Mrs. Isaac L. Lyon in Chicago.[14] Her presence in the city doubtless accounts for the unusual duration of Cyrus McCormick's visit.

By September 23 the inventor was in New York, hinting mysteriously to his brother of receiving an "important document from Chicago—more anon—till then 'nuff said.'" If these words alone remained to illuminate these months, the student of McCormick's career, hitherto accustomed to letters filled with prosaic details of lawsuits, manufacturing, and

[11] *Idem* to *idem*, Aug. 7 and 21, 1857. W. S. McCormick to T. J. Paterson, Aug. 28, 1857, L.P.C.B. No. 8, p. 595.
[12] W. S. McCormick to W. T. Rush, Sept. 5, 1857. L.P.C.B. No. 8, p. 538.
[13] L.P.C.B. No. 8, p. 521. J. B. to W. S. McCormick, Aug. 30, 1857.
[14] Her parents were Melzar and Clarissa S. Fowler, and she was born at Brownsville, Jefferson County, N. Y., on Feb. 8, 1835. Tradition has it that Cyrus McCormick first met her in June, 1857, at a party in Leander's home. She sang in the choir of the North Presbyterian Church which he attended, and he was captivated by her contralto voice. It is remembered that after the first meeting he often stopped, during the noon hour, at the Lyons' home to hear her sing. His interest in vocal and instrumental music had never waned since his boyhood in Virginia, when he played the fiddle and led the singing in the church. Miss Fowler's father was a general storekeeper and manufacturer of potash and soda at Brownsville. He died when she was seven months of age and her mother died when she was seven. She then lived with her grandmother at Clayton, N. Y., and was educated at private schools in Fulton and Troy. She taught school for at least one year. MS. of Maria Lyon, "Recollections of Mrs. Cyrus H. McCormick (Nancy Maria Fowler)"; MS. "Genealogical History of Jennie Fowler Bates."

Nancy Fowler McCormick about 1870

reaper mechanics, would realize that something unprecedented had happened to lead the inventor to write so light-heartedly, and with even an unheard-of dash of slang. In truth, the courtship, begun in Chicago, had been continued by letter, and McCormick joyfully confided to his brother that he had experienced the customary qualms of a suitor after he had despatched the marriage proposal through the mail. "It is *gone,* and I *suppose* I'm in for it," he wrote on September 25.[15]

Miss Fowler agreed to an early date for the marriage, but the Manny case before the Supreme Court kept McCormick impatiently waiting in Washington. January 26, 1858, was tentatively set for the ceremony and, fortunately for this arrangement, he was able to reach Chicago on time. On Christmas Day, 1857, he wrote to his brother William:

> I trust that, under Providence, in the anticipated change in my mode of living, I shall realize a blessing. . . . It would afford me *great pleasure* if, in view particularly of the contemplated change . . . I could settle down with you all, that we might be . . . all together, as a united family, and I hope this may yet be the case ere long. But while rather retired quiet would be to me desirable, we should always make the position that *duty* assigns to us acceptable and agreeable.[16]

Cyrus McCormick and Nancy Fowler were married at noon on January 26 at the Lyons' home; by the Rev. Nathan L. Rice of the North Presbyterian Church. Few guests were invited to witness the ceremony, but that evening about five hundred friends of the bride and groom gathered at the home of William

[15] C. H. to W. S. McCormick, from New York, Dec. 7, 1857: "Now that I regard it [the marriage] as a *fixed fact,* the next step is the one to be looked at. And I suppose you and L[eander] will fix up *considerably* your houses, etc. . . . And I suppose you and L. J. will between you now at least get a new carriage." *Idem* to *idem,* from New York, Dec. 16 and 21, 1857. W. S. McCormick to Emma Grigsby (his sister-in-law), Jan. 4, 1858, L.P.C.B. No. 10, p. 141.

[16] See also, W. S. to C. H. McCormick, Jan. 11 and 18, 1858, in L.P.C.B. No. 10, pp. 216 and 323.

McCormick to offer their congratulations. A reporter for the "Chicago Daily Press" waxed eloquent in his description of this reception:

One of the most pleasant and hospitable residences in the North Division was thrown open last evening, and despite the unfavorable weather . . . the guests gathered and filled the apartments to overflowing. They came and seemed scarcely to add to the number, they went and were little missed, as carriage after carriage deposited its freight of fair women and brave men to take their places. Within, all was gaiety and the sound of music, and the murmur of conversation, and the merry laugh. . . .

The party was the largest, and one of the most brilliant of the season, and will be marked and memorable in festive annals.

If our townsman, unknown to himself, has delayed the ceremonies for a few more years than is customary, for the express purpose of linking his fate with the one who now bears his name, we risk nothing in pronouncing the prize well worth his waiting, and in *reaping* one of the fairest flowers our city can boast, he has but added the orange blossoms to the laurels of his world famous title of nobility.

Our lady readers will be on tip-toe to learn of the bride, and how she was dressed, and who was there and how they were dressed, and who was the belle of the evening,—who besides the beautiful bride was the observed of observers. We suppose all who were there have informed those in the immediate vicinity, who were in this respect less favored, that the bride wore a white silk dress with an over-dress of *tulle,* that those who had heard of the rich trosseau [sic] looked to see diamonds and saw nothing of ornament to add to, without increasing, the simplest and therefore the highest of adornment of beauty, a simple wreath and boquet [sic] of white flowers.

Of the wedding gifts, and diamonds we have small need to speak. To wings fleeter than ever vouchsafed to local items—(will the ladies, dear angels, forgive us if we say it)—have been given the report of the generous richness of the trosseau, and we have no mind to spoil by anticipating, the telling of the same, for any of our fair readers. . . .[17]

[17] "Chicago Daily Press," Jan. 27, 1858.

After the reception Cyrus McCormick and his bride left Chicago, to spend the rest of the winter and the spring in Washington. They were present in the court-room when the unfavorable verdict in the Manny case was delivered, in March, and the inventor was also unsuccessful at this time in his effort to secure a patent-extension from Congress. In May, 1858, his brother William was told that the "Old Gentleman with his small family comprising his wife and her cousin are living as comfortably and pleasantly as you could imagine." [18]

Mrs. McCormick was in complete sympathy with her husband and his enterprise, and ably supported him in all of his endeavors during their twenty-six years of life together. As one of the family circle, as a hostess, and as a business counselor, she was equally in her element. During the later years of Cyrus McCormick's career, in the management of his vast interests, he came to rely more and more upon her skilled judgment. Under her influence his philosophy of life became more tolerant and kindly, and she led him to share and to find enjoyment in the society of his time.

Although the inventor had changed much in economic and social status between 1845 and 1858, there were certain constants in his life as characteristic of these years as of his youth. A maximum of work from his employees and loyalty to the firm were demanded, but free time must be given to all who wished to go to "Wednesday evening meeting." [19] Besides his devotion to his business and his concern for his family, of which he always considered himself the head, another most influential guiding principle was his Calvinistic faith. The stern doctrines of Presbyterianism, learned in his boyhood, were a comfort and an aid to him when he had attained large

[18] J. Campbell to W. S. McCormick, May 8, 1858. W. S. McCormick to R. G. Payne, Feb. 22, 1858, L.P.C.B. No. 10, p. 766, and to J. B. McCormick, Apr. 6, 1858, ibid., No. 12, p. 586.

[19] C. H. to W. S. McCormick, from Cleveland, O., Dec. 10, 1853. Supra, Chap. I, pp. 11 ff.

success as a manufacturer of reapers. In fact, his religion and his vocation blended, and the intense faith he always displayed in his reaper and in himself, found merely another manifestation in his love for his church. "Business is not inconsistent with Christianity," he wrote in 1845, "but the latter ought to be a help to the former, giving a confidence and resignation, after using all *proper means*." [20]

His faith required him to make the utmost effort to attain his purpose honestly; but if he failed, his lack of success was ascribed to an overruling and inscrutable Providence which knew best, and against which it was sinful to complain. This deep conviction spurred him to fight to the finish for an extension of his patent and against those who pirated his inventions; but once defeated, he could go ahead with few regrets that he had failed. It had been meant so, and his mounting success, despite these apparent checks, was ample proof to him that Providence was on his side. In the same letter from which a quotation has just been made he added:

This is the point that should be aimed at, the feeling that should be cherished, unconditional submission and resignation to the will and hand of Providence; and with His smiles the most crooked ways may be made straight, chastisements converted into blessings. But for the fact that Providence has seemed to assist me in our business, it has at times seemed that I would almost sink under the weight of responsibility hanging upon me. But I believe the Lord will help us out. How grateful should we be. How humble on account of unworthiness. And yet how rejoicing that unworthy as we are, the law has been satisfied, and we may be saved by *faith*.

The following words of McCormick, written twelve years later, might well have been a continuation of the foregoing: "So that on the whole, after doing the best that can be, there is abundant cause to thank God and take courage. *My hope*

[20] C. H. to W. S. McCormick, from Cincinnati, May 15, 1845.

you know was always large, while I think that Providence is with us and will defend us as heretofore. Let us be thankful as we should and of good cheer." [21] With such a helper, McCormick found need for few other advisers on questions of large moment. He was a solitary and forceful figure by 1855.

Believing so unreservedly in the efficacy of Calvinism both as a guide in life and as a way to heaven, McCormick naturally sought by all the means in his power to promote the spread of his denomination. The state of religion, and of Presbyterianism in particular, in the cities and towns of the United States which he visited in the course of his business were often the subject for comment in his letters. An inspiring sermon led him to send the text to his brothers and to write a paragraph or more about the preacher's discourse. He was active in the religious life of his neighborhood in Virginia, and his removal to Chicago in 1848 furnished him an opportunity to promote Presbyterianism in a field where that denomination was not so completely a master as in his native valley. He contributed generously to the church and was instrumental in increasing its influence and its membership. Since he believed that religion was a remedy for all the ills of life, he was confident that the slavery agitation could be stilled by the voice of the pulpit. In the pursuit of this ideal, he succeeded in transferring to Chicago an Indiana school for the training of Presbyterian ministers. This institution was later called the McCormick Theological Seminary, and was the first large beneficiary of the inventor's philanthropy.[22]

Cyrus McCormick had no desire to hold public office before the period of the Civil War. Even after 1860, when he began to play an influential rôle in Illinois politics, he was moved by a wish to do his share toward restoring peace between the

---

[21] C. H. to W. S. McCormick, from Washington, D. C., Dec. 25, 1857.
[22] For minor examples of his generosity see Wm. S. Plumer of Allegheny City, Pa., to C. H. McCormick, June 27, 1855; C. H. McCormick to Rachel D. W. McClung, Sept. 24, 1858, L.P.C.B. No. 14, p. 801.

North and South rather than by the ambition to add the title of statesman to his honors as inventor and manufacturer. His character did not fit him for the public forum. He was always a stanch Democrat, and as early as 1840 was a member of the Rockbridge County Democratic Committee organized to help reëlect President Van Buren.[23] The emotionalism of that campaign, played up by the Whigs, repelled him. He wrote scornfully to a neighbor of the "humbugs of the Log-Cabin, hard-cider, coon-skins, and ginger-cake party,—expenditure—furniture—union of purse and sword—one currency for the government, another for the people—corruption, etc., etc." [24]

From that time until the Civil War, very few references to political events are found in his correspondence. Although a Democrat and a Southerner, he was not stirred by the Mexican War, and he expected the reaper business to go on as usual notwithstanding the calls for recruits. In short, his energy was always focused upon a few subjects—his reaper, his factory, his family, and his church. Other matters which required attention during this formative period were distractions hardly to be tolerated.

Although Cyrus McCormick did not participate in the political life of the ante-bellum period, in his letters to his brothers he occasionally made known his attitude toward national issues. He had no sympathy for the Republican program and was considerably concerned about the political orthodoxy of those intimately associated with him in business and church affairs in Chicago. The election of 1856 found him a loyal supporter of Buchanan, and he was disappointed when J. L. Wilson, a trusted employee, was elected sheriff of Cook County, Illinois, on the Republican ticket. He urged his brothers to vote for

---

[23] "Richmond Enquirer," Mch. 31, 1840.
[24] These were the stock arguments of the Whigs. C. H. McCormick to Wm. Massie, Aug. 29, 1840, and June 11, 1841. Rockbridge County was normally Whig. Kellar, pp. 347-349.

Buchanan, although there was no reason to feel anxious about their preference in that campaign.[25] He wrote on October 7, 1856, from Philadelphia:

I am not surprised to hear of Spring and Henry [his Chicago pastor] going for Fremont, though I should have preferred that the latter at least had taken or expressed *no part*. I *regret* his position, though it is not decided Abolitionist. He had been charged with being tainted, you may recollect, but disclaimed,—goes with our Church on the main question of non-interference I presume yet. I hope *Buck* will be elected *though not certain* of the *people*. . . . And it may be expected that I should *contribute* to the election. . . . I wish *you* to see Douglas, or the Editor of the *Times,* the *democratic* paper, and any other democrats, and suggest that as I could not be there yet. I had written you to see if funds were needed (and expected) and if so contribute for me and *yourself,*— you agreeing etc. And still it may be a matter of doubt what course to take. It might be well to give $1000. You can talk about the campaign, . . . while I prefer not having it *known at all* by others that anything is done, for the present.[26]

William McCormick did talk and write about the election to agents of the company with whom he was intimately acquainted, although no positive pressure was applied to direct their votes.[27]

McCormick opposed a high protective tariff all of his life.[28] It is doubtful whether his attitude would have been different if he had been a manufacturer of a commodity which encountered foreign competition within the United States. Cer-

---

[25] C. H. to W. S. McCormick, from Baltimore, Oct. 1, 1856.

[26] *Idem* to *idem,* from New York, Oct. 7, 1856.

[27] W. S. McCormick to S. H. Myer, Smithville, O., Oct. 1, 1856; to T. J. Paterson, Rochester, N. Y., Oct. 1, 1856; to Messrs. Fairbanks, Concord, Ill., Oct. 16, 1856; to Thornton Berry, Clines Mills, Va., Nov. 12, 1856; and to Chester Weed, Muscatine, Ia., Nov. 19, 1856; L.P.C.B. No. 3, pp. 471, 480, 595, No. 4, pp. 215, 216, 265, respectively.

[28] He wrote to George S. Bowen, May 23, 1878, "So far as my recollection extends, I have been uniformly in favor of a Revenue Tariff, economically applied, and so as to afford incidental protection to American manufacturing."

tainly his importations of iron from England for factory use did not influence his point of view on this issue. His attitude was merely another expression of his whole outlook upon life. Dominantly individualistic in all things, he wished no aid in his business from a paternalistic Government.[29] To one who believed so strongly that Providence was his ally, assistance from the State was inconsequential. His reapers were a blessing to the farmers, and it was his mission to teach them to lay aside their scythes, and to guard them against less efficient machines which rivals were trying to foist upon them. Forging ahead in this way, with his eyes constantly on his goal, combining inventive genius with extraordinary business ability, and bringing to his whole task the spirit of an old Covenanter, it is not strange that he found success in an America which was rapidly becoming one of the largest wheat countries of the world.

So many factors combined, in the decade before the Civil War, to increase the production of small grains and to promote urban life in the United States that it is impossible to measure accurately the influence of each. The reaper must unquestionably be given much emphasis in any discussion of the expansion of the farming area, although it is probable that its fullest influence in this regard was not felt until the war years and afterward. Any conclusions reached after an attempt to estimate the importance of the one hundred thousand machines sold in the period prior to 1859 are subject to doubt. Cause and effect are so intertwined that they cannot be separated. Railroad mileage trebled during the fifties and the great grain area of the Old Northwest was a chief beneficiary of this expansion.[30] Ocean, lake, and river transportation lines

[29] His wish for patent-protection may seem at variance with this position, but here it is a question of a merited reward for his inventive skill, without which he would not have an equal chance with his competitors.

[30] For example, track mileage in Illinois increased from 60 in 1847 to 2,867 in 1860. T. J. Walker, agent at Belleville, Ill., wrote to C. M. McCormick on May 22, 1856: "If the *coon dog* and *butcher knife* tribe can

boomed; manufacturing grew apace in the cities, and more and more farmers who had formerly eked out a precarious hand-to-mouth existence now had money to invest in new lands or in capitalistic enterprises.

It is significant in the history of the United States that the railroad, the reaper, important inventions in the field of manufacturing, and an unprecedented immigration from Europe, came simultaneously. These influences and others, of which cheap and abundant land is possibly the chief, combined to thrust American life toward the West with a drive and speed unexampled in history. The balance of trade turned in favor of the United States, and European peasants, toiling by hand and unable to compete in their own markets with grain harvested cheaply by machinery, hastened to the mill towns of their own country, or to the land whose people had well-nigh reduced them to starvation by their efficiency.[31]

The reaper was not the only new agricultural machine which revolutionized the economy of the farm. Harvesting implements of all kinds were in use by the time of the Civil War, but it is slight exaggeration to assert that they all incorporated some of the principles which had made the McCormick reaper a success.[32] New fertilizers, better crop-rotation systems, and

ever be rooted out or killed off who occupy the best lands along the [Illinois] Central we might hope to do something with Reapers and wheat drills, improved plows, etc., in that region, but not until then or until new farms are opened up by more enterprising farmers. The present population are pretty smart raising castor beans and chickens but that is all they can do."

[31] Wm. E. Dodd, "The Passing of the Old United States," in the "Century," Nov., 1929, p. 42.

[32] "Prairie Farmer," Oct., 1849, p. 317, letter of "Silex" of Castle Comfort, Dubuque County, Ia.: "Perhaps it is not too much to say that this is emphatically the *golden age* of agriculture. The introduction of machinery for harvesting forms a new era in farming on the prairies, and had the inventors chanced to live in old Greece or Rome they would have held a high place in mythology. . . . One such practical man, as McCormick, does more for his kind than a thousand theorizers on guano."

improved seeds and stock also played their part in the agricultural renaissance.

The importance of the reaper was clearly foreseen by many who lived during its infancy. In fact, some enthusiasts at that time and later, forgetful of the accompanying factors essential to its widespread use, attributed to it an influence beyond the bounds of reason. These writers have extolled it as the invention which made Chicago the greatest grain port in the world, which brought cheap bread and banished famine from the world.[33] William H. Seward exclaimed in 1854:

The Reaper derives importance from economy in relation to the market. It brings wheat from the prairies of Michigan, Illinois, Indiana, and Wisconsin, while it permits the banks of the Hudson and the Delaware to be covered with pastures and gardens. The Reaper derives importance from considerations of economy in regard to the seasons. The harvest season is short. . . . The farmer now plunges boldly with his reaper into the field, whether it is a field of ten acres, or twenty acres, or one hundred acres, or one thousand acres, and gathers the harvest within a period almost as short as that in which he formerly stood, with cradle in hand, studying the phases of the moon for auspices of the weather. . . .

No General or Consul drawn in a chariot through the streets of Rome by order of the Senate, ever conferred upon mankind benefits so great as he [McCormick] who thus vindicated the genius of our country at the World's Exhibition of Art in the Metropolis of the British Empire.[34]

Its effect has been likened with much truth to that of the cotton-gin in the South.[35] As a Yankee gave the lower South a

[33] "Farm Life" (Chicago), Mch., 1909, p. 9. "Chicago Record-Herald," Feb. 14, 1909. "Eastern Dealer" (Phila.), Feb. 18, 1909. "Harper's Weekly," July 31, 1909. "The Wall Street Journal" (N. Y.), Jan. 31, 1909. "Cincinnati Enquirer," July 1, 1909. "Pennsylvania Farm Journal," May, 1855.

[34] Seward, pp. 1, 2, 20. See also the arguments of Reverdy Johnson and E. N. Dickerson in "McCormick Extension Case, Patent of 1845," pp. 1, 5, 8, 11, 14.

[35] "Prairie Farmer," Jan., 1848, pp. 26, 27; Aug., 1849, p. 257; Oct., 1849, p. 317; June, 1850, p. 174. "Ohio Cultivator," Oct. 1, 1849, p. 298.

machine so basic to its ante-bellum civilization, so also a slave-holder furnished the North with an implement which was to do much for the cause of human freedom.

When Cyrus McCormick sought an extension of his 1845 patent in 1858, his application was supported by many testimonials from Western farmers. These generally agreed that the McCormick reaper was worth ten times its cost to the grain-grower; that the wheat acreage had doubled in sections where it was used; that many farmers were turning from corn to small grains because of its existence, and were thereby increasing the value of their lands; that it had compelled better husbandry and had made its owner a mechanic; that it had stimulated the invention of other agricultural machinery; that it had done much to solve the labor-shortage problem; that it was less wasteful of ripe grain than the cradle, and that McCormick's easy credit system, as well as the value of his implement, permitted many farmers to enlarge their farms and pay their debts with the return from their increased crops.[36]

If doubt is expressed as to the value of this solicited testimony, it is an easy task to assemble numerous letters of the same tenor sent voluntarily by farmers to agricultural magazines between 1845 and 1860.[37] In 1858, Cyrus McCormick, certainly with some inaccuracy, contended that the estimated 73,200 reapers sold since 1845, which legally or illegally incorporated the mechanical principles of his invention, had

"Albany Cultivator," Sept., 1850, p. 313; Jan., 1851, pp. 41, 42. H. Howe, "Adventures and Achievements of Americans," pp. 156-157. Chas. W. Burkett, "History of Ohio Agriculture" (Concord, N. H., 1900), pp. 163-166.

[36] "McCormick Extension Case, Patent of 1845," pp. 1-168, 352, 557, 563-566.

[37] "American Farmer," Sept., 1852, pp. 102, 103. "N. Y. Farmer and Mechanic," Aug. 21, 1852, p. 418. "Ohio Cultivator," Apr. 5, 1847, p. 64. "Chicago Daily Democrat," June 30, 1847; Oct. 13, 1848; Aug. 18, 1851, and Dec. 23, 1851. "Chicago Daily Journal," July 2, 1846, and July 21, 1848.

doubled the Western wheat acreage where they were used, and that their money value to the country, including the worth of the grain saved, and the economy of manual labor, totaled over $130,000,000.[38] Reverdy Johnson judged that these implements annually added $55,000,000 to the wealth of the United States.[39] Compared with these figures, the $1,000,000 which Cyrus McCormick had accumulated by 1860, through wise manufacturing policies, seems very small. As early as 1852, a committee of the United States Senate hailed the McCormick reaper as "one of those great and valuable inventions which commence a new era in the progress of improvement, and whose beneficial influence is felt in all coming time." [40]

The United States census returns of 1850 and 1860 indicate that the percentage of wheat output increased as much during the decade in those counties of the Middle West which did not use many McCormick reapers as in those which did. However, the counties that furnished the largest markets for the McCormick reaper grew by far the most wheat, and the percentage of wheat increase generally much exceeded the percentage

[38] McCormick Extension Case, Patent of 1845," pp. 11-15, 565. "Prairie Farmer," Feb. 3, 1859, p. 73. Of the 73,200 reapers, McCormick had made 23,200.

[39] "McCormick Extension Case, Patent of 1845," pp. 1, 5, 8, 11, 14. See also the opinion of D. P. Holloway, Commr. of Patents, Oct. 20, 1861, in "McCormick Extension Case, Patent of 1847," p. 347.

[40] Senate, 1st Sess., 32d Cong., "Repts. of Committees," No. 160. Jos. Holt, Commr. of Patents, stated on Jan. 28, 1859: "In our country of fertile and cheap lands and sparse population, the reaping machine, operated by animal labor, ranks probably next to the plough in its value as an agricultural implement. . . . As a public benefactor, the measure of his [McCormick's] fame is already great, and is perhaps still enlarging, while the colossal fortune in his hands is proof conclusive of the lavish liberality with which his labors have been requited. He has been so fortunate as to link his name indissolubly with a machine which, unless outstripped in the race of progress, may endure as a proud memorial, so long as the ripening grain shall wave over the boundless plains of the West, or the songs of the reaper shall be heard in the harvest fields." Holt's decision had been adverse to McCormick's petition for patent-extension.

of population growth. These bumper wheat regions often had no better transportation facilities in 1860 than in 1850. Using these conclusions to supplement the testimony of farmers, already given, there is little reason to doubt that there was a direct relationship between the amount of grain harvested and the number of reapers used.[41] If records were available to show the sales distribution in the Midwest, of harvesting machines other than the McCormick, it would be possible to write with more assurance of the effect of mechanical reaping upon the production of cereals. And yet, even if statistics were altogether lacking, it could hardly be questioned that a machine which harvested grain more thoroughly, and seven times more rapidly than the cradle; with one half the labor force; with an original cost of about $130, and a life of from five to ten years, inclined farmers to grow a larger acreage of a crop that had a certain market.

Cyrus McCormick contributed to the fullness of American life from 1845 to 1860. While pioneers of women's rights labored amid the ridicule of the many whom they endeavored to aid, McCormick sought to persuade the public that he had a machine which would relieve the farmer's wife of the heavy toil of the harvest season. As the forty-niner forged his way westward to pan for gold in the Sacramento Valley, reapers were stowed below decks on Boston clipper-ships bound around the Horn to 'Frisco, to aid in the convalescence of California from the fever of mining.[42] McCormick's machine was working in Iowa, Wisconsin, Minnesota, and Oregon while they were still Territories.[43] Border ruffians and Northern bush-

---

[41] H. W. Quaintance, "The Influence of Farm Machinery on Production and Labor" in "Publications of American Economic Association" (N. Y., 1904), 3d ser., Vol. V, No. 4.

[42] C. H. to W. S. McCormick, Sept. 4, 1855: "I shall require, I think, at least one hundred machines for California." Letter of C. H. McCormick in "Albany Cultivator," July, 1851, p. 253.

[43] Alfred Kinney, Pleasant Grove, Minn. Ter., to C. H. McCormick, Mch. 21, 1856; J. L. Walker to T. Chapman, Frankford, Minn. Ter.,

whackers fought in Kansas as the reaper peacefully harvested the grain at Shawnee Mission.[44]

In the day when the Abolitionists talked less of Liberia and more of underground railways, forcible rescues, and the sins of the slaveholder, Cyrus McCormick, a native of Virginia, perfected an implement that was destined to do more for the cause of free men, in the war which was coming, than the eloquence of Garrison and Phillips. The use of the reaper demanded intelligent operation and it could not be used profitably where labor was cheap. The men that could be spared from the harvests during the Civil War, because they were no longer needed to swing scythes, would help to swell the armies of the North. The reaper made it possible to produce grain sufficient for export, and surplus wheat was to fight decisively for Lincoln in the impending conflict.

Mch. 21, 1857, and to W. H. Harrington, Winona, Minn. Ter., Mch. 27, 1857, L.P.C.B. No. 5, pp. 488, 661, 725, 821. John L. Wilson, from Cordova, Ia., Dec. 17, 1854; Hugh Allen & Co., from New York, Feb. 10, 1855.

[44] Father J. B. Duerinck, St. Mary's Mission, Kan. Ter., to C. H. McCormick, Feb. 29, 1856; J. L. Walker to Duerinck, Mch. 9, 1857, L.P.C.B. No. 5, p. 461.

BIBLIOGRAPHICAL GUIDE

The full title of each source given below will be found by referring to the designated page and foot-note of the text. Works infrequently cited in the biography are not included in this list.

	PAGE	FOOT-NOTE
"Agricultural Chronicle, Machinery, and Horticultural Gazette,"	57	14
"Albany Cultivator,"	29	2
"American Agriculturist,"	34	20
"American Farmer,"	28	1
"American Gardener's Magazine,"	82	22
"American Inventor,"	57	14
"American Quarterly Review,"	29	2
"American Railroad Journal,"	44	60
Andreas,	252	3
Anjou,	6	4
Ardrey, "American Agricultural Implements,"	55	8
Ardrey, "The Harvesting Machine Industry,"	55	5
Aultman vs. Holley,	155	15
"British Agriculturist,"	52	2
Casson, "Cyrus Hall McCormick,"	14	30
"C. H. McCormick's Statement, 1874,"	77	7
Craven,	49	1
"Dollar Farmer,"	193	46
Egle,	6	5
"Factory and Farm,"	112	49
"Farmer and Planter,"	409	3
"Farmers' Advance,"	84	30
"Farmers' Cabinet,"	151	4
"Farmer's Magazine" (Edinburgh),	36	27
"Farmer's Magazine" (London),	65	31

	PAGE	FOOT-NOTE
"Staunton Spectator,"	31	12
Swift,	52	2
"Transactions of Highland Society,"	65	29
"Transactions of New York State Agricultural Society,"	237	25
"The Plough, The Loom, and The Anvil,"	325	87
"The Plow,"	329	3
"Union Agriculturist and Western Prairie Farmer,"	158	23
"Valley Star,"	117	65
Waddell,	8	12
"Western Farmer and Gardener,"	157	19
"Wisconsin Farmer and Northwestern Cultivator,"	318	59
Woodcroft,	55	8

NOTE: All manuscripts cited in the foot-notes, unless otherwise noted, are in the McCormick Historical Association Library, Chicago.

INDEX

Date Due

MAY 1 1 '53			
MAY 1 4 '56			
MAY 1 4 '58			
MAY 20 '58			
MAR 30 '63			
APR 27 '65			
MAY 4 '65			